The Making and Remaking of Australasia

Empire's Other Histories

Empire's Other Histories is an innovative series devoted to the shared and diverse experiences of the marginalised, dispossessed and disenfranchised in modern imperial and colonial histories. It responds to an ever-growing academic and popular interest in the histories of those erased, dismissed, or ignored in traditional historiographies of empire. It will elaborate on and analyse new questions of perspective, identity, agency, motilities, intersectionality and power relations.

Published

Unhomely Empire: Whiteness and Belonging, c.1760–1830, Onni Gust, 2020

Extreme Violence and the 'British Way': Colonial Warfare in Perak, Sierra Leone and Sudan, Michelle Gordon, 2020

Unexpected Voices in Imperial Parliaments, edited by José María Portillo, Josep M. Fradera, Teresa Segura-Garcia, 2021

Forthcoming

Spiritual Colonialism in a Globalizing World, Christina Petterson

Vagrant Lives in Colonial Australasia: Regulating Mobility and Movement 1840–1920, Catherine Coleborne

Gender, Violence and Criminal Justice in the Colonial Pacific, Kate Stevens

Across Colonial Lines: Commodities, Networks and Empire Building, edited by Devyani Gupta and Purba Hossain

Arctic Circles and Imperial Knowledge: The Franklin Family, Indigenous Intermediaries, and the Politics of Truth, Annaliese Jacobs Claydon

Imperial Gallows: Murder, Violence and the Death Penalty in British Colonial Africa, c.1915–60, Stacey Hynd

Anti-Colonialism and the Crises of Interwar Fascism, Michael Oritz

The Making and Remaking of Australasia

Texts, Mobility and 'Southern Circulations'

Edited by Tony Ballantyne

BLOOMSBURY ACADEMIC

LONDON • NEW YORK • OXFORD • NEW DELHI • SYDNEY

BLOOMSBURY ACADEMIC
Bloomsbury Publishing Plc
50 Bedford Square, London, WC1B 3DP, UK
1385 Broadway, New York, NY 10018, USA
29 Earlsfort Terrace, Dublin 2, Ireland

BLOOMSBURY, BLOOMSBURY ACADEMIC and the Diana logo are trademarks of
Bloomsbury Publishing Plc

First published in Great Britain 2023

Cover image: Australia &c. (with) Colony of New South Wales. (with) Van Dieman's Land.
Published by D. Lizars, Edinburgh. (1831?). Courtesy David Rumsey Map Collection.

A catalogue record for this book is available from the British Library.
A catalog record for this book is available from the Library of Congress.

ISBN: HB: 978-1-3502-6416-8
        ePDF: 978-1-3502-6417-5
        eBook: 978-1-3502-6418-2

Series: Empire's Other Histories

Typeset by RefineCatch Limited, Bungay, Suffolk

To find out more about our authors and books visit www.bloomsbury.com
and sign up for our newsletters.

For Sue and Alan Henderson, Australasians at heart

Contents

Illustrations

Figures

Maps

Tables

Contributors

Kate Bagnall is a social historian whose research focuses on family, migration and the law in Australia and New Zealand. Kate is best known for her work in Chinese Australian history, and her most recent book is *Locating Chinese Women: Historical Mobility between China and Australia* (Hong Kong University Press, 2021), co-edited with Julia Martínez. Kate joined the University of Tasmania in 2019 as Senior Lecturer in Humanities (History), before which she was ARC DECRA Research Fellow at the University of Wollongong. Her DECRA project investigated the history of Chinese naturalization in colonial Australia, New Zealand and Canada.

Tony Ballantyne is Professor of History and Deputy Vice-Chancellor, External Engagement at the University of Otago. He has published widely on empires in modern world history, the cultural history of the British Empire in the nineteenth century, and colonialism and its consequences in New Zealand. His most recent monograph is *Entanglements of Empire: Missionaries, Māori and the Question of the Body* (Duke University Press and Auckland University Press, 2014) and he is co-editor, with Lachy Paterson and Angela Wanhalla, of *Indigenous Textual Cultures: Reading and Writing in the Age of Global Empire* (also from Duke, 2020).

Frank Bongiorno is Professor of History at the Australian National University and was Head of History for three years from 2018 to 2021. He is the author of books on politics, sexuality, society and culture in Australia, and is a Fellow of the Royal Historical Society, the Australian Academy of the Humanities and the Academy of the Social Sciences in Australia. He has previously taught at King's College London, the University of New England and Griffith University, and was Smuts Visiting Fellow in Commonwealth Studies at the University of Cambridge. He is a member of the Order of Australia.

Antoinette Burton is Professor of History at the University of Illinois, Urbana-Champaign. Her most recent book is *Animalia: An Anti-Imperial Bestiary for Our Times* (Duke University Press, 2020), co-edited with Renisa Mawani. She and Tony Ballantyne are co-editors of *World Histories from Below* (Bloomsbury, 2nd edition, 2022).

Sarah Comyn is Assistant Professor and Ad Astra Fellow at University College Dublin. Her publications include *Political Economy and the Novel: A Literary History of 'Homo Economicus'* (Palgrave, 2018), *Early Public Libraries and Colonial Citizenship in the British Southern Hemisphere* (Palgrave, 2019; with Lara Atkin et al.) and *Worlding the South: Nineteenth-Century Literary Culture and the Southern Settler Colonies*

(Manchester University Press, 2021; edited with Porscha Fermanis). She is currently working on a monograph entitled *A New Reading Public: The Mechanics' Institute on the Goldfields of Victoria, 1851–1901*.

Porscha Fermanis is Professor of Romantic Literature at University College Dublin. Her latest books are *Worlding the South: Nineteenth-Century Literary Culture and the Southern Settler Colonies* (Manchester University Press, 2021; edited with Sarah Comyn) and *Romantic Pasts: History, Fiction and Feeling in Britain, 1790–1850* (Edinburgh University Press, 2022). She is Principal Investigator of the European Research Council project 'SouthHem' and is currently completing a book on nineteenth-century settler fiction and southern spatial imaginaries.

Helen Gardner is Honorary Associate Professor affiliated to Deakin University, Melbourne. She has published on the history of Oceania and the nineteenth-century relationship between Pacific-based missionaries and armchair theorists of anthropology in the metropole. More recently she has explored the decolonization of the Pacific Islands with a focus on the independence generation of the 1970s. She is interested in the deployment of anthropological theories in the narratives of nation throughout the Pacific. She is currently the chair of the *Journal of Pacific History*.

James Keating is a historian of nineteenth- and twentieth-century Australia and New Zealand. Tracing the stories and material legacies of Australasian activists, his research interrogates local, national and international feminist movements to understand the history and memory of transnational organizing. He has written on suffrage, campaigns against the Contagious Diseases Acts, world's fairs and welfare. His first book was *Distant Sisters: Australasian Women and the International Struggle for the Vote, 1880–1914* (Manchester University Press, 2020).

Thomas McLean is Associate Professor in English at the University of Otago. He is the editor of *Further Letters of Joanna Baillie* (Rowman & Littlefield, 2010), author of *The Other East and Nineteenth-Century British Literature: Imagining Poland and the Russian Empire* (Palgrave Macmillan, 2012) and co-editor, with Ruth Knezevich, of Jane Porter's 1803 novel *Thaddeus of Warsaw* (Edinburgh University Press, 2019). The recipient of research fellowships from Harvard, Yale, UCLA and ANU, he has written on art, music and literature for *North & South*, *The Conversation UK* and *Los Angeles Review of Books*.

Grace Moore is Associate Professor of English at the University of Otago. Her research interests include Victorian crime fiction, Dickens, Trollope, the History of Emotions, and the Environmental Humanities. She is the author of *Dickens and Empire* (Routledge, 2004; shortlisted for the NSW Premier's Award for Literary Scholarship in 2006) and *The Victorian Novel in Context* (Continuum, 2012). Her most recent book is the co-edited collection, *Victorian Environments* (Palgrave, 2018; with Michelle J. Smith). Grace's current book project is on Anthony Trollope and the Environment, and she is completing a study of settler bushfire literature.

Fiona Paisley is Professor Emeritus in History at Griffith University, Brisbane. She works on progressive debates regarding the reform of settler colonialism during the first half of the twentieth century. Her books include *Writing Transnational History*, co-written with Pamela Scully (Bloomsbury, 2019), *Critical Perspective on Colonialism: Writing the Empire from Below*, co-edited with Kirsty Reid (Routledge, 2014), *The Lone Protestor: AM Fernando in Australia and Europe* (Aboriginal Studies Press, 2012) and *Glamour in the Pacific: Cultural Internationalism and Race Politics in the Women's Pan-Pacific* (University of Hawai'i Press, 2009). Her current project is a study of Pan-Pacific internationalism, education and 'race' in the interwar years.

Rachel Standfield a non-Indigenous historian of colonialism and race relations histories in Australia, New Zealand and the Pacific, lecturing in the Indigenous Studies Program at the University of Melbourne. Her research focuses on colonial histories, histories of Indigenous agency to protect country and culture, and Indigenous mobilities between Aotearoa me Te Wai Pounamu/New Zealand, the Pacific and Australia. She has worked with Indigenous peoples in Australia and New Zealand, including with Wurundjeri Elders in the Melbourne region and Kāi Tahu people on ancestors' travels and lives in Australia.

Frances Steel teaches at the University of Otago. Her research focuses on the history of the Pacific world, with a particular emphasis on colonial networks, oceanic mobilities and transnational labour cultures. Her publications include *Oceania under Steam: Sea Transport and the Cultures of Colonialism, c. 1870-1914* (Manchester University Press, 2011), the joint-authored volume *Colonialism and Male Domestic Service across the Asia Pacific* (Bloomsbury, 2019) and the edited collection *New Zealand and the Sea: Historical Perspectives* (Bridget Williams Books, 2018).

Gillen D'Arcy Wood is Professor of Environmental Humanities and English at the University of Illinois, Urbana-Champaign, where he is also director of the Environmental Writing Program. He is the author of five books and numerous articles on nineteenth-century literature, culture and environmental history, including the award-winning *Tambora: The Eruption that Changed the World* (Princeton University Press, 2014) and, most recently, *Land of Wondrous Cold: The Race to Discover Antarctica and the Secrets of its Ice* (also Princeton, 2020). His current research on the *HMS Challenger* expedition, for which he has received a 2021–22 Carnegie Fellowship, focuses on our deteriorating oceans and the Victorian origins of marine science.

Acknowledgements

This book explores the emergence of the idea of Australasia, competing visions of what constituted (or constitutes) that region and the cultural forces that shaped these spatial imaginaries. My interest in the subject of Australasia not only reflects the importance of connections between New Zealand, Australia and the Pacific in the life of my family and in my own career, but has also been shaped by two ongoing questions that have engaged me as a historian for the last couple of decades: first, how understandings of space and culture are shaped by the movement of ideas, arguments and texts within imperial systems; and, second, the various interrelationships between historical writing on New Zealand, Australia, the Pacific and Asia. Thinking through the production of Australasia is an excellent way of exploring these issues and I was delighted to be able to convene a research workshop in Dunedin to bring together historians and literary scholars to reflect upon on 'Southern Circulations: Texts, Mobility and the Production of Australasia'. From that workshop, this volume took shape and I am very grateful to Maddie Holder and Abigail Lane at Bloomsbury for their very positive engagement with this project. I am also very appreciative of the extremely useful commentaries provided by the readers of both the proposal and the final manuscript.

That initial symposium was funded by the University of Otago's Centre for Research on Colonial Culture (CRoCC). I am grateful for that funding; for almost a decade CRoCC was an important part of my work as a historian. Sue Lang, the administrator in the History Programme at Otago, provided excellent support for the organization of the workshop. The gathering was held at Hocken Collections in Dunedin – an outstanding heritage institution whose own rich holdings are both a product of 'southern circulations' and document the movement of people, texts and things. Under the leadership of Sharon Dell, there was a strong relationship between the Hocken and CRoCC, and it was a fantastic site for the workshop.

I would like to make a special acknowledgement of the volume's contributors for their patience and persistence. The workshop was held in mid-December 2019, just before COVID-19 began to transform our world. All of the contributors have worked around lockdowns and various other measures designed to control the pandemic and I have been really appreciative of their commitment and good humour in disrupted and uncertain times.

I have been very lucky to work with Richard Ley-Hamilton as a research assistant in the final stages of this project. I greatly appreciate his thoughtfulness, eye for detail and efficiency – his work has been indispensable to the completion of the volume.

As ever, I am very grateful to my family – Sally, Evie and Clara – for their love and support. I am very pleased to dedicate this volume to my parents-in-law. Although they were both raised in Southland in New Zealand, they have a deep attachment to Australia and their movement to and fro across the Tasman is testament to the enduring power of some of the connections at the heart of this book.

Part One

Framings

Introduction. Southern Circulations and the Making and Remaking of Australasia

Tony Ballantyne

This book explores the emergence of 'Australasia' as a way of thinking about the culture and geography of a large portion of the southern hemisphere. Although it is frequently understood today as only applying to Australia and New Zealand, Australasia as a concept has had a long and messy history. This notion emerged in the middle of the eighteenth century in both French and British writing – most notably in Charles des Brosses's *Histoire des navigations aux terres australes* (1756) and John Callender's *Terra australis cognita* (1766–8) – as European empires extended their reach into Asia and the Pacific. The idea was intimately connected with imperial aspirations: for commercial opportunities with adjacent Asian port cities and European colonial outposts; for valuable new resources and commodities that could be drawn into the circulations of world-spanning empires; for land that could be settled by colonists, turned into plantations and farms; and for strategic advantage within the context of the protracted rivalries and conflicts between these empire-building powers, especially Britain and France.

The essays gathered in this volume demonstrate that the idea of Australasia was never entirely fixed or stable. It was imagined in a variety of ways, and while definitions of the region often had common elements, there were significant variations in emphasis and recurrent disagreement over the region's precise boundaries. While Australia and New Zealand were often seen as the core of the region, throughout the long nineteenth century the idea remained both flexible and contested as different political agendas and cultural visions imagined Australasia as reaching to varying extents into the Pacific or towards Antarctica. This volume offers a rich series of case studies which explore how Australasia was imagined and brought into being in particular cultural locations, within specific texts or broader traditions of writing, by activists, politicians and poets who articulated a range of commitments and aspirations. Taken together they suggest that Australasia should not be understood simply as an idea, as an intellectual construct that was generated and refined by writers and ideologues, but as the product of imperial orders that had mobility and circulation at their heart. Australasia was a way of trying to make sense of the distinctive type of southern-ness of a particular part of the world.

Within the context of European empire-building, Australasia was produced through circulations, through the movement of people, commodities, things, capital, texts and ideas. These circulations are a key theme that run through this volume and which set it apart from existing work on Australasia, which has typically operated within a textually focused approach to the history of ideas. Conversely, many of the chapters gathered here show that Australasia as a region emerged out of the circulation of people and texts on the move, both in the southern hemisphere and in the imperial metropole, where a range of competing interest groups articulated often quite divergent visions of the southern parts of the British Empire, their significance and meaning.

Australasia: emergence and development

Australasia was, by origin, a European idea, one that bore no relationship to any indigenous framing of the sea, the land or human community. It was first articulated by Charles de Brosses, the Burgundian parliamentarian, who had built a significant reputation as a Classical scholar, letter writer and humanist. De Brosses was eager to collate and order European understandings of the southern Pacific, its lands and peoples. To do so, he gathered all of the key navigational texts and narratives of European exploration he could locate into a two-volume compendium *Histoire des navigations aux terres australes*, published in 1756. Drawing upon the knowledge conveyed within these accounts, de Brosses developed a new vision of the geography and culture. He summed this up in the following way:

> Our globe is made up of three large expanses of land, Asia, Africa and America, and three large expanses of sea, the Ethiopian or Indian Ocean, the Atlantic or Northern Ocean, the Pacific or Southern Ocean. In relation to this, we can even divide the unknown southern world into three parts, lying to the south of the three mentioned above. One in the Indian Ocean to the south of Asia that I will call for that reason Australasia.[1]

The other parts of the 'southern world' were named by de Brosses the 'Magellanic' and 'Polynesia'. De Brosses gave the name 'Polynesia' 'because of the many islands it encompasses' and he saw this as an expansive domain that included 'everything contained in the vast Pacific Ocean'.[2] The first chapter of the volume demonstrates that these names, and de Brosses's associated reflections on the lands and peoples of these regions, powerfully inflected European understandings over the coming decades. As Tom Ryan has argued, de Brosses 'indelibly influenced the way late-18th-century Occidentals interpreted and represented the sea, land and humanscapes of that extension of the Orient that today is most often reconstituted as "Oceania"'.[3]

Histoire des navigations aux terres australes was an important example of the Enlightenment impetus to synthesize, catalogue and systematize.[4] The great scholar of Pacific exploration O. H. K. Spate summarized the significance of de Brosses's text in this way: 'The importance of his *Histoire* was that for the first time the fragmented references to an Austral Continent, previously scattered in individual narratives or buried in massive compilations, were brought together, logically arranged, and accompanied by analyses of the advantages and problems of discovery and colonisation.'[5]

Thus, the *Histoire* of de Brosses was an important pivot point. Its encyclopedic aspiration marked a turn away from the speculative sensibility that had been so central in earlier European depictions of the Pacific Ocean, its waters, lands and peoples. The mythic great southern continent, *Terra Australis*, was pushed aside by de Brosses's new framework, which was imprinted by the Enlightenment's deep preoccupation with classification. It also helped propel a new age of European imperial exploration. His bulky tome was carried on both the expedition to circumnavigate the world by Louis-Antoine, Comte de Bougainville, that commenced in 1766 and Lieutenant James Cook's *Endeavour* on its Pacific voyage.[6] De Brosses saw the Pacific as full of imperial possibilities: in fact, the one aspect of de Brosses's text that maintained an attachment to speculation was his conviction that there were many islands in the northern Pacific as yet undiscovered by Europeans and these were likely to be rich in spices.[7]

De Brosses's notion of Australasia was swiftly translated and picked up in Britain and had wide currency across Europe in the late eighteenth century. From that period on, visions of Australasia were continually contested and reshaped. Initially there was a strong emphasis on the region's propinquity to Asia: de Brosses's neologism referred to the region's location to the south of Asia. Within the context of Asia's emergence as an increasingly central focus for European imperial enterprise, the commercial and strategic advantages that would flow to European powers from this proximity were an important driver that shaped the emergence of this vision of space.[8]

This emphasis became less prominent as the shape of European imperial systems in the region shifted and took more enduring forms. While there were important links to Asian commercial entrepôts, and the interests of the East India Company and Calcutta merchants were significant forces in moulding the development of British imperial extraction and trade, processes of migration and settlement increasingly dominated discussions of Australasia's significance and potential. As Britain's dominance in the region was solidified in the 1830s and 1840s and colonization was seen as a key mode of imperial activity, visions of Australasia increasingly focused on Australia and New Zealand, downplaying or even excising the relationship to Asia. During this period, parts of the south-west and southern Pacific were still frequently seen as part of the region, but there was no consensus on Australasia's precise boundaries and some Pacific islands were typically seen as a kind of frontier or extension rather than the core of Australasia. As the nineteenth century drew to a close, significant parts of Melanesia and Polynesia were often completely erased as understandings of Australasia often narrowed to encompass only the two large British settler colonies, Australia and New Zealand. In the 1880s and 1890s Australasia had its greatest purchase as a concept. It was widely used and increasingly it was tied to the emergence of progressive social reform movements in Australia and New Zealand that gained real political authority from the late 1880s.[9]

But this consolidation of meaning was never complete or unchallenged. In the early part of the twentieth century, Australasia remained both variable and contested as different political agendas and cultural visions imagined Australasia as reaching into the Pacific or towards Antarctica. Most importantly, the purchase of the idea began to weaken as the authority of national politics was consolidated, especially after the federation of the Australian colonies in 1901. New Zealand's refusal to enter into federation, the consolidation of a heightened sense of Australia's political coherence, and New Zealand's status as a Dominion from 1907 meant the emphasis on commonalities and connectedness between Australia and New Zealand that was so common in the 1890s, and which underwrote the particular reach of the idea of Australasia, was no longer so plausible.

Historical and historiographical recuperations

In the mid-1980s, Donald Denoon offered a searching critique of what he described as the 'isolation of Australian history'. Although Denoon suggested that Australian history had developed into a sophisticated field and was in good health, he believed a range of factors had contracted its intellectual horizons. Denoon here identified shifting patterns in publishing, the weakness and growing irrelevance of the imperial history tradition (something that would shift over the following decade), and a persistent indifference to work that either attempted to reframe Australia's history in comparative terms or within larger geographical or cultural frameworks. Taken together, he suggested, these forces produced an inward-looking sensibility.[10] In passing, Denoon noted the salience of Australasia as a more expansive model. Its importance was revealed, Denoon suggested, in the political currents of the 1880s and 1890s, progressive forces that in the New Zealand case produced 'a sober, fully enfranchised, colour-blind, domesticated society'. Although Denoon's reading of race would not be widely accepted now, he believed that there was much to be gained by an appreciation of the common currents that shaped political culture either side of the Tasman Sea, the connections that he saw as central to Australasia. But this story, he argued, had largely been forgotten because of 'the tyranny of national boundaries, and their projection backwards in time' in historical scholarship.[11]

Denoon subsequently elaborated on this suggestion as he forwarded a solution to some of these historiographical issues: a new focus on Australia's relationships with some of its 'geographical neighbours'. More specifically, Denoon wanted to direct attention to what he described as an important 'repressed memory – the Australasian dimension' of Australia's 'past and present'.[12] This argument had significant political dimensions. Denoon highlighted what he saw as a 'powerful sense of mis-placement' that had gripped Australian politics and culture. This found expression in the recurrent insistence on Australia's 'separateness' from its 'northern neighbours', anti-Asian sentiment and a persistent lack of interest in New Zealand. These dynamics co-existed with the related 'popular view' that Australia's '"natural" region' to connect with was western Europe.[13] Denoon suggested that this reluctance – which at times became a 'hysterical denial' – for Australians to identify as part of a wider Australasia was a result of a deep-seated set of cultural and political realignments that occurred in the wake of the Federation of Australia in 1901.[14] (Some of these dynamics are carefully reassessed in Frank Bongiorno's chapter in this volume.)

Denoon made this argument in 2003 at a moment where there was a growing interest in the possibilities of history beyond the nation and in transnational historical writing. The turn to global history or larger regional histories initially struggled to gain traction in Australia and New Zealand, in contrast to historians of the Pacific who were more routinely interested in both the history of connections and a broader regional perspective. In the years either side of the millennium, historians of empire who worked on Australia and New Zealand were important innovators in pushing against the limits of a national frame; but their approach was initially greeted by a degree of scepticism that reflected the enduring authority of national history.[15]

But from around 2005, historians had increasingly turned to transnational and connected histories. In Australia, a key shift was signalled by the publication of Marilyn Lake and Ann Curthoy's important collection *Connected Worlds: History in Transnational Perspective* (2005), which was reinforced by Lake's landmark collaboration with Henry Reynolds, *Drawing the Global Colour Line* (2008).[16] Much of that new transnational work was particularly interested in histories of race, feminism and gender and there was less attention to links with either Asia or across the Tasman to New Zealand, or to the Pacific.[17] But that changed quickly. The work of the historians associated with the Dragon Tails conference have subsequently produced a rich and substantial body of work that explores Australia's connections to China, and Margaret Allen, Kama Maclean and Samia Khatun have been at the forefront of work that has reconnected Australia to South Asia.[18] At the same time there has also been a flowering of scholarship on Australia's complex and shifting relationships with the Pacific, including its Pacific empire, work that was particularly catalysed by the late Tracey Banivanua Mar.[19]

In the New Zealand context, there has been a similar pattern of development. Significant seams of work have developed on connections to China and India, including work that explores South Asian connections to both Australia and New Zealand.[20] A more prominent and influential body of work has developed on New Zealand's Pacific histories, scholarship that has been particularly influenced by Damon Salesa's arguments about the double nature of New Zealand's relationship to the region; that New Zealand was located in the Pacific, but colonists and their descendants had routinely denied that Pacific-ness partially in order to justify the construction of New Zealand's own empire in the region.[21] It is also important to note the work of Frances Steel, who has explored New Zealand's connections to the Pacific, championed the importance of maritime history, and who has also worked on the transportation, economic and cultural links that underpinned Australia's relations with the Pacific as well.[22] This maritime dimension to New Zealand's past has animated some significant recent work on the Tasman Sea and trans-Tasman mobilities by David Haines, Michael Stevens, Jonathan West and Rachel Standfield.[23]

As more historians looked beyond the national past in Australia and New Zealand, Philippa Mein Smith made an important but often overlooked contribution through her arguments for the utility of Australasia as a unit of analysis. In a 2009 historiographical essay, Mein Smith emphasized the early origins of the term 'Australasia', stressing that it predates the idea of 'Australia' and precedes the modern nations of Australia and New Zealand. She carried onto to argue that 'Australasia' has

> special explanatory power for conceptualising a shared Australian and New Zealand history that also extends to communities and encounters in the South Pacific. In this history Australia and New Zealand began life as a common colonial

entity, part of the expanding southern British world of the eighteenth century. The two landmasses were linked by explorers' voyages followed by British colonisation and the establishment of white settler colonies with a shared British heritage.

James Cook is the common ancestral cultural hero of both nations; he connects them through his first voyage of exploration in 1769–1770 and his encounters with Maori and Aboriginal Australians. Both countries revere him, though Australia has been quicker to query whether Cook is actually marginal to Australian history since he only visited once and showed no subsequent interest. Yet despite a history of connections in the modern world, Australians and New Zealanders have until recently chosen not to acknowledge each other when telling their national stories in a pattern that is typical of post-colonial histories in former colonies of settlement.[24]

Mein Smith's essay was a significant manifesto that built upon the integrative narrative history of Australia, New Zealand and the Pacific, which she published in 2000 with Donald Denoon.[25] That work appeared just prior to the turn to transnational and connected histories recounted above and as such had limited purchase, but nevertheless it was an important demonstration of the utility of a larger geographic and cultural frame for historical writing. Of course, the kind of work that Denoon and Mein Smith championed enlarged upon texts such as Keith Sinclair's edited collection *Tasman Relations* (1987).[26] It is also important to recognize that although New Zealand may not figure prominently in any rendering of Australian national history, relationships with Australia were critical elements of the national histories of New Zealand produced by Keith Sinclair – whose 1959 *A History of New Zealand* featured an opening chapter entitled 'Australian Colony' – and in James Belich's *Making Peoples* (1996), which popularized the notion of the 'Tasman World'.[27] The power of the 'Tasman World' as an analytical frame has been most clearly demonstrated by Rachel Standfield's history of racial thought between the late 1760s and early 1840s.[28] For a slightly later period, Kristyn Harman's *Cleansing the Colony: Transporting Convicts from New Zealand to Van Diemen's Land* is important in its recovery of the connections between New Zealand and the Australian penal colonies, including the circulation of trading vessels, colonial constables and convicts across the Tasman Sea.[29] It has also been effectively mobilized on a broader canvas still in the synthetic history produced by Mein Smith herself in collaboration with Peter Hempenstall and Shaun Goldfinch.[30] In recent times there has been a flowering of quality work that explores both the comparisons and connections that link Australian and New Zealand histories, ranging from works on the history of natural disasters[31] to historical memory,[32] from architectural history[33] to histories of migration and mental health.[34]

Space, circulation and southern-ness

Within this historiographic context, where there are growing bodies of scholarship that explore the relationships between Australia, New Zealand and the Pacific and a strong interest in history beyond the nation, there is a real need for critical work on Australasia. Australasia was not only a key spatial formation produced by the rise of European imperial power, but as the foregoing historiographical discussion suggests, it is also an important antecedent to our contemporary interest in thinking though larger regional framings. Central to the approach developed in this volume is a concern with space and circulation. Circulation – ordered, repeated patterns of movement – is central in the production of space and underwrites the emergence of spatial constructs like Australasia.[35] An imagined space has credibility because it reflects and represents patterns of movement and circulation that are seen to define that space. Although the idea of Australasia predated its formal incorporation into European imperial regimes or its colonial settlement, its cultural authority was consolidated in the nineteenth century because complex circuits of trade, cultural mobility and colonial settlement could be identified that aligned with its imagined contours.

The movement of people was a key circulation that gave shape to imperial systems in the Pacific and these were integral to the making of Australasia. In thinking about empire and circulation, we might take Damon Salesa's argument that empires and colonialism redirected the 'circuitry' of mobility within Pacific communities as a key starting point. He has shown how Samoan patterns of mobility and exchange, moulded by a history of migration and close connections to the ocean, were always dynamic. In the nineteenth century, novel ways of moving and new connections emerged as whaling ships called into the island group, mission stations were established that depended on oceanic connections, and Sāmoans themselves increasingly travelled to parts of the Pacific that were beyond the extensive indigenous maritime networks, and out into the wider world. Commercial networks were also critical in recalibrating pathways of movement, particularly after the world-spanning Hamburg firm Godeffroy und Sohn based its Pacific operations at Apia in 1857. Steam navigation soon followed, lacing Sāmoa into more regular connection with Hawai'i, but also Australia and New Zealand, making it an integral part of the circuitry of Australasia, even if it often fell off the eastern margins of the maps of the imagined region.[36]

Salesa offered a useful schematic overview of the importance of the reordering of circuits of mobility in the colonial period, processes that were shaped by the intrusions of Europeans (Papālagi) but also by significant internal shifts within indigenous communities:

> The making and remaking of nodes or paths within the circuit created fractures and generated new associations, not only between islanders and Papalagi, but also among different groupings on all sides. Not simply a means of connecting people and places, the circuitry had high stakes: not merely shaping the destinations of people, but influencing also their collective and individual destinies. It was hardly surprising, then, that control over the mobility of islanders, as with island sovereignty and the control of island resources, animated relations of power. Localities were brought into new relations with places and peoples, new mechanisms and formations of power, often on a different scale or different register than before.[37]

My own earlier work has stressed the ways in which empires functioned as dynamic weblike structures that operated through the creation of interdependence and exchange. The nature of these connections could change over time, but the work of imperial networks often modified existing patterns of indigenous mobility and connection and created economic and cultural entanglements that had enduring consequences. I have also shown that in New Zealand, Māori patterns of movement underwent rapid change in the early nineteenth century, in part because of new engagements with missionaries, whalers and traders.[38] From the 1790s to the 1830s, Māori travellers voyaged to other parts of the Pacific, Asia and Europe, but most frequently to the Australian colonies, creating important lines of indigenous connection that spanned the Tasman Sea, creating pathways followed by later generations, which were a significant element in the making of Australasia.[39] At the same time, intra- and inter-kin group dynamics were also powerful spurs to movement in an age where warfare, displacement and migration rewrote the geography of indigenous social relationships across the motu (islands) that make up New Zealand.

As I have argued elsewhere, mobility and circulation were the very foundations of settler colonialism. The process of colonization – planting colonists – was dependent on two fundamentally important and related processes: first, the alienation of indigenous land and sovereignty; and second, the movement of colonists across the world and subsequently within the colony to 'settle' that land. This brings us to the fundamental contradiction that underwrote colonization: 'settlers' by their very nature were unsettled and mobility was one of their defining characteristics.[40] Australasian colonies were part of an imperial maritime order that drew together a range of colonial territorial holdings, ports and zones of influence, a system dependent on the movement of vessels, large and small, over both short distances and in world-spanning voyages. In this context, ports were like the beating heart of colonial life, pumping people, money and commodities into each British colony, propelling the circulations that were vital to the growth of the colony while simultaneously connecting that site into a much larger global set of circulations.[41] As this volume shows, these included the critically important networks of mobility and exchange that defined the contours of Australasia.

Ultimately, however, the regulation of mobility was an important element that eroded the power of Australasia as a spatial concept. Developing colonial nation states exercised their power through the creation of borders and controlling the people that crossed them. Radhika Mongia has demonstrated that Canada defined visions of the nation in particular in response to the supposed 'threat' of the mobility of Asian communities in the late-nineteenth century; an argument that accords with the work of Henry Reynolds and Marilyn Lake on Australia, and myself on New Zealand.[42] The racialized control of mobility was thus central in constituting national borders: while the mobility of 'white' colonists was celebrated, the movement of non-white people was pathologized and policed. The real connections that had developed between Australasian settlements and the Cantonese world were at the forefront of these anxieties. Chinese circulations reached out from Guangdong not just to South East Asia, but also to the goldfields of Victoria and Otago, to Australasian port cities and commercial centres.[43]

In important ways, these Chinese circulations intersected with, and in turn were given shape by, the wider circuitry of transportation networks, commercial relationships and flows of people that made Australasia. The regulation of these flows, especially through the racialized policing of borders, was pivotal in the creation and definition of fledgling nations. Important mechanisms of immigration control as well as arguments for the restriction of the mobility of non-white peoples were shared within and between white settler colonies, particularly Australia and New Zealand. The landmark *State Experiments in Australia and New Zealand* (1902), written by William Pember Reeves, the leading Fabian Socialist, journalist, historian and an influential architect of progressive reform in New Zealand, argued that the passage of anti-Chinese immigration acts marked the beginnings of 'interesting experiments in law and administration'. For Reeves, both nationhood and the possibility of social progress depended on the exclusion of Chinese.[44]

Thus, controlling mobility across the border was a central element in exercising the powers of the nation state. In the New Zealand case, Matthew Henry has shown that the early twentieth century saw the state exercising increasing control over the nation's borders through immigration law and the operation of a passport and permit system, a system that itself was part of the growing international regulation of human mobility by states and a mechanism that was central to the production of citizenship across the globe.[45] Similar dynamics played out in Australia. One of the key features of Australasia, at least as it was commonly understood at the end of the nineteenth century, was that it had become a privileged space for white colonists, a privilege that was manifest in the relative freedom of their mobility at the precise point where the mobility of non-white groups was pathologized and restricted.[46]

Reeves's work highlighted the strong connections between Australia and New Zealand and the very strong intellectual links that wove the colonies together. These policies themselves emerged out of a wider set of debates across Australasia (and beyond), debates that were underpinned by a heavily intertextual press system that made extensive use of cut-and-paste journalism and by the circulation of tracts on questions of civilization, race and nationhood. These transnational processes were integral to the calcification of national boundaries, an irony that echoes C. A. Bayly's observation that nations insisted on their distinctiveness and difference, but through a common set of arguments and symbols.[47] The development of more clearly bounded national communities in the decade either side of 1900 was critical in initiating the erosion of Australasia's cultural currency, a shift that is clearly captured in a Google N-gram analysis of the Google Books corpus:

Figure 0.1 Usage of 'Australasia' as reflected by a Google N-gram analysis of the Google Books corpus, https://books.google.com/ngrams. Source: Public Domain.

The nation state's consolidation was and is dependent on projecting and actualizing a nation-space. As I have argued elsewhere, this was a complex set of processes driven by various elements of colonial states as government officials and departments projected and policed the authority of the state over the nation-space.[48] State agents were also significant actors in the much wider process of producing the array of cultural artefacts, frequently printed, that defined the nation's landscapes and limits, and disseminated visions of the nation as a territorial unit that was coherent and clearly defined. The sophisticated cartographic apparatus of atlases, maps and charts that were integral to this process were reinforced by the symbolic repertoire of currency, stamps, a coat of arms, a flag and a national anthem that states fashioned for their young nation.

Economic circulations – labour, capital, commodities and technologies – were also integral in the making and remaking of Australasia. My chapter in this volume demonstrates that from its genesis the idea of Australasia was intimately connected with imperial territorial ambition and commercial aspirations. Exploration, resource extraction, evangelization, commercial activity and formal colonial settlement drew these into imperial circulations, and created new patterns of exchange, new markets, and new circuits for the movement of people, goods and money. Important work in the last generation has begun to refocus our attention on the economic dimensions of colonial development, including Peter Gibbons on trade and the making of New Zealand; Michael Stevens on indigenous material culture, exchange networks and their interface with the colonial economy; James Belich and Felicity Barnes on the cultural dimensions of New Zealand's economic ties to Britain; Alecia Simmonds and Jennifer Newell on trade between Australia and the Pacific; and the call of Hannah Forsyth and Sophie Loy-Wilson for a new attentiveness to material factors in the history of Australia and its relations with the world.[49] Taken together, the contributions in this volume also point to the disjunctures and disconnects that can develop between economic and cultural forms (like historical writing) or political identities. Denoon underscored this very important point when he observed that '[t]he real cultural and historical connections between northern Australia and Southeast Asia' have remained 'buried under generations of denial', as historical and political visions of Australia have prioritized the importance of relationships with Europe, neglecting or erasing these Asian connections.[50]

A sharper focus on the operation of mobility and circulation at varying scales – the locality, the district, the region, the colony and larger spatial formations such as Australasia – enriches our understanding of the operation of empires and the development of colonial cultures; an undertaking that a number of the chapters in this volume advance. The movement of texts was one very important aspect of these circulations, the whole system underpinned by the shuffling and shuttling of paper, whether official documents, newspapers, argumentative pamphlets, ethnographic texts, travel narratives, or various forms of fiction.[51] Competing arguments about the capacity of Indigenous peoples, the imperial potential of various lands and resources, plans for colonization and visions of imagined futures were dependent on writing, printing and paper. Thus, rather than imagining these texts as primarily articulating 'ideas' or as politically interested forms of 'representation', we can also think of them as material forms, designed to be mobile, to be shared, to be sent, to be stored and retrieved; they were accumulated, ordered, combined and compared, and disseminated.[52]

Paper's very distinctive materiality – its lightness, portability and plasticity – meant that it was in Harold Innis's terms a 'space-binding' technology, perfectly suited to the spatially dispersed orders fashioned by modern maritime empire.[53] These mobile inscriptions physically moved across the empire and they fundamentally shaped its development.[54] Paper moved more quickly from the 1840s, as the power of steam, developing rail networks, steamer routes and telegraph lines expanded communication networks and greatly accelerated the movement of news and information.[55]

Such connections have become central to writing the history of empires. Since the 1990s it has become common to treat imperial metropoles and their colonies in a single frame. My earlier work insisted that historians of empire could go further than this, however, and explore the 'horizontal' connections between colonies as well as the 'vertical' links between any given colony and the imperial centre. While there is significant interest throughout the volume in the 'horizontal' connections between Australia, New Zealand and the Pacific, it offers particular insights into how these 'vertical' connections took shape and were conceived. A number of the contributors focus particularly on the question of the south, taking their cues from the etymology of 'Australasia'. With its connotations of southern-ness, it directs us to the importance of relationality in this geographical construct: the south and southern-ness are defined in connection to their relation to the north, to Europe, and frequently to Britain in particular. A number of chapters explore this dimension of Australasia, but also its interplay with other associated ideas: the 'south', the 'antipodes', the 'South Pacific' and 'Oceania'. This approach is energized by a growing body of work in literary studies that has been particularly concerned with how the southern hemisphere has been constituted not just through texts but in literary culture and explores what is distinctive about writing from the south.[56] A number of the key proponents of this approach contribute to and enable this volume to offer a unique interdisciplinary conversation about how space was produced, contested and reformulated.

This volume is organized into three sections. The first, 'Circulating People and the Production of Space', examines the ways in which human mobility was central in the production of the idea of Australasia. In exploring the movement of people within and across the imagined region, it explores how the region's boundaries were understood, borders were policed and the ways it jostled with other spatial formations, including the calcifying nation states of Australia and New Zealand as well as ideas about the Pacific region more broadly. Here we get a clear sense of how people on the move made Australasia, both as a space of routinized mobility and as an imagined space, created and contested by the visions produced out of these dynamic southern circulations of officials and administrators, traders and colonists, tourists and activists, Indigenous peoples and members of Asian diasporic communities. These chapters can be usefully read alongside Raymond Williams's insight that mobility, or 'traffic' in his formulation, 'is a form of consciousness and a form of social relations'.[57]

The middle section of the volume offers three chapters on 'Environmental Transformations', which explore the distinctive land- and seascapes of the south and the ways in which they were understood within the context of empire. Although these pieces are anchored in literary analysis (and thus link nicely to the third section of the volume), they offer important perspectives on the limits of 'improvement' – the great energizing idea of colonization – highlighting the unruly circulations of seeds, the connection between agricultural development and colonial violence, and the catastrophic environmental change propelled by empire-building. These chapters illuminate critically important dimensions of the colonization of this region's distinctive environments and the ways in which these landscapes and seascapes inflected understandings of its southern-ness. They can be read productively alongside landmark studies of environmental history by the likes of Alfred Crosby, Tom Griffiths, Libby Robbins and Tom Brooking.[58] But it is also possible to read these chapters in dialogue with recent important work on the 'eco-cultural networks' that spanned the Tasman, but which also reached out further still to the Pacific and Asia. James Beattie has played an important role in highlighting the significance of these connections, but his earlier work on environmental anxiety, which itself traced important circulations between India, Australia and New Zealand, has also pointed to the productive space where the study of environmental change can interact with intellectual and cultural history, a space that this section engages with as well.[59]

The third section of the volume, 'Texts in Motion', connects circulation and a concern with southern-ness through critical readings of a number of texts. This section clearly underscores the *relational* nature of Australasia as a concept; the ways in which it was embedded in oppositions and contrasts between the south and the north, Europe and the Antipodes. These chapters are also unified in their concern with mobility and exchange as they trace the cultural visions articulated with important southern circulations of literary texts, excavating a range of readings of Australasia, the Antipodes and the colonial dominions of Australia and New Zealand. They do important work in connecting representation and materiality, particularly within the context of the transformations and disruptions of European empire-building.

By reading Australasia in multiple contexts and alongside a number of other regional imaginaries, the contributions gathered here return this spatial imaginary to the range of cultural fields from which it took shape. Written from a variety of angles of vision, they capture a diverse array of arguments and perspectives, producing a composite piece of the making and continuous remaking of Australasia. They do not suggest in the manner of Denoon or Mein Smith that Australasia is a privileged analytical frame, but rather they recognize the significance of this conception within the context of European empire-building and settler colonialism. Framed by imperial aspirations, the idea of Australasia was continuously remade by the changing shape of the networks and circuitry of empires and by evolving colonial orders that developed within this region. Although the currency and purchase of Australasia is now attenuated, we must recognize the critical importance of this understanding of space in enabling Europeans to claim significant portions of the world and its oceans, and in the justifications they offered for imperial dominance.

Notes

1   Charles de Brosses, *Histoire des navigations aux terres australes: contenant ce que l'on sait des mœurs & des productions des Contrées découvertes jusqu'à ce jour ; & où il est traité de l'utilité d'y faire de plus amples découvertes, & des moyens d'y former un*

établissement (Paris: Durand, 1756), 80. 'Notre globe est formé de trois grandes pièces de terre, Asie, Afrique & Amérique, & de trois grandes pièces de mer, éthiopique ou des Indes, atlantique ou du nord, pacifique ou du sud. Rélativement à ceci on peut de même diviser le monde austral inconnu en trois portions, chacune au sud des trois ci-dessus. L'une dans l'océan des Indes au sud de l'Asie que j'appellerai par cette raison *australasie*.'

2   Ibid., 80: 'tout ce que contient le vaste océan pacifique, & je donnerai à celle-ci le nom *polynésie* à cause de la multiplicité d'isles qu'elle renferme'.

3   Tom Ryan, '"Le Président des Terres Australes": Charles de Brosses and the French Enlightenment Beginnings of Oceanic Anthropology', *The Journal of Pacific History* 37:2 (2002): 160.

4   Thomas Hankins, *Science and the Enlightenment* (Cambridge: Cambridge University Press, 1985), 21, 29, 49, 61; Richard Yeo, *Encyclopaedic Visions: Scientific Dictionaries and Enlightenment Culture* (Cambridge: Cambridge University Press, 2001).

5   O. H. K. Spate, *Paradise Found and Lost* (Sydney: ANU Press, 1987), 71–2.

6   John Robson, 'A comparison of the charts produced during the Pacific voyages of Louis de Antoine de Bougainville and James Cook', in *Captain Cook: Explorations and Reassessments*, ed. Glyndwr Williams (Woodbridge: Boydell Press, 2004), 137.

7   De Brosses, *Histoire*, 4: 'il n'est pas possible qu'entre le Japon & l'Amérique il n'y ait, dans le vaste océan pacifique, un grand nombre d'isles riches en épiceries'.

8   Vincent T. Harlow, *The Founding of the Second British Empire, 1763-1793*, 2 vols (London: Longmans, Green & Co, 1952-64); C. A. Bayly, *Imperial Meridian: The British Empire and the World, 1780-1830* (London: Longman 1989).

9   E.g. Michael Davitt, *Life and Progress in Australasia* (London: Methuen, 1898); T. A. Coghlan, *The Progress of Australasia in the Nineteenth Century* (Edinburgh: W. & R. Chambers, 1903); William Pember Reeves, *State Experiments in Australia and New Zealand*, 2 vols (London: G. Richards, 1902).

10 Donald Denoon, 'The isolation of Australian history: historical reconsiderations', *Historical Studies* 22:87 (1986): 252-60.

11 Ibid.

12 Donald Denoon, 'Re-Membering Australasia: A repressed memory', *Australian Historical Studies* 34:122 (2003), 290.

13 Ibid., 291.

14 Ibid., 292.

15 E.g. Tony Ballantyne, *Orientalism and Race: Aryanism in the British Empire* (Basingstoke: Palgrave, 2002); Angela Woollacott, *To Try Her Fortune in London: Australian Women, Colonialism, and Modernity* (New York: Oxford University Press 2001). For a sceptical response to transnational approaches anchored in the political and cultural weight of the nation, see Ann Curthoys, 'We've Just Started Making National Histories, and You Want Us to Stop Already?', in *After the Imperial Turn: Thinking with and through the Nation*, ed. Antoinette Burton (Durham, NC: Duke University Press, 2003), 70–89.

16 Ann Curthoys and Marilyn Lake, eds, *Connected Worlds: History in Transnational Perspective* (Canberra: ANU E Press, 2005); Marilyn Lake and Henry Reynolds, *Drawing the Global Colour Line: White Men's Countries and the International Challenge of Racial Equality* (Cambridge: Cambridge University Press, 2008). See also the discussion in Alecia Simmonds, Anne Rees, and Anna Clark, 'Testing the Boundaries: Reflections on Transnationalism in Australian History', in Clark, Rees, and Simmonds, eds, *Transnationalism, Nationalism and Australian History* (Singapore: Palgrave Macmillan, 2017), 1–14, here 1–2.

17 One notable exception of work that had foregrounded a range of Asian connections within an imperial context was James Broadbent, Margaret Steven and Suzanne Rickard, *India, China, Australia: Trade and Society 1788–1850* (Glebe, NSW: Historic Houses Trust of New South Wales, 2003).

18 For important examples of the work of the scholars associated with the Dragon Tails conferences, see Sophie Couchman and Kate Bagnall, eds, *Chinese Australians: Politics, Engagement and Resistance* (Leiden: Brill, 2015); Kate Bagnall and Julia T. Martínez, *Locating Chinese Women: Historical Mobility Between China and Australia* (Hong Kong: Hong Kong University Press, 2021); Sophie Loy-Wilson, *Australians in Shanghai: Race, Rights and Nation in Treaty Port China* (London: Routledge, 2017). On South Asian connections, see e.g. Margaret Allen, 'Otim Singh in White Australia', in *Something Rich and Strange: Sea Changes, Beaches and the Littoral in the Antipodes*, ed. Susan Hosking et al. (Adelaide: Wakefield Press, 2009) 195–212; Kama Maclean, *British India, White Australia Overseas Indians, Intercolonial Relations and the Empire, 1901–1947* (Sydney: New South Books, 2001); Samia Khatun, *Australianama: The South Asian Odyssey in Australia* (London: Hurst & Company, 2020).

19 Key starting points are: Tracey Banivanua Mar, *Violence and Colonial Dialogue: The Australian-Pacific Indentured Labor Trade* (Honolulu: University of Hawai'i Press, 2007); *Decolonisation and the Pacific: Indigenous Globalisation and the Ends of Empire* (Cambridge: Cambridge University Press, 2016).

20 E.g. Sekhar Bandyopadhyay, *India in New Zealand: Local Identities, Global Relations* (Dunedin: Otago University Press, 2010); Sekhar Bandyopadhyay and Jane Buckingham, *Indians and the Antipodes: Networks, Boundaries, and Circulation* (New Delhi: Oxford University Press, 2018); Jacqueline Leckie, *Indian Settlers: The Story of a New Zealand South Asian Community* (Dunedin: Otago University Press, 2007). The most important entry point for scholarship on Chinese-New Zealand history remains James Ng, *Windows on a Chinese past*, 4 vols (Dunedin: Otago Heritage Books,1993), although a number of important essays have been produced more recently by Brian Moloughney and James Beattie. Also see Manying Ip, *Unfolding History, Evolving Identity: The Chinese in New Zealand* (Auckland: Auckland University Press, 2003).

21 See, especially, Damon Salesa, 'New Zealand's Pacific', in *The New Oxford History of New Zealand*, ed. Giselle Byrnes (Melbourne: Oxford University Press, 2009), 149–72; *Island Time: New Zealand's Pacific Futures* (Wellington: Bridget Williams Books, 2017); Sean Mallon, Kolokesa Mahina-Tuai and Damon Salesa, eds, *Tangata o le Moana: New Zealand and the People of the Pacific* (Wellington: Te Papa Press, 2012).

22 Frances Steel, *Oceania under Steam: Sea Transport and the Cultures of Colonialism, c.1870–1914* (Manchester: Manchester University Press, 2011); editor of *New Zealand and the Sea: Historical Perspectives* (Wellington, New Zealand: Bridget Williams, 2019). Also see her 'Re-routing empire? Steam-age circulations and the making of an Anglo Pacific, c. 1850–90', *Australian Historical Studies* 46:3 (2015): 356–73.

23 David Haines and Jonathan West, 'Crew Cultures in the Tasman World', in *New Zealand and the Sea: Historical Perspectives*, ed. Frances Steel; Michael Stevens, '"A Defining Characteristic of the Southern People": Southern Māori Mobility and the Tasman World', in *Indigenous Mobilities: Across and Beyond the Antipodes*, ed. Rachel Standfield (Canberra: ANU Press, 2018); and Rachel Stanfield, *Race and Identity in the Tasman World, 1769–1840* (London: Pickering & Chatto, 2012), and her edited collection, *Indigenous Mobilities*.

24 Philippa Mein Smith, 'Mapping Australasia', *History Compass* 7 (2009): 3. Mein Smith's characterization of Cook as being 'revered' was not convincing in 2009 and is certainly not tenable now.

25 Donald Denoon and Philippa Mein Smith with Marivic Wyndham, *A History of Australia, New Zealand, and the Pacific* (Oxford: Blackwell, 2000).

26 Keith Sinclair, ed., *Tasman Relations: New Zealand and Australia, 1788–1988* (Auckland: Auckland University Press, 1987).

27 James Belich, *Making Peoples: A History of the New Zealanders: From Polynesian Settlement to the End of the Nineteenth Century* (London: Allen Lane, 1996), 131–2, 187, 348.

28 Standfield, *Race and Identity in the Tasman World*.

29 Kristyn Harman, *Cleansing the Colony: Transporting Convicts from New Zealand to Van Diemen's Land* (Dunedin Otago University Press, 2017).

30 Ibid.; Philippa Mein Smith, Peter J. Hempenstall and Shaun Goldfinch, *Remaking the Tasman World* (Christchurch: Canterbury University Press, 2008).

31 Scott McKinnon and Margaret Cook, *Disasters in Australia and New Zealand: Historical Approaches to Understanding Catastrophe* (Singapore: Palgrave Macmillan, 2020).

32 Klaus Neumann, Nicholas Thomas and Hilary Ericksen, eds, *Quicksands: Foundational Histories in Australia & Aotearoa New Zealand* (Sydney: UNSW Press, 1999).

33 Andrew Leach, Antony Moulis and Nicole Sully, *Shifting Views: Selected Essays on the Architectural History of Australia and New Zealand* (St Lucia, Queensland: University of Queensland Press, 2008).

34 Catharine Coleborne, *Madness in the Family: Insanity and Institutions in the Australasian Colonial World, 1860–1914* (Basingstoke: Palgrave, 2010); *Insanity, Identity and Empire: Immigrants and Institutional Confinement in Australia and New Zealand, 1873–1910* (Manchester: Manchester University Press, 2021); Jennifer S. Kain, *Insanity and Immigration Control in New Zealand and Australia, 1860–1930* (Cham: Palgrave Macmillan, 2019).

35 See Tony Ballantyne, 'On place, space and mobility in nineteenth-century New Zealand', *New Zealand Journal of History* 45:1 (2011). These arguments also draw from Doreen Massey, 'Places and Their Pasts', *History Workshop Journal* 39:1 (1995): 182–92; *Space, Place and Gender* (Minneapolis: University of Minnesota Press, 1994); and *For Space* (London: Sage, 2005).

36 Damon Ieremia Salesa, '"Travel-happy" Samoa: colonialism, Samoan migration and a "brown Pacific"', *New Zealand Journal of History* 37:2 (2003): 172–3.

37 Ibid., 172.

38 Ballantyne, 'On place, space and mobility'; Ballantyne, 'Entangled Mobilities: Missions, Māori and the Reshaping of Te Ao Hurihuri', in Standfield, ed., *Indigenous Mobilities*, 115–44; *Webs of Empire: Locating New Zealand's Colonial Past* (Wellington: Bridget Williams Books, 2012); *Entanglements of Empire: Missionaries, Māori, and the Question of the Body* (Durham, NC: Duke University Press, 2014).

39 Judith Binney, 'Tuki's Universe', in Keith Sinclair, ed., *Tasman Relations*, 15–33; Vincent O'Malley, *Haerenga: Early Māori Journeys Across the Globe* (Wellington: Bridget Williams Books, 2015); Stevens, '"A Defining Characteristic of the Southern People", 79–114.

40 Ballantyne, 'Mobility, Empire, Colonisation', *History Australia* 11:2 (2014): 7–37.

41 Ballantyne, 'Maritime Connections and the Colonisation of New Zealand' in Steel, ed., *New Zealand and the Sea*.

42 Lake and Reynolds, *Drawing the Global Colour Line*; Ballantyne, 'Mobility, Empire, Colonisation'.

43 Eric Tagliacozzo, *Chinese Circulations: Capital, Commodities, and Networks in Southeast Asia* (Durham, NC: Duke University Press, 2001); Adam McKeown, 'Global Migration 1846–1940', *Journal of World History* 15:2 (2004).

44 Reeves, *State Experiments in Australia and New Zealand*, I, v.

45 Matthew Henry, 'Border Geostrategies: Imagining and Administering New Zealand's Post-World War One Borders', *New Zealand Geographer* 64:3 (2008): 194–204; Radhika Mongia, 'Race, Nationality, Mobility: A History of the Passport', *Public Culture* 11:3 (1999): 527–56; 'Historicizing State Sovereignty: Inequality and the Form of Equivalence', *Comparative Studies in Society and History* 49:2 (2007): 384–411; Adam McKeown, *Melancholy Order: Asian Migration and the Globalization of Borders, 1834–1929* (New York: Columbia University Press, 2008); Craig Robertson, *The Passport in America: The History of a Document* (New York: Oxford University Press, 2010).

46 Jane McCabe, 'Working the permit system: Anglo-Indian immigration to New Zealand, 1920–1940', *New Zealand Journal of History* 48:2 (2014): 27–49.

47 C. A. Bayly, *The Birth of the Modern World, 1780–1914: Global Connections and Comparisons* (Oxford: Blackwell, 2004), 1–2.

48 Ballantyne, 'On place, space and mobility'.

49 Peter Gibbons, 'The far side of the search for identity: reconsidering New Zealand history', *New Zealand Journal of History* 37:1 (2003): 38–49; Stevens, '"A Defining Characteristic of the Southern People"', 79–114, and 'A "Useful" Approach to Māori History', *New Zealand Journal of History* 49:1 (2015): 54–77; Belich, *Making Peoples*; Felicity Barnes, *New Zealand's London: A Colony and its Metropolis* (Auckland: Auckland University Press, 2012); Jennifer Newell, *Trading Nature: Tahitians, Europeans and Ecological Exchange* (Honolulu: University of Hawai'i Press, 2010); Alecia Simmonds, 'Trading Sentiments: Friendship and Commerce in John Turnbull's Voyages (1800–1813)', *The Journal of Pacific History* 48:4 (2013): 369–85; Hannah Forsyth and Sophie Loy-Wilson, 'Seeking a New Materialism in Australian History', *Australian Historical Studies* 48:2 (2017): 169–88.

50 Denoon, 'Re-Membering Australasia', 291.

51 Tony Ballantyne, 'Indien und die Globalisierung Kolonialen Wissens', in *Von Käfern, Märkten und Menschen: Kolonialismus und Wissen in der Moderne*, ed. Rebekka Habermas and Alexandra Przyrembel (Göttingen: Vandenhoeck & Ruprecht, 2013), 115.

52 Ballantyne, 'On place, space and mobility'.

53 The distinctions between time-binding and space-binding media (and the attendant political orders they support) was explored in Harold A. Innis, *The Bias of Communication* (Toronto: University of Toronto Press, 1951) and *Empire and Communications* (Oxford: Oxford University Press, 1950).

54 Bruno Latour, 'Visualisation and Cognition: Drawing Things Together', in H. Kuklick, ed., *Knowledge and Society: Studies in the Sociology of Culture Past and Present*, Jai Press vol. 6 (1986): 1–40.

55 Martin Moir, 'Kaghazi Raj: Notes on the Documentary Basis of Company Rule, 1771–1858', *Indo-British Review* 21 (1993): 185–93. For more regionally focused studies, see Richard Saumarez Smith, *Rule by Records: Land Registration and Village Custom in Early British Panjab* (Delhi: Oxford University Press, 1996); Bhavani Raman, *Document Raj: Writing and Scribes in Early Colonial South India* (Chicago: The University of Chicago Press, 2012).

56 Lara Atkin, Sarah Comyn, Porscha Fermanis and Nathan Garvey, *Early Public Libraries and Colonial Citizenship in the British Southern Hemisphere* (Basingstoke: Palgrave Macmillan, 2019); Sarah Comyn and Porscha Fermanis, eds, *Worlding the South: Nineteenth-Century Literary Culture and the Southern British Colonies* (Manchester: Manchester University Press, 2020); 'Writing southern spaces: or, Grappling with Patriarchy in Darkest Africa: Elleke Boehmer in conversation with Gillian Dooley and others', *Writers in Conversation* 6:2 (August 2019).

57 Raymond Williams, *The Country and the City* (Oxford: Oxford University Press, 1973), 296.

58 Alfred W. Crosby, *Ecological Imperialism: The Biological Expansion of Europe, 900– 1900* (Cambridge: Cambridge University Press, 1986); Tom Griffiths and Libby Robin, *Ecology and Empire: Environmental History of Settler Societies* (Edinburgh: Keele University Press, 1997); Tom Griffiths, *Forests of Ash: An Environmental History* (Cambridge: Cambridge University Press, 2001); Eric Pawson and Tom Brooking, eds, *Making a New Land: Environmental Histories of New Zealand* (Dunedin: University of Otago Press, 2013); Tom Brooking, Eric Pawson and Paul Star, *Seeds of Empire: The Environmental Transformation of New Zealand* (London: I.B. Tauris, 2011).

59 James Beattie, Edward D. Melillo and Emily O'Gorman, eds, *Eco-cultural Networks and the British Empire: New Views on Environmental History* (London: Bloomsbury Academic, 2015); James Beattie, 'Plants, Animals and Environmental Transformation: Indian-New Zealand Biological and Landscape Connections, 1830s–1890s', in Vinita Damodaran, Anna Winterbottom and Alan Lester, eds, *The East India Company and the Natural World* (Basingstoke: Palgrave Macmillan, 2015), 219–48; James Beattie, 'Biota barons, "neo-eurasias" and Indian-New Zealand informal eco-cultural networks, 1830s–1870s', *Global Environment* 13:1 (2020): 133–65. On environmental anxiety: James Beattie, *Empire and Environmental Anxiety: Health, Science, Art and Conservation in South Asia and Australasia, 1800–1920* (Basingstoke: Palgrave Macmillan, 2011).

1

Framing Australasia: Empire, Colonization and the Cartographic Imagination

Tony Ballantyne

This chapter explores the interplay between imperial aspirations and the geographic construction of Australasia from the middle of the eighteenth century through to the beginning of the twentieth century. It suggests that a cartographic imagination was central to British understandings of both space and culture within an age where Asia and the Pacific became key domains for British imperial trade, exploration, evangelization, war-making and colonial settlement. This cartographic imagination was manifest in the variety of ways in which ethnology and geography were woven together as well as through an imperial culture that was saturated by geographic artefacts – maps, atlases, globes, textbooks, travel narratives, postcards, board games and biscuit tins – that used cartography to demonstrate and celebrate the global reach of British imperial power.

Within this context, 'Australasia' was created, framed and repeatedly reframed. I demonstrate that this idea was shaped by a number of European geographers and mapmakers in addition to the work of agents of the British Empire, but underscore the ways in which representations of the region of Australasia were increasingly dominated by British imperatives and aspirations, especially as British colonies were established in Australia and New Zealand. This chapter traces some of these key transition points. The foundation of my argument is established in the opening section, which discusses the emergence of the idea of 'Australasia', reading it against long traditions of British and European thought about *Terra Australis Incognita*, the Great Unknown Southern Continent. In addition to sketching the ways in which British understandings of Terra Australis were inflected by visions of early modern empire-building, my discussion turns to the work of the Burgundian Charles de Brosses, the scholar who first articulated the idea that a significant portion of the southern hemisphere should be best understood as 'Australasia'. I highlight the swift translation of this idea into British thought within the context of Britain's growing imperial interest and investment in both Asia and the Pacific. I also trace the interactions between this idea and the influential model of racial geography of the Pacific developed by the French explorer Jules-Sébastien-César Dumont d'Urville in the 1820s and 1830s. The chapter then turns to focus on shifting cartographic representations of Australasia – its composition and boundaries – through the nineteenth century, highlighting significant arguments about its borders and the ways in which Australia and New Zealand were increasingly dominant in understandings of what constituted the region. It concludes with some reflections on the interplay between how this broader region was imagined and depicted and the rising authority of national spatial imaginaries promoted by these consolidating colonial nations.

The genesis of Australasia

The Introduction to this volume noted the pivotal role of Charles de Brosses's *Histoire des navigations aux terres australes* (1756) in the genesis of Australasia as a concept. But de Brosses's work was shaped not only by shifting political dynamics and cultural currents within Europe, but also moulded by a longer arc of argumentation about geography and the human population. In particular, the idea of a large land mass deep in the southern oceans, a great southern land, had long been central in European beliefs about the nature of the geography of the world.

Bronwen Douglas has provided the richest reconstruction of the complex interplay between geographical thought, cartographic conventions, imperial exploration and developing European commercial knowledge in shaping understandings of Terra Australis in European thought through to the eighteenth century. She notes that the 'idea of an antipodean *terra incognita*' gained traction during the late fifteenth century as Renaissance scholars were energized by the application of new printing technologies to older cartographic traditions.[1] Against this backdrop, as well as the flow of new geographical information from European exploratory expeditions through the sixteenth century, the idea of Terra Australis was elaborated and gained greater intellectual purchase. We can see it being refined and rearticulated in a number of important cartographic artefacts: in the globe that featured a large southern land mass, part of which was named 'Terra Australis', produced by the Nuremberg mathematician and astronomer Johannes Schöner; the Parisian mathematician Oronce Finé's 1531 world map that featured a southern continent named *Terra Australis*; and in the mappa mundi featuring a huge southern continent in the 1570 atlas created by the Brabantian cartographer Abraham Ortelius – it was labelled *Terra Australis nondum cognita* ('The Southern Land not yet known').[2]

In the British case, the idea of Terra Australis was intimately connected with developing imperial aspirations. Sir Francis Drake's circumnavigation of the globe was not only propelled by a desire to check Spain's global power and to explore areas suitable for planting English colonies, but also to access the unknown wealth promised by Terra Australis. Drake was connected to John Dee, the great 'Magus' or 'Arch Conjuror' of the Elizabethan age. An astrologer, astronomer, mathematician and political advisor to Queen Elizabeth, Dee was strongly connected to the foremost European mapmakers in addition to being a cartographer himself. Dee produced fine maps that synthesized knowledge of the Atlantic world that was increasingly central in English thought, commerce and strategy.[3] Dee, who popularized the very term 'British Empire', also was convinced that there was a Terra Australis in the southern hemisphere, a great continent that would balance the known land masses, providing the symmetry of number and proportion that was central to his vision of Creation.[4]

This understanding was all the more important given that Dee was a proponent of what David Armitage has described as a 'maritime ideology'. He imagined Great Britain as not just England, Scotland, Ireland and the Orkneys, and also the surrounding seas; it was a polity that also had in his view legitimate claim over Iceland, Friesland and Greenland in addition to North America's eastern seaboard. Dee believed that as an oceanic *imperium*, Britain's commercial destiny was dependent on maritime connections and the cultivation of sea power through the development of its navy.[5]

Drake was an important early English player in a much wider set of European voyages, texts and maps that began to sketch the great ocean that Magellan named 'the Pacific', a process that fundamentally transformed European understandings of geography and which brought what Oskar Spate called 'The World Without the Pacific' to an end.[6] In the middle of the eighteenth century, the idea of Terra Australis remained central to European understandings of the Pacific despite the scepticism expressed by a range of navigators and cartographers. In the wake of Abel Janszoon Tasman's voyages in the 1640s, for example, the Dutch cartographer and publisher Pieter Goos rejected the idea that a large continent lay hidden in the southern ocean, suggesting that Tasman's discoveries south of New Guinea constituted the key element of Terra Australis, and he left the remainder of the southern ocean blank.[7] But the draw of an imagined great southern continent was persistent and powerful. Douglas offers this useful assessment:

> despite its ever-shrinking reality, the mirage of *Terra Australis* captivated savants up to and including the mid-18th-century compilers of collections of voyage texts, John Campbell, Charles de Brosses, and Alexander Dalrymple. Moreover, *Terra Australis* remained a well-nigh universal goal for maritime exploring expeditions until the return in 1775 of Cook's iconoclastic second voyage which definitively reduced it to roughly the modern contours of Australia and Antarctica.[8]

Spanish, French, Dutch and British navigation in the Pacific enabled a few partial coastlines to be tentatively sketched on European maps of the Pacific in the seventeenth and eighteenth centuries, but as Douglas suggests, these developments did not resolve the question of Terra Australis. This partial knowledge posed questions, but also raised hopes within a Europe that was hungry for land, commercial opportunities and new markets. Well into the eighteenth century, as Alfred Hiatt has observed, 'imagination and exploration shared a close kinship' and both animated a powerful interest in the possibilities of empire-building.[9]

De Brosses and 'Australasie'

While the *Histoire* of de Brosses drew upon these European traditions of exploration and geography, it also marked a significant turning point. Although de Brosses accepted the tradition of believing that lands in the far south had to act as a 'counterweight' to the better-known northern lands, he argued that there was not simply one great undifferentiated land mass. Rather than an 'immense' continent existing deep in the southern ocean, he suggested that there were three great regions. He conjectured that there was a land mass to the south of South America and this he named 'Magellanique'. The two other regions he graced with the neologisms 'Australasie' ('Australasia') and 'Polynésie' ('Polynesia'), the latter of which encompassed the regions that we now think of as Micronesia, Melanesia and Polynesia.[10]

In Tom Ryan's view, these arguments of de Brosses inaugurated a threefold shift. First, Ryan suggests that the volume was an important example of Enlightenment scholarship: 'This work, *Histoire des navigations aux terres australes*, for the first time ever systematically translated, summarized and analysed 250 years of written accounts by European voyagers to the southern hemisphere.'[11] Secondly, Ryan argues, de Brosses's *Histoire* catalysed a more rigorous and scholarly approach to thinking about the Pacific and the southern parts of the world: here, the tight bond between imagination and exploration identified by Hiatt began to be severed.[12] Ryan stresses that this new way of thinking predated Cook and Bougainville, and notes that it calls into question common scholarly arguments which posit that 'French anthropological thinking about the peoples of the South Pacific began to coalesce only after 1800'.[13] Third, and more importantly for us here, Ryan contends that de Brosses's text was central in not only systematizing accounts of European navigation, but also in advocating that the region be systematically explored and that it would be well-suited to European settlement. Ryan suggests that these arguments by de Brosses were important in galvanizing a European interest in exploring the Pacific: 'Without the efforts of de Brosses ... the voyages of Bougainville and Cook may not have occurred when and as they did, and Western imaginings of and interventions in this part of the globe may have taken a quite different – and not necessarily better – course.'[14]

This reading of de Brosses by Ryan is a significant argument which emphasizes the intellectual shifts he helped instigate. Ultimately, what was critically important about de Brosses is that his *Histoire* offered a vision of Australasia that was inflected by a deep interest in its imperial potential. Serge Tcherkézoff has suggested: 'De Brosses was less concerned with proposing a geographic nomenclature than he was with furthering strategic, political, even colonial goals. He wanted to encourage the French court to send expeditions towards the "Austral Lands" – lands that he maintained should be discovered without delay.'[15] Early in his text, de Brosses suggested that it was 'impossible for there not to be, in the immense Pacific Ocean, between Japan and America, a large number of islands rich in spiceries', a suggestion encoded by imperial ambition.[16]

But de Brosses was far from unique in expressing such desires for territory, wealth and influence. A strong interest in commercial opportunities and the possibilities of 'new' lands offered unified British and French interest in the Pacific. Even against the backdrop of the global conflict that was the Seven Years War, there were strong connections between the European rivals, and important scholarly and literary connections meant that there was a steady traffic in texts and knowledge across the Channel and between the two imperial systems.[17] De Brosses's *Historie* was quickly woven into that traffic, even though it offered a strong articulation of French imperial interests, highlighting the commercial opportunities, the strategic advantages, and even the possibilities that might be afforded to the Jesuits, if Australasia was explored. The need was pressing, he suggested, because of the way in which Britain was asserting its 'universal monarchy of the sea'.[18]

Translating 'Australasie': John Callander and Australasia

Australasia emerged in French as 'Australasie', but became a broadly European concept with it being shaped by Belgian, German ('Australasien'), Dutch ('Australasië') and Italian cartographers and authors as well.[19] It gained particular purchase in Britain, however, as it was swiftly adopted and deployed within the context of Britain's powerful global ambitions. De Brosses's *Histoire* was recycled and repackaged across the Channel by John Callander, a prolific Scottish antiquary, under the title *Terra Australis Cognita*. Callander followed de Brosses by introducing the idea of 'Australasia', rendering de Brosses's geographical sketch in the following way:

> As our globe is formed of three great pieces of earth, Asia, Africa, and America, and of three great pieces of water, the Indian, Atlantic, and Pacific Oceans, so we can naturally divide the great southern world into three districts, each of which lies to the south of the three before mentioned. The first in the Indian Ocean to the south of Asia, which, for this reason we shall call Australasia. The second lying in the North Sea, from the south point of America, we shall call Magellanica, from the name of the first discoverer; and in this tract we comprehend all that may be found to lie beyond the south of Africa, though no great extent of coast has yet been found on that side. We call the third division Polynesia, being composed of all those islands, which are found dispersed in the vast Pacific Ocean.[20]

Callander's volume essentially offered an unacknowledged translation of de Brosses's French text, but with a reworked interpretative frame that stressed the imperial potential of the Pacific for British interests. The first volume opened with a note 'To the Reader':

> We here offer to the Publick, the First Volume of our Collection of Voyages, to a distant, and hitherto little known Part of the Globe. The Editor flatters himself, that the following Journals, (many of which never appeared in *English* before) may be of Use to advance the Knowledge of Geography and Navigation; and thus tend to promote the Commercial Interests of *Great Britain*, and extend her Naval Power.[21]

Britain was presented with a particular strategic opportunity, Callander argued, because France was now a 'nation which is so far from being able to prosecute new discoveries, that they have been stripped, by the late war, of the best foreign settlements they possessed; and by the ruin of their marine, seem totally disabled at present to attempt any thing of [the] moment in this way'.[22] Callander suggested that within such a context Britain should look south:

> The extensive countries of the *Terra Australis*, hitherto untouched, open to us a field worthy of our attention in every respect. Establishments may be here formed without quarrelling with our neighbours. The spice-trade, hitherto possessed by our envious neighbours the *Dutch*, would be immediately within our reach, not only from our nearness to the islands whence these precious drugs come at present,

but also because these commodities are to be found in the countries which are the object of our present inquiries.[23]

Callander contended that these lands offered a particular opportunity to extend trade with Asia, 'if we consider the immense tracts of country that now lie before us, and which, by the parallels under which they are situated, must produce every valuable article that constitutes at present the *Indian* commerce'.[24] This was a timely argument given the crisis that had gripped Britain's Atlantic empire and the emergence of the East India Company as a territorial power in Bengal, Bihar and Orissa in 1765.

To a modern reader, one of the striking passages of Callander's work was where he suggested that the texts assembled could be understood as an '*Antartick* history of our globe'.[25] Here 'Antartick' was used an adjective, an invocation of southern-ness, and it pointed towards a kind of relational history. A similar project could, Callander noted, be undertaken to produce a history of the '*Artick Circle*', but those northern zones were much closer to Europe and better known. The opportunity, both for knowledge-gathering and empire-building, lay in the south. Callander's text was seen as an important guide to that potential: Cook carried a copy with him on the *Endeavour* on his first Pacific voyage.

Callander's reputation, however, did not endure so well in the long term. His career was blighted by the growing awareness of his willingness to copy, borrow, recycle and even invent.[26] The 1878 catalogue of German-born British bookseller and collector Bernard Quaritch pointedly characterized Callander's compendium of voyages as an 'impudent plagiarism',[27] while more recently Glyndwr Williams and P. J. Marshall suggested that Callander 'plundered' de Brosses,[28] and Spate dubbed Callander the 'piratical Scot'.[29] But Callander's creative strategies as an author were only questioned towards the end of his career and his collection appeared just at the moment where there was a significant reorientation in British imperial interest, anticipating and contributing to a growing interest in both Asia and the Pacific, a reorientation that Vincent Harlow identified as 'a swing to the east' in British imperial interest.[30] In this age of imperial ambition and competition, Williams and Marshall suggested that Britain and France were both caught up in a 'Pacific craze'.[31]

Elsewhere I have argued that the 1760s were pivotal in marking the emergence of an age of imperial globalization and that in Britain the culture that emerged out of these economic and political currents was strongly imprinted by a cartographic consciousness. Cartography enabled the emergence and circulation of truly global images of the world, images that were the product of the world-spanning nature of European imperial activity. Britons increasingly came to imagine the world generally, and their empire more specifically, within a global framework shaped by a geographic consciousness framed by maps, atlases and globes. This was a profound change where the map of the world and the globe became potent symbols of British commercial reach and imperial power.[32]

Within this context, the term and concept 'Australasia' jostled with a range of related terms: 'Australia' and 'New Holland' for what we know think of as Australia, the 'antipodes' for either or both Australia and New Zealand, and 'Oceania' (and associated variations such as 'Oceanica') or the 'Pacific' for the wider region. A good example of some of these uncertain distinctions is George Shaw's 1794 assessment of the zoology of Australia – a land which he suggested 'seems to abound in scenes of peculiar wildness and sterility' – which began invoking a range of names that might cover this land: 'the vast Island or rather Continent of Australia, Australasia, or New Holland'.[33]

In the preface to his survey of Australasia, first published in 1879, Alfred Russel Wallace, the influential naturalist and geographer, noted the persistent ambiguity of this geographical concept:

> The term Australasia has been used in very different senses. In the original German edition of this work it included the whole area as above defined, except the Malay Islands west of New Guinea, which were united with Asia. In the last edition of the *Encyclopaedia Britannica* (now publishing) it is held to comprise only Australia and New Zealand, with the large islands as far as New Guinea and the New Hebrides. Oceania is the word often used by continental geographers to describe the great world of islands we are now entering upon; but, as defining one of the six great divisions of the globe, Australasia harmonises better with the names of the other divisions, and at the same time serves to recall its essential characteristics – firstly, that it is geographically a southern extension of Asia; and, secondly, that the great island-continent of Australia forms its central and most important feature.[34]

Wallace's own research pointed to the blurred nature of Australasia's boundaries. In his influential work that identified a marked faunal divide in the Malay archipelago, a divide now known as the 'Wallace Line', he suggested that the eastern portion of the archipelago had strong connections with Australasia, an insight that explains his insistence on Australasia's status as a 'southern extension of Asia' above.

Cartography, ethnology and race

Some commentators saw cartography and ethnology or anthropology converging in the definition of Australasia. For these commentators, human difference was understood as intimately related to geography. This is well conveyed in the volume entitled *A geographical description of Australasia* (1830), written by the proponent of colonization S. H. Collins. Collins explained some of the key connections between human cultural variation and geography, later explored by Wallace, in the following way:

> Nor is there any difficulty in drawing the line of separation between those two divisions [Australasia and Polynesia]; though it is not quite so easy to mark the distinct boundary between the Australasian and the Asiatic Islands, where they melt into each other, about the Equator, at the north-west extremity of Papua or New Guinea. In a geographical view, the small islands of Waygiou, Salwatty, Batanta, Mysol, and Timorlaut, ought strictly to belong to Australasia; but peopled, as they are, by Asiatics of the Malay tribe, and under the influence of the Dutch Islands, it may, perhaps, be more proper, in a moral and political point of view, to consider them as belonging to the Asiatic Islands; more particularly, as we shall

then have all the Australasian population, with very few exceptions, marked with the African or Negro character.[35]

Collins believed that within the Pacific there was a fundamental divide among Indigenous peoples: in his view, Australasia was unified ethnologically by the common African origins of indigenous communities. Collins listed the elements of Australasia in the following way:

1. Notasia, or New Holland.
2. Van Dieman's Land.
3. Papua, or New Guinea.
4. New Britain, New Ireland, and neighbouring Islands.
5. Solomon's Islands.
6. New Hebrides.
7. New Caledonia.
8. New Zealand, and Isles to the southward.
9. Kerguelen's Islands, or Islands of Desolation.
10. St. Paul and Amsterdam.
11. Numerous reefs and islets of coral scattered over the Australasian Sea.[36]

What is striking about this formulation is the extent to which there was a complete concordance between race and geography: Australasia as a geographic space neatly mapped onto a racial formation. The ethnological identifications in this argument would not be dominant, however. In New Zealand, there were a few commentators who posited an African or Hamitic origin for Māori, or, more commonly, suggested a two-race theory of settlement. More common positions, however, used language, material culture and traditional narratives to identify Māori as Polynesians and as part of a broader Polynesian race, which was commonly seen as having Aryan origins.[37]

It is also interesting to note the unusual occurrence of 'Notasia' as a designation for Australia in Collins's work. The most likely derivation for this toponym was the Greek *notos* ('south; the south wind'), aligning the term quite closely with 'Australasia'.[38] 'Notasia' appeared in a small number of texts and maps in the early nineteenth century – including Italian maps from the 1820s – but it occasionally resurfaced later in the century, including in the title of the 1888 pamphlet, *Heroes of Notasia: A Record of Australian Exploration*.[39] As Peder Gammeltoft has noted, this was a 'cartographic curiosity', one that reminds us of the fluidity of naming systems, a fluidity that persisted well beyond the formal colonization of the region.[40]

It is important to note that some colonists in the region were sceptical of these framings. A short article in the *Hobart Town Gazette* in 1826 pointedly argued:

That part of the world situated in the great ocean between Africa, Asia, and America, has been very justly denominated OCEANICA – a name which must supersede, and in the mouths of the learned and polite has already superseded the unmeaning and inaccurate terms of Australasia, Notasia, Austral India, and Australia. New Holland and Van Diemen's Land have not one Asiatic feature, and as to the designation Austral or Southern this great fifth part of the world extends both north and south above 40 degrees on both sides of the equator.[41]

Although the *Hobart Town Gazette* was committed to the idea that Van Diemen's Land was not part of Australasia, the island produced other notable publications with 'Australasia' in the title, including *The Austral-Asiatic Review* and its successor *The Austral-Asiatic Review, Tasmanian and Australian Advertiser* in the 1830s and 1840s, and the *Australasian Friend in* the 1880s. In some quarters that investment persisted into the twentieth century: Launceston's *Daily Telegraph* was committed to promoting Tasmania and produced a colour poster proclaiming 'The Port of Hobart: the finest deep-water port in Australasia' in 1912.[42]

This critique from the 1820s does suggest both the uncertainty of both the limits and meanings of these geographic constructs. But over the century and a half following de Brosses and Callander there was generally a separation and delineation of terms. The *Hobart Town Gazette*'s advocacy for 'Oceanica' as its broad framing of the southern part of the world was quite unusual but was made at a time when its proximate form 'Oceania' had considerable authority. Bronwen Douglas has traced the evolution of this term in the early nineteenth century. In 1804 the French geographers Edme Mentelle and Conrad Malte-Brun suggested 'Océanique' in the place of (the French form) 'Terra Australes', seeing it as a rough equivalent of the broad geographical labels 'Amérique' ('America') and 'Afrique' ('Africa'). A decade later, another French cartographer, Adrien-Hubert Brué, replaced 'Océanique' with 'Océanie' ('Oceania') as a preferred regional framing and Douglas suggests that Brué worked with de Brosses's names for the constituent elements of Océanie.[43]

The naturalist, navigator and naval leader Jules-Sébastien-César Dumont d'Urville offered the most influential framework for interpreting the ethnology and geography of the Pacific in 1832. D'Urville's vision of Océanie was expansive, with a western boundary running through the 'Straits of Malacca, the China Sea, the eastern coasts of the islands of Formosa and Liu-Kiu, and Japan'.[44] Drawing on existing works and his own observations, d'Urville was keen to offer a definitive interpretation of the Pacific and suggested that Océanie was made up of 'four main divisions': 'Malaisie' ('Malaysia'), 'Mélanésie' ('Melanesia'), 'Micronésie' ('Micronesia') and 'Polynésie' (Polynesia).[45] In this theory, 'Australie' (Australia) belonged to Mélanésie as he argued, like S. H. Collins in 1830, that indigenous Australians were clearly part of the 'black race', which he saw as expressing strong continuities with African peoples and believed that they shared a common origin.[46] In this vision, race was fundamental in interpreting geography. Douglas suggests that 'the concept Océanie is a synecdoche for the fertile marriage of geography and raciology that characterised the science of race from its emergence at the dawn of the 19th century'.[47] Of course, as the nineteenth century progressed, Australasia did become racialized in another fashion, as for many Europeans it essentially was Australia and New Zealand, two settler colonies which had come to be seen by some as 'white men's countries'.[48]

D'Urville's theory of cultural and racial divisions proved powerful: it quickly became 'common knowledge' in France, was taught in French schools in the 1840s, and rapidly disseminated throughout Europe and in learned circles.[49] It continues to provide an enduring framework today (albeit with some of his racial assumptions stripped back), and shapes both popular and scholarly apprehensions of the region. But d'Urville's vision of an expansive Océanie/Oceania was less durable and the idea of Australasia continued to have power even if he rejected its usefulness. Through the nineteenth century, a growing divide marked island South East Asia, d'Urville's 'Malaysia', off from the rest of Oceania: its lands and peoples were seen as belonging to Asia rather than to the Pacific. As Denoon has observed, 'Oceania continued to shrink' through the second two-thirds of the nineteenth century. This growing focus on the islands of the central and southern Pacific helped enable Epeli Hau'ofa, in his landmark revisioning of the Pacific, to argue for a rehabilitation of 'Oceania', seeing it as a way of thinking that converged with his own revisioning, arguing that '"Oceania" denotes a sea of islands with their inhabitants'.[50]

I have noted how Callander saw Australasia as belonging to the broader 'Antartick' history of the globe. This formulation worked within deep traditions of Western thought that reached back to Greek and Roman thinkers who imagined lands deep in the south as a counterpoint to the northern lands. These lines of thought both shaped, and intersected with, later discussions of Terra Australis.[51] By the early nineteenth century, Terra Australis had lost currency and through this process was 'decomposed', to use William Eisler's phrase, into its constituent parts, whether Australia, New Zealand, Papua New Guinea and the Antarctic, or broader regional framings – Melanesia, Polynesia and Australasia – all of which had greater currency than the now antiquated Terra Australis.[52] But as Rip Bulkeley has noted in his discussion of the naming of Antarctica, such transitions could be protracted, rather than a sharp transition occurring between the older traditions of speculative geography and those based on imperial exploration. He notes the long persistence of Greek- and Latin-derived framings of southern land masses and waterways, but suggests that a key shift in the meaning of the adjective 'antarctic' from 'southern' to 'far southern' was initiated in the middle of the 1840s after Joseph Dalton Hooker published his *Flora Antarctica*, based on James Clark Ross's expedition, where Hooker stipulated that Antarctica should only be used for territories south of 50°S.[53] This, together with the adoption of the name 'Antarctica', was central in delineating key divisions, separating Antarctica from Australasia.[54]

Maps: shifting framings

The first graphic representation of 'Australia' – in fact 'l'Australasie' – came in a 1756 map in de Brosses's *Histoire des navigations aux terres australes* by the noted Parisian cartographer Gilles Robert de Vaugondy. De Vaugondy and his son Didier Robert had inherited a share in the establishment and materials of Nicolas Sanson (1600–67). While making use of inherited material was an important element of their practice, they also sought the newest intelligence and worked hard to verify and record their sources. De Vaugondy's 'l'Australasie' was based on a 1753 map by the hydrographer Jacques Bellin. Bellin's map, however, was of 'Terra Australes', where de Vaugondy's map

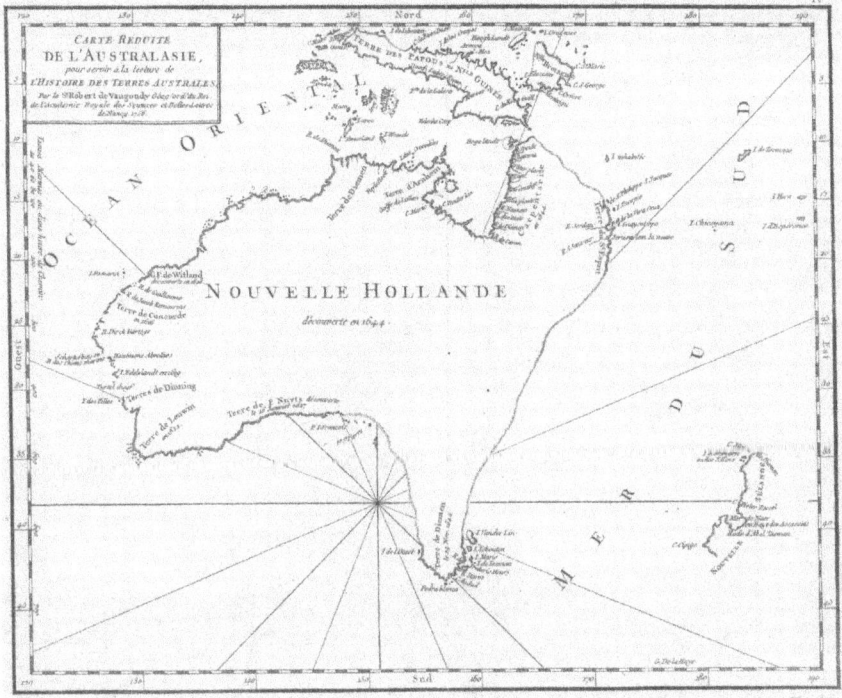

Map 1.1 'Carte Réduite de l'Australasie', from Charles de Brosses' *Histoire des navigations aux terres australes*, 1756. National Library of Australia, 1769324.

depicted de Brosses's notion of 'l'Australasie'. In this new vision, de Vaugondy amended several aspects of Bellin's map and excised some of its more mythic and speculative elements, even though he was unsure about the contours of the east coast of Australia and imagined some of the locations already discovered on Van Diemen's Land as part of the mainland of 'Nouvelle Hollande'.[55] This map imagined Australasia as primarily being made up of Australia, a partially explored New Zealand, Papua New Guinea and some of the islands in the Banda, Timor and Arafura Seas, including Timor-Leste ('I. Timorland'). Both Louis-Antoine, Comte de Bougainville, and Lieutenant James Cook were familiar with de Vaugondy's map. Cook's first voyage, with its circumnavigation of New Zealand and careful charting of Australia's east coast, rapidly extended European understandings of the geography of the Pacific and propelled rapid advances in European mapmaking. Bougainville's voyage cast doubt on the possibility of a large Terra Australis sitting undiscovered in the Pacific and also corrected a number of European misapprehensions, most notably confirming that the land 'discovered' by the Spaniard Quirós in 1606, which he named 'Australia de Espiritu Santo', was in fact part of an island group (Vanuatu) which was in fact, contrary to Quirós, unconnected to the Australian land mass.[56]

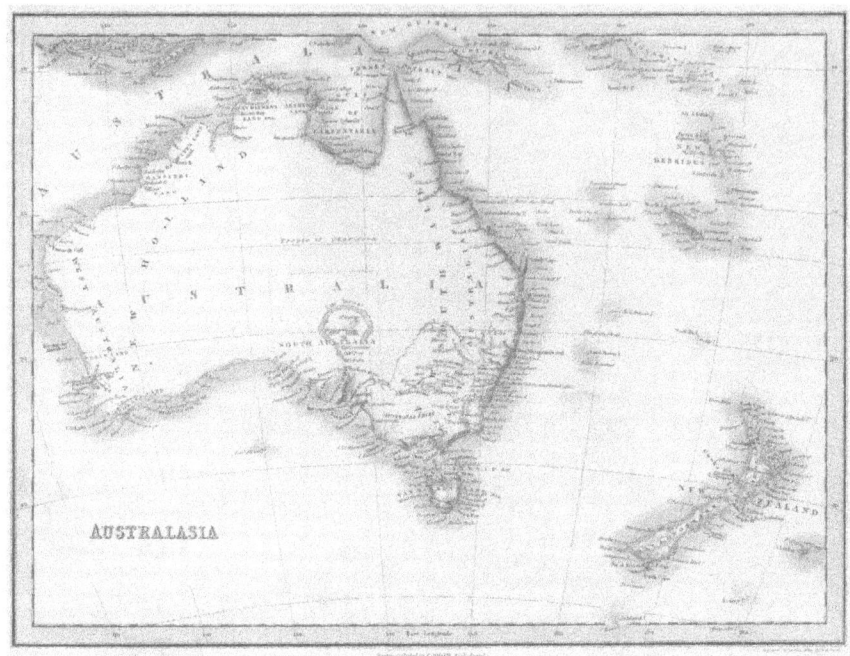

Map 1.2 'Australasia', *Smith's new general atlas containing distinct maps of all the principal empires, kingdoms & states* (London: C. Smith, 1843), plate 42. National Library of Australia digitised item. MAP T 1538 copy.

By the 1840s, representations of Australasia began to privilege Australia and New Zealand and the relationships between these two British colonial possessions. A good example of this shift is the 1843 map of Australasia engraved by W. R. Gardiner for the *Smith's New General Atlas* published in London, a volume which contained 'distinct maps of all the principal empires, kingdoms & states' as well as key regions such as Australasia.[57] Australia and New Zealand dominate the map, although a portion of the southern coast of Papua New Guinea intrudes into the top margin of the image and it features a number of key islands, including Timor in the north-west of the map, the Solomons in the north-east, the New Hebrides (now Vanuatu) and New Caledonia in the east. This map offered readers some important additional historical detail: Port Jackson, for example, was accompanied by a small notation '(Colony established 1788)' and on the eastern coast of South Australia was inscribed 'Discov^d by Flinders 1802'. It is also notable that this map's depiction of New Zealand drew on old material from Cook's first voyage. Bank's Peninsula is rendered as an island and Rakiura or Stewart Island is depicted as attached to the south-east corner of the South Island (Europeans had finally realized it was a separate island in 1804). It also inscribes Cook's renderings of Māori names 'Tavaipoenammo' (Te Wai Pounamu – the greenstone waters) and 'Eaheinomauwe' (perhaps He-mea-hī-nō-Māui – the things fished up by Māui) on

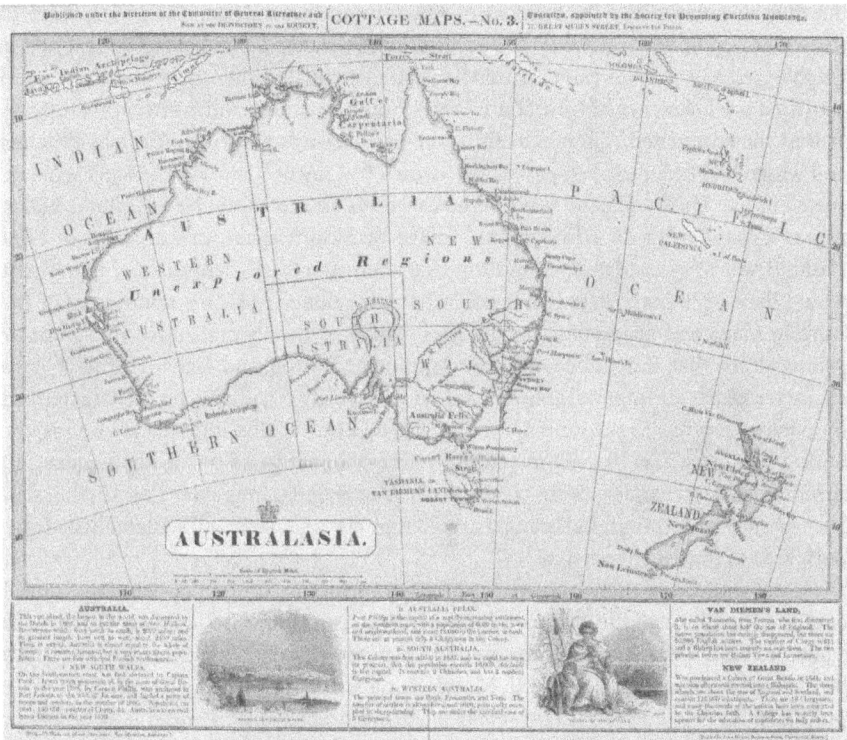

Map 1.3 'Australasia', 1863. Published under the direction of the Committee of General Literature and Education, appointed by the Society for Promoting Christian Knowledge, printed by John Bishop, Camberwell, Surrey, National Library of Australia, MAP T 1184.

what are now called the South and North Islands, respectively, underlining the persistence of old conventions, especially those associated with the celebrated British navigator.

An even sharper focus on Australia and New Zealand is delivered in an 1863 map. It was the third instalment in a series of four maps that depicted key elements of the British Empire: Canada, India and West Indies were the other maps in the series and these had been printed since at least the mid-1840s.[58] The Society for Promoting Christian Knowledge (SPCK) was an important agent in shaping Britons' sense of the empire, its geography and ethnology through its maps, popular narratives and children's texts.[59] One of the key features of this map is the top border tightly framing Australia's north coast, a device that effectively elided key waterways, islands and land masses to the north, especially New Guinea. This echoes the long-standing elision of the importance of connections across the Torres Strait, and the Timor and Arafura Seas in Australian historical writing, linkages that have been foregrounded in important recent work.[60] The illustrations and narratives provided at the bottom of this map not only were in keeping with the SPCK's awareness of the power of text and image together, but they also underlined the primacy of Australia and New Zealand in giving shape to the wider region of 'Australasia'. The account of Australia, divided over two text boxes, emphasized its scale ('in extent Australia is almost equal to the whole of Europe') and provided brief sketches of New South Wales, South Australia and Western Australia as well as the antiquated 'Australia Felix' – the pasturelands named by Thomas Mitchell and which had become a key part of the Crown Colony of Victoria in 1851. A separate sketch of Van Diemen's Land was offered as well as an account of New Zealand, which was associated with an ethnographic image of Māori: again, this account of New Zealand was very outdated, suggesting that there were '18 Clergymen', a figure that would have been inaccurate by the mid-1840s, let alone 1863. This reminds us of the ways in maps and geographic imaginaries remained deeply embedded in a popular print culture that functioned as what Antoinette Burton and Isabel Hofmeyr have characterized as an 'imperial commons', a pool of widely circulating texts characterized by extensive copying, reuse and upcycling.[61] In addition to this 'imperial commons', the notion of Australasia was reinforced through a wide range of printed ephemera and commercial merchandise, from cigarette cards to popular engravings of Australasian 'scenes' (sheep farming, bushrangers, gold miners and colonial settlements), from postcards to tourist advertising.

Along with maps, dictionaries have been powerful instruments of defining cultural communities through the identification of a distinct and common language that unifies a people. Australasia, according to some late-nineteenth-century authorities, could also be defined by language. Edward E. Morris, Professor at the University of Melbourne, produced *Austral English: A Dictionary of Australasian Words, Phrases and Usages* in 1898.[62] The noted Classicist H. A. Strong, who had also taught at the University of Melbourne, noted in a review that Morris's work was significant as it not only recorded the impact of te reo Māori and the indigenous languages of Australia on the versions of English spoken in Australasia, but it was also an archive of the names given by the colonists to the flora and fauna they encountered across the region. Strong noted that for readers based in Britain this environmental language was really only of 'secondary' interest, but that such readers were particularly engaged with the 'new coinages due to Australasia, and to the old words which have received new meaning under the Southern Cross'.[63] Here again the meaning of Australasia was compressed to focus on Australia and New Zealand alone and these two colonial societies were seen as the defining features of the region.

Some maps continued to offer an inclusive view of Australasia, offering a broad image of South East Asia and the south-west and southern Pacific. An excellent example of this is the 1880 map of Australasia produced by the Glasgow printing and publishing house Blackie & Son, a firm that had a global reach through its offices in Canada, Australia and India and produced popular children's annuals as well as atlases and maps.[64] The Blackie & Son map is particularly expansive, encompassing not only all of what we would now think of as South East Asia, but much of coastal East Asia, parts of the Pacific north of Micronesia, and across to the Marquesas, the Society Islands in contemporary French Polynesia and Pitcairn Island in the central Pacific. Despite this very expansive vision of what constituted Australasia, Australia dominates this map, not simply because of the relative size of its land mass but also because of the two large

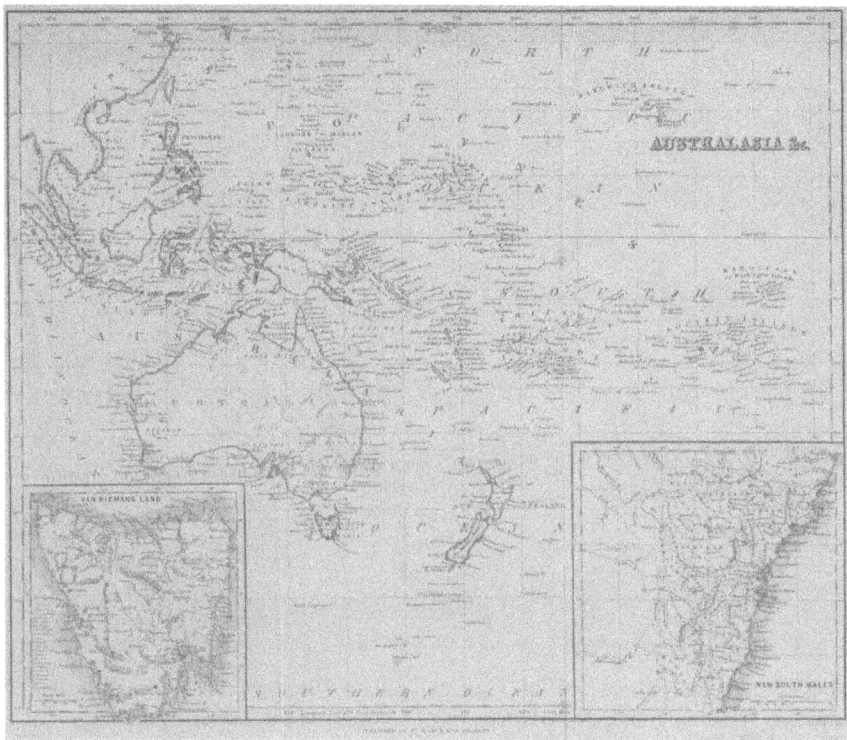

Map 1.4 'Australasia &c.' (Blackie & Son, *c.* 1880), Tooley Collection; Map T1462, National Library of Australia.

inset maps in the bottom corners. In the left, a very large inset offers a detailed depiction of Van Diemen's Land or Tasmania, rendered at almost the same size as the main image of Australia. In the bottom right, an even larger inset shows the coast of New South Wales, overshadowing the adjacent image of New Zealand in the main body of the map. So although this map certainly imagines Australasia within the context of both Asia and the Pacific, Australia is presented as the most important and defining element in this regional imaginary.

In the Introduction to this volume, I argued that circulation is a powerful analytical lens for making sense of Australasia. Through this chapter, we have seen how the notion of Australasia was developed, translated and reworked in a variety of contexts as ideas and concepts travelled. But maps of Australasia also underlined that the region itself was a space defined and made by circulation. An excellent example of this is the map of Australasian industries and communication networks, depicting the region as laced together by transportation routes and the commodities that circulated within (and beyond) its boundaries: people, money, animals and things on the move made the region and gave it shape.

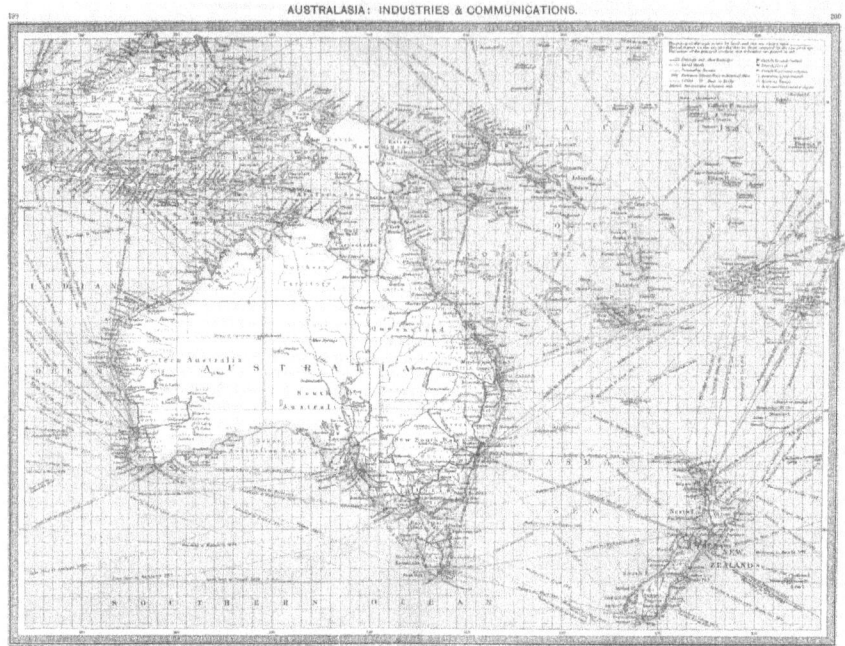

Map 1.5 'Australasia: Industries and Communications', *Harmsworth Universal Atlas and Gazetteer* (London: Amalgamated Press, 1906). Courtesy of the University of Otago Library.

Conclusion

By the time this image appeared in London in 1906, the concept of Australasia was beginning to lose its purchase. Australia federated in 1901 and New Zealand was on the path to Dominion status, which was proclaimed in 1907. These changes were products of quite divergent processes: as Frank Bongiorno shows elsewhere in this volume, the Federation of Australia was subject to sustained and impassioned debate, including across the Tasman. The possibility that New Zealand might join the Federation enjoyed considerable currency, but was ultimately rejected, particularly in light of farmers' concerns about tariffs restricting the circulation of their products in Australian markets. New Zealand's Dominion status, however, was ultimately the outcome of the interplay between British imperial politics and the ambition of New Zealand Prime Minister Joseph Ward: it did not capture the public imagination. It was very significant, however, in further stoking New Zealand's imperial aspirations in the Pacific: Ward believed New Zealand was 'the natural centre for the government of the South Pacific'.[65] In New Zealand's case, colonial nationhood and imperial aspirations were firmly laced together; these connections helped to make the notion of Australasia less relevant.[66] And New Zealand's rejection of the possibility of Federation meant that in turn Australia increasingly turned away from its trans-Tasman neighbour.

Donald Denoon has argued that while the precise boundaries and composition of Australasia were contested and shifted over time, Australia and New Zealand came to define it as a geographical imaginary. This chapter has delineated that process and it has reaffirmed Denoon's other key insight, that Australasia was a way of imagining space that was intimately connected with empire. Denoon argued: 'Despite its elastic boundaries, Australasia was a political and cultural reality, expressing the shared interests of British colonists and governors, relying on the Royal Navy for security, London for capital, Westminster for legitimacy, and Christianity for salvation.'[67]

As we have seen, those interests shifted over time as did the circuitry that linked Australia, New Zealand and the Pacific Islands. The imperial cartographic imaginary that initially shaped the idea of Australasia was anchored in European aspirations for empire in distant southern waters and lands. As the political and cultural visions of colonial governments and colonists shifted, so too did their cartographic imaginations.

Visions of nationhood or Pacific empires controlled by Australia or New Zealand eroded the authority of Australasia in the twentieth century. As we have seen, visions of Australasia were elaborated through a range of media including maps, statistics and histories, forms that were later central in the process of building modern states and were foundational to their national imaginaries. Of course, the symbolic repertoire mobilized to stress national distinctiveness shared common features: as C. A. Bayly noted, the insistence on uniqueness of nations is one of the great uniformities at the heart of modernity.[68] In a world of nation states, Australasia lost much of its appeal and for decades attracted little historical interest. Building on a generation of work on imperial connections and transnational histories, the chapters in the remainder of this volume reveal many different iterations of this vision of space and culture and its embeddedness in the mobile, restless and fundamentally unequal world of empire.

Notes

1 Bronwen Douglas, '"Terra Australis" to Oceania: Racial Geography in the "Fifth Part of the World"', *The Journal of Pacific History* 45:2 (2010): 183.

2 Ibid., 186–7.

3 Glyn Parry, *The Arch Conjuror of England: John Dee* (London: Yale University Press, 2011); E. G. R. Taylor, 'Master John Dee, Drake and the Straits of Anian', *The Mariner's Mirror* 15:2 (1929): 125–30; E. G. R. Taylor, *Tudor Geography, 1485–1583* (New York: Octagon Books 1968), 118–19; Ken MacMillan, *Sovereignty and Possession in the English New World: The Legal Foundations of Empire, 1576-1640* (Cambridge: Cambridge University Press, 2006), 153–5.

4 David Armitage, *The Ideological Origins of the British Empire* (Cambridge: Cambridge University Press, 2000), especially 47, 105; Margaret Small, 'From Thought to Action: Gilbert, Davis, and Dee's Theories behind the Search for the Northwest Passage', *The Sixteenth Century Journal* 44:4 (2013): 1041–58, especially 1049–50.

5 Armitage, *Ideological Origins*, 105–8.

6 O. H. K. Spate, *The Spanish Lake* (1979; Canberra: ANU Press, 2004), 1–24. For Spate's reflections on the Eurocentrism of this framing, see ibid., ix–x.

7 Douglas, 'Terra Australis to Oceania', 196.

8 Ibid.

9 Alfred Hiatt, 'Terra Australis and the Idea of the Antipodes', in *European Perceptions of Terra Australis*, ed. Anne M. Scott, Alfred Hiatt, Claire McIlroy and Christopher Wortham (Farnham: Ashgate, 2011), 10.

10 Douglas, 'Terra Australis to Oceania', 196.

11 Tom Ryan '"Le Président des Terres Australes": Charles de Brosses and the French Enlightenment Beginnings of Oceanic Anthropology', *Journal of Pacific History* 37:2 (2002): 157.

12 Hiatt, 'Terra Australis and the Idea of the Antipodes', 10.

13 Ryan, '"Le Président des Terres Australes"', 158. He identifies this argument around a later shift with Maurice Blackman, ed., *Australian Aborigines and the French* (Kensington, NSW: University of New South Wales, 1990); also Jean Copans and Jean Jamin, eds, *Aux origines de l'anthropologie française: Les mémoires de la Société des observateurs de l'homme en l'an VIII* (Paris: Jean Michel Place, 1994).

14 Ryan, '"Le Président des Terres Australes"', 158.

15 Serge Tcherkézoff, 'A Long and Unfortunate Voyage Towards the "Invention" of the Melanesia/Polynesia Distinction 1595–1832', translated from French by Isabel Ollivier, *The Journal of Pacific History* 38:2 (2003): 179.

16 Charles de Brosses, *Histoire des navigations aux terres australes* . . . (Paris: Durand, 1756), 4: 'il n'est pas possible qu'entre le Japon & l'Amérique il n'y ait, dans le vaste océan pacifique, un grand nombre d'isles riches en épiceries.'

17 Richard Drayton, 'Apprendre des Français: les sciences et le deuxième empire britannique (1783-1830)', *Revue française d'histoire d'outre-mer* 86 (1999): 91–118.

18 John Gascoigne, 'The Globe Encompassed: France and Pacific Convergences in the Age of the Enlightenment', in *Discovery and Empire: the French in the South Seas*, ed. John West-Sooby (Adelaide: University of Adelaide Press, 2013), 29.

19 M. (Pierre) Lapie map of c.1820, *Océanie ou Australasie et Polynésie* (MAP RM 591). Courtesy of the National Library of Australia; *Carte de l'Australie (partie sud-ouest de l'Océanie) of Hubert Brué* (1826); Louis Vigouroux, *L'évolution sociale en Australasie* (Paris: A. Colin, 1902); E. Pollet, *Australasie: colonie de Victoria, Nouvelle-Galles du Sud, Queensland, Australie de l'Ouest, Australie du Sud, Tasmanie, Nouvelle-Zélande* (Bruxelle : P. Weissenbruch, 1898); Carlo Rossari, *Oceanica* (Milano: C. Rossari, 1824); Stephen Bauer, *Arbeiterfragen und Lohnpolitik in Australasien* (Jena : Gustav Fischer, 1891); Alfred Manes, *Politisches und Wirtschaftliches aus Australasien* (Berlin: L. Simion, 1910); P. L. van der Byl, *Een kolonist op rei: in Australasië, de Vereenigde Staten, en Engeland* (Kaapstad: J. C. Juta & Co. 1887).

20 John Callander, *Terra Australis Cognita: or, voyages to the Terra Australis, or Southern hemisphere, during the sixteenth, seventeenth, and eighteenth centuries* (Edinburgh: A. Donaldson, 1766–8).

21 'To the reader', ibid., vol. 1, unpaginated.

22 Ibid., vol. 1, ii–iii.

23 Ibid., vol. 1, iii.

24 Ibid., vol. 1, iv.

25 Ibid., vol. 1, viii.

26 T. F. Henderson and Alexander Du Toit, 'Callander, John (b. in or after 1721, d. 1789), antiquary', *Oxford Dictionary of National Biography*, 23 September 2004; accessed 30 May 2021, https://www.oxforddnb.com/view/10.1093/ref:odnb/9780198614128.001.0001/odnb-9780198614128-e-4395.

27 Bernard Quaritch, *Catalogue of Works on European Philology and the Minor European Languages* (London: Bernard Quaritch, 1878), 1166.

28 P. J. Marshall and Glyndwr Williams, *The Great Map of Mankind: Perceptions of New Worlds in the Age of Enlightenment* (London: Dent, 1982), 260.

29 Spate, *Paradise Found and Lost*, 75.

30 Vincent Harlow, *The Founding of the Second British Empire, 1763–1793*, 2 vols (London: Longmans, Green & Co., 1952–64).

31 Marshall and Williams, *The Great Map of Mankind*, 258.

32 Tony Ballantyne, 'Empire, Knowledge and Culture: from Proto-Globalization to Modern Globalization', in *Globalization in World History*, ed. A. G. Hopkins (W. W. Norton & Co.: New York, 2002), 115–40.

33 George Shaw, *Zoology of New Holland* (London: J. Sowerby, 1794).

34 Alfred Russel Wallace, *Australasia*, 3rd edition (London, E. Stanford, 1883), 1–2.

35 S. H. Collins, *A geographical description of Australasia: comprising New Holland, Van Dieman's Land, New South Wales, the Swan River Settlement, &c. &c. and including a faithful account of the first discoveries* (Hull: Joseph Noble, 1830), 36–7.

36 Ibid., 37–8.

37 Tony Ballantyne, *Orientalism and Race: Aryanism in the British Empire* (Basingstoke: Palgrave, 2002).

38 Jan Tent, 'The Early Names of Australia's Coastal Regions', *ANPS Occasional Paper*, No. 2, (2017): 6–7; Jan Tent, 'Two unusual names for the Australian continent. Part I'. *Placenames Australia*, March 2010, 6.

39 Rossari, *Oceanica*; Christian Gottlieb Theophit Reichard, *Oceanica: Projezione di Mercatore disegnata da C.G. Reichard* (Venezia: Dalla tipografia di Alvisopoli, 1829); Dio, *Heroes of Notasia: A Record of Australian Exploration* (Hobart: Mercury, 1888).

40 Peder Gammeltoft, 'Island Names', in *The Oxford Handbook of Names and Naming* (Oxford: Oxford University Press, 2016), 130. For the instructive case of 'Ulimaroa' as an alternative name for Australia, see Jan Tent and Paul Geraghty, 'Where in the World is Ulimaroa? Or, How a Pacific Island Became the Australian Continent', *The Journal of Pacific History* 47:1 (2012): 1–20.

41 *The Hobart Town Gazette*, 30 December 1826, 2–3.

42 *The Port of Hobart: the finest deep-water port in Australasia* (Launceston: Daily Telegraph, 1912).

43 Douglas bases this reading on Adrien-Hubert Brué, 'Océanie ou cinquième partie du monde .. ', engraving, in *Grand atlas universel . . .*, carte 36, 2nd edition (1815; Paris: Desray, Libraire-Editeur, 1816), David Rumsey Map Collection, Fulton, MD. Available online at http://www.davidrumsey.com/detail?id=1-1-25585-1040021&name=Oceanie. Douglas, 'Terra Australis to Oceania', 197.

44 Jules-Sébastien-César Dumont d'Urville, 'On the Islands of the Great Ocean', Isabel Ollivier, Antoine de Biran and Geoffrey Clark trans, *Journal of Pacific History* 38:2 (2003): 163. This was originally published as 'Sur les îles du Grand Océan', *Bulletin de la Société de Géographie* 17 (1832): 1–21.

45 Tcherkézoff, 'A Long and Unfortunate Voyage', 175–96.

46 D'Urville, 'On the Islands of the Great Ocean', 165, 173.

47 Douglas, 'Terra Australis to Oceania', 202.

48 Marilyn Lake and Henry Reynolds, *Drawing the Global Colour Line: White Men's Countries and the Question of Racial Equality* (Cambridge: Cambridge University Press, 2008).

49 Tcherkézoff, 'A Long and Unfortunate Voyage', 175–96.

50 Epeli Hau'ofa, 'Our Sea of Islands', in *We Are the Ocean: Selected Works* (Honolulu: University of Hawai'i Press, 2008), 32.

51 Rip Bulkeley, 'Naming Antarctica', *Polar Record* 52:262 (2016): 2–15; Alfred Hiatt, *Terra Incognita: Mapping the Antipodes Before 1600* (London: British Library, 2008), 297.

52 William Lawrence Eisler, *The Furthest Shore: Images of Terra Australis from the Middle Ages to Captain Cook* (Cambridge: Cambridge University Press, 1995), 154.

53 Bulkeley, 'Naming Antarctica', 2–3; J. D. Hooker, *The botany of the Antarctic voyage of H.M. discovery ships 'Erebus' and 'Terror' in the years 1839–1843: Flora Antarctica* (London: Reeve Brothers, 1844–60).

54 Bulkeley, 'Naming Antarctica'.

55 Jacques Nicolas Bellin, *Carte Reduite des Terres Australes* (Paris: Chez Didot, 1753); *Australia in Maps: Great Maps in Australia's History from the National Library's Collection* (Canberra: National Library of Australia, 2008), 46–8; Kenneth Morgan, *Navigating by the Southern Cross: A History of the European Discovery and Exploration of Australia* (London: Bloomsbury, 2021), 88–9.

56 John Robson, 'A comparison of the charts produced during the Pacific voyages of Louis-Antoine de Bougainville and James Cook', in *Captain Cook: Explorations and Reassessments*, ed. Glyndwr Williams (Woodbridge: Boydell Press, 2004), 137, 156.

57 'Australasia', in *Smith's new general atlas containing distinct maps of all the principal empires, kingdoms & states* (London: C. Smith, 1843), plate 42.

58 *Report of the Society for Promoting Christian Knowledge for 1857* (London: Society for Promoting Christian Knowledge, 1857), 211; *The Christian's monthly magazine and universal review* 1 (1844): 494.

59 Megan A. Norcia, *X Marks the Spot: Women Writers Map the Empire for British Children, 1790–1895* (Athens, OH: Ohio University Press, 2010), 7, 12, 15; Hilary M. Carey, *God's Empire: Religion and Colonialism in the British World, c.1801–1908* (Cambridge: Cambridge University Press, 2011), 54–6, 80 n. 13, 94, 107, 309.

60 E.g. Henry Reynolds, *North of Capricorn: The Untold Story of Australia's North* (Crows Nest, NSW: Allen & Unwin, 2003); Campbell Macknight, 'The view from Marege': Australian knowledge of Makassar and the impact of the trepang industry across two centuries', *Aboriginal History* 35 (2011): 121–43.

    For the broader regional context of these islands and seas, see the classic study: James Francis Warren, *The Sulu Zone, 1768–1898: The Dynamics of External Trade, Slavery, and Ethnicity in the Transformation of a Southeast Asian Maritime State* (Singapore: Singapore University Press, 1981).

61 Antoinette Burton and Isabel Hofmeyr, 'Introduction: the spine of empire? Books and the Making of an Imperial Commons', in *Ten Books That Shaped the British Empire: Creating an Imperial Commons*, ed. Burton and Hofmeyr (Durham, NC: Duke University Press, 2014), 1–28; Tony Ballantyne, 'Remaking the Empire from Newgate: Wakefield's *A Letter from Sydney*', in *Ten Books*, 42–4.

62 Edward E. Morris, *Austral English: A Dictionary of Australasian Words, Phrases and Usages* (London: Macmillan, 1898).

63 H. A. Strong, 'Austral English and Slang', *The University Extension Journal*, February 1898, 70.

64 John Wilson, *Australasia &c* (Glasgow: Blackie & Son, c.1880); accessed 30 May 2021, http://nla.gov.au/nla.obj-232671467.

65 Reginald Ernest Horsley, *New Zealand* (Edinburgh: T. C. & E. C. Jack, 1908), 316.

66 Tony Ballantyne, 'The State, Politics, and Power, 1769–1893', in *The New Oxford History of New Zealand*, ed. Giselle Byrnes (Melbourne: Oxford University Press, 2009), 99–125.

67 Donald Denoon, 'Re-Membering Australasia: A repressed memory', *Australian Historical Studies* 34:122 (2003): 293.

68 C. A. Bayly, *The Birth of the Modern World, 1780–1914: Global Connections and Comparisons* (Oxford: Blackwell, 2004).

Part Two

Circulating People and the Production of Space

2

Circulating Texts on Circulating People: Mobilities, Epistemic Injustice and the Creation of the Imagined Australasian

Rachel Standfield

In investigating the history of Australasia as a region, chapters in this volume investigate the creation of a regional identity that is the product of, and helps shape, an ongoing settler-colonial history. This regional identity has at its heart a project to bring settler colonists together, creating a sense of similarity and connection between settler colonists living on opposite sides of the Tasman Sea.

Emigration texts play a vital role in settler colonies. In supporting immigration and championing its benefits, they work to people colonies. As Lorenzo Veracini argues, textual representations work to set up the possibility of 'mass transfer', on which the very project of settler colonialism depends.[1] Jude Piesse, researching settler emigration literature, has argued that the period from the 1830s 'constituted a distinct period of settler empire history'. This period brought in a 'new settler ideology', which sought to replicate Anglo culture at the point of destination and served to redeem immigration, at least partially, from older negative associations with exile, criminality, and national depletion'.[2] This chapter investigates emigration texts from the 1830s onwards and examines the way that immigration was presented. The authors of these texts attempted to 'redeem' immigration from the negative associations with convicts that had so dominated the representation of Australia, in particular. I also explore how literature, as Tamara S. Wagner has written, 'continually redefined those spaces in and beyond the empire that did not easily fit into established parameters'.[3] Texts examined in this chapter suggest contestation and reshaping of the sense of the region, as highlighted in the Introduction – the relationships between Australia and New Zealand compared to relationships with other places – and debate and contestation about the nature of the non-Indigenous populations of the two countries.

Emigration texts opened up colonial space to those contemplating immigration or preparing for the move, providing more knowledge, administering advice, and making the journey and processes of settlement seem possible and achievable. I delve here into how selected emigration texts constructed a white British person as the naturally mobile subject who could legitimately travel to and across Australasia, eventually settling on lands which are, of course, Indigenous lands, but which were rarely explicitly recognized as such within the texts. The texts created a sense of inevitability of non-Indigenous possession of land throughout the region. The texts set out ideas about the use-value of Australia and New Zealand as colonies and put forward different perspectives on Australia and New Zealand as claimable within the British Empire, but simultaneously marginalize Indigenous land ownership and in some cases work to deny any Indigenous presence.

Emigration texts about southern regions of the globe were also shaped by complex associations between culture and geography. Deborah Bird Rose has explored the ways that Western geography works as a cultural system that naturalizes hierarchy between the 'north' of the world and 'the antipodes', one that for centuries has placed the south in an inferior position associated with savagery, places to be exploited.[4] Non-Indigenous settler colonists were and are 'ambiguously positioned' to both the north as 'Home' and to adopted southern lands, a struggle continuing through generations. Rose articulated this struggle in this way: in the 'role as colonisers they represent Home; the discontinuity between home and colony positions them on the side of Home and thus alienates them from the place where they actually live and from the Indigenous people whose homes are here'.[5] The texts examined here include multiple examples of how authors worked to maintain the connection between metropole and periphery via immigration while marginalizing Indigenous peoples – for example, by refusing to recognize Indigenous peoples and their lands, creating conditions that exacerbate violent conflict, or – what seems far more mundane but has important implications for how we now understand settler-colonial histories – working to crowd out stories of and understandings of Indigenous movement.

This chapter analyses four texts focused on regional mobilities, published either side of the colonization of New Zealand. The first of these is James Busby's *Authentic information relative to New South Wales, and New Zealand*, published in 1832. Busby was British Resident in New Zealand from 1833 and helped draft the Treaty of Waitangi in 1840. The purpose of his *Authentic information* was to influence emigration policies and advise intending immigrants, but also discussed Māori people and Māori travel. Busby saw Māori travel as central to the region, and as, at least on some level, agentic and 'meaning-expressing' – Māori circulation through the region was creating the region itself. Patrick Matthew's *Emigration fields*, published in 1839 on the cusp of colonization in New Zealand, is likewise focused on emigration. Despite considering both Australia and New Zealand, Matthew remained unconvinced about the two forming a region. In 1851, the Van Diemen's Land newspaper owner Henry Melville published his text, *The present state of Australasia*, offering advice to intending immigrants and perspectives on convict transportation.[6] The following year medical doctor John Shaw published his beautifully titled *A tramp to the diggings: being notes of a ramble in Australia and New Zealand in 1852*, which incorporated a travel narrative with a summation of the state of the colonies. Within these texts, there was increasing use of the term 'Australasia' over time, including in the title of Melville's book, but I argue that there is no inevitable linear development in how the region was imagined and what the term 'Australasia' might incorporate or elide.

The depiction of a mobile British subject, the white, and generally male, immigrant, is central to the texts examined in this chapter. The moral redemption of the unemployed poor white male through processes of immigration is a recurring theme. As Piesse notes '[u]nlike other migrant groups in history, the vast majority' of British immigrants during the period of the 'British settler emigration' were '"ordinary" people of working- or middle-class origins who had elected to emigrate on a permanent basis'.[7] This, it was imagined, would simultaneously solve problems for Britain and the Australasian colonies, and thus we see attempts to reiterate, and strengthen, a relationship between the centre and periphery of empire. In working to create a regional identity, the texts create relations of solidarity between disparate settler-colonial populations, identities that are not natural or neutral, and indeed, as one of the texts examined within suggests, not necessarily inevitable or desired.

In constructing a vision of the appropriate mobile Australasian subject as white, British and male, the texts work to erase Indigenous presence. Indigenous peoples are discussed through use of several tropes – Aboriginal peoples are depicted as no longer of landscapes; Māori, after the formal colonization of New Zealand, are seen undergoing rapid and mysterious depopulation.[8] At its heart, the very making of regional identity for Australia and New Zealand is about creating a connected white settler-colonial space, the region as a white person's expanse. These texts firstly do this via racialized language, in a way that is relatively obvious to us as contemporary readers, and I will discuss some of these racialized depictions within this essay. Piesse argues that 'acknowledging the dangerous Eurocentrism of these perspectives remains morally and politically imperative'.[9] I argue here, though, that the emigration texts do something further and more subtle than demonstrate Eurocentrism, and that is repress other stories of movement. Thus, they play an important epistemic function that continues to impact understandings of the region and on scholarship on its history.

As part of recent developments within historical mobilities studies, historians in Australia and New Zealand are working to understand histories of Indigenous mobilities. This chapter is part of work in historical Indigenous mobilities that seeks to contribute to this broader scholarly project, completed by a team of Aboriginal, Torres Strait Islander, Māori, Pasifika and settler scholars who work in history, geography, Indigenous studies and sociology. Together we are seeking to uncover histories of Indigenous movement to and through Australia and attempt to do so in ways that foreground the perspectives of the travellers themselves and their descendants.[10] But, writing these histories, as historians from either side of the Tasman have noted, is often a challenging task, as the nature of the archives makes the primary business of even tracing Indigenous mobility difficult. Journeys may not be recorded in archives, or the archives may not record identifying details of travellers that allow their stories to be traced. Even when details are recorded, extant depictions of Indigenous travellers may mask an understanding of diverse Indigenous epistemologies of movement.[11]

Thus, when discussing the history of the conceptualization of a region as a settler-colonial space, scholars must remain vigilant not to continue to erase Indigenous peoples and perpetuate what I argue within this chapter is a process of epistemic repression and injustice. Like many other representations of Australian and regional Indigeneity, I argue that these texts support epistemological ignorance, where histories of Aboriginal mobilities and Māori travel and immigration to Australia have been effectively silenced within both historical and contemporary public discourse and historical writing. The development of representation that downplays Aboriginal and Māori movement creates what Miranda Fricker has termed 'hermeneutical injustice': when 'collective interpretive resources puts someone at an unfair disadvantage when it comes to making sense of their social experiences'.[12] José Medina writes that one aspect of this injustice is that the subject's agency 'in meaning-making and meaning-expressing is compromised (if not eliminated altogether)'.[13] The colonial archive contributes to later epistemic hiding, and it makes the experiences of some subjects 'invisible and inaudible'.[14] My argument here is that Indigenous mobilities were not, could not and cannot be completely repressed. Indigenous mobilities continue to be recognized in some of the texts I analyse, particularly at the margins of the writing. It is not an erasure, but can be conceptualized more as a repression, founded in epistemic non-alignment.[15] Diverse epistemologies of Indigenous mobilities continue, and it is these epistemologies that need to be brought into research on historical Indigenous travel.

There is value, however, I would argue, in understanding how imperial and colonial authors work through their writing to silence Indigenous epistemic life, in violent processes of erasure. In these texts, that erasure takes the form of naturalizing non-Indigenous life in the region, erasing the recognition of Māori movement through the region and life in Australia, and reinscribing the foundation of *terra nullius* on which the Australian invasion was and is based. Wiradjuri writer and scholar Jeanine Leane writes, following literary critic Barbara Johnson, 'if we believe that texts present major claims which attempt to dominate, erase, or distort various "other" claims whose traces, nevertheless, remain detectable to a reader, then reading in its extended sense is deeply involved with questions of authority and power'.[16] In her work on the representation of Aboriginal peoples within Australian settler-colonial novels, Leane argues that reading should be like tracking: 'It is not just about seeing and hearing what *is* there; it is as much about what is *not* there.'[17] She argues that the settler authors she analyses 'make tracks over time and place and as they displace and replace, dispossess and repossess Aboriginal people in their quests, still writing nation from Country'.[18]

To take just one example which can alert us to this silencing and displacement, in the context of Indigenous mobilities, Sir Tipene O'Regan, the most senior Kāi Tahu kaumātua, himself a historian, has stressed that for Kāi Tahu 'the voyage west has always been more attractive ... than the journey north'. O'Regan writes: 'Since the early nineteenth century when we first learnt about muskets, potatoes and whaleboats ... Ngai Tahu have been crossing the Tasman to trade, to settle and to marry'.[19] This sense of the importance of the voyage west is something that Michael Stevens and I foreground in our research when tracing Kāi Tahu travel through archives working to silence and ignore it, remembering that the movement is there, even though it might be hidden. We employ Mike's knowledge as a Kāi Tahu person to help us uncover travellers through whakapapa-based approaches, while we focus on understanding travel through Kāi Tahu epistemologies of movement.[20]

Authentic information relative to New South Wales,
and New Zealand

James Busby's 1832 text, *Authentic information relative to New South Wales, and New Zealand*, was a 'selection from his papers' which he had compiled in response to being 'repeatedly urged' to publish information respecting New South Wales 'as would tend to place upon their real footing, the inducements it holds out to Emigration from this country'.[21] He included his 'Memoir on New Zealand' because 'the present state of New Zealand cannot be without interest to those who are contemplating a residence in New South Wales'. New Zealand was only of 'interest' to those contemplating New South Wales because it was yet to become an official site of British settlement. Busby himself would play a vital role in the colonization of New Zealand. By the time the book was published, his author byline was 'formerly collector of the internal revenue and land board in New South Wales; now British Resident at New Zealand'.[22]

The first paper collected in Busby's text was a letter he had sent to the English MP Robert Wilmot Horton, responding to Horton's 'Inquiry into the Causes and Remedies of Pauperism'.[23] Horton had brought before Parliament a bill to promote emigration, principally to Canada and other North American sites and Australia.[24] In his letter Busby was a strong promoter of emigration from the United Kingdom to Australia, writing 'no other single measure, perhaps no combination of measures, is capable of benefiting these Colonies so extensively as this, if conducted on sound principles and with a due attention to the wants of the Colonies, and to the physical and moral qualities of the persons whose emigration it is proposed to encourage'.[25]

Busby's focus was clearly on moral uplift for the non-Indigenous population and saw migration of the correct type of person as key to change within colonial society overall. He stressed that benefit for the colony 'will depend upon the moral character of the individuals selected'. New South Wales had 'a right to look to the mother country for every assistance she can possibly afford towards a renovation of its moral character, by infusing a more healthy population into the corrupted mass of its present inhabitants'.[26] He included detailed ideas about what created this 'corrupted mass': the cheapness of provisions meant people did not have to work diligently 'to better their condition in life', choosing to work less and spending 'the greater part of their time' in 'sloth and dissipation; – or if a greater portion of their time be given to labour, it is only that they may plunge the deeper in debauchery during the remainder'.[27] Busby was confident to state that workmen had 'indolent and depraved habits'.[28] Busby calculated that up to 4,000 men could be accommodated in New South Wales over the next three years: 1,500 to 2,000 'married mechanics, with their wives, and as many married shepherds and labourers in husbandry, with their wives'. His conclusions on New South Wales society were not favourable, and immigration was his answer to fix the problem. Robert Grant has written about how this was a common thread of immigration debate. New South Wales was considered, for free immigrants as much as convicts, a dangerous place: '"[B]ush" life appeared to be ineluctably regressive in its force … With high wages, laborers could work one third or one quarter of their time and still earn an ample livelihood.'[29] In terms of both the promotion of emigration for Britain's poor and working class, and the attempt to redeem immigration from negative associations, such as those connected to previous arrivals in Australia, Busby's text fits neatly with Jude Piesse's analysis in *British Settler Emigration in Print*.[30]

Busby then aimed to bring about the moral uplift of non-Indigenous society in New South Wales, and his text provides detailed discussion and information to promote such immigration. He described Australian processes of 'settlement' as uncontrolled and indiscriminate compared to Canada, the United States and South Africa. In those colonies, Busby wrote, governments controlled settlement into delineated areas that had already been surveyed.[31] In New South Wales, by contrast, 'the Government have considered that the wealth of this country does not consist in immeasurable tracts of rich arable land ... but in the excellence of its natural pasturage, which requires a widespread population to reap its advantages'.[32] The irony is that Aboriginal peoples created this pasturage as part of their land management practices of caring for Country physically and spiritually, and the description of pasturage as 'natural' was a silencing of Aboriginal life in Country.[33] Colonists as invaders of Country spread out everywhere all at once. In order to 'allow settlers to avail themselves' of the pastoral land 'to the utmost extent, an immense territory is thrown open'.[34] Emigrants were required to select their land within four months of arrival, 'which period is considered sufficient to allow enough to be seen of the colony to select a grant'.[35]

Busby described a process of unrestrained and chaotic movement, highlighting how difficult it was – he wrote it was 'perplexing' for emigrants to know whether their land was good land and well-watered.[36] The process threw newly arrived emigrants to land far removed from developing cities and towns, funnelling them straight to frontiers of settlement where they ran well ahead of the reach of governments, even of surveys. The work of this text then, and Busby's appeal to British MPs like Horton to increase immigration, was to encourage and facilitate emigrant arrivals. In doing so he obscured the violence that this process unleashed. In fact, he did not even admit to it.

Busby mentioned Aboriginal people twice in his text. At one point Busby compared Māori explicitly and favourably to Native American, Pacific and Aboriginal peoples.[37] He later included an excerpt from a 'Copy of a *Minute* of the Committee of the Missionaries attached to the Church Missionary settlement at New Zealand',[38] which denied the creation of a Māori settlement in New South Wales on the basis that Māori, like 'the Aborigines of New Holland, being so near the Europeans, could be kept under no restraint by the Missionaries, but would be continually liable to stray'.[39] It was not unusual for Aboriginal peoples to be written out of emigration texts. Terra Walston Joseph notes that Charles Dickens, while providing a different and contradictory vision of emigration to the New South Wales philanthropist and champion of immigrants Caroline Chisholm in *Bleak House*, follows Chisholm in 'omitting aboriginal peoples from the Australian landscape altogether'.[40] Lisa Chilton, writing of Chisholm, specifically described how 'emigrators ... literally wrote out other racial and ethnic groups out of the colonial setting, their unsettling presence in the colonies symbolically denied'.[41] Robert Grant also alerts us to the ways that Busby's representation of landscape ready for colonists to 'avail themselves' of the 'excellence' of pastoral land was characteristic of emigration texts more generally, displaying 'numbing optimism in their accretive force'. The 'evocation of colonial landscapes calculated to convey how readily land might be converted from wilderness to farmland, picturing each destination as welcoming and familiar, or at least as being capable of ready conversion to some ideal of the old country'.[42] Within this context, where even Aboriginal presence was refused, it seems inconceivable that Aboriginal epistemologies of movement could be recognized, even while mobilities remains such a central focus of the texts. Movement of Ancestral beings as vital to the very creation of Country, the gathering of people together to ensure the health and vitality of those Countries, the use of sophisticated protocols for crossing boundaries and acknowledging the ownership of other Indigenous nations – all of these would require a level of engagement far beyond the scope of the texts.[43]

These forms of representation also, however, have immensely practical and intensely violent implications. For example, Busby's text provides detailed information about processes for proving financial means or bureaucratic processes for transferring land, but not what would happen when an emigrant needed to 'take' that land. An arriving emigrant reading Busby would not even know that Aboriginal peoples existed on the land they were travelling to take up; Aboriginal peoples for whom the land was, and remains, the basis of culture, kin and life, people who would go on to defend that Country with their lives. There is no place here for Aboriginal epistemologies of travel.

As one of the emigration texts which supports the mass settler emigration of the period, we can see the effects of the period of emigration mapped on the Australian land mass on the *Colonial Frontier Massacre Map*. Map 2.1 shows a proliferation of yellow dots of 'Aboriginal or Torres Strait Islander people massacred' from 1835 to 1845, spreading out into areas between Sydney and Brisbane and inland from the coast in New South Wales and South-East Queensland, to the south of Sydney along the Murray River, right across Victoria and beginning in South Australia and Western Australia. The image is only a snapshot, not including the earlier intense violence of

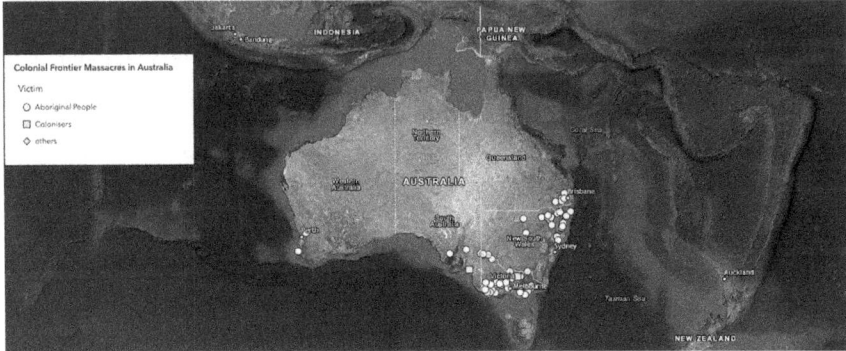

Map 2.1 'Colonial Frontier Massacres, Australia, 1780 to 1930', date range 1835–45, Centre for 21st Century Humanities, University of Newcastle, Australia, https://c21ch.newcastle. edu.au/colonialmassacres/map.php. Permission courtesy of the University of Newcastle. The research team acknowledges the Traditional Owners of Country and pay their respects to Elders past, present and emerging.

places like Van Diemen's Land. This visual representation of the intense physical violence of colonization is connected to and arises from, but has far more immediate impact than, the repression and erasure of representation.

In contrast to the complete silence on Aboriginal peoples, Māori figure prominently in Busby's text. He provided a detailed discussion of Māori travel, and Māori feature as travellers to Australia. Busby does not use the term 'Australasia' or depict the two countries as a region, but in his 'Memoir on New Zealand', the economic connections between the two sites were clearly articulated through descriptions of the flax trade, whale and seal fisheries, and spar and timber procurement. Along with other trans-Tasman travellers such as missionaries and traders, Māori bridged the divide between Australia and New Zealand and created it as a region in practice. Busby drew on the notion of Māori engagement with 'civilisation' in Sydney as a marker of intelligence. Māori who had

> visited Sydney, have often evinced a curiosity and penetration which would have been considered as the characteristics of an educated foreigner, rather than of an unenlightened savage. Some of these visitors, who were treated with a degree of respect which enabled them to satisfy their curiosity without danger of insult, were observed to exhibit, by the objects which arrested their attention, a very high degree of mental activity and acuteness. They would examine most minutely into the construction of a piece of mechanism; and they were not satisfied to admire the shewy colours of an English carpet, without also comparing its texture with that of the mats manufactured by their own women. On the whole, their admiration of every thing they witnessed, and of those who possessed such things, was unbounded.[44]

Māori were mobile, and for Busby, they were appropriately mobile subjects, with Māori travel and responses to new environments a sign of their worth as people. We see Māori – while the Ngā Puhi chief Hongi Hika is named, Busby states that 'chiefs . . . have visited Sydney, from almost every part of the coast' – depicted as active agents. In this text, we see representation of people undertaking meaning-making activities, examining new technologies and manufactures. It is possible to see meaning-expressing, even if it must be accessed through Busby's description. Travel was a marker of interest, of engagement, of potential for a group who at this time were visible within texts.

Emigration fields

In 1839, the year before the British colonization of New Zealand, the Scottish natural historian and champion of both empire and ideas of natural selection, Patrick Matthew, published two texts on New Zealand. While it is believed he never travelled to New Zealand himself, he was a strong advocate of colonization to the country. In August 1839 he presided as chairman of a meeting in Perth, Scotland, and his *Prospectus of the Scots New Zealand Land Company* and the resulting company would later take up land around Auckland.[45] The *Prospectus* quoted his other text, *Emigration fields: North*

America, the Cape, Australia, and New Zealand, describing these countries, and giving a comparative view of the advantages they present to British settlers, examined here.[46] Although Matthew did not become a director of that company, two of his sons would emigrate to New Zealand in 1851.[47]

Matthew depicted immigration as mitigating poverty, as an economic good, but also as racial destiny. Economics was making immigration necessary. In Britain, the changing nature of work meant declining demand for labour and increasing poverty. The 'excessive toil and insufficient remuneration of the working-men in Britain' was well understood, he wrote.[48] Migrating to 'fruitful new lands' was the method 'by which our paupers would be transformed into rich customers (our greatest evil turned to our greatest good)'.[49] The potential was such that 'the whole of the unpeopled regions of the earth may now be said to be British ground, and the gate is opened to an exceedingly improved field for human labour and vast increase of British race'.[50] The text was strongly grounded in racialized discourse, and a strong sense of British racial superiority. Matthew was an early proponent of natural selection. In his first book *On Naval Timber and Arboriculture*, published in 1831, an appendix published notes on natural selection that would be acknowledged in editions of Darwin's *The Origin of Species* from 1860.[51]

So, Matthew used both economic and racial reasons to justify empire and settler-colonial expansion. He was clearly focused on expounding the benefits of New Zealand, and while his text discussed North America, the Cape Colony, Australia and New Zealand, the latter was his primary interest. According to Matthew, it was his publisher who had urged a regional approach: '[H]e objected to the limitation of the subject and advised me to treat also of the neighbouring country, Australia.'[52] 'This led me to reflect,' Matthew wrote, 'whether I had not such a knowledge of the subject of our colonies generally, as might be of use to my countrymen who were inclined to emigrate, and whether I could not shew how very important an element emigration might be rendered in our national economy.'[53] Matthew resisted the regional perspective, ignored the publisher's view, and expanded his vision to include North America and the Cape. He justified this through the development of travel technologies and, in doing so, oriented New Zealand towards North America rather than Australia:

> The proposed Pacific steam-communication *via* the Isthmus of Darien, will soon bring New Zealand, and the fine countries on the West Coast of North America, within little more than a month's voyage. In regard to New Zealand in particular, there is, I would almost say, a wilful blindness to its importance as a commercial and maritime station, and invaluable raw-material field of supply.[54]

In doing so, Matthew's text demonstrates a point noted by scholars of emigration literature, that the 'Anglo world' did not only include current colonies, or, in the case of New Zealand, an emergent colony, but those that were 'lost' to the British Empire.[55] These colonies remain linked by both 'race' and their foundation in the dispossession and subjugation of Indigenous peoples.

Matthew depicted Māori as valuable to the British Empire. His chapter 'Especial reasons for Colonising New Zealand' emphasized benefits to Māori. Māori constituted 'at least the most striking instance, of a thin and scattered population which would not necessarily suffer, but might greatly benefit by the immigration of Europeans into their country'.[56] The benefit which would supposedly accrue to Māori was because they were not '*hunters*' like Native American and Australian Aboriginal peoples, but practised agriculture. Assessed as 'very industrious cultivators for savages', Māori had not peopled the land densely enough because of 'their ferocity and by anarchy'.[57] Elsewhere in the text, writing on Australia, Matthew had described Aboriginal peoples in bluntly racialized terms as 'a race of savages, perhaps the farthest removed from civilised man of any in existence'.[58] New Zealand, however, was 'an anomalous case'; Māori were 'a very scant agricultural population' occupying only 'straggling' and 'petty districts' of land, the rest of the 'extensive' country was 'to them entirely useless'. Not only that but Māori were, according to Matthew, 'even fast decreasing in numbers', due to 'defects in the social order and other circumstances'. A 'steady general government' brought by emigrants 'would, in all probability, remedy the consuming evils under which the race is disappearing'. Colonization was thus conceptualized as 'reason, humanity, justice'.[59] It would support 'our overflowing population' and it would save Māori, who, due to the Europeans already there, were 'actually retrograding'.[60] Māori suffered more injury from the 'dissolute crews of whaling vessels and roaming sailors, convicts and emancipists' than could be outweighed by the 'benefit derived from the Christian missions'.[61] Like Busby's depictions of New South Wales society, some previous travellers were to have had wholly negative influences outweighing the assumed positive influences of missionaries.

Matthew was not enthusiastic in depicting the two countries as a region, as the depiction of people – convicts, emancipists, expirees, sailors, whalers – most easily associated with Australia, and his refusal to take on his publisher's suggestion to write of Australia together with New Zealand, might suggest. He believed a colony in New Zealand would benefit Australia due to the southern whale fishery and as a granary for the Australian colonies in times of drought. The benefits, however, only flowed one way. Matthew did not express any sense that New Zealand would benefit from Australia.[62]

Nor did Matthew depict Māori as equal partners in New Zealand or as governing themselves. Iwi, he wrote, were 'numerous tribes' in 'perpetual hostilities, kept up by the savage principle of honour – *revenge*'.[63] As 'a warlike maritime race', however, Māori were 'capable of forming excellent seamen and shipwrights, and as such would be most valuable auxiliaries'.[64] He quoted British observers who drew on the proficiency of Māori as sailors and as better sailors than British peers.[65] Matthew thus saw Māori as forming a specific class within a British-controlled society rather than travelling people under their own cultural and social direction. Their mobility would be directed and shaped as part of a labouring class of maritime workers. Colonizers would utilize Māori as a labour force in the name of 'civilising', where labour would transform those traits judged 'savage' by Matthew. This language justified the colonial appropriation of Māori labour, just as the notion of the scattered population quoted above justified the colonization of Māori land.[66] Māori would be relegated to helpers in the settler-colonial project, becoming 'valuable auxiliaries', moving settler populations between colonial sites. A maritime Māori labour force would support settler populations moving between New Zealand and North America, the Cape, and Australia.

In terms of their textual representation within *Emigration fields*, Matthew's writing constitutes a shift from the Busby text. Māori were no longer a group of known people such as those observed and respected by Busby, people who, when Matthew published his text, Busby was working with. Matthew, having not travelled in the region, wrote in broad brushstrokes about the role that Māori might play in colonization. Matthew saw Māori as becoming a working class supporting the travel of others and not self-determining political groups directing their own mobility. Māori, compared to their depiction in Busby's text as active in directing their movement, are stripped of agency here. These textual depictions do not mean that people were not travelling across Australasia as a region on their own terms, nor did they mean people were not making meaning of their travel within their epistemologies. This shift from seeing Māori as a political class to their incorporation as a labouring class is a factor, however, that contributes to the invisibility of Māori as travellers during this and later historical periods. As Mike Stevens and I have written, ships' captains leave few records compared to the government authorities and missionaries who authored the early archives on Māori travel. Often Indigenous sailors were not identified.[67] Sailors may have been employed from different iwi, so even connecting unidentified individuals more generally to families, communities and lands may not be possible.[68] For Stevens's people, Kāi Tahu, whose ancestors also often include mobile Pākehā labourers such as sealers and whalers, both Indigenous and non-Indigenous ancestors can appear as 'little more than ghosts in the colonial archive'.[69] As such, in Matthew's text, we can see the seeds of what makes later historical scholarship on Indigenous mobilities challenging. There is a shift from individuals or groups of people being specifically identified – and even at times representing themselves, even though this may be mediated – to a labouring class below decks, often unnamed or given only racialized 'nicknames', not identified with their people, never asked what travel meant to them or why they were undertaking it. Matthew's text envisioned a future where Māori became subaltern, a labour force used to support the efficient populating of various settler-colonial sites. His rendering of Māori as without their own functioning societies, as awaiting a colonial intervention to save them from savagery and warfare, also helps set the conditions for future hermeneutical injustice by stripping agency and meaning-making.

The present state of Australasia

Henry Melville's text, *The present state of Australasia*, was published in 1851, after the formal British colonization of New Zealand. It depicts a clear sense of Australasia as a region; the term is in the title and those intending to immigrate are addressed as though they weighed up any Australian colonies or New Zealand as their destination. Melville stated in his text that 'New Zealand it is true does not properly belong to Australia, yet it is nevertheless the last portion of Australasia that has been selected by the mother country for the purpose of carrying out emigration, and consequently requires notice in this work'.[70] A chapter dedicated to New Zealand is sandwiched between one assessing Victoria and a weighty treatment of Van Diemen's Land that reflected Melville's long association with that colony. *The present state of Australasia* was published from London after Melville departed from Van Diemen's Land in 1849. He had first come to Van Diemen's Land in the late 1820s and had owned newspapers, literary magazines and publishing ventures, incurring the disapproval of the government for his criticism of the George Arthur regime.[71]

The present state of Australasia discussed, as had the other texts before, the benefits of Australasian colonies for 'pauper immigrants'.[72] Melville's text differed from the earlier texts examined when he outlined the history of the imperial relationship between Australia and New Zealand. This history of connection across the Tasman was depicted as flowing one way, only from Australia towards New Zealand. He discussed flax production, for example, as being 'prepared by the natives ready for shipment', not as being brought to Australia by Māori. He did not recount histories of Māori coming to Australia, which had been central to Busby's assessment of Māori civilization.[73] Nor does Melville mention Māori as maritime peoples, a representation of which had been crucial to the futures imagined for Māori by Matthew.

Melville, as Matthew had, employed a representation of Māori decline, attributable to colonization.[74] 'Through the instrumentality of the Europeans, the tribes have within the last twenty years been lamentably reduced,' Melville wrote. Māori communities had been 'instigated to war with each other' and sold weaponry by settler colonists.[75] In this description, Melville can be understood as mirroring his earlier writing about Aboriginal peoples. Johanna Perheentupa argues that Melville followed other nineteenth-century Australian historians by describing 'Aboriginal people as naturally friendly people who had been provoked to hostilities by violent treatment, not by dispossession'.[76]

These depictions of Māori as a 'dying race' provided a sense that the land was ripe for the taking. In this respect, Māori appeared destined to suffer the same fate as the author assumed had befallen Tasmanian Aboriginal peoples, to whom the final chapter of Melville's text was devoted – the author considering it 'desirable to devote a few pages to the history of the Aborigines of Van Diemen's Land, and thus record the lamentable fate of that unfortunate race of human beings'.[77] His descriptions were grounded in blunt racialized and derogatory language that ranged across topics such as skin colour, hair and facial features, and people's movement through Country.[78] The deeply racialized language justified his conclusions that Tasmanian Aboriginal peoples were 'perhaps, of all creatures that wear the human form . . . according to the European standard in these matters . . . justly placed in the lowest scale'.[79] Melville's assessments of Aboriginal culture, physical characteristics and cultural life led to recounting the Black War's history and the removal and exile of Tasmanian Aboriginal peoples, first to Flinders Island, and then back to the mainland. Melville was deeply critical of colonial authorities and the way they conducted the war against Tasmanian Aboriginal peoples. Ultimately, though, Perheentupa argues: 'The underlying narrative describing frontier conflict followed the logic of colonial discourse whereby the actions of Europeans, who were superior beings, determined how the relationship between white and Aboriginal people would develop.'[80] The sense of Māori as declining and of Tasmanian Aboriginal peoples as extinct lent weight to the sense of inevitability of the region as a non-Indigenous space, ready for the taking by new emigrants who could choose either Australia or New Zealand as their destination.

There was no discussion of Māori as migrants or travellers in Australia. There was an example, however, of a Māori man in Van Diemen's Land, a young man called a 'lad' and a 'boy' by Melville, who appears in the text only to illustrate an argument about failures in the colonial legal system. The man, unidentified except for being called a 'New Zealander', was called to give evidence when a young woman was found drowned in the Derwent River in Hobart. He 'lived as one of the servants on the premises where the deceased had resided'.[81] The young man was 'unable to speak the English language' and 'an interpreter was engaged'.[82] In Melville's text he remains an example of the problems of witnesses giving evidence multiple times, before a magistrate first, and later in the trial. The anecdote, however, prompts us to remember that silence in the text on Māori as migrants or travellers does not mean that Māori no longer crossed the Tasman.

A tramp to the diggings

John Shaw, a medical doctor and member of the Geological and Linnean Societies and the Botanical Society of Edinburgh,[83] published three travel narratives, the first of which was *A tramp to the diggings*, published in 1852.[84] The text provides a lively account of Shaw's travels. Like Henry Melville's text, Shaw places heavy emphasis on the idea of Australasia, opening the book with the following statement: 'AUSTRALASIA, or Australia, consists of the Continent of New Holland, or Australia, the island of Tasmania, or Van Diemen's Land, and the islands of New Zealand.'[85] A travel narrative, it included immigration advice, and provided examples of people arriving in Australia and New Zealand with nothing, who were able to, in the colonies, gather 'abundance, as to make them as independent, as ladies and gentlemen in England'.[86] He believed that 'much has been done for the people of England latterly' but that immigration to Australia and New Zealand should be encouraged through the alleviation of poverty and ignorance:

> [T]ell all the ignorant that they are capable of becoming valuable members of society in Australia and New Zealand, and send them there if they are willing to go. Provide all the enlightened (many of whom are too anxious to go) with a purse sufficient to land them in these beautiful countries.[87]

Shaw's promotion of immigration, however, took a different tone to the other texts examined. He deliberately undermined negative racial depictions of Indigenous peoples and stressed Indigenous agency.

Shaw included significant discussions of both Aboriginal peoples and Māori, and within the text attempted to undermine racialized depictions of Indigenous peoples, especially Aboriginal peoples, even as he emphasized that Indigenous populations were undergoing population decline. He had a particular interest in Indigenous religious beliefs. He spent time describing 'the *tabu*' as a Māori 'sacred prohibition' that 'exists among them, as among other Malayan races of the South Seas', and the spirits of the dead travelling to 'Parengarenga', Cape Reinga.[88] And while he felt that Aboriginal peoples had only 'so exceedingly vague' a sense of religion 'that they may be said scarcely to have an opinion upon it', he emphasized that 'in all other respects, they exhibit considerable intelligence'. He specifically negated racialized and derogatory depictions of Aboriginal peoples, writing that 'it has been customary among some writers to dignify the Australian natives by the appellation of "human monkeys"' but writing back to these representations, bringing evidence from 'enlightened travellers' into his text to counter negative discourses of Aboriginality.[89] He emphasized Aboriginal intelligence, assessed Aboriginal technologies as appropriate to their needs rather than lacking by comparison with other peoples, and stressed that Aboriginal peoples were valued employees. It was in this capacity that Aboriginal mobility was also addressed: '[M]any of them have been advantageously employed,' he wrote, as shepherds, hut-keepers or police, 'but their love for a roaming life, and the calls of their tribe, prevent them from permanently leading a civilised life.'[90] It is within a significant section recounting ethnographic knowledge of Aboriginal peoples that Shaw wrote bluntly of dispossession: 'Cases of infanticide do not appear to have taken place among the natives until the arrival of the white man, who has stolen their lands and killed or driven away the animals upon which they subsisted.'[91]

Shaw also returned to an earlier discursive construction, more akin to Busby's depictions, that viewed Māori as active agents within the region. He highlighted colonial desire to 'treat this intelligent and high-spirited people with justice and kindness'. Māori were characterized as 'aborigines ... perhaps, superior to any in the world'. Shaw provided evidence that Māori were taking on civilization, writing: 'They make excellent seamen and mechanics; and in the settlements they dispose of the produce they raise. Many of them are possessed of property in farms and trading vessels, and have considerable sums in the savings' banks.'[92]

Shaw's text is an example of an emigration text that did not remove Aboriginal peoples from their places, exclude them from movement, or deny their intelligence or agency. His emphasis on immigration as a strategy to solve British poverty continued to encourage mass transfer in the service of settler colonization, supporting dispossession just as the other texts. In Shaw's rendition, however, British people were not the only ones who could legitimately traverse Australasia as a region; Indigenous peoples were also active agents, working for their communities, travelling under their own steam.

Goenpul Scholar Aileen Moreton-Robinson has called for academic disciplines to resist trajectories that disavow Indigenous sovereignty by seeing the 'nation ... socially and culturally constructed as a white possession'.[93] In coming to understand the history of a regional identity, the ways that Australasia came to be constructed, it is imperative that scholars explicitly recognize that this is entangled with settler colonialism as a project of connecting non-Indigenous populations invading the lands of Indigenous peoples.

There is no Australasia as we know it now without settler colonialism, and emigration texts aimed to create the conditions by which prospective settler-invaders would thrive in these southern colonies; the glaring issue of Indigenous land ownership and the sovereignty of Indigenous peoples was barely mentioned. A common strategy of the first three texts at least was to refuse to recognize Aboriginal presence, either by overlooking it completely or focusing on the belief that Tasmanian Aboriginal peoples were extinct. Within this rendering, the notion that Aboriginal movement between

Countries was a meaningful experience of cross-cultural engagement was inconceivable, beyond the scope of the authors to comprehend. In relation to New Zealand, discourses that Māori were a dying race rendered colonization as 'justice'. Within Busby's text, Māori experience in Australia was employed in his portrayal of Māori as civilizable people. For Matthew and Melville, Māori were portrayed as static, fixed in New Zealand, even as presence in Australia occasionally slipped into a text. Likewise, the mention of Māori-owned trading vessels within Shaw's text demonstrates the premium that might be placed on travel, and desires to control the means of travel. In placing British travel at the heart of human mobility, the texts work to suppress Indigenous peoples' movement, the overall effect of which is hermeneutical marginalization, precluding Indigenous access to such 'significant area(s) of social experience' as human mobility and travel.[94]

Notes

1   Lorenzo Veracini, *Settler Colonialism: A Theoretical Overview* (New York: Springer, 2010), 33.
2   Jude Piesse, *British Settler Emigration in Print, 1832–1877* (Oxford: Oxford University Press, 2015), 8.
3   Tamara S. Wagner, 'Introduction: The Nineteenth-Century Pacific Rim: Victorian Transoceanic Studies Beyond the Postcolonial Matrix', *Victorian Literature and Culture* 43:2 (2015): 225.
4   Deborah Bird Rose, *Reports from a Wild Country: Ethics for Decolonisation* (Sydney: UNSW Press, 2004), 42.
5   Rose, *Reports from a Wild Country*, 43. See also Ann Curthoys, 'Expulsion, exodus and exile in white Australian historical mythology', *Journal of Australian Studies* 23:61 (1999): 1–19; Andrew Lattas, 'Aborigines in Contemporary Australian Nationalism: Primordiality and the Cultural Politics of Otherness', *Social Analysis: The International Journal of Anthropology*, no. 27 (April 1990), 'Writing Australian Culture: Text, Society, and National Identity'.
6   E. Flinn, 'Melville, Henry (1799–1873)', *Australian Dictionary of Biography*, National Centre of Biography, Australian National University, https://adb.anu.edu.au/biography/melville-henry-2445.
7   Piesse, *British Settler Emigration in Print*, 8.
8   The depiction of Australian landscapes as being without their people is a feature of Australian colonial discourses and is based in colonization as proceeding on the basis that the land was *terra nullius*. On dying race discourses, see Patrick Brantlinger, *Dark Vanishings: Discourse on the Extinction of Primitive Races, 1800–1930* (Ithaca: Cornell University Press, 2003).
9   Piesse, *British Settler Emigration in Print*, 10.
10   Barry Judd, Julie Andrews, Elia Shugg, Michael Stevens, Lynn Mitchell, Ruth Faleolo, Kat Ellinghaus, Alan Lester, Sianan Healy and myself comprise the Australian Research Council 2020 Discovery Project DP 2020103269, 'Indigenous Mobilities to and through Australia: Agency and Sovereignties'.
11   Lachy Paterson, 'The Similarity of Hue Constituted No Special Bond of Intimacy between Them', *Journal of New Zealand Studies* 14 (2013): 19–20; Maria Nugent, 'Jacky Jacky and the politics of Aboriginal Testimony', in *Indigenous Intermediaries: New*

Perspectives on Exploration Archives, ed. Shino Konishi, Maria Nugent and Tiffany Shellam (Canberra: ANU Press, 2015), 67–84; Rachel Standfield and Michael Stevens, 'New Histories But Old Patterns: Kāi Tahu in Australia', in *Labour Lines and Colonial Power: Indigenous and Pacific Islander Labour Mobility in Australia*, ed. Victoria Stead and Jon Altman (Canberra: ANU Press, 2019), 103–31; Rachel Standfield, 'Reading Māori and Aboriginal Mobilities and Encounters in Newcastle, 1853', *Australian Historical Studies* 51:1 (2020): 4–18.

12 Miranda Fricker, *Epistemic Injustice: Power and the Ethics of Knowing* (Oxford: Oxford University Press, 2007), 1.

13 José Medina, 'Epistemic Injustice and Epistemologies of Ignorance', in *The Routledge Companion to the Philosophy of Race*, ed. Paul C. Taylor, Linda Martin Alcoff and Luvell Anderson (New York: Routledge, 2017).

14 Medina, 'Epistemic Injustice and Epistemologies of Ignorance'.

15 My thanks to the members of the symposium for the discussion which drew out these ideas.

16 Jeanine Leane, 'Tracking Our Country in Settler Literature', *JASAL: Journal of the Association for the Study of Australian Literature* 14:3 (2014): 1, drawing on Barbara Johnson, 'Writing', in *Critical Terms for Literary Study*, ed. Frank Lentricchia and Thomas McLaughlin (Chicago: The University of Chicago Press, 1990).

17 Leane, 'Tracking Our Country in Settler Literature', 1.

18 Ibid., 15.

19 Tīpene O'Regan, 'The Dimension of Kinship', in *States of Mind: Australia and New Zealand 1901–2001,* ed. Arthur Grimes, Lydia Wevers and Ginny Sullivan (Wellington: Institute of Policy Studies, Victoria University of Wellington, 2002), 36.

20 Standfield and Stevens, 'New Histories but Old Patterns'.

21 James Busby, *Authentic information relative to New South Wales, and New Zealand* (London: Joseph Cross, 1832), v.

22 Busby, *Authentic information relative to New South Wales, and New Zealand*, title page.

23 Ibid., 1.

24 Ibid.

25 Ibid.

26 Ibid., 20.

27 Ibid., 4.

28 Ibid., 3.

29 Robert Grant, '"The Fit and Unfit": Suitable Settlers for Britain's Mid-Nineteenth-Century Colonial Possessions', *Victorian Literature and Culture* 33:1 (2005): 170.

30 Piesse, *British Settler Emigration in Print, 1832–1877*, introduction.

31 Busby, *Authentic information relative to New South Wales, and New Zealand*, 39.

32 Ibid., 40.

33 Bruce Pascoe, *Dark Emu: Aboriginal People and the Birth of Agriculture* (Broome, Western Australia: Magabala Books, 2018); Bill Gammage, *The Biggest Estate on Earth: How Aborigines Made Australia* (Crows Nest, NSW: Allen & Unwin, 2011).

34 Busby, *Authentic information relative to New South Wales, and New Zealand*, 40.

35 Ibid., 38.

36 Ibid., 39.

37 Ibid., 62–3.

38 Ibid., 70–2.

39 Ibid., 71.

40 Terra Walston Joseph, '"Saving British Natives": Family Emigration and the logic of Settler Colonialism in Charles Dickens and Caroline Chisholm', *Victorian Literature and Culture* 43:2 (2015): 262.

41 Lisa Chilton, *Agents of Empire: British Female Migration to Canada and Australia, 1860s–1930* (Toronto: University of Toronto Press, 2007), 12, quoted in Terra Walston Joseph, '"Saving British Natives"', 269.

42 Grant, '"The Fit and Unfit"', 178.

43 Amanda Kearney and John J. Bradley, '"When a long way in a bark canoe is a quick trip in a boat": relationships to sea country & changes to Yanyuwa watercraft', *Quaternary International* 385 (2015): 166–76; Samia Khatun, 'Beyond blank spaces: Five tracks to late-nineteenth century Beltana', *Transfers* 5:3 (2015), 68–86; Nicolas Peterson, 'Myth of the "walkabout": Movement in the Aboriginal domain', in *Population Mobility and Indigenous Peoples in Australasia and North America*, ed. John Taylor and Martin Bell (London: Routledge, 2004), 223–38; Heather Goodall and Allison Cadzow, *Rivers and Resilience: Aboriginal People on Sydney's Georges River* (Sydney: UNSW Press, 2009); Shino Konishi, 'Crossing Boundaries: Tracing Indigenous Mobility and Territory in the Exploration of South-Eastern Australia', in *Indigenous Mobilities: Across and Beyond the Antipodes*, ed. Rachel Standfield (Canberra: ANU Press, 2018), 35–55; Rachel Standfield, 'Introduction: Looking Across, Moving Beyond', in *Indigenous Mobilities: Across and Beyond the Antipodes*, 1–33.

44 Busby, *Authentic information relative to New South Wales, and New Zealand*, 63.

45 Patrick Matthew, *Prospectus of the Scots New Zealand Land Company* (Edinburgh: Adam and Charles Black, 1839).

46 Patrick Matthew, *Emigration fields: North America, the Cape, Australia, and New Zealand, describing these countries, and giving a comparative view of the advantages they present to British settlers* (Edinburgh: Adam and Charles Black, 1839).

47 G. J. Tee, 'Reviews: Patrick Matthew and Natural Selection', *New Zealand Journal of History* 18:1 (1984), 66–7.

48 Matthew, *Emigration fields*, vii.

49 Ibid., 6.

50 Ibid.

51 Patrick Matthew, *On Naval Timber and Arboriculture: With Critical Notes on Authors who Have Recently Treated the Subject of Planting* (Edinburgh: Adam Black, 1831); Tee, 'Reviews: Patrick Matthew and Natural Selection', 66.

52 Matthew, *Emigration fields*, v.

53 Ibid.

54 Ibid., vi.

55 Wagner, 'Introduction: The Nineteenth-Century Pacific Rim', 229.

56 Matthew, *Emigration fields*, 126.

57 Ibid., 126–7. The concept of Māori as 'very industrious cultivators' was a quote from J. L. Nicholas to the British Parliament, included in a footnote on page 127.

58 Ibid., 100.

59 Ibid., 128.

60 Ibid., 128, 133.

61 Ibid., 133.

62 Ibid., 122.

63 Ibid., 129–30.

64 Ibid., 121.

65 Ibid.

66 See Victoria Stead and Jon Altman, 'Labour Lines and Colonial Power', in *Labour Lines and Colonial Power: Indigenous and Pacific Islander Labour Mobility in Australia*, ed. Victoria Stead and Jon Altman (Canberra: ANU Press, 2019), 1–26.

67 Standfield and Stevens, '"New Histories but Old Patterns"', 124.

68 Standfield, 'Reading Māori and Aboriginal Mobilities and Encounters in Newcastle, 1853', 12.

69 Michael J. Stevens, '"The Ocean is Our Only Highway and Means of Communication": Maritime Culture in Colonial Southern New Zealand', *Journal of New Zealand Studies* 12 (2011): 157.

70 Henry Melville, *The present state of Australasia: including New South Wales, Western Australia, South Australia, Victoria, and New Zealand: with practical hints on emigration; also, Remarks on prison discipline: with suggestions for obviating the difficulties attending the transportation of convicts; to which are added the land regulations, and description of the aborigines and their habits* (London: G. Willis, 1851), 79.

71 Flinn, 'Melville, Henry (1799–1873)', *Australian Dictionary of Biography*.

72 Melville, *The present state of Australasia*, 91.

73 Ibid., 83.

74 Brantlinger, *Dark vanishings*.

75 Melville, *The present state of Australasia*, 83, 84.

76 Johanna Perheentupa, 'Victims of the Past? White–Aboriginal relations in Australian historiography in the nineteenth century', *ZFA – Zeitschrift für Allgemeinmedizin* 23 (2009): 31.

77 Melville, *The present state of Australasia*, 345.

78 Ibid., 346.

79 Ibid., 345–6.

80 Perheentupa, 'Victims of the Past?', 31.

81 Melville, *The present state of Australasia*, 174.

82 Ibid., 175.

83 Author Record, 'John Shaw', AustLit, St Lucia: The University of Queensland, 2002. https://www.austlit.edu.au/austlit/page/21956755.

84 John Shaw, *A tramp to the diggings: being notes of a ramble in Australia and New Zealand in 1852* (London: Richard Bentley, 1852); John Shaw, *A ramble through the United States, Canada, and the West Indies* (London: J. F. Hope, 1856); John Shaw, *A gallop to the Antipodes, returning overland through India* (London: J. F. Hope, 1858).

85 Shaw, *A tramp to the diggings*, 1.

86 Ibid., 273.

87 Ibid., 274.

88 Ibid., 35.

89 Ibid., 16–17.

90 Ibid., 17.

91 Ibid., 21.

92 Ibid., 34.

93 Aileen Moreton-Robinson, *The White Possessive: Property, Power, and Indigenous Sovereignty* (Minneapolis–Saint Paul: University of Minnesota Press, 2015), xxi.

94 Fricker, *Epistemic Injustice*, 153, quoted in Luvell Anderson, 'Epistemic Injustice and the Philosophy of Race', in *The Routledge Handbook of Epistemic Injustice*, ed. Ian James Kidd, José Medina and Gaile Pohlhaus Jr. (London: Routledge, 2017), 140.

3

Triangular Formation: Fiji, New Zealand and Australia

Frances Steel

Fiji's geographical position as 'the natural centre of the British Islands in the Pacific Ocean', its Governor asserted in 1909, appeared to offer promise it would take a 'not unimportant share with Australia and New Zealand in forming that one great portion of the British Empire – call it Australasia or what you will – which will hereafter occupy that quarter of the world'.[1] This centring of Fiji was by this time familiar to colonists in Australia and New Zealand, who had long regarded the island group as a 'crossroads' in the western Pacific and a gateway to Polynesia and beyond. Framed strategically in this way, Fiji's location positioned the group differently in imaginings of Australasia than other islands annexed to the 'British Pacific', such as New Guinea. It was folded more routinely into shared visions of Australasia and its potential futures, and more frequently envisaged as a sister colony, rather than a dependency.

This chapter approaches the history of Australasia as a regional construction through the lens of connections between Fiji, New Zealand and Australia. Placing Fiji at the apex of the triangle, it explores the ways in which these three sites have interacted and influenced each other, recognizing also the prominence of their pairings along each side of the triangle, i.e. Fiji–Australia, Fiji–New Zealand and Australia–New Zealand. This captures a sense of their multidirectional interactions, whether through traffic and exchange, as well as notions of mutual dependence and rivalry. It also works to show how these close engagements fostered comparative assessments, including in ways that might help to probe Fiji's colonial 'difference' in the wider imperial setting. As the colony's 'dealings are principally with self-governing Dominions', reflected Assistant Under-Secretary of State for the Colonies, Sir Charles Lucas, who toured the region in 1909, the Crown Colony system 'is here, so to speak, constantly being put on its trial, and tested by contrast'.[2] Conversely, this also invites us to consider how the self-governing Dominions may have been 'tested by contrast' through their engagements with Fiji. This 'triangular formation' is, however, not meant to enclose, and I am attentive here to the ways in which their relations were always mediated by wider connections – to Britain as well as the United States, to India and to other islands in the Pacific.

In what follows, I sketch a brief history of this intercolonial relationship, before turning to a series of federal moments in Australasia in the late nineteenth century.

Scholarship has often treated the decline of political debates and agitation for the formal unification of Fiji with the self-governing colonies as an analytic end point. This chapter also aims to demonstrate how an idea of Australasia that bound Australia, New Zealand and Fiji together persisted, as did arguments about its limits, articulated most starkly with respect to perceived racial capacities for political citizenship. Beyond the realm of formal constitutional arrangements, however, we might explore how the infrastructures of commerce and shipping, and the mobilities they fostered, channelled regional connections and continued to give legibility to this triangular formation. Attending to seaborne linkages across Australasia can direct us to commercial complicities with, as well as interrogations of, political boundary-making over time. This chapter aims to untangle some of these complexities.

Annexation to federation

Colonial relations between Fiji, Australia and New Zealand have largely been addressed within histories of early colonial Fiji, or in the course of wider surveys of settler-colonial aspirations in the Pacific.[3] Because Fiji was never formally incorporated into the island empires of either Australia or New Zealand, there is, unsurprisingly, a comparatively richer body of work on the islands brought under their respective rule, i.e. Papua and New Guinea, the Cook Islands, Niue and Sāmoa. Interestingly, the index entry for 'Australasia' in Angus Ross's *New Zealand Aspirations in the Pacific*, directs the reader to 'see Australia' – suggestive of the ways in which these histories have been examined, in line with consolidating national history approaches, often from an analytic base on one side of the Tasman with the occasional comparative glance across it.

More focused scholarship on these transcolonial ties has tended to proceed along one side of the triangle, without a tradition of work that places the three sites together in the same frame at any length. Such studies typically emphasize discrete episodes, notably the path to Fiji's cession to Britain in 1874, or political movements for the formal incorporation of Fiji, particularly the 1900–2 campaign of New Zealand premier Richard Seddon.[4] Moreover, much of the close empirical analysis lies unpublished in dissertations written in the 1960s and 1970s.[5] This research tends to be focused on high politics, particularly discussions between key colonial and imperial statesmen about the limits of Australia and New Zealand's autonomy vis-à-vis Britain.

Fiji often rates a brief mention in the historical scholarship of the federation movement that led ultimately to the inauguration of the Australian Commonwealth in 1901, given it was formally represented at one convention and was a member of the Federal Council of Australasia established in 1885. New Zealand's decision not to join the Commonwealth has produced a sustained body of scholarship, and while Fiji's disinclination never propelled the same level of attention at the time or since, there has been little to no consideration of why it participated in the movement in the first place. In a valuable survey chapter, Helen Irving refers to Fiji as 'an unlikely co-federationist' and 'never a realistic prospect as a State of the Commonwealth', with these asides presented as self-evident, rather than inviting further enquiry.[6]

To approach a history of this triangular formation thus requires addressing Fiji's relative submergence in the more general surveys of settler-colonial island empire, on the one hand, and in the historiography of Australian federation, on the other. It also means working with historical fragments, impeded somewhat by work skewed to distinct nation-centred accounts of Australia and New Zealand in the Pacific. I endeavour here to pull some of these threads together in order to draw out understandings of the shifting attempts to forge connections and mark out boundaries in the late nineteenth century as a way to make sense of the relations and preoccupations that endured in the first decades of the twentieth century.

Australasia, when approached as encompassing the Australian continent, New Zealand and islands in the western Pacific, distinguishes British (and prospective British) territory in the Pacific – a 'colonising ideology' as Donald Denoon remarks.[7] From the mid-nineteenth century this was an ideology championed increasingly by the settler colonies, as they asserted their own colonizing capacities in the wider region. Fiji was an early shared field of engagement and endeavour, and this arguably distinguished it in the colonial imagination. The establishment of the Polynesia Company in Melbourne in 1868, which paid off a leading chief's long-standing debt to the US government in return for land and trading rights, was followed by what has been termed the 'Great Fiji Rush' of 1870–1 to develop cotton plantations first established in the wake of the US Civil War.[8] There were over 150 ship arrivals in Fiji in one year, the majority from Sydney, Melbourne and Auckland, carrying migrants seeking plantation fortunes. Much of this traffic was short-lived, and many planters failed and deserted Fiji.

This brought into enduring tension two broad strands of representation, with Fiji decried, on the one hand, as a marginal and disorderly site, wracked by white settler ruin and disappointment; and conversely, this trajectory of white mobility from the colonial 'homelands' was understood to set a course to their political unification. The first might be epitomized by Litton Forbes, a Sydney doctor in Levuka in 1871, who in referring to a rising white 'semi-criminal class' in the islands remarked: '[T]he very name of Fiji was looked on in Sydney and Melbourne with loathing and contempt. "Gone to Fiji" bore the same significance in Australia as "Gone to Texas" did in America a few years ago.'[9] The second found expression in the reports of journalist Henry Britton, special correspondent in Fiji for the Melbourne *Argus*, who asserted in 1870 that the islands 'belong to Australia':

> They are, by their geographical position, the birthright of Australians; they are being peopled from our shores, and our hold of them will be in the close affection which grows from common names, kindred blood, and from equal political privileges. When the federation of the Australian colonies has been accomplished, and we form one great nation, Fiji must be included in the commonwealth.[10]

Similar assertions were aired in New Zealand. Frederick Moss, who had joined the rush to Fiji and would later serve as a colonial administrator in the Cook Islands, argued that New Zealand needed tropical territory to provide some form of balance, for Australia had enough of its own.[11] Still, others saw potential for joint rule for their mutual protection against foreign encroachment.[12] Beginning with the 1870 Intercolonial Conference at Melbourne, the colonies of New South Wales, Victoria and New Zealand kept their interests in Fiji's future in Britain's sights, variously emphasizing their Anglo-Saxon racial heritage, geographical proximity, their long-standing investments in the region and their domestic experience of colonization – which all spoke to a common, if not directly articulated, belief in Australasia as an expansionist regional platform.[13]

The close interest of the Australian and New Zealand colonies would partly propel the British annexation of Fiji in 1874. Secretary of State for the Colonies, Lord Carnarvon, weighed up the presence of English settlers, capital and crime and the imminent prospect of 'chaos'; the abuses of plantation labour recruitment in Melanesia; Fiji's strategic location as a 'convenient stepping stone' across the Pacific; and the desire of Australia and New Zealand that the islands become British.[14] If their collective pressure and agitation informed Britain's actions, their recent histories also profoundly shaped the nature of Crown Colony rule in Fiji. The first Governor, Sir Arthur Gordon, declared that Fiji was 'emphatically not a white man's colony', arguing that indigenous demographic and landholding dominance meant 'it is idle to think that the interests of some few hundred settlers are alone to be thought of'.[15] This 'anti-settler' sentiment and the policies that followed from it reflected a desire to avoid reproducing the racial conflict and land loss witnessed in New Zealand and Australia, 'a transcolonial system of reference', as Lorenzo Veracini puts it.[16] While annexation may have quelled the self-governing colonies' security concerns, it created new insecurities for the Europeans in Fiji who sought self-government rather than Crown Colony rule. In this respect, John Young concludes: 'Fiji proved to be not a stage in the process of the continuous expansion of Australasia but its cultural terminus.'[17]

The Australasian federation movement represented a possible release from these perceived constraints. The *Fiji Times*, a vehicle for settler grievances, saw it as offering the colony relief 'from the Crown colonial incubus which at present fetters her progress and retards her advancement'.[18] Yet intercolonial forums held to discuss a federal future more readily exposed rifts within Fiji, and tensions about who could best represent its affairs. An intercolonial conference held in Sydney in 1881 did not include Fiji yet would discuss issues that directly concerned it. A tabled report on the Pacific labour trade reproduced anonymous accounts from the popular press accusing leniency towards Islanders who attacked Europeans and undue harshness towards British perpetrators.[19] Sir Arthur Gordon, now Governor of New Zealand but retaining the position of High Commissioner for the Western Pacific, expressed outrage that the conference would reprint and officially circulate views highly ignorant of the Commission's mandate and authority. These views would potentially prejudice attitudes towards Fiji's judicial authorities. Moreover, they contained 'a good deal of severe censure' of Fiji's internal administration that he was forced to correct.[20] As 'an Australasian colony' Fiji was as sensitive to its rights and dignity as its neighbours, he argued, and thus asks 'why if her affairs were to be a topic of discussion' its government was not invited to take part.[21]

Fears about such meetings giving unchallenged voice to aggrieved white settlers spilled over to the federal convention held in 1883. It met in the aftermath of Queensland's failed attempt to annex New Guinea. The convention aimed to pressure the imperial government to forestall German encroachment in New Guinea, but also engaged broader questions of island annexations in the Pacific. In the minds of many delegates, though promoted more vocally by representatives from Victoria, the movement towards federation and island annexations were linked, and said to reflect a 'newborn spirit of Australasian patriotism'.[22]

Governor of Victoria, James Service, issued an invitation to Fiji. This was publicized in the *Fiji Times* and prompted meetings to promote a settler delegation and petitions to the Queen and the convention for the incorporation of Fiji in any future Australasian Federation. The settler movement led by R. Beckwith Leefe, a planter from Ra province, and made up of planters, merchants and industrialists, felt hardest hit by government controls on land claims, indigenous labour protections, and by a government not sufficiently responsive to its interests. Fiji's governor, Sir William Des Voeux, ultimately attended the convention, remarking to the Colonial Office that colonial politicians held erroneous views about Fiji that needed correcting.[23] While Leefe hoped to enter as a special delegate, this was not entertained, nor was the settlers' petition tabled, Des Voeux making it clear he would not speak to the 'unauthorised' settler movement in Fiji.[24] He also worked to temper the annexationist zeal, submitting a lengthy report in which he challenged any extension of plantations and the labour trade in the Pacific.[25] This was reported favourably by the *New Zealand Herald* as a 'dispassionate review of the whole question of Anglo-Saxon colonization in the South Seas' and that his views run counter 'to all our preconceived theories with reference to colonization'.[26] From this perspective, the Fiji governor's presence and contribution was a tempering one, an important foil to rampant 'Anglo Saxon colonization'.

The Federal Council of Australasia, established following the 1883 convention, was made up of representatives from Western Australia, Queensland, Tasmania and Victoria, and later for a time by South Australia. Neither New South Wales nor New Zealand joined, although Fiji did. The council, which had no executive authority and no revenue, met in alternate years until 1899. Its legislative powers, of which it made little use, covered a limited range of subjects, including relations with islands of the Pacific, prevention of the influx of criminals, and fisheries beyond territorial limits.[27] It appears Fiji was not in regular attendance, or at least did not place much store on it, with Governor Charles Mitchell relaying in 1887 that 'from a social standpoint he would chiefly represent a race that has nothing in common with the Anglo-Saxon communities of Australasia'.[28] With whiteness a unifying feature of the federal movement, Fiji's position became increasingly anomalous, and exposed simmering tensions between the government's official commitment to the paramountcy of native interests and the power and reach of white settler interests.

Concurrent with these developments, New Zealand's political leaders attempted to forge a distinctive path for a future island empire through its Confederation and Annexation Bill, which passed in mid-1883 and awaited imperial assent. It gave white settlers in Fiji confidence that if they approached New Zealand 'they would find support, sympathy and salvation'. Indeed, Leefe had corresponded with Sir George Grey as he drafted the bill.[29] After the rebuff at the 1883 convention, Leefe petitioned the New Zealand delegates, again without success, for leaders recognized the difficulties in the absence of support from Fiji's officials or the Colonial Office. Remarking of the

New Zealand legislation, Fiji's Colonial Secretary John Thurston decried, 'The British Jingo is pretty bad property, but he isn't a "circumstance" as sailors say, to the Colonial Jingo ... stupendous cheek and insolence!', a disparaging tone more characteristic of the imperial metropole.[30] In any case the imperial government's refusal to ratify the Confederation and Annexation Act in 1885 made clear its position on New Zealand's ambitions.

The Fiji settler lobby renewed its petitioning, approaching New Zealand again in 1885 and then Victoria in 1887 without success. By the late 1880s, Alan Atkinson suggests, the 'archipelagic vision' that earlier informed the broader federal movement in the Australian colonies was beginning to hold less appeal to younger men coming into power who wanted 'the bright symmetry of a single landmass' and not what he characterized as 'a mess of islands'.[31] The Federal Council was not regarded as suited to grappling with the different emerging views, and conferences were held in 1890 and 1891 to forge a new path to establish basic constitutional principles. Fiji was invited to the first conference and planned to attend but ultimately did not, while at the second its representation was only figurative, depicted along with New Guinea and the white settler colonies on the illustrated banquet menu.[32] Representing New Zealand, Captain William Russell remarked on the good feelings between the colonies, yet argued that 'it would be absurd to deny the fact that when circumstances are so different as between the sister colonies of New Zealand, Fiji, and Australia, it is impossible to say at this moment that the people of the two former colonies would at once join in any scheme of federation'.[33] Such differences confirmed their absence in later forums held between 1897 and 1898, with the question of federation put to the Australian people and finally passed in 1899.

As New Zealand turned its back on the six Australian colonies, its own expansionist agenda was now being championed by Premier Richard Seddon, augmented by an island tour in 1900 which ignited his interest in Fiji. He was the guest of honour at a banquet in Suva, where it was proposed New Zealand and Fiji unite. Seddon was receptive, and a Fiji Federation League was formed with whom Seddon corresponded on his return to New Zealand.[34] His campaign would soon champion dual aims – federation with Fiji in the interests of New Zealand's security, trade and prestige, and constitutional reform in Fiji to achieve representative government. As D. K. Fieldhouse notes, if the first aim failed, he could fall back on the second, which in turn held the prospect of a self-governing Fiji voting for union with New Zealand.[35]

Domestic opposition in New Zealand turned keenly on questions of race, labour and colonial difference. Seddon believed the disaffected white settlers were worthy of assistance not least because many of them were New Zealanders and have 'enjoyed freedom'. New Zealand was 'practically their parent colony' and had an obligation to them.[36] There were particular anxieties about the circulation of Indian and other colonial labour, though this was seen to rest on the form that union would take – whether a 'federation' of the colonies or the 'incorporation' of Fiji as part of New Zealand. The latter would seem to preclude laws to control the movement of non-white labour between them, but federation would allow for differentiated laws to prevent it.[37] Still, federation would mean New Zealand tolerating 'coolie' labour within its realm. There were related concerns about the extension of political representation to non-white subjects, who might 'almost control the Federal Parliament' and hence 'the laws of New Zealand', as Russell put it.[38] Picking up on this theme, the *New Zealand Herald* argued that the proportionate vote of Fijians and Indians 'could turn the scale against every New Zealander north of the Waikato'. This prospect would also hamper any future move to join the Australian Commonwealth, others feared, given its constitution imposed race barriers to political representation.[39]

At the same time Seddon's proposals elicited strong protests from New South Wales to the Colonial Office, citing the extensive investment of Australian firms and shippers in the island group. The Fiji trade was triangular; most of its imports came from Sydney, while New Zealand was its primary export market. Sydney traders naturally feared the prospect of tariff barriers if 'the triangle became a straight line'.[40] In any case, the Colonial Office had no intention of entertaining Seddon's proposals, and in 1902 all correspondence on the issue ceased. This date has also marked a kind of scholarly terminus, with little sustained attention to this triangular formation following the campaigns for federation and the renegotiation of boundaries upon the advent of white Australia. The granting of Dominion status in 1907 in turn seemed to magnify a sense of separation, it being asserted that 'no New Zealander would wish his country to be confused with the Fijis, the Jamaicas, and the Sierra Leones of the Empire', places where the Englishman was 'only in exile, even though he is ruler and master'. The new designation would, it was hoped, also help to distinguish New Zealand, so easily subsumed by the phrase 'the Australasian colonies'.[41] The *Fiji Times,* however, regarded it as a rupture, for 'the "Colony" of New Zealand' was 'not a great time ago included as one of the various groups of islands comprising the "South Sea Islands"'.[42]

Whereas Seddon's proposals raised the spectre of Indian mobility and political representation, in subsequent years Fiji was increasingly regarded as a rising 'Asiatic' stronghold. This overshadowed questions about the political status of whites in Fiji and reflected anxieties back on the racial preservation of the white Dominions. In 1913, for instance, J. S. Griffiths described Fiji as '[t]he eastern outpost of Australia', arguing that it was imperative Australia govern Fiji to prevent it becoming 'a sugar estate worked by coolies'.[43] For others the first step was to 'materialise the aspiration of a White Australia, not to speak of a White Papua'. In Fiji the Indian could be declared 'the coming man', which 'only serves to bring home to us with increased emphasis the urgency of strengthening our grip on Australia' through immigration restriction.[44] Incidents in Fiji might be sensationalized to caution against the relaxation of such laws, such as a 1912 cover of the *Bulletin* depicting a violent incident in Fiji involving three Indian lighthouse keepers.[45] Speculative reports of Indian uprisings in Fiji were commonplace in Australia and New Zealand in the early twentieth century, leading Fiji's Commissioner of Lands, Dyson Blair, to squash such rumours during a visit to New Zealand in 1909 as 'utter nonsense'.[46]

At the same time, Australian travellers in Fiji in the first decades of the twentieth century seldom looked beyond a 'coolie' stereotype, their observations of Indians 'overwhelmingly negative', although some began to question indenture as dehumanizing.[47] Others were unsettled by racial hierarchies and the forms of white mastery that upheld them. John Bell Thompson, hospital superintendent in Arrowtown, New Zealand, travelled in 1908 on an island round-trip steamer from Auckland to

Sydney, via Fiji, Tonga and Sāmoa. When a group of plantation overseers joined the ship at Suva for Sydney, conversation in the smoking room about 'wool and butter gave way to copra and sugar cane'. This provoked a heated argument about the treatment of Indian labourers, one planter bearing a facial scar from the slash of a worker's cane knife: 'We outsiders said nothing but thought a lot', he recorded.[48]

Not all Australians shared fears of an Asiatic peril. In their work lobbying for the rights of Indians overseas and for the end of indenture, former Anglican clergymen Charles F. Andrews and William W. Pearson visited Fiji in 1915, travelling via Australia. Fiona Paisley notes they ascertained a 'new attitude' among Australian progressives towards 'India as a civilisation' and as a result of the united war effort. They held the view that Fiji fared better as 'Australians and New Zealanders were less racist than their counterparts in South Africa'.[49] However, Andrews was more circumspect about Australian attitudes on a second visit in 1918, according to Kama Maclean, and in private remarked how firmly politicians held to their exclusionary immigration policy.[50]

Divergent views of Fiji's racial future became more marked with a growing anticolonial agitation in India and rising Indian demands in Fiji for more political rights and opportunities. A strike in 1920 by Indian workers in Suva for better wages and living conditions prompted the Fiji Government to request military reinforcements from Australia and New Zealand. This assistance was justified in New Zealand on the grounds of protecting Europeans, yet it elicited protests among labour leaders there, while in India it was regarded as an action 'calculated to arouse or maintain bitter racial feeling', given the marginal status of Indian residents in New Zealand.[51] In 1925 a Fiji Indian deputation to the first conference of the Institute of Pacific Relations in Honolulu stressed that their treatment in Fiji was 'part of a great Empire problem' but also a question of 'racial contacts', noting their desire 'to live on friendly and neighbourly terms with New Zealand and Australia'. Reported in a Sydney newspaper, the account, however, concluded with comments from prominent Fiji resident Sir Maynard Hedstrom of the danger of Fiji becoming 'Asiatic in settlement' and 'a place in which few Europeans would care to live'.[52]

Race relations in Fiji continued to be heavily influenced by resident Australians and New Zealanders. James R. Pearson, the first Secretary of Indian Affairs in Fiji, appointed in 1927 after a career in the Indian Civil Service, saw his role in part to educate 'these Colonials' about the 'advantages both Imperial and local of adopting the Fiji Indian into the Colonial family and helping them along'. He felt that 'New Zealanders, who have successfully handled their Maori problem, are much more understanding than the Australians, though many of them are I think pretty reasonable'. They need only see 'they have these people in their pockets', and by 'fostering and controlling' their advancement they might prevent them turning instead to 'advanced and semi-hostile politicians in India'.[53] He went on:

> I sometimes wonder if the importance of the Indian problem here is not increased by the fact that it is one Colony where Indians are in direct contact with the big British Colonies in the Southern Hemisphere. It may count for something in Imperial politics to give Australia a practical demonstration of the possibility of the two races living together on amicable terms.[54]

If Fiji, from one strand of thought, needed to be 'recovered' from Indians rather than embraced for its ethnic and racial diversity, this particular moment in Fiji's development also suggested opportunities to reflect back on the white Dominions to pose a different way forward; they were being 'tested by contrast'. Warwick Anderson has shown that about the same time a number of white Australian intellectuals, enamoured of what they saw of race-mixing in Hawai'i, were beginning to question the 'fetish of whiteness' and sense there were possible anti-racist solutions to Australia's population problems.[55] Yet Fiji was – and was at – a different kind of crossroads. More directly entangled with Australia and New Zealand, this racial boundary arguably held a different import and immediacy for its white neighbours.

Transoceanic ties

As the preceding section has shown, Fiji posed a repeated conundrum – did its white settler population set it on a course to unification with the self-governing colonies, or would this undermine the dominant white identity of Australia and New Zealand? If the latter, the question then became how to facilitate connections that profited the white Dominions without entangling them too closely with Fiji. Intercolonial ties were not formalized through federation, yet there were deep investments in maintaining connections to facilitate flows of capital and goods. Shipping networks emblematized such connections; indeed, shipping came up repeatedly in annexation and federation debates and retained its triangular importance long after they ended. As a journalist observed in 1909, the Fiji trade moved 'in two sharply-divided compartments' – in red-funnelled steamers to Auckland, and black-funnelled ships to Sydney, while 'nearly everything that Fiji uses comes from Sydney. That is Australia's interest in Fiji'.[56]

This reference to red and black funnels spoke to the decades-long engagement of the Union Steam Ship Company of New Zealand (Union Co), and the Australasian United Steam Navigation Company (AUSNCo, a merger of Sydney- and Brisbane-based shipping interests). Routes from Sydney, Melbourne and Auckland to Fiji were inaugurated during the 1870s and augmented the following decade by Union Co's monthly round-trip services from Sydney to Auckland (and vice versa) via Fiji, Tonga and Sāmoa. In addition to these circuitries, Fiji was included as a port of call on transpacific routes that linked Australia and New Zealand with the US and Canada. In the years preceding British annexation in 1874, arguments for Fiji's strategic importance repeatedly centred on its prospects as an intermediate point and coaling station between Australia and North America. This was a key consideration for Colonel W. J. Smythe, sent to Fiji in 1860 to investigate the first offer of cession, with the focus being a prospective route between Sydney and Panama. Upon the completion of the transcontinental US railroad in 1869, the focus shifted north to San Francisco, and this redirected attention to an intermediary port in Fiji. Beginning in the early 1870s and put on a more secure footing from 1875, a transpacific network from Sydney to San Francisco included Galoa Habour in Kadavu in southern Fiji. Every alternate month a steamer departed Sydney or Auckland for San Francisco and in alternate months each colony would send a branch steamer to carry passengers and goods to connect with it at Kadavu. This was triangulation quite literally at work, as both Australia and New Zealand had access to a monthly transpacific service. It was through Fiji, then, that these settler colonies sought to forge closer exchanges with their 'white brethren' and fellow empire-builders on the other side of the Pacific.[57] Whereas Fiji was not envisaged as a white man's colony, its strategic importance, as Paisley notes, worked to bolster 'Australia's place as a white nation in the Pacific', as it did New Zealand's.[58]

There were realignments and adjustments in the transpacific trades. From 1885 the Union Co assumed operation of the Sydney–San Francisco service, one that now bypassed Fiji, in conjunction with the American-owned Oceanic Steam Ship Company. From 1893 another route, opened by Australian shipowner James Huddart, linked Sydney and Vancouver via Brisbane, Suva, Honolulu and Victoria. It was known as the Canadian Australian Line or the 'All Red Route' in that the service linked British territory. A branch line between Suva and Auckland connected this route to New Zealand until 1911, when the Union Co assumed its operation and Auckland replaced Brisbane as a port of call (and the service renamed the Canadian Australasian Line). In the meantime, the Union Co had been forced off the Sydney–San Francisco route altogether in 1900 when Hawai'i was designated a coastal port of the US and foreign ships were now excluded from trading between Honolulu and San Francisco. This was an enduring source of bitterness, for it was an important part of Pacific trade which the Union Co considered 'they had created and built up by pioneer effort'.[59]

From the 1920s, British Dominion maritime activity in the Pacific was further overshadowed by a handsomely subsidized American seaborne imperialism, encroaching beyond Hawai'i and further south to Fiji, New Zealand and Australia. In 1925 the Oceanic Company expanded its transpacific route (San Francisco–Honolulu–Pago Pago–Sydney) to include a call at Suva before Sydney. In this way it re-established a connection between Fiji and the US, abandoned after Kadavu was dropped from the San Francisco route in the 1880s.

The Union Co was concerned that colonial passengers might choose to travel by the American line between Sydney and Fiji in preference to its own ships. Little could be done unless Australia and New Zealand legislated to replicate 'American conditions' between the Dominions and the Pacific Islands, i.e. protecting those stretches of the ocean as 'coastal' shipping.[60] In 1931 Oceanic, now incorporated within the Matson Line, went a step further, interposing a call at Auckland between Suva and Sydney, arguing a call at New Zealand was vital to entice American travellers into the Pacific.[61] It professed initially to be interested only in the transpacific through-traffic and not in trans-Tasman passengers, but soon reversed its decision, apparently in response to numerous requests from Auckland residents.[62]

With the long shadow cast by America's maritime push into the Pacific, New Zealand and Australia could not level the playing field together, let alone individually, and Fiji now became central to their stakes in this competition. The comparatively short distances from Fiji to Auckland and to Sydney, one newspaper argued, 'may more reasonably be treated as lying within a "Domestic-Trade" Zone, than the staggering distances included as belonging to the "Coastal" trade of the US'.[63] Yet because Suva, Auckland and Sydney were not under the jurisdiction of a single government, it would take a multilateral agreement to exclude American shipping. Both the Australian and New Zealand governments initially hoped Britain would take the lead.

From another view, however, Australia's heightened protectionism against Fiji had left the region vulnerable to US incursion. Former New Zealand Minister of Marine, J. D. Gray, drew a link between Matson's entry to Suva and the Commonwealth's decision in 1921 to increase tariffs on Fiji bananas. Bananas were the mainstay of the AUSNCo's Fiji trade, but with a move to protect Australian growers the company's steamers were forced off the line. Matson soon entered the Fiji–Australia trade, 'and now, after an appropriate interval' directed its offensive against 'another branch of our own trade'. The Union Co privately concurred with this assessment. In this instance, the impact of tariffs reached beyond the targeted commodity to affect wider commercial interests and trigger heightened competition in seemingly unrelated sectors.[64]

An earlier attempt to reserve a 'colonial sea' in the south-west Pacific had, ironically, a different catalyst. In 1910 the premier British firm P&O extended its route between Britain and Sydney to Auckland in order to relieve an unremunerative lull while its ships berthed in Sydney. P&O's reliance on lascar (Indian) crew paid lower wages than white seafarers prompted New Zealand to draft legislation to extend the meaning of coasting, so that ships trading between New Zealand and either Australia or the Cook Islands (annexed to New Zealand in 1901) would follow local manning and wage rates. The Secretary of State for the Colonies opposed it on the grounds it went beyond New Zealand's legislative power.[65] Some two decades later, New Zealand sought to build a maritime fortress against the incursions of their 'white' brethren across the Pacific, with 'Britishness' mobilized now as a shared, binding heritage. To extend the irony, in 1933 P&O added Suva to its tourist cruise programme from Sydney, complementing existing cruises to Papua and Noumea, to counter Matson's growing monopoly of the excursion traffic between Australia and Fiji.[66] While the Union Co feared Matson could use this as 'counter propaganda', they appreciated 'the desirability of shewing the Flag and maintaining the prestige of the British Mercantile Marine'.[67] In 1934 P&O extended its Australian cruises also to New Zealand, but agreed not to carry local passengers across the Tasman. Matson rejected a challenge to do likewise, insisting that its service between Australia and New Zealand was 'part of a long established and regular through line between America and Australia', thus implying that P&O was an outsider and latecomer to this supposedly 'British sea'.[68]

P&O was about the extent of British involvement and support to which there were strict limits. Britain was more concerned for its global interests and had no wish to take on US shipping interests in the western Pacific. British shipping was 'very vulnerable' in the US because it carried more American foreign trade than American ships. Ports in the Philippines were still 'international' under US law, but should the US retaliate by bringing the Philippines under its coastal laws, Britain would be excluded from the 'substantial' US–Philippines trade. Britain's reluctance to act in the western Pacific came as a 'great disappointment' to Australia and New Zealand, but as Australia's prime minister put it, '[W]e are willing and indeed anxious not to embarrass you.'[69]

Britain eventually relaxed its resistance to Dominion-led agitation and in 1936 New Zealand passed the Protection of British Shipping Bill to restrict trans-Tasman passenger shipping to vessels of nations that imposed no restrictions on British shipping. It could not be made law until Australia passed similar legislation. Commentators in Fiji were certain that Britain would not ask them to fall into line by designating the Fiji–Australia or Fiji–New Zealand trades as coastal. While Fiji's sympathies lay with British shipping, Matson offered a valuable service to the colony, introduced some welcome competition, and also induced greater tourist traffic from Australia and New Zealand.[70] 'It is all very well having the satisfaction of being thoroughly British in this matter', remarked the *Fiji Times*, yet Fiji would have the most to lose by enclosing the sea.[71] From this perspective, therefore, Fiji was at best a reluctant Australasian entity. In the end the legislation was put on the backburner pending a wider British enquiry into its shipping position in the Pacific completed shortly before World War II.

Conclusion

Different ideas of Britishness shaped Australasia as a regional formation over time, and a key point of fracture was how these ideas gelled or not with assertions of white dominance in Australia and New Zealand. The triangular relationship weakened from the mid-1880s, as settler agitation against Crown Colony rule in Fiji struggled to gain traction, and Fiji's officials used intercolonial forums to temper settler-colonial expansionism. Yet seaborne networks continued to give legibility to forms of exchange; from a maritime angle of vision Australasia survived the project of political separation. A British sea offered new expressions of common interest when embraced to push back against American incursions in the south-west Pacific. Yet there was a persistent inner boundary that limited political and cultural connection with Fiji, whose own triangulation of race repeatedly challenged Dominion visions of a white future.

Notes

1   Cited in Charles Lucas, 'Note on a Visit to Australia, New Zealand, and Fiji, in 1909', Colonial Office series, Dominions No. 1 [Cd. 5100], 9.
2   Lucas, 'Note on a Visit', 8.
3   Angus Ross, *New Zealand Aspirations in the Pacific in the Nineteenth Century* (Oxford: Clarendon Press, 1964); Roger Thompson, *Australian Imperialism in the Pacific: The Expansionist Era, 1820–1920* (Melbourne: Melbourne University Press, 1980); John Young, *Australia's Pacific Frontier: Economic and Cultural Expansion into the Pacific, 1795–1885* (Melbourne: Cassell, 1967); Merze Tate, 'The Australasian Monroe Doctrine', *Political Science Quarterly* 76:2 (1961): 264–84.
4   For example, D. K. Fieldhouse, 'New Zealand, Fiji and the Colonial Office', *Historical Studies: Australia and New Zealand* 8:30 (1958): 113–30; John Young, *Adventurous Spirits: Australian Migrant Society in Pre-Cession Fiji* (St Lucia: University of Queensland Press, 1984).
5   Ahmed Ali, 'The federation movement in Fiji, 1880–1902: Causes and courses' (MA thesis, University of Auckland, 1969); Marguerite Ashford, 'Seddon v O'Brien. An incident in New Zealand–Fijian Relations, 1900–1902' (Postgraduate Diploma in Arts,

University of Otago, 1975); I. D. Borrie, 'Opinions on Fijian Federation with NZ 1900–1903' (MA thesis, University of Otago, 1963); F. M. Caughey, 'Opposition within New Zealand to Fijian Federation 1900–1902' (BA Hons thesis, University of Otago, 1972); Ruth Moses, 'The Polynesia Company Limited of Melbourne and Fiji 1868–1883; a social history' (BA Hons thesis, University of Adelaide, 1971); Max Quanchi, 'Fiji and Australasia: 1868–1888 Internal problems and political union' (BA Hons thesis, Monash University, 1972); A. M. Dobbie, 'Fijian federation with New Zealand; 1883–1885' (BA Hons thesis, University of Otago, 1973).

6   Helen Irving, 'Making the federal Commonwealth, 1890–1901', in *The Cambridge History of Australia*, ed. Alison Bashford and Stuart Macintyre (Melbourne: Cambridge University Press, 2013), 251, 257.

7   Donald Denoon, 'Re-Membering Australasia: A repressed memory', *Australian Historical Studies* 34:122 (2003): 293.

8   Evelyn Stokes, 'The Fiji cotton boom in the eighteen sixties', *New Zealand Journal of History* 2:2 (1968): 165–77.

9   Litton Forbes, *Two Years in Fiji* (London: Longmans, 1875), 277.

10   H. Britton, *Fiji in 1870* (Melbourne: Samuel Mullen, 1870), 72.

11   F. J. Moss, *A Planter's Experience in Fiji* (Auckland: Jones and Tombs, 1870), 63–4.

12   *Otago Daily Times*, 24 June 1870, 2.

13   Thompson, *Australian Imperialism in the Pacific*, 21–34; Ross, *New Zealand Aspirations*, 93–130; Julius Vogel, 'The Fiji Islands', *Appendices to the Journals of the House of Representatives* [AJHR], 1874, A-3, 10–11.

14   W. D. McIntyre, *The Imperial Frontier in the Tropics, 1865–75* (London: Macmillan, 1967), 331. See also Jane Samson, *Imperial Benevolence: Making British Authority in the Pacific Islands* (Honolulu: University of Hawai'i Press, 1998), 148–69.

15   Cited in John Young, 'Race and sex in Fiji revisited', *Journal of Pacific History* 23:2 (1988): 216.

16   Lorenzo Veracini, '"Emphatically not a white man's colony": Settler colonialism and the construction of colonial Fiji', *Journal of Pacific History* 43:2 (2008): 199. See also Deryck Scarr, 'John Bates Thurston, Commodore J. G. Goodenough, and rampant Anglo-Saxons in Fiji', *Historical Studies: Australia and New Zealand* 11:43 (1964): 361–82.

17   Young, *Australia's Pacific Frontier*, 14.

18   *Fiji Times*, 26 February 1881 and 21 May 1881.

19   'Intercolonial Conference Held at Sydney: Minutes of Proceedings' AJHR, 1881, Session I, A-03, 22–35.

20   Arthur H. Gordon, 'Memorandum', 26 February 1881, AJHR, 1881, Session I, A-03, 42.

21   Gordon, 'Memorandum', 42.

22   'The Annexation Conference', *Otago Witness*, 8 December 1883, 10. See also Marilyn Lake, 'The Australian Dream of an Island Empire: Race, reputation and resistance', *Australian Historical Studies* 46:3 (2015): 411–14; A. M. Quanchi, 'Fiji, Sixth Star for the Australasian Federation', *Pacific Islands Monthly* 47:8 (1976): 37–8.

23   *New Zealand Herald*, 31 October 1883, 5; Ali, 'The federation movement in Fiji', 96.

24   Ali, 'The federation movement in Fiji', 106–9.

25   'Memorandum by his Excellency the Governor of Fiji and Acting-High Commissioner of the Western Pacific on the future of New Guinea and Polynesia with reference to the question of Australasian Annexation or Protectorate', *Report of the Proceedings of the Intercolonial Convention, held in Sydney in November and December 1883*, AJHR, 1884, Session I, A-03, 117–25.

26 *New Zealand Herald*, 17 January 1884, 4.

27 Stuart B. Kaye, 'Forgotten source: The legislative legacy of the Federal Council of Australasia', *Newcastle Law Review* 1:2 (1996): 57–71.

28 National Archives of Fiji (NAF), Despatches from the Governor of Fiji to the Secretary of State, vol. 7, no.141, 4 November 1887; in 1895 it was noted that Fiji 'is once more not sending delegates to the sitting', *Launceston Examiner*, 23 January 1895, 5.

29 Dobbie, 'Fijian Federation with New Zealand', 5, 16.

30 Cited in Deryck Scarr, *Viceroy of the Pacific: A Life of Sir John Bates Thurston* (Canberra: Pacific Research Monograph, 1980), 106–7.

31 Alan Atkinson, *The Europeans in Australia*, vol. 3 (Sydney: UNSW Press, 2014), 175.

32 Reproduced in John Hirst, *The Sentimental Nation: The Making of the Australian Commonwealth* (Melbourne: Oxford University Press, 2000), 220.

33 *Official Record of the Proceedings and Debates of the Australasian Federation Conference, 1890* (Melbourne: Government Printer, 1890), Russell, 11 February 1890, 41.

34 Fieldhouse, 'New Zealand, Fiji and the Colonial Office', 117.

35 Fieldhouse, 'New Zealand, Fiji and the Colonial Office', 118.

36 *New Zealand Parliamentary Debates* [NZPD], vol. 115 (Wellington, 1900), 473.

37 NZPD, vol. 115, 475.

38 NZPD, vol. 115, 476. Estimates of proportional representation including sixteen for non-white subjects (including the exiting seats for Māori), while whites in Fiji would be assigned one third of a white member.

39 *New Zealand Herald*, 4 October 1900, 4, and 8 October 1900, 4.

40 Fieldhouse, 'New Zealand, Fiji and the Colonial Office', 115.

41 'Press opinions on the proposed changes', *Press*, 29 June 1907, 10.

42 *Fiji Times*, 28 September 1907.

43 *The Lone Hand*, 1 April 1913, 514.

44 'The coming man in the South Seas', *Daily Telegraph*, 15 June 1912, 12.

45 Kama Maclean, *British India, White Australia: Overseas Indians, Intercolonial Relations and the Empire* (Sydney: UNSW Press, 2020), 122–3.

46 Frances Steel, 'Servant Mobilities between Fiji and New Zealand: The transcolonial politics of domestic work and immigration restriction, c.1870–1910', *History Australia* 15:3 (2018): 537. See also Nicholas Halter, *Australian Travellers in the South Seas* (Canberra: ANU Press, 2021), 290–1.

47 Halter, *Australian Travellers*, 285–6, 292.

48 Cited in Frances Steel, 'Uncharted Waters? Cultures of sea transport and mobility in New Zealand colonial history', *Journal of New Zealand Studies* 12 (2011): 148.

49 Fiona Paisley, 'Sexuality, Nationalism, and "Race": Humanitarian Debate about Indian Indenture in Fiji, 1910–18', *Labour History* 113 (2017): 195, 197, 204.

50 Maclean, *British India, White Australia*, 125–9.

51 Frances Steel, 'Cruises and the Making of Greater New Zealand', in *New Zealand and the Sea: Historical Perspectives*, ed. Frances Steel (Wellington: Bridget Williams Books, 2018), 269.

52 'Storm cloud in Fiji: Will there be a new Kenya?', *Daily Telegraph*, 16 July 1925, 4.

53 Pearson identified the Fiji Government's antipathy to nationalism in India as part of the issue in reckoning with Indian demands, John D. Kelly, *A Politics of Virtue: Hinduism, Sexuality and Countercolonial Discourse in Fiji* (Chicago: The University of Chicago Press, 1991), 240.

54 British Library, Indians in Fiji, IOR/L/E/7/1469, File 6008(ii), 2 October 1929, James Rae Pearson, Secretariat for Indian Affairs, Suva, to S. F. Stewart, Assistant Under Secretary of State, India Office.

55 Warwick Anderson, 'Liberal Intellectuals as Pacific Supercargo: White Australian masculinity and racial thought on the boarder-lands', *Australian Historical Studies* 46:3 (2015): 426.

56 C. E. W. Bean, *With the Flagship of the South* (Sydney: William Brooks, 1909), 63.

57 Frances Steel, 'Re-routing Empire? Steam age circulations and the making of an Anglo Pacific, c.1850–90', *Australian Historical Studies* 46:3 (2015): 356–73.

58 Paisley, 'Sexuality, Nationalism, and "Race"', 196.

59 Libraries and Archives Canada, RG25, vol.1790, file no. 318 AE, Imperial Conference 1937, Pacific Shipping, enclosure Paper No. 3 Memorandum on British Shipping, 12 May 1936 – Appendix: historic overview of trans-pacific trade.

60 Hocken Collections, Union Co Records, AG-292-005-002/002, Holdsworth to Aiken, 14 February 1929.

61 Hocken Collections, Union Co Records, AG-292-005-004/181, Holdsworth to Aiken, 17 October 1928; Wellington City Archives (WCA), Union Co Records, AF066:7:1, Aiken to Carter, 10 June 1929.

62 WCA, Union Co Records, AF080:85:1, Back to Aiken, 8 July 1931.

63 *Wellington Times* [NSW], 4 April 1932, 5.

64 *New Zealand Herald*, 23 May 1931, 14. See also C. F. Yong, 'The banana trade and the Chinese in NSW and Victoria 1901–1921', *ANU Historical Journal* 1:2 (1964): 28–35.

65 Frances Steel, *Oceania under Steam: Sea Transport and the Cultures of Colonialism, 1870–1914* (Manchester: Manchester University Press, 2011), 41–2.

66 WCA, Union Co Records, AF080:331:6, James to Aiken, 7 July 1933.

67 WCA, Union Co Records, AF066:3, Aiken to Shaw, 8 August 1933.

68 National Archives UK, BT 188/266, Pacific Shipping. Documents handed to Sir H. Mackinder by the Board of Trade, enclosed notes by 'AS'.

69 National Archives New Zealand, Coates, Joseph Gordon Papers, MS-Papers-1785-053, Matson Shipping Line, 1932–34, Secretary of State for Dominion Affairs to Governor General of New Zealand, 18 May 1934.

70 NAF, 64/24, Union Co and CA Line mail subsidy agreement, Hedstrom to Bailey, Vice President of Matson, 3 March 1936.

71 *Fiji Times*, 30 July 1932, 4.

4

'A Splendid Thing': Imagining Australasian Federation

Frank Bongiorno

Armidale, in the New England region of northern New South Wales, had to wait until mid-February 1901 to celebrate the federation of the Australian colonies in a manner befitting that accomplishment. Queen Victoria's death had inaugurated a period of mourning. But the festivities were worth waiting for: local newspapers called the occasion '[t]he greatest and most imposing demonstration ever seen in Armidale', one that foretold a 'bright and glorious future for Federated Australia'. Alongside the flags, bunting and streamers were banners bearing slogans such as 'One Flag', 'One People', 'One King' and 'One Destiny'. A procession involved local organizations: the Irish National Association's display included a 'monster kangaroo representing the Federated States, with a disjoined tail as a symbol of New Zealand's stand-offness'. And among the most spectacular of sights was the splendid Amazon Fire Brigade, an all-female outfit, carried along on a fire truck in their dark blue uniforms while the tableau behind them had young girls representing each of the federated colonies. New Zealand, a reluctant fairy, trailed behind, 'as if anxious to join, but not yet quite decided'.[1]

To the extent that Australians think about their federation at all, some still imagine an alternative nation that includes New Zealand. The wording of the constitution itself does a little work to encourage such whimsy, since it provides 'for the admission into the Commonwealth of other Australasian Colonies and possessions of the Queen'; New Zealand itself maintains a ghostly presence in the definition of 'The States' conditional, naturally, on it joining the Commonwealth. But in the most influential modern account of federation, produced to coincide with its centenary, this counterfactual is given short shrift. John Hirst declared: 'God wanted Australia to be a nation'. Not Australasia: Hirst's reference was to the sense of destiny that impelled the founders of a specifically *Australian* federation, their conviction that it was a sacred cause and that they were doing God's will.[2] Ignoring Tasmania, Australia's physical existence 'as a single geographical unit' could be presented as an exhibit in defence of such a case: this 'home … girt by sea', as the eventual national anthem *Advance Australia Fair*, a song first performed in 1878, would say.[3] While allowing for the wider empire to which the federating colonies belonged, Australia nonetheless seemed to patriots made for the nationhood theorized by Mazzini and won by Garibaldi. Yet, as the kangaroo tail and reluctant fairy of the Armidale celebrations hinted, God's creation could have been otherwise. Destiny might have dictated a different kind of nation state, one more oceanic than continental, an Australasian rather than an Australian federation.

This chapter will explore these alternative imaginaries, from an Australian perspective – a gap in the literature. It acknowledges the case Tony Ballantyne argues in the Introduction to this collection: 'the idea of Australasia was never entirely fixed or stable'. There is already a substantial literature attempting to explain why New Zealand did not join the Commonwealth but almost all of it emerged out of New Zealand historiography, even when acknowledging the need for a trans-Tasman perspective.[4] One landmark in the field was an article by the Australian-born New Zealand professor of history, F. L. W. ('Freddie') Wood, asking: 'Why did New Zealand not join the Australian Commonwealth in 1900-1901?' Wood was one of those urging the wider perspective, arguing that 'there was really nothing to differentiate New Zealand significantly from the Australasian community as a whole', and that the question was really not why New Zealand stayed out, but why the 'Australians, who had as many reasons as New Zealanders to be cagey, nevertheless went ahead'.[5] Wood's foundational contribution emphasized the spoiling role of Premier Richard Seddon, but Miles Fairburn persuasively argued that the matter had been largely resolved by the time Seddon was in charge: 'New Zealand had always been the least active and the most reluctant participant in federation movements before Seddon's ascendancy.' That New Zealand would not join was already clear by 1891. Fairburn's case rested largely on material causes. The lack of economic incentives fostered indifference: 'Apathy was always the dominant sentiment.'[6] New Zealand, instead, as a loyal and affectionate member of the British Empire, looked for its trade and defence to Great Britain.

This debate occurred in some of the earliest issues of the *New Zealand Journal of History*: indeed, that journal's establishment in 1967 signalled the consolidation of a national historiography in New Zealand, one that could be considered neither merely as an aspect of British Empire history nor the history of Australasia and the Pacific. National historiographies had emerged initially as fragments of imperial history but by the 1960s, as more fully developed fields in their own right. One result would be bemoaned by historians of empire, who wondered whether it would be possible to put the Humpty Dumpty of imperial history together again.[7] Another, as Philippa Mein Smith has suggested, was the submergence of Australasia, a meaningful 'political and cultural entity' which, in the globalizing era of recent decades, has reasserted its presence.[8]

Until 1967 the major outlet for scholarly research in both Australian and New Zealand history had been the Melbourne-based *Historical Studies: Australia and New Zealand*, founded in 1940, and becoming plain *Historical Studies* with the appearance of the new journal across the Tasman. In 1952 it had published an earlier article on the same topic by E. J. Tapp, a London-born historian educated in New Zealand who made his academic career in Australia.[9] Tapp argued that New Zealand's decision to remain aloof was born of a separate history, strong allegiance to the mother country, isolation that fostered a sense of individuality, pride in social and political development and conquest, and ambition for further dominion in the Pacific.[10] This would be a rare excursion into a genuinely trans-Tasman history of federation, and neither New Zealand nor Australasia has figured prominently in Australian federation historiography since that time.[11] Hirst registered New Zealand's fitful presence, although only briefly. But it was important for him to be able to do so because he also stressed the strength of federalist notions that 'the island continent was the natural boundary of the new nation';[12] the most enthusiastic of them, such as Alfred Deakin, presented internal boundaries as largely artificial, 'imaginary lines ... we are a people one in blood, race, religion, and aspirations'.[13]

Hirst's account plays up the force of these ideas and plays down alternative imaginaries. It is not that New Zealand nearly joined the federation, for it did not. New Zealand was not the reluctant fairy who needed just a little more coaxing. In his treatment of the issue, Hirst echoes the New Zealand historian Keith Sinclair's explanation of why his compatriots had not joined the federation: 'two distinct though similar nationalisms were being formed in Australia and New Zealand'. For Sinclair, as for Hirst, New Zealanders did not regard themselves as Australians: rather, those on either side of the Tasman believed they each had a destiny to become a nation.[14] It is in line with his general approach to federation as essentially Australian nationalist business that Hirst only takes up the story of New Zealand and federation in the context of the manoeuvrings of the late 1890s, the fraught London negotiations in 1900 in which Deakin and the other federalist delegates believed New Zealand to be playing the role of dog in the manger – obstructing a federation that they had played little part in making and had no intention of joining.[15] During 1899, once it became clear that federation was now likely to occur, some interest in it revived in New Zealand, largely driven by commercial entities worried about matters of moment such as whether New Zealand would be able to sell its oats, but Seddon did nothing to encourage the flurry. 'If New Zealand joined the Commonwealth,' Hirst remarked, 'the continental trope would have to be dropped ... The movement still officially kept the name "Australasian" so that New Zealand was not forgotten, although strictly the term was also necessary to embrace Tasmania.' For Hirst, the various arguments for New Zealand federation 'became lame because they were not knitted together and fired by a sense that union was destiny'.[16]

Hirst does not ask another question that might have suggested itself in this context: did Australian federalists also think of themselves as Australasians? His analysis implies that their attachment to the term 'Australasia', which they used persistently throughout the 1890s in the name of their leagues and their conventions, was a pragmatic concession to their brethren across the Tasman: a mere signal that they had not been forgotten rather than expressive of any deeper belonging. This would be so if they did, as Hirst suggests, now habitually think in terms of a 'nation for a continent, and a continent for a nation', to use Edmund Barton's phrase.[17] But even then, there would still be a puzzle: how and why had this essentially landed and continental conception come into being? Why did these people who now thought of themselves as Australians see a 'home ... girt by sea' rather than an archipelago or ocean as the basis of their nationhood? Philippa Mein Smith has argued that a conception of Australasia had survived in the New Zealand mind, evident for instance in testimony to the New Zealand Federation Commission appointed by Seddon in 1900. Yet, to what extent such Australasian thinking was influential on the Australian side of the Tasman is, as in Hirst's work, left unresolved.[18]

Older visions of federation in the south seas had been more oceanic, or at least less continental. John Dunmore Lang, the Presbyterian clergyman writing in the 1850s in *Freedom and Independence for the Golden Lands of Australia*, envisaged a future republic that would be composed of the eastern Australian colonies of New South Wales (which then included what is today Queensland), Victoria, South Australia and Tasmania. It would not include Western Australia, at that time a convict colony with a small settler population: 'For as the eastern and western portions of the Great South Land are separated from each other by a great central desert, like those of Africa and Arabia, of at least a thousand miles in extent, it must be evident that the eastern and western divisions of that land must each be under a separate *régime*.' It was seemingly no less significant for Lang that Swan River (now Perth) had been transformed into a penal settlement, a 'condition which all the eastern colonies strongly repudiate'. Lang thought it likely the British government would establish further settlements of this kind along the coast: 'There is, therefore, as complete a separation of the eastern and western divisions of the continent as if a wide ocean had rolled between them.' Yet, perhaps paradoxically, Lang did not regard the existence of a literal ocean as an insuperable barrier to union between the colonies of eastern Australia and New Zealand. If there were to be 'a National Government established for the united provinces of Australia', he predicted, within three years New Zealand would be petitioning to join.[19]

This was an oceanic vision of 'Australasia'.[20] Visions of Australasia were also imperial and, no less than the continental nationalism that later dominated, they rested on racial hierarchy. John West, the Tasmanian newspaper editor and anti-transportationist, writing under the pseudonym 'John Adams' in 1854, imagined a federation formed by 'the Anglo-Saxon race, which will give to the whole the practical consistency and energy of one empire. In Europe, the United Kingdom, in British America, the United Colonies; on the Atlantic and Pacific Oceans, the United States; in New Zealand, the United Province; and in New Holland, the United Australias!'. For West, such an entity could only work if it recognized self-government based on recognition of 'local rights and personal independence'.[21] Here was the essence of his federal vision, which was at once global, oceanic, imperial, racial, national, regional and local. West often used the term 'The Australias' to refer to the three mainland colonies of New South Wales, Victoria and South Australia, plus Tasmania. Still, the anti-transportation league he led from 1851 was called the Australasian League, adopted a southern cross flag with the Union Jack in the canton, and devised the motto, 'The Australias are One'. There was a league across the Tasman, in Christchurch: 'Thus the five colonies', explained West in his 1852 history of Tasmania, 'answering to the stars of the Southern Cross, had raised that sign of hope and union.'[22]

These ways of thinking about federation reflected the oceanic character of colonial life itself. Historians such as Geoffrey Blainey and Frank Broeze have drawn attention to the way early settlers looked predominantly out to the sea rather than to the interior of the continent. Australia's famous bush nationalism would evolve in time, but as the product of a political economy in which sheep replaced whales, and in which the theft of Indigenous land became the foundation of territorial empire and a pillar of settler prosperity. As Broeze remarks, it was an 'inward-looking', racially defined and continentally based nationalism 'in which the sea was seen as a fence shutting out unwanted intrusions from the surrounding region'.[23] Such nationalism played a part in the movement towards federation in the late nineteenth century, but there were other, probably equally powerful impulses. There was a desire for recognition, identity and status, a resistance to being thought colonial and inferior.[24] 'Why should not the name of an Australian be equal to that of a Briton?' Henry Parkes asked the 1890 Australasian Federation Conference in Melbourne.[25]

Alternatively, Broeze suggests, Australia may be viewed as 'an archipelago of "islands" of settlement rather than as a continent'.[26] We might see this approach to understanding space and identity as the point at which the idea of 'Australia' shades into that of 'Australasia', a less bounded and more oceanic understanding of geographical space. This understanding was there, too, in the titles and content of commercial publications that aimed to instruct Australians about their country, such as in *The Picturesque Atlas of Australasia* (1886–8) and *Cassell's Picturesque Australasia* (1889). But the preface written by the *Picturesque Atlas*'s editor, Andrew Garran, addressed readers as if they were being introduced to a book about Australia, which 'though populated for centuries, was a blank in history until it was discovered by Europeans'.[27] The multipart serial of three volumes was, moreover, slanted towards treatment of 'Australia' at the expense of any vivid sense of a broader spatial imaginary, even while providing details of the history, economies, ethnology, climate, geology, flora and fauna of various places in the Pacific. We can see here what Ballantyne refers to in the Introduction as 'an erosion of Australasia's cultural currency'. It is perhaps for this reason that scholarship on the *Picturesque Atlas* has emphasized its representation of Australia – with titles such as *Paper Nation* and *Picturing a Nation* – rather than Australasia as a less bounded oceanic entity.[28] New Zealand and other parts of the Pacific, such as New Guinea, Fiji and a host of Pacific Islands, even including French New Caledonia – collectively dubbed 'insular Australasia' – did figure in the third and final volume, which also looked forward to the day when Australia, 'set apart in a pleasant sea to work out our destiny untroubled by the distraction of contemporary politics', would 'unite upon a common basis of federation'. 'So far there has not been that unanimity of action and of policy which alone can secure solid political progress all along the line,' the journalist Frank J. Donohoe explained, but the day would soon arrive 'when a united Australia would evolve itself from the federated colonies.' The 'Australasian story', he concluded confusingly, suggested that such a dream was not 'over-sanguine'.[29]

If the image of Australasia was already somewhat attenuated in these reflections, it was still nonetheless alive. And as the first effort to create an Australasian federation by the Victorians in the 1880s would indicate, it was an imaginary shaped by imperialism and race. Denis McLean is perhaps, therefore, only partly right in suggesting the empire provided Australians and New Zealanders with their 'grand design', and that no room existed 'for the development of an alternative strategic vision, in the shape of a united "Australasia"'.[30] Not as 'an alternative', to be sure: but it is more accurate to see imaginings of the British Empire and Australasia as entangled and increasingly, too, saturated in the wider global identity of whiteness.[31] The creation of the Federal Council of Australasia in the mid-1880s – it first met in 1886 – is usually recalled for being a failed experiment, a premature and ill-fated exercise in federalism. New South Wales never joined; Fiji joined but disappeared after the first meeting; South Australia held out and then only attended once.[32] Driven by Victorian premier James Service's desire for British annexation of Pacific islands as yet unclaimed by empire lying between New Guinea and Fiji, the Victorian-led movement to federate was motivated by colonial hostility to the ambitions and policies of European powers towards the Pacific. The Queensland government sent a police magistrate to Port Moresby in 1883 to annex eastern New Guinea, its actions being, however, repudiated by an imperial government that subsequently agreed to a carve-up of the territory with Germany. Of more direct concern to Service and Victoria was French policy towards the New Hebrides and New Caledonia, with the latter due to receive a large boost in its population of criminals sent from France, 'the moral filth of that country', as Service indelicately put it – the subject of convicts was necessarily a touchy one for Australians.[33] Both New Zealand and Fiji were represented at the conference held in November 1883 in Sydney that resolved to create a council. But the delegates could agree to only a weak body, without executive powers or revenue. Still, Service did his best to persuade New Zealand that distance was no barrier to further participation: 'I have heard it said that New Zealand is too far away from Australia to have the same interest that our Australian Colonies have in union, but in these days of rapid steam communication such an argument can have no weight.' But it did seemingly carry weight with the New Zealand political elite, as did the opposition of New South Wales to the scheme and the fear among leading New Zealand politicians of a loss of autonomy.[34]

Despite its still-birth, Service's vision of 'Federation and all the islands' still had some purchase when the new federal movement emerged after 1889 following Henry Parkes's address at Tenterfield. One of the Tasmanian delegates at the Melbourne Federation Conference in 1890, Bolton Stafford Bird, articulated an explicitly Australasian vision, being 'so anxious … to see the foundations of a great empire in these Southern seas laid broad and deep that I desire the constitution of this proposed Confederation to be such that all the British possessions which cluster around Australia … should eventually be drawn in as members of the Dominion of Australasia'. He envisaged the New Hebrides, Fiji and other islands 'which are the natural adjuncts of an Australasian Empire' being joined together under 'the flag of a United Australasia'.[35] Perhaps as a Tasmanian, Bird was more comfortable with a maritime federation. Elliott Lewis, Tasmanian premier, would tell the New Zealand Federation Royal Commission a decade later that 'to have the whole of the Australasian Colonies united would be a splendid thing'.[36]

Other Australians would also articulate an Australasian federal vision as a counterpoint to the unquestionably dominant continental version. Edward Dowling, secretary of the Australasian Federation League of New South Wales, told the New Zealand federation commissioners in 1901: 'Australasia should have a kind of protectorate over all the islands on this side of the equator, leaving the United States to look after those adjacent to America.'[37] William McMillan, a leading conservative Free Trader from New South Wales and soon to be elected to the federal parliament, provided an imperial context, arguing that 'if the British Empire is to hold together there must be three great Confederations, putting aside the Asiatics and others' under allegiance to the crown: Canada, South Africa and Australasia. He thought that a New Zealand-led Pacific federation would imperil empire by sowing discord with Australia, and a united Australasian voice would carry greater weight in imperial affairs.[38] Richard O'Connor, a Protectionist cabinet minister and future High Court judge, considered in 1901 that as 'a set-off against the development of tropical Australia, I think we ought to look forward to the time when Oceania will be embraced in Australasia. All those islands will probably be attached in some degree to the Commonwealth, and New Zealand will be much closer to them than the continent is.' O'Connor's vision here seems to have been largely sub-imperial: two white men's countries would join together in exercising dominion over the Pacific on behalf of the British Empire.[39]

Yet, despite the presence of two New Zealand delegates at the 1890 conference in Melbourne, and three at the National Australasian Convention in Sydney in 1891, such visions of federation were rarely articulated by Australians on these occasions. The South Australian liberal and future premier, Charles Cameron Kingston, was one who did venture into this territory at the 1891 convention, arguing that although it was desirable to provide for New Zealand's admission, delegates should not lose sight of the possibility of extending 'the jurisdiction of a united Australia to all British colonies in the Pacific'. He cited the failed effort to annex New Guinea in 1883 as a lesson in the disadvantage of the lack of a government able to speak for 'the whole of Australasia'.[40] The Tasmanian delegate, Nicholas Brown, praised the 'graceful and charming speech' of one of the New Zealand delegates, Captain William Russell, which 'recalled to our minds the fact that this is an Australasian Convention'. It would 'be deplorable if one important member of these Australasian communities should, for any reason, think it necessary to stand out'.[41] Perhaps so, but Brown's choice of words suggested that delegates needed reminding of their convention's 'Australasian' character, and New Zealand's participation was desirable rather than essential.

One of the leading younger federalists, Alfred Deakin, was even more sceptical about the possibility of creating a political unit that would include New Zealand. In his later account of the federal movement, Deakin praised the 'courtesy' of the New Zealand delegates in Melbourne in 1890, Russell and Sir John Hall, the former premier, which 'if it did not conceal at all events sweetened their unruffled good sense and friendly criticism as of onlookers rather than actual participants or even prospective partners'. In a similar vein, he would describe New Zealand as being 'only represented by courtesy' in Sydney; indeed, he resented that two of the three delegates had voted on a key division bearing on the respective powers of the House of Representatives and the Senate.[42]

Certainly, the New Zealand delegates in Melbourne and Sydney made it clear enough that their colony would not be joining in the near future. At Melbourne in 1890, both Hall and Russell were happy enough to talk vaguely of a 'Federated Australasia', but each made it clear that New Zealand was unlikely, as Russell put it, to 'submit ourselves to a Government in which we should have so unimportant a part'.[43] They suggested, and had accepted by the conference, a change in the motions to be adopted from the achievement of 'Australasian' to 'Australian' federation, with the rider that 'the remoter Australasian Colonies shall be entitled to admission at such times and on such conditions as may hereafter be agreed upon'.[44] At Sydney in 1891, Russell reiterated his arguments of the previous year, defending New Zealand aloofness while his colleague, the elderly Sir George Grey, was so preoccupied with long-winded speech-making, name-dropping and pressing pet causes, such as the abolition of plural voting and an elective governor general, that his contribution was entirely ineffectual.[45] The ailing former New Zealand premier, Sir Harry Atkinson, also present in 1891, spoke rarely through what Deakin called his 'failing strength and disinclination as an outsider to interfere with continental developments'.[46]

For Deakin himself, federation was a national destiny to be realized; it would be accomplished by creating a union that expressed an existing feeling of fellowship and belonging. By way of contrast, for Russell, federation was a process more than it was an end or goal; one that, if handled rightly – that is, as 'federation' and not 'unification' – would allow each of the free peoples of Australasia to work out its own development while advancing their common dominion over the Pacific. The islands of that ocean could fall under the influence of either Australasia or the United States: what was needed was an arrangement sufficiently loose 'that we shall attract all these various atoms to ourselves, rather than allow them to fly off to the great continent of America'.[47]

What was at stake in these competing versions of federation was different 'cartographic imaginaries'.[48] Maps express understandings of collective identity and geographical space and through wide dissemination and repeated exposure – such as in mass culture and the education system – they are likely to exercise influence over how people imagine their world. Alan Atkinson has argued that, to those who learn how to read them, maps tell stories of 'ownership and control', suggesting 'hierarchies of place and space'. In Atkinson's telling, the map is a technology that facilitates a mental and cultural process by which the small place is connected to the larger, the very essence of forming a federal nation.[49]

This was true of the maps delineating the British Empire that emerged from the 1830s, as of those published of Australasia, New Zealand and Australia.[50] Sir John Hall's declaration at the Melbourne conference of 1890 – 'Nature has made 1,200 impediments to the inclusion of New Zealand in any such Federation in the 1,200 miles of stormy ocean which lie between us and our brethren in Australia' – would be cited repeatedly in the years that followed, to demonstrate why New Zealand remained aloof.[51] But it was a statement that embodied an understanding of how Australia and New Zealand related to one another that could perhaps be most vividly captured in a map. 'Democratic government must be a government not only for the people, and by the people ... it must be in sight and within hearing of the people,' declared Hall.[52] But as Nicholas Aroney has pointed out, the delegate of another colony, South Australia, that, like New Zealand, had good reason to fear being swamped, Sir John Cockburn, said something very similar: '[T]here can be no government by the people if the Government is far distant from the people.'[53] Marilyn Lake has shown how the Sydney feminist, Rose Scott, argued against federation in similar terms: it would install another elite and centralize power in a distant parliament, one remote from the communities, families and homes where women lived – the negation, she thought, of true self-government.[54]

The New Zealanders' arguments about distance, then, are intriguing not because they were peculiar to the New Zealanders but because they expressed in sharpest form key tensions at the heart of making a federation – notably those between small and large colonies, and between diversity and local self-government, on the one hand, and common central institutions expressing the unity of democratic nationhood, on the other.[55] After all, the New Zealanders' fears about those 1,200 miles could be easily countered by the observation that the journey from Western Australia to the east coast was a rather longer one than from New Zealand. The Western Australian delegates had taken eleven days to reach Sydney, by sea, for the 1891 convention, which began before they got there.[56] Edmund Barton, by 1901 Australian prime minister, told the New Zealand federation commissioners: '[Y]ou might as well say there were twenty-five hundred reasons in the case of Western Australia, but they have been got over.'[57]

New Zealanders' evocations of literal physical distance served as proxy for a different and deeper sense of 'distance': that based on race and place. New Zealanders distinguished themselves as a hardy 'island race' or 'insular race' from Australians who formed a 'continental' one – and that with a dubious convict past, and a dubious piebald future. For the New Zealanders especially, history and geography conspired to create a people in Australia who were different from themselves. The consolidation of national identities on each side between the 1870s and 1890s enfeebled a shared feeling of Australasian similarity and belonging.[58] In New Zealand, the ambitious public works programme initiated by Julius Vogel in the 1870s, the end of provincial government in that decade, the economic depression of the 1880s, and the progressive social, political and industrial legislation of the *fin de siècle* generated a sense of national distinctiveness within a wider British world.[59] In Australia, too, there was a rising nationalism that was popularly associated with the belief in a distinctive Australian 'type'. The 'typical Australian' was most commonly imagined as male, but there was also discussion centred on the 'Australian Girl' and the 'New Woman', all seen as emerging out of the country's unique blend of demographic, physical and social circumstances.[60]

Despite the obvious commitment of their brethren across the Tasman to a White Australia, some New Zealanders – like some Australians – thought the continent's northern climate would dictate a mixed-race population because of the unsuitability of the tropics to British settlement and labour.[61] The character of a people was seen as the product of climate and landscape and there was a suspicion, strong among New Zealanders, that for this reason distinctive types were already emerging on either side of the Tasman. Historians such as K. R. Howe and Tony Ballantyne have also pointed to the ways that the theory of common Aryan origins between Pākehā and Māori could be used to project a shared imperial, racial and national destiny based on what Ballantyne calls 'an Indocentric cultural vision' of Aryan diffusion from South Asia, an understanding with some echoes in the concept of Māori as honorary whites identified by James Bennett.[62] While parallel racial theorizing did occur in Australia, where Aboriginal peoples at the turn of the century were sometimes presented as primitive Caucasians, it had less cultural resonance. Aboriginal peoples were seen as unworthy of inclusion within the political community, pointedly excluded from the franchise in 1902, and held to be a dying race.[63]

In this way, New Zealand and Australian whiteness carried different cultural and political meanings, complicating the idea of an Australasian community.[64] In 'native administration', for instance, Russell told the Melbourne federation conference that

were we to hand over that question to a Federal Parliament – to an elective body, mostly Australians, that cares nothing and knows nothing about native administration, and the members of which have dealt with native races in a much more summary manner than we have ventured to deal with ours in New Zealand – the difficulty which precluded settlement for years in the North Island might again appear.[65]

Here, as in other times and places, a New Zealander was appealing to a distinctive experience of colonization to explain national individuality. To the extent that 'Australasia' was seen as a shared geographical and cultural space, it was also understood to contain different colonial, racial and, increasingly, national histories.

Conclusion

The point has been made often that the two national communities that developed as a result of the formation of separate states on either side of the Tasman at the turn of the century have been projected backwards into earlier times in an anachronistic manner that has provided a misleading understanding of the historical development of both – although one suspects that it is understanding of the larger entity, Australia, that has most suffered. But the fate of Australasia is an even more peculiar one than the story of historiographical estrangement between the two dominions. While New Zealand would largely drop out of the federal movement in the early 1890s and would not participate in the conventions of 1897 and 1898 that made the Commonwealth, the term 'Australasia' itself was ubiquitous in public discourse. It was also there in the nomenclature and rhetoric of the federal movement itself. But understanding the place of Australasia in the mental maps of those who made that federation is a harder task than identifying its traces in popular culture and discourse. The best explanation for its elusiveness seems to be that for a range of reasons that have figured in federation historiography, such as the spread of railway and telegraph, the movement of people between colonies and the emergence of national markets, media, literature and institutions, the *fin de siècle* would witness a powerful consolidation of a continental Australian nationalism aspiring to an alignment of 'literature, land, and nation'.[66] An oceanic, archipelagic conception of national space that was sometimes understood as 'Australasia' was a casualty of this recalibration and reimagining. But the era of more intensive globalization that came in the late twentieth century would often remind Australians that the oceans surrounding their nation are conduits as well as barriers.

Notes

1   *Armidale Chronicle*, 16 February 1901; *Armidale Express*, 15 February 1901.
2   John Hirst, *The Sentimental Nation: The Making of the Australian Commonwealth* (South Melbourne: Oxford University Press, 2000), 4.
3   Ibid., 15.
4   Ged Martin, *Australia, New Zealand and Federation, 1883–1901* (London: Menzies Centre for Australian Studies, King's College London, 2001).

5   F. L. W. Wood, 'Why did New Zealand not join the Australian Commonwealth in 1900-1901?', *New Zealand Journal of History* 2:2 (1968): 115–16.

6   Miles Fairburn, 'New Zealand and Australasian Federation, 1883-1901: Another View', *New Zealand Journal of History* 4:2 (1970): 139, 156.

7   D. K. Fieldhouse, 'Can the Humpty Dumpty Be Put Together Again? Imperial History in the 1980s', *Journal of Imperial and Commonwealth History* 12:2 (1984): 9–23.

8   Philippa Mein Smith, 'New Zealand Federation Commissioners in Australia: One Past, Two Historiographies', *Australian Historical Studies* 34:122 (2003): 308.

9   Don Beer, *A History of History: The Department of History at the New England University College and the University of New England, 1938-1997* (Armidale: Department of History, University of New England, 1998): 4–5.

10 E. J. Tapp, 'New Zealand and Australian Federation', *Historical Studies: Australia and New Zealand* 5:19 (1952): 244–57.

11 See, for instance, J. A. La Nauze, *The Making of the Australian Constitution* (Carlton: Melbourne University Press, 1972) and William Oliver Coleman, *Their Fiery Cross of Union: A Retelling of the Creation of the Australian Federation, 1889-1914* (Redland Bay: Connor Court Publishing, 2021). The eight issues of the *New Federalist*, published over 1998–2001 for the Centenary of Federation, contained just one 4-page article on New Zealand and Federation, provided by a former New Zealand prime minister, Mike Moore, 'New Zealand: A Federation Partner, Then and Now', *New Federalist*, no. 1 (June 1998): 63–6.

12 Hirst, *Sentimental Nation*, 201.

13 *Official Record of the Proceedings and Debates of the Australasian Federation Conference, 1890, held in The Parliament House, Melbourne* (Melbourne: Robert S. Brain, Government Printer, 1890), 77.

14 Keith Sinclair, 'Why New Zealanders are not Australians: New Zealand and the Australian Federal Movement 1881-1901', in *Tasman Relations: New Zealand and Australia, 1788-1988*, ed. Keith Sinclair (Auckland: Auckland University Press, 1988), 102. See also Joanne Smith, 'Twelve Hundred Reasons Why There is No Australasia: How Colonisation Influenced Federation', *Australian Cultural History* 27:1 (April 2009): 35–45.

15 Alfred Deakin, *'And Be One People': Alfred Deakin's Federal Story*, ed. Stuart Macintyre (Carlton South: Melbourne University Press, 1995), 154.

16 Hirst, *Sentimental Nation*, 221, 222.

17 Ibid., 201, 221.

18 Mein Smith, 'New Zealand Federation Commissioners in Australia', 311.

19 John Dunmore Lang, *Freedom and Independence for the Golden Lands of Australia; the Right of Colonies and the Interest of Britain and of the World* (Sydney: F. Cunninghame, 1857), 41–2, 392.

20 Ibid., 97.

21 'John Adams' [John West], 'Union of the Colonies VI', in *John West's Union of the Colonies: Essays on Federation published under the pseudonym of John Adams in 1854*, ed. Patricia Fitzgerald Ratcliff (Launceston: Queen Victoria Museum and Art Gallery, 2000), 51–2.

22 John West, *The History of Tasmania, with copious information respecting the Colonies of New South Wales, Victoria, South Australia, &c., &c., &c.* (1852; Sydney: Angus & Robertson Publishers, 1971), 240.

23 Geoffrey Blainey, *The Tyranny of Distance: How Distance Shaped Australia's History* (Melbourne: Sun Books, 1966); Frank Broeze, *Island Nation: A History of Australians*

and the Sea (St Leonards: Allen & Unwin, 1998), 12; Russel Ward, *The Australian Legend* (Melbourne: Oxford University Press, 1958).

24 Hirst, *Sentimental Nation*, chapter 2.

25 *Official Record of the Proceedings and Debates of the Australasian Federation Conference, 1890*, 225.

26 Ibid.

27 Andrew Garran, 'Preface', in *The Picturesque Atlas of Australasia*, ed. Andrew Garran, Vol. 3 (Melbourne: The Picturesque Atlas Publishing Company, 1886-8), iii.

28 Tony Hughes-d'Aeth, *Paper Nation: The Story of the Picturesque Atlas of Australasia 1886-1888* (Carlton: Melbourne University Press, 2001); Gary Werskey, *Picturing a Nation: The Art and Life of A.H. Fullwood* (Sydney: NewSouth Publishing, 2021). I am indebted to Dr Werskey for his insights on *The Picturesque Atlas of Australasia*.

29 Frank J. Donohoe, 'The People of Australasia', in Garran, ed., *The Picturesque Atlas of Australasia* 3, 798.

30 Denis McLean, *The Prickly Pair: Making Nationalism in Australia and New Zealand* (Dunedin: University of Otago Press, 2003), 70.

31 Marilyn Lake and Henry Reynolds, *Drawing the Global Colour Line: White Men's Countries and the International Challenge of Racial Equality* (Cambridge: Cambridge University Press, 2008).

32 Victor Isaacs, 'Hope Deferred: The Federal Council of Australasia', *New Federalist*, no. 5 (June 2000): 81-6.

33 Geoffrey Serle, 'The Victorian Government's Campaign for Federation, 1883-1889', in *Essays in Australian Federation*, ed. A. W. Martin (Carlton: Melbourne University Press, 1969), 7.

34 Tapp, 'New Zealand and Australian Federation', 246-7.

35 *Official Record of the Proceedings and Debates of the Australasian Federation Conference, 1890*, 164-5.

36 Neil Elliott Lewis, Evidence, Q. 410, *Report of the Royal Commission on Federation, Together with Minutes of Proceedings and Evidence, and Appendices* (Wellington: John Mackay, Government Printer, 1901), 567.

37 Edward Dowling, Evidence, 25 March, 1901, Q. 820, ibid., 524.

38 William McMillan, 20 March, 1901, Evidence, Q. 323, ibid., 496.

39 R. E. O'Connor, 16 March, 1901, Evidence, Q. 18, ibid., 473-4.

40 *Official Record of the Proceedings and Debates of the National Australasian Convention, held in the Parliament House, Sydney, New South Wales, in the Months of March and April, 1891* (Sydney: George Stephen Chapman, Acting Government Printer, 1891), 74-5.

41 Ibid., 100.

42 Deakin, 'And Be One People', 32, 44.

43 *Official Record of the Proceedings and Debates of the Australasian Federation Conference, 1890*, 123, 125.

44 Ibid., 129.

45 Nicholas Aroney, 'New Zealand, Australasia and Federation', *Canterbury Law Review* 16:1 (2010): 39-42.

46 Deakin, 'And Be One People', 45.

47 *National Australasian Convention, Official Record 1891*, 32-33, 400.

48 Robert Dixon, '"A Nation for a Continent": Australian Literature and the Cartographic Imaginary of the Federation Era', *Antipodes* 28:1 (June 2014): 142.

49 Alan Atkinson, *The Europeans in Australia, Volume Three: Nation* (Sydney: NewSouth Publishing, 2014), 111.

50 Zoë Laidlaw, *Colonial Connections 1815–45: Patronage, the Information Revolution and Colonial Government* (Manchester: Manchester University Press, 2005), 187–8; Philippa Mein Smith and Peter Hempenstall, 'Rediscovering the Tasman World', in *Remaking the Tasman World*, ed. Philippa Mein Smith, Peter Hempenstall and Shaun Goldfinch with Stuart McMillan and Rosemary Bird (Christchurch: Canterbury University Press, 2008), 16–18.

51 *Official Record of the Proceedings and Debates of the Australasian Federation Conference, 1890*, 175.

52 Ibid., 176.

53 Aroney, 'New Zealand, Australasia and Federation', 35.

54 Marilyn Lake, '"In the Interests of the Home": Rose Scott's Feminist Opposition to Federation', in *Makers of Miracles: The Cast of the Federation Story*, ed. David Headon and John Williams (Carlton: Melbourne University Press, 2000), 123–31.

55 Atkinson, *Europeans in Australia*, Vol. 3, 173–5, 192–3.

56 B. de Garis, 'Western Australia', in *The Emergence of the Australian Party System*, ed. P. Loveday, A. W. Martin and R. S. Parker (Sydney: Hale & Iremonger, 1977), 299.

57 Edmund Barton, Evidence, 16 March, Q. 171, *Report of the Royal Commission on Federation*, 487.

58 Adrian Chan, 'New Zealand, the Australian Commonwealth and "Plain Nonsense"', *New Zealand Journal of History* 3:2 (1969): 190–5; Philippa Mein Smith, 'The Cartoon History of Tasman Relations', in Mein Smith, Hempenstall and Goldfinch with McMillan and Bird, eds, *Remaking the Tasman World*, 44–5.

59 Raewyn Dalziel, *Julius Vogel: Business Politician* (Auckland: Auckland University Press/ Oxford University Press, 1986); André Brett, *Acknowledge No Frontier: The Creation and Demise of New Zealand's Provinces, 1853–76* (Dunedin: Otago University Press, 2016); Tom Brooking, *Richard Seddon: King of God's Own: The Life and Times of New Zealand's Longest-serving Prime Minister* (Auckland: Penguin, 2014).

60 Ward, *Australian Legend*; Richard White, *Inventing Australia: Images and Identity 1688–1980* (Sydney: George Allen & Unwin, 1981), ch. 5.

61 Warwick Anderson, *The Cultivation of Whiteness: Science, Health and Racial Destiny in Australia* (Carlton: Melbourne University Press, 2002).

62 K. R. Howe, *Singer in a Songless Land: A Life of Edward Tregear 1846–1931* (Auckland: Auckland University Press, 1991), 13, 34, 52, 62, 64, 67; Tony Ballantyne, *Orientalism and Race: Aryanism in the British Empire* (Basingstoke: Palgrave Macmillan, 2002), 76–7; James Bennett, 'Maori as Honorary Members of the White Tribe', *Journal of Imperial and Commonwealth History* 29:3 (2001): 33–54.

63 Russell McGregor, 'An Aboriginal Caucasian: Some Uses for Racial Kinship in Early Twentieth Century Australia', *Australian Aboriginal Studies* 1 (1996): 11–20; Frank Bongiorno, 'Aboriginality and Historical Consciousness: Bernard O'Dowd and the Creation of an Australian National Imaginary', *Aboriginal History* 24 (2000): 39–61.

64 Smith, 'The Cartoon History of Tasman Relations', 40–5.

65 *Official Record of the Proceedings and Debates of the Australasian Federation Conference, 1890*, 126.

66 Dixon, '"A Nation for a Continent"', 142.

5

Cosmopolitan Pacific: Pan-Pacific Internationalisms in the Mid-Twentieth Century

Fiona Paisley and Helen Gardner

This chapter concerns contrasting visions of a cosmopolitan 'Pan-Pacific' circulating internationally during the mid-twentieth century. Our first example comes from the interwar years when Western internationalists saw in the formation of Pan-Pacific networks an opportunity for Pacific Rim nations to shape modernization in the region. In collaboration with counterparts from Japan and China, Anglo Dominion and North American progressives envisaged an 'East–West' collaboration that would work on behalf of, and to some extent in partnership with, Pacific Islander peoples experiencing disruptions to their ways of life following the war. Our second example stands as an implicit critique of this earlier narrative. Announced at the United Nations (UN) in 1970 in the name of an emerging Pacific Islander regionalism, this Pan-Pacific identity claimed to build on the resources of a long-standing, dynamic Indigenous cosmopolitanism only latterly in dialogue with the West. By assimilating European forms of democratic liberalism to its own needs, moreover, this Pan-Pacific ideology intended to finally realize the hitherto failed claims of Western civilization and thus contribute to a global remaking of modernity itself.

As is already evident from this brief sketch, our two cases differ in several significant ways. The limits of the interwar Pacific ideal would be all too evident in its hierarchies of advancement relative to Europe, and in its framing of modernization as a problem for those beyond the West that would have to be managed with the support of former and current colonial powers. In contrast, the Pacific ideal promoted decades later at the UN asserted the historical and cultural capacity of peoples and emerging nations within the region, as evidenced by their intention to engage with the world – including former colonizers – on their own terms. Put simply, the Pacific regionalism originating in the interwar decades (and as we discuss below, with its continuation into the 1950s and beyond) concerns southern circulations viewed 'from above', while the latter illustrates the political intervention inherent to 'histories from below'.[1]

Even though our two Pan-Pacific regionalisms differ in their temporalities and scales and in their political purpose, in the following we set out to consider them in critical relationship. We have been inspired by recent scholarship on the longer emergence of the Pan-Pacific from the nineteenth century as a dynamic field not only of interconnected colonial formations but of emergent anticolonial critiques.[2] The emergence in the interwar years of a cross-cultural cooperation imagined between Pacific Rim nations and Pacific Islander peoples, with their many imperial, colonial and migratory entanglements, reflects also a distancing by its proponents from the earlier concept of 'Australasia' that was explicitly Anglo-Saxon and settlerist in its intentions (several examples of which are discussed by other contributors to this collection).[3] In the following, we investigate instead some of the overlapping yet distinct expressions of a cosmopolitan world view in each of our Pan-Pacifics.

By reading these two Pan-Pacifics in proximity, we aim to foreground their shared interest in reinventing or overturning dominant narratives of racial and/or colonial difference. As we point out, each of these distinctly articulated utopian imaginaries sought to reframe the relationship of colonial pasts to the globalizing present. Both ideologies argued that if the Pacific was geographically distant, it was historically and politically interpolated within the present and future of Europe and could provide a model of cooperative thinking and acting for the whole world.[4] We will show that each asserted the need for a politics of mutual recognition based on intercultural respect – although, as we show, the interwar vision of a Pan-Pacific did so within racializing forms of cultural hierarchy inherently reiterating colonialist frameworks of gradualism and paternalism. Yet, by relocating these within the region itself, Pan-Pacific cultural internationalism opened up to critical investigation the question of (self-) representation. In what might be called a genealogy of anticolonial agency, Pacific Islanders joined these networks and conferences and hence were advocates as well as critics seeking to extend the agenda towards their own interests as Indigenous representatives of the Pacific world. Before the United Nations in 1970, one of their newly national leaders would proclaim an Indigenous form of decolonization by incorporating elements of European political thought into a uniquely Pacific account of internationalism. In both of our examples, therefore, intersecting histories of colonization, migration and indenture shaped the region, but also became the contexts within which renewed relationships between cultural identity and autonomy were enacted in international fora by national delegations. Becoming national was one basis on which the right to speak for one's own was articulated.[5] Ultimately, each of our case studies provides evidence of Indigenous voice internationalizing the Pacific in ways that sought to disrupt imperial and colonial frameworks through an assertion of regional identity as a counterpoint to the dominance of Europe.

In pursuing these continuities and disjunctures, the following is informed by histories of internationalism and cosmopolitics that have insisted upon the colonial and postcolonial formations of European cosmopolitanism.[6] Thus our chapter navigates away from the vestiges of 'colonial cosmopolitanism' reflected in the construction of the Pacific as a desirable travel destination, towards those 'new cosmopolitanisms' that expressed a plurality of cosmopolitics including through their southern formations.[7] Critical studies of progressive internationalism and liberalism in this era have pointed to the mobilizations of internationalism by anticolonial activists aiming to engage world opinion.[8] Susan Pedersen has argued that rights agendas circulating through the League of Nations should be treated distinctly from questions of the success or failure of the League as an institution.[9] Other scholars of this period have pointed to myriad conferences and diverse international venues at which liberal reform agendas became radicalized by the involvement of people of colour, anticolonialists and Indigenous representatives.[10] Through such networks and via interpersonal exchange, numbers of white reformers became critics of empire through interaction with anticolonial commentators who articulated alternative forms of nationalism in the context of internationalism based not on white 'civilization' nor the racial homogeneity of white nations, but on the idea of intersectional communities united by shared values.[11] Writing of interwar London, Leila Gandhi has described activists and commentators with intersecting anticolonial and progressive critiques of empire engaged in an affective 'politics of friendship'.[12] According to Elleke Boehmer, this relational process produced a plurality of modernisms.[13] And for Priyamvada Gopal, such relationality became a form of 'reverse tutelage' that refracted the tutelary claims of the League of Nations mandates system and aimed at 'rehumanizing the metropole'.[14] Recent studies have pointed similarly to the possibilities (as well as the limits) of Pan-Asian and Pan-African networks emerging at this time.[15] As we argue here, the Pan-Pacific region figures as another locale in which the 'politics of friendship' was played out in self-conscious fashion.[16]

But as soon became evident, the interwar Pan-Pacific was far from the inert space that many white proponents had assumed. Transnational and international studies have begun to investigate the diversity of Indigenous modernities, mobilities and liberalisms active in these decades[17] – native Hawai'ian suffrage networks formed in the 1910s and 1920s, for example.[18] The Pan-Pacifics in our chapter were but two among a myriad of intersecting networks of exchange, ideas, print cultures, mobility and movement in which peoples Indigenous to this dynamic region were involved, and of which many more were undoubtedly aware. In their study of Indigenous voices in anthropological discourse, Jason Gibson and Helen Gardner have illustrated the importance of adopting a dialogic model when investigating predominantly one-sided accounts of contact.[19] Likewise, we approach Pan-Pacific networks emerging in the 1920s through the lens of a small but influential number of Pacific Islanders who were contributors to its agenda.

Writing of the entangled histories of colonization and contact in early colonial New Zealand, Tony Ballantyne has pointed to investments in the concept of 'improvement' held in common between Māori elites and local missionaries.[20] Tracey Banivanua Mar has also brought to light the 'imperial literacies' and 'shadow networks' through which Indigenous leaderships in the Pacific sought to engage world opinion.[21] Likewise, we conclude that Pacific Islanders who attended Pan-Pacific conferences found some usefulness, and perhaps also familiarity, in the ideals of cooperation, interracial 'friendship' and 'intercultural exchange' they enacted alongside Asian and Anglo counterparts. There was certainly some purpose in attending for the opportunities they afforded to engage with other Islander leaders. Reflecting on the world views of two contemporary Māori intellectuals and statesmen – Āpirana Ngata, a member of New Zealand parliament, who spoke at the Institute of Pacific Relations (IPR) in 1927, and Te Rangihīroa (Peter Buck), the director of the Bishop Museum in Honolulu – Miranda Johnson notes their interest in progressive agendas such as these.[22] Fiona Paisley has argued elsewhere that a shared interest in advancement and modernization was apparent among Pan-Pacific delegates attending the Pan-Pacific Women's Association

(PPWA) between the 1920s and 1950s.[23] As Nicholas Hoare concludes from his study of domestic anti-imperialism and anticolonialism in New Zealand at this time, such collaborations across cultural divides were necessarily always limited by the colonial contexts within which they took place.[24]

Additional studies of circulation and knowledge production have pointed to the mobilities of print culture across the imperial world, intersecting with those produced by Indigenous communities themselves.[25] According to Antoinette Burton and Isabel Hofmeyr, an imperial commons was available to a diversity of readerships, including through ephemeral forms such as scrapbooks, and newspapers.[26] From the interwar years, Pan-Pacific conferences and research were reported regularly in newspapers and widely circulating popular magazines such as *The Mid Pacific*. In these pages, the business of cross-cultural internationalism sat alongside reports of the burgeoning tourist industry by which the region was becoming 'known' to increasing numbers of middle-class white travellers.[27] These print cultures were available to Pacific Island readerships as well, and thus the Pan-Pacific ideal circulated beyond the confines of conferences themselves.

In the first section of this chapter, we consider the aims of two key networks engaged in promoting a cultural internationalism in the interwar Pacific. As we show, the IPR and the PPWA sought to put into practice a cross-cultural internationalism primarily advantageous to Pacific Rim nations and white settlers within the region, but also seeking the involvement of Pacific Islanders themselves. Through annual conferences, publications and research promoted as both humane and scientific, they hoped to bring international recognition to the Pacific as a location in which to carry out the kind of liberal, humanitarian imperialist ethics that animated progressive internationalist thought more broadly in the League of Nations era.[28] As Duncan Bell has pointed out, in previous decades progressive Anglo utopianism reaching across the Pacific had asserted itself on the grounds of white exceptionalism.[29] This previously Australasian, now increasingly Anglo, world order had been given reality in a brotherhood of white nations exchanging expertise and policies designed in part to exclude non-white immigrants and to manage 'native' populations, while proclaiming a progressive role within the British Commonwealth in international affairs.[30] At the same time, some of those involved hoped to rehumanize Western modernity tainted by colonialism and slavery, and the kinds of aggressive nationalisms resulting in world war. Such a reframing of world history might finally realize a post-imperial future by revising the relationship between local and global, ending racism and establishing a politics of mutual respect. According to Jeanne Morefield, such claims for the universal application of Anglo-Saxon standards of civilization, however, did little more than direct attention away from 'Empire's acts of imperialising' by rehearsing 'the liberal, democratic character and nature of Empire itself'.[31] The interwar Pan-Pacific movement that took shape in the 1920s professed a more inclusive version but enacted a similar deflection, rehearsing long-standing notions of 'civilization' towards the creation of a new, cultural internationalist Pacific.[32]

At Pan-Pacific conferences Anglo internationalists aimed to share professional expertise while enacting new deportments that relied on the presence of non-white delegates. Seeking to reconfigure the region away from its Australasian pasts – by casting it as relatively free of racial antagonisms and histories of colonial oppression – Pan-Pacific idealists drew from the latest anthropological and sociological theories and studies that declared 'race' to be hierarchies of relative advancement shaped by environment. Such accounts of difference as relative rather than innately biological enhanced internationalist assertions of the importance of meeting within the Pacific region itself. For here they could exchange knowledge and viewpoints, attend cultural events and enjoy personal interaction with a diversity of colleagues from Asian to Pacific Islander, each with their own contributions towards the formation of 'interracial friendship'.[33] More technically speaking, as outlined further below, friendly exchange required careful management, and this was codified for participants as The Way. Thereby, roundtable sessions would channel even the most controversial topics towards the desired aim of mutual understanding.

During these decades as internationalist ideas circulated in popular culture, women from beyond Europe became significant figures in liberal, progressive networks promoting ideas of peace, cooperation and equity.[34] Pacific Islander women were especially valued in Pan-Pacific circles, for example, as their presence appeared to confirm the value and success of the women's cultural internationalist project. And yet this desired outcome was tempered also by the authority of racialized views of capacity within internationalist circles. Among members of the supposedly more advanced Polynesian race, Māori women were relatively early among Pacific Islander delegates to the PPWA, becoming significant conference figures from the 1930s.[35] The occasional involvement of Native American and Native Hawai'ian delegates was considered noteworthy also.[36] While in contrast, women from Fiji in the western Pacific or Melanesia – a subregion declared less racially advanced – were not directly involved until the 1950s. As we show later in the chapter, the practice of British women speaking for the 'women of Fiji' only came to an end following the war.[37]

We conclude our chapter by reflecting on the Pacific regionalism presented at the UN by the first prime minister of Fiji, Ratu Sir Kamasese Mara, in 1970. As we outline, Mara invoked a Pacific regionalism by which Islander peoples asserted their communalism as an alternative form of global relations. His address has been associated with the first international articulation of The Pacific Way, a specifically Pacific Island mode of address that drew from long-standing communal methods of finding resolution in the face of conflicting interests. This Pan-Pacific way of being and knowing in the world, and of living on the land, while impacted upon by a shared experience of colonial rule, celebrated the resilience of local political forms throughout the colonial period. In this decade of decolonization,[38] Mara presented Fiji's capacity for cosmopolitanism as inherently Indigenous, offering it as a potent adjunct to European democratic principles by which, he stated, Fiji's own path towards independence had been strengthened. He argued that his country's adaption of European democratic traditions had helped it to achieve a peaceful and equitable transition towards independence. Implicit to his claim for interracial harmony was equitable representation also for the resident Indian Fijian population.[39] One of the themes in this chapter is that both interwar Pacific internationalism and post-war Fijian nationalism gestured towards inclusive agendas while prioritizing certain histories of place and belonging over others.[40] Ranging from the 1920s to 1970, this chapter moves from what has been called 'colonial cosmopolitanism' towards a cosmopolitics of decolonization,[41] two modalities of 'internationalism' and their relationship with the Pacific.

Pan-Pacific meeting ground (1920s and 1930s)

Vanessa Smith has pointed out that the idea of a friendly Pacific predated first contact and was central in the formation of European discourses of modernity and tradition. However, in the wake of the death of Cook and following the arrival of missionaries, the trope of 'friendliness' quickly fell away to be replaced by one of 'savagery'.[42] By the early decades of the last century, the Pacific would be once again cast as a site of friendly exchange. In this case, a network of North American Christian progressives headquartered in Hawai'i declared the region relatively 'untouched' by the antagonistic legacies of slavery and colonial rule they considered increasingly evident in other parts of the world. In this imagined Pacific it would be possible, they contended, to replace anachronistic forms of white superiority with a more modern, culturally engaged set of race relations through which the Anglo world would be better equipped to assume its responsibilities for the guidance of other peoples considered less advanced.[43] Such an agenda was promoted by the North American Alexander Hume Ford through a 'Hands-Around-the-Pacific' movement he established in Honolulu before World War I. Ford's intention was to build on what he saw as the recent successes of modern world missionary work in Japan through strategic engagements with local culture.[44] The Young Men's and Young Women's Christian Associations (YMCA and YWCA), also active in the Pacific and Asia, claimed likewise to combine Christian leadership with cross-cultural awareness. Their networks were to contribute significantly to the formation of the IPR and PPWA.[45]

From the mid-1920s the IPR and the PPWA convened annual conferences within the Pacific that attracted delegations from a range of countries including Australia and New Zealand. Along with their counterparts in an 'awakening' Asia, these Pan-Pacific internationalists argued for a new mode of collective and interpersonal exchange that would seek to apply some of the insights of contemporary anthropology and sociology to the practicalities of governance and development across cultural and racial difference. Internationally influential books such as *Patterns of Culture* (1934) by Ruth Benedict circulated within these Pan-Pacific networks on conference reading lists or more broadly as texts shared among the global elite of professionals and activists in its membership.[46] Thus 'race' was to be rendered interpretable through a schema of cultural or national 'types' whose world views could be decoded relative to one's own, and thereby 'understood' relationally. Managing differences of opinion (with their origins in human difference as well as colonial history) would require also a willingness for self-reflection. Whiteness was itself to be a subject for scrutiny, hence bringing into question racist ways of thinking and acting that for many critics had long characterized imperial rule.

In her comprehensive study of the IPR, Tomoko Akami notes that the Pan-Pacific movement was committed to an ideal of 'free and frank discussions to solve racial conflict'.[47] The question was how to carry this out. Holding conferences in the region or along the Pacific Rim was considered one element in achieving this goal. Honolulu was chosen as the headquarters of both organizations, reflecting the importance of 'interracial' Hawai'i to the Pan-Pacific project of the sort being promoted by studies of intercultural interaction undertaken by American racial scientists at the university, including by S. D. Porteus, formerly of Australia.[48] New Zealand was also important in this mapping of the region as an experiment in modern interracial techniques, and was routinely commended in Pan-Pacific circles for having supposedly achieved 'interracial harmony' on the basis of its Māori education and health policies, and Māori representation in parliament.[49]

Such an account of New Zealand, and of the Pacific more generally, necessarily elided the multiple settler-colonial and territorial interests it contained, such as those of the US in Hawai'i, the Philippines and Sāmoa. While under the League of Nations mandate system (in addition to their territory in Papua) Australia and New Zealand had recently assumed governance of former German colonies.[50] In promoting itself as a 'Geneva in the Pacific', the Pan-Pacific movement aimed to progress its own trusteeship agendas in the south as a model for Europe. In a 1925 editorial published in *The Pacific* (another popular magazine promoting the Pan-Pacific ideal), the newly formed IPR announced its intention to establish a 'common mode of exchange' between the peoples of the Pacific. This was intended to bring about a dialogue between those Anglos or Asians who had 'adopted' the region as their own, and the Indigenous Islander peoples themselves. Once informed of local cultures and world views, those among the supposedly more advanced incomers would work to ensure 'the furtherance of the best interests of the land of their adoption, and ... spread about the Pacific the friendly spirit of inter-racial co-operation'.[51]

A second strategy was to be enacted at conferences through the kinds of embodied deportments considered necessary for the management of 'difference' across diverse political and racial contexts. Conference guidelines for roundtable debate indicate that this practice of exchange needed to be carefully orchestrated. Referred to as The Way and discussed in more detail in the following section, these instructions aimed to channel the emotions of opinion into rational forms of debate via compromise or by finding common ground where differences of perspective or opinion seemed otherwise insurmountable. One way to enable this communication was to understand each other through the lens of racial or national types. Histories of internationalism in this era have pointed out that such deployment of racial typologies reiterated aspects of the very imperial and colonial hierarchies they claimed to supersede. Ranking Pacific Islanders as more or less 'primitive' was commonplace and entailed comparing them, firstly, against each other and, then, collectively against the supposedly more advanced Pacific Rim 'civilizations'.[52] This mobilization of 'culture' as a universal condition of humanity on the one hand, but a distinguishing factor between peoples on the other, provided the logic for a Pan-Pacific regionalism that needed guidance from the West. Such hierarchies were central to the IPR and the PPWA, informing their representations of the Pacific as an experimental zone in which to learn about demography and science, but also in experiential terms to observe new forms of whiteness in action.

Less schematically but equally importantly, the work of international 'friendship' was to be encouraged by sharing accommodation or attending conference cultural events and outings. In their studies of the IPR, James Cotton and Tomoko Akami have pointed to the rational and objective yet also idealistic aims of the organization.[53] John Davidann, writing of this era, adds that central to the attractiveness of internationalism was its emotional yield.[54] Carrying out interracial friendship alongside a self-critique of whiteness invoked the larger place of affect and the spirit in this era of reformulating world affairs.[55] Writing in his acclaimed contemporary book *The Third British Empire* about a reordering of whiteness for the modern world, Alfred Zimmern (a leading figure in the League) declared this new spirit force to be no more exemplified than in the 'familial bonds' of the British Commonwealth.[56] Such a world view might find its greatest resource in the Pacific: Warwick Anderson has shown that numbers of leading Australians, for example, when attending early IPR conferences, emerged with new perceptions of themselves as white men, having encountered other ways of managing 'race contact' than the restrictive immigration policies adopted within their own countries.[57] For many, aspects of what they considered to be characteristics of the 'traditional' lives of Pacific peoples, such as community connection and handicrafts, appeared to contrast with the regimentation and alienation of the 'machine age' in the West.[58] White women also reported transformative experiences at conferences in the Pacific, although these often led nevertheless to a reinvestment in the idea of Western-led progress through cross-cultural means. Having attended the first IPR conference in 1925, for example, Janet Mitchell spoke of her renewed respect for what she saw as the progressive influence of Western civilization.[59]

Science offered new insights into non-Western counterparts. As they prepared for conferences, Anglo and Asian delegates to the IPR and PPWA were encouraged to read some of the latest studies of the 'South Seas' by leading anthropologists and social scientists. Among them were New Zealanders Marie and Felix Keesing, also members of the IPR and PPWA.[60] These and other progressive social scientists pointed to something more radical than guiding non-Western progress, and that was the politics of self-representation. Integral to the initial cultural internationalist ideal had been that tutelage and guidance would eventually empower Pacific Islanders to speak for themselves. In the meantime, some among them could practise their skills and become more confident in negotiating their place in the world by attending international fora hosted by the IPR and PPWA. Daniel Gorman has declared a feminization of the international sphere in this era during which women entered in unprecedented numbers into the social sciences and were involved through international networks in promoting new ideas about world cooperation and 'the nation' as a progressive force in world affairs.[61] In the Pan-Pacific movement also, women's expertise in the social sciences and their asserted proclivities as 'women' for cooperative exchange saw them described as highly suited to the cross-cultural internationalist project. Pacific Islander women would be part of this broader feminization.

Furthermore, some delegates in these networks envisaged the Pacific as a laboratory for hybridization not just knowledge exchange. Warwick Anderson has pointed to interest in miscegenation and hybridity among Australians and others involved in the IPR.[62] And Jane Carey has described the interests of Pacific Islander anthropology also in this regard, noting that Te Rangihīroa (the leading Māori anthropologist and director of the Bishop Museum in Honolulu) was an advocate of racial mixing and hence for cultural hybridization in New Zealand.[63] As will be discussed in the next section, Marie Keesing was another such enthusiast. Before turning to specific examples of Pacific Islander women's participation at the PPWA, the next section describes the white, gendered ethos of a Pacific Way articulated in the interwar Pan-Pacific.

The Way, women internationalists, and world culture

Aiming to provide a cross-cultural mode of friendly exchange, The Way provided conference participants with specific instructions for roundtables. And by extension, they indicated broader expectations for conference-goers regarding intercultural deportment. Particularly British Dominion and North American delegates would need to develop a more culturally aware outlook when in the company of non-Western or non-white counterparts with whom they might, at some point in the future, establish business or other forms of partnership in the region. In his 1929 report, the US academic W. H. Kilpatrick opened his account of the potential of the IPR by asserting that The Way offered a commonplace set of knowledges aimed at the kinds of mutual recognition essential to meaningful cross-cultural exchange. False (racist) assumptions about others could be overcome through getting to know people personally. And so, conferences should include ample time for social and cultural events alongside its formal programme of roundtable discussions. According to Kilpatrick, the 'spiritual' aspect of this social learning would be one of the most important contributions the IPR could make to world peace.[64]

The roundtable method of speaking in turn, and of asking questions designed to encourage honest exchange but ultimately facilitate compromise, had been deployed previously by the Round Table group in London. This organization claimed to have staged potentially divisive debate between members of the British Commonwealth without allowing internal division to obstruct collective decision-making or endanger unity.[65] By adapting the technique for use in the Pacific, the IPR and PPWA sought to enable intercultural and interracial exchange by which imperial and colonial relations would be further reformulated. To engage with non-white colleagues in meaningful discussion, white delegates would have to unlearn their assumption of racial superiority, at the same time as enabling their non-Western colleagues to develop their own skills in the formalities of debate.[66]

At the 1929 PPWA conference, for example, observers reported that The Way had enabled Japanese and Chinese delegates, in spite of hostilities between their national governments, to discuss the recent invasion of Manchuria by Japanese forces.[67] The Way also offered a framework in 1937, it was reported, for Australian and Japanese delegates at that year's PPWA conference to exchange very different views on White Australia, the Japanese delegates asking pointed questions about Australian racism, and Australians proffering a map of the continent supposedly illustrating the vulnerability of the northern half of the continent to invasion. They contended that immigration restriction was, moreover, a humane response to a level of resistance that Asian immigrants would experience from mainstream white Australia.[68]

Roundtables provided spaces in which Asian and Anglo members might unite, however, over the question of 'native' people deemed as yet insufficiently advanced to manage their own affairs. At a PPWA Round Table on 'Cultural Relations and the Dependencies', for example, agreement was reached that forcing 'native' labour in the dependencies, although regrettable, was a necessity for progress and was in any case allowed under international agreement in certain mandates.[69] The forcing of labour among mandated peoples was far from uncontroversial at this time, however. During these years Australia and New Zealand reported to the Permanent Mandates Commission (PMC) at the League of Nations concerning its management of a number of such Level C mandates where forced labour was allowed in certain circumstances. International as well as national commentary routinely criticized Australia's regime in New Guinea and Nauru, as well as its treatment of the Indigenous peoples within its borders.[70] As the South Australian delegate Constance Ternent Cooke reminded delegates at the PPWA conference in 1930, much of the critical international press raising questions about government policies and settlers' treatment of the Aboriginal population within Australia had been alerted by activists involved in Australian women's networks.[71]

A brief survey of roundtable topics suggests that, within international circles, it was widely agreed that only some Islander peoples would ever reach independent status. In 1931, for example, IPR organizers proposed questions for roundtables at the forthcoming conference such as: 'What is the basis of the right of a governing country to control a dependency?' But also: 'How far is self-determination to be encouraged among native peoples?'[72] At the IPR conference in 1927, for example, Jerome Greene, an American businessman involved in its formation and the first chairman of its American Council, commended to fellow attendees the value of using hierarchical typologies in order to better understand and thus govern non-Western peoples and 'races'. He reasoned that while universal standards and global progressive agendas were commendable, they would only succeed if modified to suit specific cultural contexts. In his opinion, any proposal for modernization would need to take into account the relative advancement of the people in question.[73]

During these decades increasing numbers of predominantly white women found professional employment in social work and the social sciences. The PPWA offered an opportunity to discuss with peers the process of modernization in the region. One contemporary observer reported admiringly of what she described as the PPWA's 'evolution' of The Way. After attending the first PPWA conference in Honolulu in 1928, Elizabeth Green (Secretary of the IPR) wrote up her observations for fellow IPR members and readers of *Pacific Affairs*, another leading journal that regularly reported on Pan-Pacific conferences. In her article titled 'The Pacific Technique: New Clinical Notes on its Evolution', Green reported that the PPWA 'is employing and to some degree modifying the conference mechanism ... [that] the Institute [IPR] pioneered for the Pacific area'. In Green's opinion, PPWA delegates brought important new insight to The Way as professional women with direct knowledge of the issues facing government and industry in the areas of health, education and social work. Moreover, she considered that, being women, they were naturally skilled in exchange and mediation. The PPWA's version of 'the Pacific Technique', she wrote, was especially effective because its residential conferences included time for 'exchanging experience' as well as social programmes including cultural performances and trips to sites of interest. The result was the forming of friendships and a degree of self-reflection that could be confronting as 'many of the women [delegates were] ... new to the international conference method ... [and being] outside their own respective countries for the first time ... [they were brought] into intimate intellectual contact with women of other races'. Underlining the fact that she referred here to white women, Green continued by asserting that many among them had put aside their false sense of 'superiority' as a result.[74]

For some, the ideal of a cross-cultural Pacific went beyond individual revelation or national cooperation. It would contribute to a new 'planetary' civilization. As a member of the PPWA's organizing committee for the 1939 conference, the anthropologist Marie Keesing precirculated a study outline for those participating in a roundtable on 'Cultural Contributions of Pacific Countries'. They should consider in preparation the compelling question of how Indigenous cultures would contribute to the 'planetary civilization ... [now] in its birth throes'. She encouraged them to think about the Pacific on three levels: first, 'local cultures' of people 'recently in the stone age'; secondly, civilizations of the Orient; and, thirdly, the Occident 'in which science and industrialism have their more immediate roots'. Each would contribute according to their strengths to a new 'common civilization' destined to emerge out of an interracial and cross-cultural Pacific. Once the innovation of cross-cultural exchange had been applied to the reality of global socio-economic interdependence, she asserted, a form of harmonious hybridity would follow, answering many of the problems facing the modern West. One of these was an increasing disconnection between individual and collective creative expression. Creativity should not be left in the hands of specialists, Keesing warned, as had become the norm in 'machine civilization'. Through interaction with other cultures still connected to creative and community life, Westerners would be brought back to the importance of cultural expression as 'a function of the human spirit'.[75]

In an address she made during the conference itself, Marie Keesing spoke further on the significance of cultural understanding for a peaceful and equitable world order. World history had shown that cultural exchange seeded progress: Europe had been a meeting place for a diversity of cultural influences, she stated, which had led to its current ascendancy in world affairs. In the shadow of the recent world war, that trajectory seemed less certain. Now it was the time for the Pacific to be recognized as the world's next crossroads leading the way forward.[76] As a recipient in the 1920s with her husband of the Rockefeller Memorial Fellowship to study the Māori and the 'Polynesian' Pacific, both Marie and Felix Keesing had become advocates for 'integration' between European and Indigenous cultures, the two greatly influenced in this respect by leading Māori advocating this same outcome.[77] She and Felix promoted this agenda through the IPR and PPWA. In his book on education in the Pacific published in 1937, Felix asserted likewise that the creation of a new, syncretic world civilization was not only inevitable but should be welcomed. It would entail 'some blend between old and new which would meet the needs of life in a changing world, and which would be based on a critical approach to all existing cultures'.[78] Ten years later, following another world war, Felix Keesing would write with approval of what he saw as elite Pacific Islanders' growing capacity to succeed in both their own and European culture.[79]

The next section concerns the question of Indigenous self-representation. The IPR and the PPWA proclaimed its ethics of engagement based on mutual recognition, exchange and cooperation partly on the basis of relative advancement but also through the need to reform colonial relations and modernity itself. While Pacific islands had been colonized from the 1850s and the task was completed by the early twentieth century, the region was widely considered sufficiently free from the history of formal colonization. Therefore, it was anticipated that new 'race' relations might emerge from within its bounds. Such an expectation required the suppression of complex histories of migration that intersected with colonization, such as indenture of Indian labour into Fiji, and that interrupted progressive narratives of anticolonial nationalism.[80] Through the example of Fiji representation at the PPWA between the 1930s and 1950s, we consider in the next section some of the implications for Pacific Islander women internationalists as they negotiated some of these evident contradictions within the cultural internationalist world view. We conclude with the Pan-Pacific as it was articulated by the new president of an independent Fiji before the UN in 1970.

The 'women of Fiji'

Accounts of a primitive Fiji were rehearsed routinely in Pan-Pacific networks. In correspondence with the IPR, for example, the Royal Institute of International Affairs in London declared of this era that – aside from Fiji – the 'problem' of '"self-Government" could hardly be said to arise' in regard to the western Pacific.[81] Such assumptions of relative advancement were evident at early PPWA conferences where white delegates spoke on behalf of Fijian women. In their accounts, Indigenous contact with Europeans was often represented as negatively impacting on cultural cohesion and thus revealing the destructive effects of modernization. In 1930, for example, a British Australian resident, Miss A. M. Griffin, offered a brief account of Fijian society and culture before declaring that unregulated contact with Europeans had resulted in youth delinquency.[82] A second British Fijian delegate that year, Olive Meek reiterated the theory of racial incapacity by warning that, without stronger guidance, such 'a simple-minded . . . race' still living in the 'Stone Age' would become demoralized and ultimately fade away in the face of rapid modernization.[83] In 1937, Miss Gwen Atherton, a British woman also living in Fiji, spoke of Fijian women in explicitly racialist terms as 'happy, docile, friendly and hospitable'.[84]

Towards the end of World War II, however, questions were being raised about 'alien' women speaking on the behalf of their local counterparts. In a pamphlet titled *Pacific Islands in War and Peace*, published in 1944, Marie Keesing noted that before the war any Fijian woman simply wishing to attend conferences needed permission from the British governor. Such was unlikely to continue, she concluded, because experience of the war and living in closer contact with Europeans now meant that increasingly 'natives' would 'feel constricted by alien control'. Having come into contact with ideas of 'equality and freedom' during those years, they would be less 'submissive to white domination'. Some native peoples, she continued, might require ongoing guidance given they were 'strung out at all stages on the road to modernity'. But in future, Pacific Island peoples as a group could be expected to claim the right to negotiate their own affairs.[85]

It would not be until 1958 that Lolohea Akosita Waqairawai became the first Fijian woman delegate to a PPWA conference. She advised fellow delegates that year in Tokyo that, after growing up on a church mission, she had trained in Sydney to become a teacher. Following her return to Fiji, she worked as a child welfare officer before joining the Fijian mothercraft movement. She was awarded a British Empire Medal in 1950 for her contributions to maternal health.[86] Waqairawai's long-standing involvement in the PPWA was recognized posthumously by Eta Baro, a graduate of the University of the South Pacific, in a 1975 booklet she published with the PPWA called 'Women's Role in Fiji'. In its pages, Baro describes Waqairawai as a woman of 'international repute' who was devoutly Christian, an advocate for gradual change and a promoter of women's roles in civic affairs who spoke often of 'living in a multi-ethnic society'. She was 'multi-racial in her thinking and encouraged women to learn about other cultures as a step towards understanding each other'.[87]

Declaring the Pacific before the UN

A little over ten years later, the Pacific was presented to the UN as an Indigenous force in world affairs. Speaking of an inherent capacity for international relations at the Assembly in 1970, the prime minister of its newest member nation Fiji, Ratu Sir Kamisese Mara, proclaimed his country's leadership through offering what he referred to as 'the Pacific Way' to the world community. The Pan-Pacific that Mara described expressed the resilience of Indigenous cosmopolitan collectivity beyond the history of colonization. Yet Mara spoke not of a break with the past, but rather of a politics of worldliness that drew from European ways adapted to Pacific Islander needs. This co-option of Europe by the Pacific was no better illustrated, he told fellow members, than in what he declared to have been Fiji's friendly relations with former colonial powers throughout the process of decolonization. But equally central to this process was applying a critical view of 'civilization' itself. The British may have brought with them 'a sense of fair play, respect for rule of law, and a basic decency', but they had not always honoured those virtues. Wryly, he explained that they had not been 'immune from the failings inherent in the colonial system itself'. And they had shown a lack of respect and inflated sense of superiority by seeking to assert their own cultural norms upon the peoples and cultures over whom they governed.[88]

In a speech he gave later at the UN's Decolonization Committee, Mara continued with his theme of cooperative decolonization with a critical edge, by turning a somewhat ironic gaze towards British domestic culture. He had been initiated into 'Western rituals and tribal customs', he remarked, while studying in England as a young man. It was while there (rather than in his homeland) that he had learned from other Commonwealth students of his status as a colonized person, seemingly oppressed by 'white imperialists'.[89] Mara expanded on his theme by questioning the uniformity attributed to the colonial experience, declaring instead that it was the right of the formerly colonized to work through decolonization as they saw fit, including if they wished by remaining friendly with their former colonizers.[90] As his own country had chosen the former, he stated, it had combined liberal ideals with local communal forms.

Thus, the promise of liberal democracy might finally be realized in Fiji. His people were long used to reaching a 'common objective' beyond 'our own individual ways', he declared, having learned well before colonial rule how to negotiate with other Island peoples. As a result, he claimed that a commitment to racial equality had characterized Fiji's independence movement.[91] A brief glance at Fijian history indicates, however, that this premise had not characterized relations between I'Taukei and Indo-Fijians. A degree of mutual mistrust that characterized the lead-up to decolonization had continued in the post-independence period. Only one year later, for example, anthropologist Michael Haas concluded that Fiji had much still to achieve before it matched Hawai'i's level of racial harmony.[92] His reference to Hawai'i as an ideal in comparison to Fiji evokes the interwar Pan-Pacific internationalist vision discussed above, and similarly veils Hawai'i's own history of colonization and racial hierarchy.

Furthermore, Mara's Pacific Way asserted the value of Islander ways in a globalizing world, not as a manifestation of a 'stage' of civilization but an alternative modernity. Of particular relevance in Fiji itself was the question of traditional land tenure. From the 1930s anthropologists had declared communal land tenure a major hindrance to development. In his book *Education in Fiji* (1935), for example, commentator Cecil W. Mann argued that traditional ways persisted despite efforts at reform: the tenacity of the communal land system showed that even the younger generation of ethnic Fijians were resisting the supposedly necessary shift from communal to individual ownership, and to the kinds of family units he considered essential for success in Western-style education.[93] A few years later, the American Council of the IPR commissioned a study of Fiji by the anthropologist Laura Thompson (published in 1940 as *Fijian Frontier*). Thompson reiterated the argument that a rising generation was struggling with Westernization, especially the idea that communal land should be privately owned.[94] Indeed, following decolonization communal land tenure would be celebrated, and embedded in Pacific Island constitutions as manifestations of the Pacific – and later the Melanesian – Way to the detriment in Fiji of Indo-Fijians.[95]

By asserting the capacity of the Fiji independence movement to embrace diversity, Mara pointed to the resilience of ethnic Fijians and more broadly of Pasifika culture and knowledge. In a subsequent memoir, he wrote that he had found the politics of decolonization at the UN overly 'dogmatic and doctrinaire'. While he supported the need to confront white racism, he thought it more productive to do so through 'mutual understanding'. Echoing something of The Way applied at PPWA and IPR round tables decades earlier, Mara concluded: '[T]his issue [of racism] is capable of arousing the deepest and ... most sincere emotions ... often lead[ing] to a situation where it is impossible for any communication to take place ... This was the sort of situation where I felt we [of the Pacific] might be able to help.'[96]

In her analysis of the reception of The Way over following years, Stephanie Lawson argues that it accrued a set of explicitly anticolonial counter-hegemonic 'characteristics' not evident in Mara's original statement at the UN.[97] During a conference convened by the South Pacific Social Sciences Association in 1975, something of this accrual is evident in the enthusiasm of the educationalist Ron Crocombe, who described Mara's speech at the UN as a pivotal moment that signalled 'an emerging identity' among

Pacific Island elites and their growing confidence in Pacific regionalism. The Pacific Way, he continued, had shown itself capable of bringing 'traditional' ways of discussion into dialogue with 'foreign' elements like Christianity, proving in the process to be sufficiently flexible for a diversity of pathways towards nationhood. Furthermore, the unique yet universal quality of the Pacific Way asserted at the UN had contributed to a growing 'confidence' within the Pacific regarding its capacity to protect 'common interests' against 'neo-colonial' exploitation from the Pacific Rim.[98] Crocombe concluded that Mara's aim to 'create a common ground between different places within the Pacific region ... [had an] ... important boundary-marking function, to separate the Pacific from the non-Pacific'.[99] A few years later, this celebration of boundary formation had become an ode to separate development. The report of the 'Pacific Islands Conference: Development the Pacific Way', held at the East-West Centre, University of Hawai'i, in March 1980, predicted that economic partnerships with 'metropolitan countries' (the former colonial powers) would fall away as Pacific Island nations worked increasingly together towards 'maintaining ... [their] independence and integrity ... in the face of increasing interest and external influence' from the Pacific Rim.[100]

Reflecting more recently on the longevity of The Way as a symbol of Pan-Pacific identity, Lamont Lindstrom underlines the point that rather than an expression of 'kastom', The Way should be understood within a set of 'broader political rhetorics'. It had been part of a new emphasis on 'regional cultural heritage' taking shape in the 1970s.[101] Miranda Johnson, in her investigation of the Pacific Way in the same decade during a Pacific Island land rights case, argues conversely that engaging Europeans in Pacific world views was integral to its effectiveness. Johnson concludes that Indigenous rights movements in the Pacific had gained ground over the previous decade not least by calling upon Europeans to learn from Indigenous ways of knowing.[102]

Conclusion

According to Priyamvada Gopal, there is a long history of exchanges between anticolonial activists and white critics of empire yet to be written. In many instances, these sought to remake or ultimately overturn the colonial order.[103] We argue that Pacific internationalism offers one such history. At PPWA and IPR conferences, Pacific Islanders were measured against colonial and racial assumptions about relative advancement. But they were also highly anticipated figures, considered to embody the efficacy of the Pan-Pacific cooperative ideal. Furthermore, they contributed to that agenda not only through their presence but as resilient and outspoken representatives of their own constituencies and world views. When decades later Fiji's first prime minister announced before the UN a Pan-Pacific united in the face of colonization, he described an explicitly Indigenous approach to international relations with potential insights for a West embarking somewhat belatedly upon its own journey of decolonization. His claim for Fiji's cooperative approach to separation from Britain mirrored, he asserted, its own capacity to engage with diversity in the region, and its post-independence inclusion of diversity within its new nation. When viewed from the perspective of the interwar Pan-Pacific, Mara's account inverts the ubiquitous iteration of Europe as source of modernity and change, replacing it with a narrative of Pacific internationalism that Dipesh Chakrabarty, writing of South Asia, has termed the provincializing of European liberal thought.[104]

By adopting the long view from the 1920s through the 1950s to 1970, we have sought to uncover something of the entanglements of internationalism and cosmopolitanism within Indigenous and internationalist modernities intersecting in the Pan-Pacific. We have assumed their myriad forms including, we suggest, via the opportunities offered by organizations like the IPR and PPWA to local actors. Without limiting our investigation to questions of origin or even of competing genealogies, we have found that the idea of internationalism operated within and perhaps across these Pan-Pacifics in several ways. In the first instance, The Way stood for networks of like-minded individuals forming national delegations to attend conferences where they discussed a regionalism of their (more or less) shared invention. In the second, The Way indicated the power of regionalism as a potential site of international, anticolonial interests and their mediation between local and global. And thirdly, the Pacific Way figures as an expression of unceded sovereign polities articulated in the name of a prior polity residing within long-standing Pasifika interventions into the historical and contemporary operations of colonization. Reflecting on the intersecting terrains of critical imperial, anticolonial and nationalist politics during this same period, Simon During has concluded that the notion of the 'Global South' – of which the Pan-Pacific may be seen as one subset and, in our interpretation, antecedent – emerged in the post-World War II era when colonialism became internationalism, and thus, he argues, the 'post-colonial' is better understood as the 'international'.[105]

Each of the Pan-Pacifics described in this chapter combined elements of these three modes of the international and thus reflect also something of this international postcolonial that During suggests. They brought into critical frame the race-based claims to national identity that accompanied the imperial world and were reinvented at the supposed 'ends of empire'. At the same time as deploying differing, at times counter perspectives, scales and temporalities, we have argued the limits of the Pan-Pacific imaginary were evident in both time frames. Although never fully realized, nonetheless such internationalisms grounded in the south suggested the possibility of refashioning colonizing world views in the name of a more inclusive world order.

Notes

1   Antoinette Burton and Tony Ballantyne, 'Keywords: "World History", "Below", and "Dissent and Disruption"', in *World Histories from Below: Disruption and Dissent: 1750 to the Present*, ed. Burton and Ballantyne (London: Bloomsbury, 2016), 1–9.

2   See David Armitage and Alison Bashford, 'Introduction: the Pacific and its histories', in *Pacific Histories: Ocean Land People*, ed. David Armitage and Alison Bashford (Basingstoke: Palgrave Macmillan, 2013); and Jane Carey and Francis Steel, 'Introduction on the Critical Importance of Colonial Formations', *History Australia* 15:3 (2018): 399–412.

3   Donald Denoon, Philippa Mein-Smith and Marivic Wyndham, 'Representations of Regional, National and "Ethnic" Identities', in *A History of Australia, New Zealand and*

the Pacific, ed. Denoon, Mein-Smith and Wyndham (Oxford: Blackwell Publishers, 2000), 9–36, especially 30.

4   Miranda Johnson, 'Introduction: The Declension of History', in *Pacific Futures Past and Present*, ed. Warwick Anderson, Miranda Johnson and Barbara Brookes (Honolulu: University of Hawai'i Press, 2018), 1–14; Tony Ballantyne, 'Imperial Futures and India's Pacifics: Space, Temporality, and the Textures of Empire', in Anderson, Johnson and Brookes, eds, *Pacific Futures*, 157–77.

5   Tony Ballantyne, *Orientalism and Race: Aryanism in the British Empire* (Basingstoke: Palgrave Macmillan, 2002), 11.

6   See Gurminder K. Bhambra and John Narayan, eds, *European Cosmopolitanism: Colonial Histories and Postcolonial Societies* (London: Routledge, 2017); and Dominic Davies and Elleke Boehmer, 'Postcolonialism and South-South Relations', in *The Routledge Handbook of South-South Relations*, ed. E. Fiddian Qasmiyeh and P. Daley (London: Routledge, 2018), 48–58.

7   Pheng Cheah and Bruce Robbins, eds, *Cosmopolitics: Thinking and Feeling Beyond the Nation* (Minneapolis: University of Minnesota Press, 1998).

8   David Long and Brian C. Schmidt, eds, *Imperialism and Internationalism in the Discipline of International Relations* (Albany: SUNY Press, 2005); and Glenda Sluga, *Internationalism in the Age of Nationalism* (Philadelphia: University of Pennsylvania Press, 2013). On the interpolated hists of internationalism and empire from the perspective of the Pacific and Islander agency, see Tracey Banivanua Mar, *Decolonisation and the Pacific: Indigenous Globalisation and the Ends of Empire* (Cambridge: Cambridge University Press, 2016), especially ch. 3.

9   Susan Pedersen, 'Review Essay: Back to the League of Nations', *American Historical Review* 112:4 (2011): 1091–117.

10 Harald Fischer-Tiné, 'The Other Side of Internationalism: Switzerland as a Hub of Militant Anti-Colonialism (c. 1910–1920)', in *Colonial Switzerland: Rethinking Colonialism from the Margins*, ed. Patricia Purtschert and Harald Fischer Tiné (Basingstoke: Palgrave Macmillan, 2015), 221–58.

11 For Tagore on cooperative internationalism, see Elleke Boehmer, *Empire, the National, and the Postcolonial 1890–1920* (Oxford: Oxford University, 2010), ch. 5; and Mrinalini Sinha, 'Whatever Happened to the Third British Empire? Empire Nation Redux', in *Writing Imperial Histories*, ed. Andrew S. Thompson (Manchester: Manchester University Press, 2013), 168–87.

12 Leila Gandhi, *Affective Communities: Anticolonial Thought, Fin-de-Siècle Radicalism, and the Politics of Friendship* (Durham, NC: Duke University Press, 2006).

13 Boehmer, *Empire, the National, and the Postcolonial*.

14 Priyamvada Gopal, *Insurgent Empire: Anticolonial Resistance and British Dissent* (London and New York: Verso, 2019): 24, 26.

15 Sarah Claire Dunstan, 'Conflicts of Interest: The 1919 Pan-African Congress and the Wilsonian Moment', *Callaloo* 39:1 (2016): 133–50; Adom Getachew, *Worldmaking after Empire: The Rise and Fall of Self-Determination* (Princeton: Princeton University Press, 2019); and Conrad Sebastian and Dominic Sachsenmaier, eds, *Competing Visions of World Order: Global Moments and 1880s–1930s* (Basingstoke: Palgrave Macmillan, 2007).

16 Gandhi, *Affective Communities*, 26 ff.

17 Rachel Standfield, 'Moving Across, Looking Beyond', in *Indigenous Mobilities: Across and Beyond the Antipodes*, ed. Standfield (Canberra: ANU Press, 2018), 1–33.

18 Rumi Yasutake, 'Re-Enfranchising Women of Hawai'i, 1912–1920: The Politics of Gender, Sovereignty, Race and Rank at the Crossroads of the Pacific', in *Gendering the Trans-Pacific World*, ed. Catherine Ceniza Choy and Judy Tzu-Chun Wu (Leiden: Brill, 2020), 114–39.

19 Jason Gibson and Helen Gardner, 'Conversations on the Frontier: Finding the Dialogic in Nineteenth-Century Anthropological Archives' *History Workshop* 88 (Autumn 2019): 4–65. See also Gardner, *Gathering for God: George Brown in Oceania* (Dunedin: Otago University Press, 2006).

20 Tony Ballantyne, 'Christianity, Commerce, and the Remaking of the Māori World', in *Facing Empire: Indigenous Experiences in a Revolutionary Age*, ed. Kate Fullagar and Michael A. McDonnell (Baltimore: Johns Hopkins University Press, 2018), 193–213.

21 Tracey Banivanua Mar, *Decolonisation and the Pacific: Indigenous Globalisation and the Ends of Empire* (Cambridge: Cambridge University Press, 2016): 51 ff.; and Banivanua Mar, 'Shadowing Imperial Networks: Indigenous Mobility and Australia's Pacific Past', *Australian Historical Studies* 46:3 (2015): 340–55. See also Robbie Shilliam, *Black Pacific: Anticolonial Struggle and Oceanic Connections* (Bloomsbury: London, 2015).

22 Miranda Johnson, 'Towards a Genealogy of the Researcher as Subject in Post/ Decolonial Pacific Histories', *History and Theory* 59:3 (2020): 424. See also Patricia O'Brien, *Tautai: Samoa, World History and the Life of Ta'isi O.F. Nelson* (Honolulu: University of Hawai'i Press, 2017).

23 Fiona Paisley, *Glamour in the Pacific: Cultural Internationalism and Race Politics in the Women's Pan-Pacific* (Honolulu: University of Hawai'i Press, 2009).

24 Nicholas Hoare, 'Anticolonialism and the Politics of Friendship in New Zealand's Pacific', *History Australia* 15:3 (2018): 540–58.

25 Antoinette Burton and Isabel Hoyfmeyr, eds, *Ten Books that Shaped the British Empire: Creating an Imperial Commons* (Durham, NC: Duke University Press, 2014); and Tony Ballantyne, Lachy Paterson and Angela Walhalla, eds, *Indigenous Textual Cultures: Reading and Writing in the Age of Global Empire* (Durham, NC: Duke University Press, 2020).

26 Antoinette Burton and Isabel Hofmeyr, 'Introduction: The Spine of Empire? Books and the Making of an Imperial Commons', in Burton and Hofmeyr, eds, *Ten Books*, 1–28.

27 On how tourism contributed to modern interest in the Pacific, see Frances Steel, 'Cruises and the Making of Greater New Zealand', in *New Zealand and the Sea: Historical Perspectives*, ed. Steel (Wellington: Bridget Williams Books, 2018), 251–73; and Nicholas Halter, *Australian Travellers in the South Seas* (Canberra: ANU Press, 2021).

28 Susan Pedersen, *The Guardians: The League of Nations and the Crisis of Empire* (Oxford: Oxford University Press, 2015); Heather Streets-Salter, 'International and Global Anti-colonial Movements', in *World History from Below*, ed. Burton and Ballantyne, 47–74; and Nelson Lichtenstein and Jill M. Jensen, eds, *The ILO from Geneva to the Pacific Rim: West Meets East* (London: Palgrave Macmillan, 2016).

29 Duncan Bell, *Dreamworlds of Empire: Empire and the Utopian Destiny of the Anglo-America* (Princeton: Princeton University Press, 2020). See also Bill Schwarz, *The White Man's World: Memories of Empire* (Oxford: Oxford University Press, 2011).

30 Marilyn Lake and Henry Reynolds, *Drawing the Global Colour Line: White Men's Countries and the Question of Racial Equality* (Melbourne: Melbourne University Press, 2008).

31 Jeanne Morefield, *Empires without Imperialism: Anglo-American Decline and the Politics of Deflection* (Oxford: Oxford University Press, 2014), 101.

32 Akira Iriye, *Cultural Internationalism and World Order* (Baltimore: Johns Hopkins University Press, 2001).

33 Paisley, *Glamour in the Pacific*, 20.

34 Daniel Gorman, *The Emergence of International Society in the 1920s* (Cambridge: Cambridge University Press, 2012); and in the Australian context, see Kate Darian Smith, Catriona Elder and Fiona Paisley, eds, 'Are We Internationally Minded? Everyday Cultures of Internationalism', special issue, *Journal of Australian Studies* 43:4 (2009): 405–11.

35 Paisley, *Glamour in the Pacific*, 106 ff.

36 Such as Alice Garry, a Native American delegate at the 1926 PPWA conference. Paisley, *Glamour in the Pacific*, 85.

37 For the importance of gendered histories, see Choy and Wu, eds, *Gendering the Trans-Pacific World*.

38 Roland Bourke, *Decolonisation and the Evolution of International Human Rights* (Philadelphia: University of Pennsylvania Press, 2013). See also Dominic Davies and Elleke Boehmer, *Postcolonialism and South–South Relations* (London: Routledge, 2018).

39 For new approaches to the global histories of Indian indenture and South Asian diasporas, see, e.g. *Journal of World History* 32:1 (2021); and Diane Kirkby and Sophie Loy-Wilson, eds, 'Labour History and the "Coolie Question"', special issue, *Labour History* 113 (2017).

40 Partha Chatterjee, 'Whose Imagined Community?', *Millenium* 20:3 (1991): 521–5.

41 Jane Haggis, 'Friendship, Faith and Cosmopolitan Thought Zones on the Cusp of Empire', in *Cosmopolitan Lives on the Cusp of Empire: Interfaith, Cross-Cultural and Transnational Networks, 1860–1950*, ed. Jane Haggis, Clare Midgley, Margaret Allen and Fiona Paisley (Cham: Palgrave Macmillan, 2017), 8.

42 Vanessa Smith, *Intimate Strangers: Friendship, Exchange and Pacific Encounters* (Cambridge: Cambridge University Press, 2010); see also Madeleine Herren, Martin Ruesch and Christiane Sibille, *Transcultural History: Theories, Methods, Sources* (Heidelberg: Springer, 2012), 27.

43 Such as David Armitage and Alison Bashford, eds, *Pacific Histories: Ocean, Land, People* (Basingstoke: Palgrave Macmillan, 2014).

44 Paul Hooper, *Elusive Destiny: The Internationalist Movement in Modern Hawai'i* (Honolulu: University of Hawai'i Press, 1980); and on comparative frameworks in contemporary world missionary discourse, see Felicity Jensz, 'The 1910 Edinburgh Missionary Conference and Comparative Colonial Education', *History of Education* 47:3 (2018): 399–414.

45 Harald Fischer-Tiné and Ian Tyrrell, *Spreading Protestant Modernity: Global Perspectives on the Social Work of the YMCA and YWCA 1889–1970* (Berlin: De Gruyter, 2021); and Emily Conroy-Krutz, *Christian Imperialism: Converting the World in the Early American Republic* (Ithaca: Cornell University Press, 2015).

46 Paul B. Rich, *Race and Empire in British Politics* (Cambridge: Cambridge University Press, 1990).

47 Tomoko Akami, *Internationalising the Pacific: The United States, Japan and the Institute of Pacific Relations in War and Peace, 1919–45* (London: Routledge, 2002): 48–9.

48 Warwick Anderson, 'Racial Hybridity, Physical Anthropology and Human Biology in the Colonial Laboratories of the United States', *Current Anthropology* 53:5 (2012): 95–107.

49 Barbara Brookes, 'National Manhood: Te Akarana Maori Association and the Work of Maori Women on Chinese Market Gardens in Late 1920s New Zealand', in *Rethinking the Racial Moment: Essays on the Colonial Encounter,* ed. Alison Holland and Barbara Brookes (Newcastle upon Tyne: Cambridge Scholars Publishing, 2011), especially 157–64.

50 Patricia O'Brien, 'From Sudan to Sāmoa: Imperial Legacies and Cultures in New Zealand's Rule over the Mandated Territory of Western Samoa', in *New Zealand's Empire*, ed. Katie Pickles and Catharine Coleborne (Manchester: Manchester University Press, 2016), 127–46.

51 Editorial, *The Pacific,* 15 January 1925, 25; and 'The Hands-Around-the-Pacific-Movement', *Review of Reviews* (December 1913): 1009.

52 Akami, *Internationalizing the Pacific*, 28.

53 James Cotton, *The Australian School of International Relations* (New York: Palgrave Macmillan, 2013); Akami, *Internationalizing the Pacific*.

54 Jon Davidann, 'Citadels of Civilization: U.S. and Japanese Visions of World Order in the Interwar Period', in *Transpacific Relations: America, Europe, and Asia in the Twentieth Century,* ed. Richard Jensen, John Davidann and Yoneyuki Sugita (Westport, CT: Praeger, 2003), 21–44.

55 Erez Manela, *The Wilsonian Moment: Self-Determination and the International Origins of Anticolonial Nationalism* (Oxford: Oxford University Press, 2007), xi.

56 Jeanne Morefield, '"A Liberal in a Muddle": Alfred Zimmern on Nationality, Internationality, and Commonwealth', in *Imperialism and Internationalism in the Discipline of International Relations*, ed. David Long and Brian C. Schmidt (Albany, NY: SUNY Press, 2005), 93–115; and Glenda Sluga, *The Nation, Psychology, and International Politics, 1870–1919* (Basingstoke: Palgrave Macmillan, 2006).

57 Warwick Anderson, 'Liberal Intellectuals as Pacific Supercargo: White Australian Masculinity and Racial Thought on the Boarder-lands', *Australian Historical Studies* 46:3 (2015): 425–39. And on the role of 'race' in the formation of American social sciences from the late nineteenth century, see Robert Vitalis, *White World Order, Black Power Politics: The Birth of American International Relations* (Ithaca: Cornell University Press, 2015).

58 Reports of the Machine Age and Culture Roundtable. Conferences Kyoto 1929 Proceedings #1, B/3/7 IPR Collection, Special Collections, University of Hawai'i Manoa.

59 Fiona Paisley, 'The Spoils of Opportunity: Janet Mitchell and Australian Internationalism in the Interwar Pacific', *History Australia* 13:4 (2016): 575–91. Prasenjit Duara describes a similarly contradictory discourse of European renewal via engagement with 'Asia'. Duara, 'The Discourse of Civilization and Decolonization', *Journal of World History* 15: 1 (2004): 1–38.

60 Felix M. Keesing, *Modern Samoa: Its Government and Changing Life* (London: George Allen & Unwin, 1934). In his book *The South Seas in the Modern World*, first published in 1941, Keesing discussed the status of 'non-native groups' across the region. Keesing, *The South Seas in the Modern World* (New York: John Day Company, 1946), ch. 13.

61 Gorman, *The Emergence of International Society*.

62 Warwick Anderson, 'Racial Conceptions in the Global South', *ISIS* 105:4 (2014): 782–92.

63 Jane Carey, 'A "happy blending"? Maori Networks, Anthropology, and "Native" Policy in New Zealand, the Pacific and Beyond', in *Indigenous Networks: Mobility, Connections and Exchange,* ed. Jane Carey and Jane Lydon (New York: Routledge, 2014), 184–215.

64　W. H. Kilpatrick, 'The Kyoto (1929) Conference of the IPR: A Critique'. Conferences Kyoto 1929 Undated Materials. B4/9 IPR Collection, Special Collections, University of Hawai'i Manoa.

65　Alex May, 'Dominion Nationalism and Imperial Federation', in *The Round Table: The Empire/Commonwealth and British Foreign Policy,* ed. Andrea Bosco and Alex May (London: Lothian Foundation Press, 1997), 225–6.

66　This proved not to be the case. Paisley, *Glamour in the Pacific,* 48.

67　Paisley, *Glamour in the Pacific,* 155.

68　Ibid., 154.

69　A similar conclusion was reached during a public meeting organized under the auspices of the IPR in Melbourne in 1934. Fiona Paisley, 'Being International at Home: Australian Public Opinion in the League Era', *Journal of Australian Studies* 43:4 (2019): 426–46.

70　Pickles and Coleborne, eds, *New Zealand's Empire*; and on controversy over Australia's early reporting to the PMC in the 1920s, see Paisley, 'To See with their Eyes and Feel with their Hearts', in *League of Nations: Histories, Legacies, Impact,* ed. Joy Damousi and Patricia O'Brien (Melbourne: Melbourne University Press, 2018), 214–36.

71　Paisley, *Glamour in the Pacific,* 89–95.

72　Preliminary List of Questions for Roundtable Discussion, n.d.. Conferences Hangchow 1931 Proceedings #5. B5/8 IPR Papers,

73　Address by Mr Jerome Greene, 29 July 1927. Conference Honolulu 1927 Proceedings #9, B/2/3 IPR Collections, Special Collections, University of Hawai'i Manoa. On the use of typologies, see Tomoko Akami, *Internationalising the Pacific,* 104–7.

74　Elizabeth Green, 'The Pacific Technique: New Clinical Notes on its Evolution', *Pacific Affairs* 1:4 (1928): 12–16.

75　Marie Keesing, 'Cultural Contributions of Pacific Countries', *Pan-Pacific* (April–June 1939): 10.

76　Notes of the Address given by Mrs M. Keesing, 1 July 1939. Mary Seaton Papers. Auckland War Museum.

77　In this, they were greatly influenced by Māori anthropologist Te Rangihīroa. See Carey, 'A "happy blending"?'.

78　Felix M. Keesing, *Education in Pacific Countries* (Shanghai: Kelly and Walsh, 1937): 48.

79　F. M. Keesing, *The South Seas,* xxiv. See also Felix M. Keesing and Marie M. Keesing, *Elite Communication in Samoa: A Study of Leadership* (Stanford: Stanford University Press, 1956). On p. 112, for example, the Keesings refer to traditional Samoan political techniques as being 'marked by a balance of power'.

80　See, e.g. Clare Anderson, ed., *A Global History of Convicts and Penal Colonies* (Bloomsbury: London, 2018); and Donna R. Gabaccia and Derek Hoerder, eds, *Connecting Seas and Connected Ocean Rims* (Brill: Leiden, 2011).

81　'Progress towards Self Government in Dependent Areas': 3. Box 310 'Pacific Relations'. IPR Collection, Columbia University.

82　Paisley, *Glamour in the Pacific,* 79.

83　Olive Meek, 'Important Factors in the Education of the Fijian Race', *The Mid-Pacific* 40:3 (1930): 226–8. And on depopulation theory, see, e.g., Russell McGregor, *Imagined Destinies: Aboriginal Australians and the Doomed Race Theory* (Carlton: Melbourne University Press, 1997).

84　Paisley, *Glamour in the Pacific,* 79.

85　Marie Keesing, *Pacific Islands in War and Peace, American Council, Institute of Pacific Relations,* Pamphlet 14 (1944): 63. Beaglehole Rare Books Collection, Victoria University, Auckland.

86   Paisley, *Glamour in the Pacific*, 79.
87   Eto Baro, 'Lolohea Akosita Waqairawai', in *Women's Role in Fiji*, ed. J. Amrathal et al. (Suva: South Pacific Social Science Association, 1975), 36–7. See also Nicole George, *Situating Women: Gender Politics and Circumstance in Fiji* (Canberra: ANU E Press, 2012), ch. 2.
88   Ratu Sir Kamisese Mara, *The Pacific Way: A Memoir* (Honolulu: University of Hawai'i Press, 1997), 240.
89   Mara, *The Pacific Way*, 106. See also Sudesh Mishra, 'Pacific Way', in *Historical Companion to Postcolonial Literatures in English*, ed. Prem Poddar and David Johnson (Edinburgh: Edinburgh University Press, 2005), 364–8. Gopal discusses the effect more broadly in relation to Caribbean activists and intellectuals in Britain. See Gopal, *Insurgent Empire*, 331–2.
90   Mara, *The Pacific Way*, 106.
91   Ibid.
92   Michael Haas, *Peace Research at the University of Hawaii: A Report to President Harlan Cleveland* (Department of Political Science, University of Hawai'i, 1971): 58.
93   Cecil W. Mann, *Education in Fiji* (Melbourne: Melbourne University Press, 1935).
94   Laura Thompson, *Fijian Frontier* (San Francisco: American Council, Institute of Pacific Relations, 1940).
95   The literature on land tenure in the Pacific is vast. For an example of the history of land tenure in the decolonizing and postcolonial Papua New Guinea, see Victoria Stead, 'Landownership as Exclusion', in *Kastom, Property and Ideology: Land Transformations in Melanesia*, ed. Siobhan McDonnell, Matthew G. Allen and Colin Filer (Acton, ACT: ANU Press, 2017).
96   Mara, *The Pacific Way*, 117.
97   Stephanie Lawson, 'The "Pacific Way" as Postcolonial Discourse', *Journal of Pacific History* 45:3 (2010): 297–314. See also Hau'ofa Epeli, 'The New South Pacific Society', in *Class and Culture in the South Pacific*, ed. Antony Hooper et al. (Auckland: Centre for Pacific Studies, and Suva: Institute of Pacific Studies, 1987), 1–12. According to Ron Crocombe, if The Way became associated with the elites of the older generation it would soon be sidelined. Crocombe, *The Pacific Way: An Emerging Identity* (Suva: Lotu Pasifika Productions, 1976), 11.
98   Crocombe, *The Pacific Way*, 1.
99   Ibid., 7.
100   Proceedings of the 'Pacific Islands Conference: Development the Pacific Way', March 26–29, 1980, Honolulu, Hawai'i: 54. Special Collections, University of Hawai'i Manoa.
101   Lamont Lindstrom, 'Custom Remade', in *The Cambridge History of Pacific Islanders*, ed. Donald Denoon et al. (Cambridge: Cambridge University Press, 1997), 408, 413.
102   Miranda Johnson, 'The Pacific Way', in *The Land in our History: Indigeneity, Law, and the Settler State,* ed. Miranda Johnson (Oxford: Oxford University Press, 2016). See also Katerina Teaiwa, 'Our Rising Sea of Islands: Pan-Pacific Regionalism in the Age of Climate Change', *Pacific Studies* 41:1–2 (2008): 26–54.
103   Gopal, 'Introduction: Enemies of Empire', in *Insurgent Empire*.
104   Dipesh Chakarbarty, *Provincialising Europe: Postcolonial Thought and Historical Difference* (Princeton: Princeton University Press, 2000).
105   Simon During, 'The Global South and Internationalism: The Geographies of Post-Subjectivity', *Postcolonial Studies* 23:4 (2020): 527–67. See also Michael Goebel, 'Vernacularising Nationalism. An Outcome Foretold?', in *Anti-Imperial Metropolis: Interwar Paris and the Seeds of Third World Nationalism* (Cambridge: Cambridge University Press, 2015), 250–77.

6

'We Seem To Shake Hands across the Seas':
Dora Meeson Coates and the Lost World of
Australasian Suffrage Activism

James Keating

On 17 June 1911, Dora Meeson Coates (1869–1955) stood on London's Victoria Embankment. She was waiting at the head of the 'imperial contingent' in the 40,000-strong Women's Coronation Procession, the largest march in the British women's suffrage campaign. Over the five hours it took demonstrators to reach the Royal Albert Hall, Meeson marched alongside Margaret Fisher, the wife of Australia's prime minister, and Lady Anna Stout, an acclaimed suffragist and the wife of a former New Zealand premier. She kept such company by virtue of the banner she had painted and, helped by three attendants, bore through balmy Westminster.[1] Meeson did not know it, but the occasion was the acme of her activist career, though not that of her most famous creation: a four-square-metre hessian canvas depicting Minerva, draped in the young Commonwealth of Australia's heraldry, imploring imperious Britannia to 'Trust The Women Mother As I Have Done'. When it was discovered, seventy years later, at the Fawcett Library – the central repository for archives from the British suffrage movement – Labor senator Susan Ryan sponsored its 'return' to Australia. Such an artefact, she argued, would fill an 'obvious gap' in the 'record [of] women's part in the early political process of this country'. In 1988, the National Women's Consultative Council (NWCC) purchased the banner for £10,000, intending it as a 'gift to the women of Australia'.[2] Almost unique among the official efforts to mine history in search of a national character as the bicentenary of the First Fleet's arrival at Botany Bay loomed, the deal was uncontroversial and effective.[3]

After its unveiling by Prime Minister Bob Hawke on International Women's Day, Meeson's banner, patched together by a London upholsterer, was sequestered for conservation. Two years later, the NWCC loaned it to the new Parliament House in Canberra, where it was displayed opposite the jewel of its collection – Tom Roberts's depiction of the inaugural federal parliament – in the Main Committee Room foyer.[4] The transfer was formalized on another moment of national reflection, the centenary of the Commonwealth Franchise Act 1902, which extended the federal vote to white women and disenfranchised most Indigenous peoples. Despite the banner's remove from the Australian suffrage movements – Meeson neither campaigned for the vote in her native

Victoria nor maintained working ties with antipodean suffragists from Britain – Senator Ryan soon realized her goal.[5] The reason for its elevation above colonial artefacts is clear. The Australasian campaigns, which transpired between the 1880s and 1908, were defined by parlour meetings, petitioning, pamphleteering, and lobbying more or less sympathetic politicians. Contrasting these decades of quiet toil, Meeson's work appeals to the popular fascination with the spectacular street politics that developed out of necessity in Britain's Edwardian suffragette movement. For those accustomed to associating suffragism with familiar objects – battle-worn banners, hunger-strike medals, arresting posters, badges and ribbons in organizational colours, or even, as in New Zealand, an iconic petition roll – the banner fills a material and emotional void.[6]

Scholars, too, have been seduced by the banner's dramatic potential. No sooner had Meeson's canvas been installed at Parliament House than historians began weaving its century-old threads into the story of a nation seeking its place in the world.[7] In 1992, the banner lent its name to a nationally touring exhibition of women in parliamentary life, and adorned the cover of Audrey Oldfield's *Woman Suffrage in Australia*, the first comprehensive history of the continent's suffrage campaigns. Ten years later, the Office of the Status of Women published a biography of Meeson to coincide with the banner's permanent transfer to the parliamentary collection, while the Royal Australian Mint issued a commemorative dollar coin adorned with her design.[8] Catalysed by the state's acquisition of her most singular work, Dora Meeson has been reimagined as a progressive icon of the pre-war Commonwealth. Despite her expatriation, in this telling she was an vital contributor to the creation of Australia's democratic values and, crucially, an agent of their dissemination in Britain, upsetting the lingering belief in a unidirectional flow of moral and political influences from metropole to periphery.[9] Rather than a protest banner, historian Clare Wright argues Meeson authored a 'founding document': an artefact that reveals as much about the 'aspirations and identity of the young nation as the still-wet constitution'.[10]

Yet, on closer inspection, Meeson seems ill-suited to bearing the weight of a nation.[11] A few years after Dora's birth in 1869, the Meeson family moved first from Melbourne to London, then to New Zealand in 1881, settling in Canterbury. Over the next decade, Meeson discovered her life's passions: painting and feminism. While she attended the Christchurch School of Art, the city became the epicentre of the women's suffrage campaign. Meeson left for London and the Slade School of Art in 1890, but illness soon forced her return to Christchurch. There, alongside her sister Amy, she added her name to the 23,968 others on the 1893 suffrage petition.[12] It is unclear if Meeson voted in that December's general election, the colony's first under the universal franchise. Nevertheless, her experiences, which she would recount at rallies in Britain, prepared her to join the metropolitan suffrage movement. By 1895 she was again on the move. After two years at Melbourne's National Gallery School of Art, Dora undertook the pilgrimage expected of a serious colonial artist: finishing in the Paris ateliers, then on to London to establish a career. There she married the portraitist George Coates, a member of her Melbourne art school cohort, and established the studio from which she would posthumously seal her place in Australian history.[13]

Cast against the backdrop of these formative Tasman years, Dora Meeson can be seen as an emblematic character whose life dovetailed with the rise and fall of the

Australasian suffrage world. Despite Meeson's Canterbury years, art historians Rex Butler and A. D. S. Donaldson's assertion that she was, 'in fact', a New Zealander might better be read as a gesture at the tradition of Tasman appropriation than a serious attempt to drag her back across the ditch.[14] Nevertheless, their claim is not unmerited. While attending the Slade, for example, Meeson deemed New Zealand 'home'. The Canterbury Society of Arts displayed her work for at least a decade after she left Christchurch and, in 1902, she exhibited for New Zealand at a London showcase of 'British Colonial Art'. Even those, like Dunedin painter Frances Hodgkins, who branded Meeson an artistic 'fraud' accepted her right to represent the colony.[15] In New Zealand, newspapers repurposed snippets from the British press to keep readers abreast of the successes achieved by Meeson, whom they habitually described as 'erstwhile of Christchurch'.[16]

Despite contemporaries' interest in her career, Meeson is absent from New Zealand historiography. She has fallen foul of the mid-twentieth century impulse to furnish the settler nation with a canon distinct from that of its 'geographical neighbours' and later feminist scholarship 'targeted at the nation-state in order to force it to change'.[17] Such sentiments can be seen in the rare instances when she was admitted to the fold. Reviewing a 1993 exhibition of Canterbury artists held to celebrate the centenary of New Zealand women's enfranchisement, the critic Judith Collard deemed Meeson's inclusion an example of the curators' 'comic comprehensiveness', joking that merely visiting Christchurch was enough to make an artist eligible for display.[18] One hundred years earlier, the city's press fêted Meeson's budding Australian career, with the *Star* reminding readers that 'although the young lady has been studying for some little time in Melbourne . . . her training was acquired here; and it was here that the bent of her talent won hearty recognition'.[19]

Contrasting her erasure in New Zealand, the installation of Meeson's banner at Parliament House transformed her reputation in Australia. In the decades since, historians have seized upon Meeson, their work united by a consensus on her Australian-ness.[20] Yet, centring the Commonwealth of Australia in Meeson's story ignores the historian Greg Dening's exhortation 'to return to the past its own present', overlooking the rudiments of her biography: the peripatetic youth, decade in New Zealand, and nearly sixty years in London.[21] Budding national identities, as scholars of the *fin de siècle* have shown, were rehearsed and refigured by antipodean settlers, especially those living in Britain. Individuals whose lives were not 'organised around the nation-state', but enmeshed in overlapping intercolonial and imperial networks, negotiated slippages between multiple identities and affiliations.[22] 'New Zealandness, Australasianism – and Britishness', as James Belich contends, had yet to become 'mutually exclusive'.[23]

Meeson, then, stands in for a cohort who – during the late-nineteenth-century moment when the 'perennial interchange' of capital, goods, migrants and ideas between Britain's antipodean colonies reached its zenith – might be read as Australasian.[24] Given the suffragists' complicity in what Rebecca Mead describes as settler progressives' project to 'defend their brave new worlds against resentful indigenes', the region is best understood as they did, in its narrowest sense, encompassing the seven colonies of settlement: New South Wales, New Zealand, Queensland, South Australia, Tasmania, Victoria and Western Australia.[25] Theirs was, as Tony Ballantyne illustrates in this volume's Introduction, a white Australasia. If, as historians of both countries have suggested, a century of 'reciprocal amnesia' has debased the term, it remains more apt than the geographically rigid 'Tasman world'.[26] During the *fin-de-siècle* years when women fought for the vote, 'Australasia' – referring to a coherent 'site of social experiment' – circulated among the bureaucrats, labourers, naturalists, reformers and writers that lived, worked and thought across colonial borders.[27] Despite the ascendance of transnational historiography, an intellectual pursuit to which historians of Australia and the international suffrage movement have been especially attentive, the pressures that have squeezed Meeson's life into a national frame have seen these intercolonial ties overlooked by antipodean scholars.[28] In response, this chapter explores the circulations and exchanges which constituted the Australasian suffrage world between the emergence of organized campaigns for the vote in the late 1880s and their conclusion, with Victorian women's enfranchisement in 1908. Then, following in Meeson's footsteps, it charts Australasia's afterlife among suffragists in the diaspora in Edwardian London.

Southern circulations: building an intercolonial suffrage movement in the Antipodes

In the case of the campaigns for women's enfranchisement, historians' inattention to Australasian connections is surprising, because it ignores the suffragists' articulation of their own struggles. In 1892, Mary Lee, secretary of the South Australian Women's Suffrage League, reflected on an erroneous report that New Zealand had enfranchised adult women. 'We, S.A., N.S.W. [New South Wales], & the other colonies have been racing each other in the noble ambition to be the first to reach the desired goal, women's suffrage. New Zealand has won . . . her victory is ours.'[29] When, the following year, New Zealand reached the milestone, Sydney's *Daily Telegraph* observed that 'for the first time in the history of Australasia, in fact of the British dominions, women are to vote'. Months later, the Womanhood Suffrage League (WSL) of New South Wales borrowed the *Telegraph*'s phrasing in its congratulations to New Zealanders.[30] The statements were not throwaway lines. Over the next decade League members framed their campaign in an Australasian context, demanding 'to be as free to vote as the women of New Zealand, South Australia, and West Australia'. When, in 1902, New South Wales women won the state vote, the veteran social reformer Catherine Helen Spence rejoiced that 'half the women in Australia are enfranchised and more than half in Australasia'.[31]

The Woman's Christian Temperance Union (WCTU) of Australasia, established in Melbourne in 1891, was an expression of, and vehicle for, regional sentiment among politically active women. By then, the American organization, which arrived in Sydney in 1882, and flourished after its first 'round-the-world missionary' landed in Auckland three years later, had become crucial to the fight for the vote across Australasia. The union's first intercolonial meeting occurred within weeks of the National Australasian Convention, which had drafted a Commonwealth constitution for ratification by all seven colonial parliaments. Likewise, at the WCTU summit delegates agreed to pool their 'forces and funds' to promote 'National Righteousness', an expansive agenda that included Sabbatarianism and the prohibition of alcohol, opium and gambling.[32] Though the constitution strategically omitted political rights, as one observer reported, 'a stranger might almost have suspected that the Australasian WCTU was a meeting for the advancement of woman suffrage'.[33] Like the first Australasian federal convention, the New Zealand delegation stood alone in its refusal to affiliate. As the colonial leadership explained it, the difficulty of trans-Tasman travel and their existing ties to the World's WCTU outweighed any benefits of federation. The decision was, nevertheless, contentious. Perhaps at the insistence of its travelling party who, undeterred by the six-week round trip, returned eager to formalize the bonds they had formed in Melbourne, the union's decision came with a caveat; members would, 'at some future time', revisit the decision and affiliate with the Australasian union.[34]

Despite New Zealand's self-exclusion from the WCTU's intercolonial hierarchy, the union's informal structures encouraged women to join the traffic that bound Britain's Australasian settlements. In 1888, Auckland branch stalwart Hannah Main attended a WCTU meeting during a visit to Sydney. She returned five times in fifteen years, enjoying the recognition afforded to her as a 'representative of the emancipated sisters of her colony'. Migrants who settled into new branches retained ties with former colleagues, posting news and literature and reporting in person if they returned. In the 1890s, Main's Auckland branch hosted twenty-three overseas speakers, mostly from the Australian colonies, and welcomed recruits from Queensland and New South Wales. Visitors from Sydney were so familiar that during busy meetings, 'no time could be allowed' for them to speak.[35] The Auckland union doubled as a training ground for grassroots leaders, like Helen Dewar – who served as a Queensland branch president, instructing members across the colony on suffrage campaigning – and Agnes Berry, who joined the Adelaide union as secretary during its final push for the vote in 1893–4.[36] The branch was not exceptional; over the next decade women experienced in the New Zealand campaign cropped up in branches and at conventions across Australia.[37]

Such exchanges encouraged the WCTU of Australasia to spend the next decade working to make the geographic descriptor in its title a political reality. From their perspective, the New Zealanders' refusal to affiliate was a setback, but not an irrevocable assertion of a separate identity. After all, despite agreeing to make 'united efforts' in pursuit of common goals, the union's Australian members complained about being 'forced together' and pursued interests that contravened intercolonial objectives.[38] At each triennial convention between 1894 and 1903, New Zealand was invited to federate, while travelling envoys like Victorian WCTU president Mary Love addressed local branches, hopeful that members would recognize the 'advantages [of] federating with Australia'.[39] They were driven by a belief in Australasia as a coherent entity and, if they could not win the vote first, the union's leaders were determined to capitalize on their neighbours' experience. Kate Sheppard, New Zealand's franchise superintendent, who had long been admired in Australian reform circles, received several requests to lead the equivalent Australasian department in the 1890s. Australasian secretary Flora Harris spoke for many in 1897 when she described the New Zealand suffrage campaign as 'an object lesson' and a reason to hold out hope that 'we may yet induce them to unite with us'.[40]

Belying Harris's optimism, and despite its promise of 1892, the New Zealand WCTU never revisited the question of intercolonial federation. Its members' reticence must be read against the WCTU of Australasia's surging enthusiasm for federation. The architect of the union's consolidation as a national body was its second president, the South Australian Elizabeth Webb Nicholls. After the Melbourne convention of 1891 she described the union as a weapon for slaying 'the strongest foe of intercolonial life ... the provincial spirit which so narrows and hinders all real progress'.[41] Three years later, upon accepting the Australasian presidency, her ambition had narrowed to the cultivation 'of a national spirit in these Australian colonies'.[42] To realize her vision of a teetotal Commonwealth 'federated in the interests of women as well as men', she launched a newspaper, *Our Federation* (1897–1903). Yet, even as she encouraged her readers to consider themselves 'nation builders', it was at Nicholls's behest that the WCTU of Australasia repeatedly invited the New Zealanders to join.[43] She saw little contradiction in these positions. More than most of her colleagues, she studied developments to the east. After South Australian women won the vote in 1894, she professed that the New Zealanders' victory 'led the way for our own'.[44] Despite the nationalist overtones of *Our Federation*'s title and masthead – a closely cropped map of the Australian mainland unmarred by colonial borders – Nicholls insisted that the paper spoke from 'an Australasian standpoint'. The following year she averred her belief in the progressive possibilities of 'clasp[ing] hands across the [Tasman] sea as enfranchised women'.[45] Nevertheless, the fact that the New Zealand union never formally considered such overtures suggests that they were less sanguine about the shift from the intercolonial terminology of 'Australasia' to the nationalist rhetoric Nicholls and her colleagues adopted as the century closed.

Still, the conviction that Australasia, however imagined, constituted an arena in which white women could pursue common goals extended beyond the WCTU. Dora Montefiore, the founder of the New South Wales WSL, pinpointed the organization's origins in her 'intimate' conversations with Sir George Grey, the former governor of South Australia, Cape Colony, and New Zealand, where he had also served as premier between 1877 and 1879. Grey, an early supporter of women's enfranchisement, advised Montefiore to follow New Zealand's example by simultaneously cultivating parliamentary allies to progress suffrage legislation and forming an extra-parliamentary pressure group to mobilize public sentiment.[46] Over the next decade, the League hosted speakers with experience in the New Zealand campaign and employed one, Miss Boyd, as an organizer.[47] Following Montefiore's example, the League's secretary, Rose Scott, looked across the Tasman for a mentor. Between 1891 and 1894 she wrote regularly to another former premier, the legislative leader of the suffrage campaign Sir John Hall. Indeed, so profound was Hall's influence that when he retired from parliament in 1893, Scott assured him that 'always and ever the women of Australia and the world ... will hold up your name in grateful remembrance as it is due to you that they have gained the first step in Political Liberty & Equality'.[48]

Hall's published speeches constituted a fraction of the print-culture circulations that animated the Australasian suffrage world. The WCTU's division of its agenda into uniform departments covering everything from 'scientific temperance instruction' to franchise work encouraged intercolonial dialogue and allowed members to request reform literature from like-minded women across the globe. A precursor to the New Zealand campaign came in 1885, when Kate Sheppard ordered a parcel of American suffrage leaflets to Christchurch. Suitably inspired, in 1888 she began writing her own. Her tracts *Sixteen Reasons for Supporting Woman's Suffrage* (1891) and *Is it Right?* (1892) quickly drew an Australian readership.[49] In return, she devoured the Australasian WCTU's *Manual of the Franchise Department*, distilling its contents into thirteen 'Hints for District Franchise Superintendents' which dictated the final years of the New Zealand campaign.[50] Such success was a function of the tracts' viral qualities: they were pithy, geographically non-specific, and encouraged intertextual borrowing. It also testified to the WCTU's efficiency as a circulatory network.[51] Both texts appeared in the Christchurch temperance newspaper *Prohibitionist*, which Sheppard swapped with sympathetic Australian editors, while the pamphlet versions her WCTU branch sent across Australia were quickly repurposed by their recipients.[52]

The forces that connected this Australasian world and denoted its geographic limits can be seen most clearly in the women's advocacy newspapers that proliferated in the 1890s. Between 1888 and 1910, dozens of titles concerning women's political rights launched in the region.[53] If politically organized women envisioned Australasia as an arena for progressive reform, editors understood that it enlarged their audience, an essential consideration for those eager to take on an enterprise as precarious as a nineteenth-century newspaper. Thus, resourceful publishers fashioned pan-colonial distribution chains. Publications like *Woman's Voice* (Sydney) and *Australian Woman's Sphere* (Melbourne) advertised two subscription prices: one for local readers and another for those across Australasia. The *Voice* went further, branding itself as an 'Australasian' newspaper, working in concert with 'our sisters (the *Dawn* in Sydney, and *Daybreak* in New Zealand)'.[54] To attract intercolonial readers, editors used local agents. Capitalizing on the lack of an equivalent New Zealand publication, Sydney's *Woman's Suffrage Journal* worked with Kate Sheppard to recruit subscribers, attracting forty in 1892 alone.[55] For publications that concealed subscription figures, correspondence columns offer clues about the distribution of their readers. Between 1892 and 1903, the region's bestselling women's political newspaper, *Dawn*, published more letters from New Zealand than anywhere but its home colony, New South Wales, and neighbouring Queensland.[56] Following a warm notice in *Woman's Voice*, Wellington's *Daybreak* began receiving letters from Australian readers and employed a Hobart correspondent.[57] For the well-read, like New South Wales WCTU secretary Alice Masterman, this dynamic print market encouraged solidarity of sentiment and a sense of collective belonging. In 1896, she likened the 'interchange' of newspapers 'throughout Australasia' to 'shak[ing]' hands across the seas'.[58]

For all Masterman's enthusiasm, the intercolonial newspaper trade was far from unbounded. Editors prioritized local readers, their efforts underwritten by local advertisers. In 1901–2, 10 per cent of the *Sphere*'s Australasian readers lived outside Victoria. Similarly, *Dawn*'s lively community of New Zealand correspondents must be put in context. Of the almost 2,500 letters the paper published over its lifetime, 92 per cent came from New South Wales, a figure that matches the distribution of readers from the paper's extant subscription figures.[59] A close analysis of these titles in the years 1894–5 and 1901–2 suggests the 'village and globe' model that predominated in the mainstream press also prevailed in women's advocacy publications. In most titles, the WCTU's explicitly national *Our Federation* aside, 40–70 per cent of the news published came from their home colony, with the remainder coming from Britain, the

United States and settlements bordering the Tasman Sea.[60] For readers, a flood of information linked New Zealand, New South Wales, South Australia and Victoria. Beyond Australia's south-east, it slowed to a trickle. This was not only, or even primarily, a product of proximity. After all, distance did not forestall coverage of significant events from afar, like the death of the American suffragist, Elizabeth Cady Stanton, in 1902. Nor did it hinder the compilation of columns – entitled 'Mild and Bitter' in *Daybreak* and 'The World Moves' in *Australian Woman's Sphere* – filled with deracinated trivia pertaining to the status of women around the world.[61] Instead, it was a function of the exchange system through which editors gathered news. Without women's newspapers from which to clip news from Queensland, Tasmania and Western Australia, developments in those colonies went unnoticed.

As Australia drew closer to federation, the ties which allowed white women to imagine themselves working in a shared enterprise frayed. Enfranchisement ended the solidarity between women with otherwise diffuse interests, but as Helen Bones has noted of Australasia as a whole, the connections between suffragists did not immediately 'end at any of the obvious points of separation.'[62] In newly federated Australia, popular apathy stymied efforts to commemorate the nation's birth, leaving a void that would be filled with a myth formed around the invasion of Gallipoli in 1915.[63] For many feminists, such sentiments took decades to awaken. Some, like Sydney's Rose Scott, threw themselves into international organizing to ward off the threat of 'national singularity'. Yet, even those amenable to centralization necessarily invested in state politics, where they could most easily advocate for reforms to marriage and divorce law, wage equality, the age of consent and the sale of intoxicants.[64] The conservative Australian Women's National League's (1904–45) efforts to rouse women's patriotism came in response to their perceived 'civic indolence', a sentiment encapsulated by the fact that the states resisted the formation of a unified National Council of Women of Australia until 1931.[65] Likewise, and despite its enthusiasm for federation, the WCTU proved reluctant to replace the regional 'Australasia' with the national 'Australia' in its title. The union only formally delimited its ambitions in 1927, a decision that coincided with its push for a federal land grant to build a headquarters in Canberra.[66] Despite such ambivalence, the wholesale enfranchisement of white women in the region within five years of federation (with the exception of Victoria in 1908) meant that they needed another basis for cooperation. Their task was complicated by the fragmentation of the suffrage coalitions along class lines, the disappearance of the once vibrant Australasian women's advocacy press after 1901 and, perhaps, a degree of self-satisfaction at the ease with which their world-leading achievements had been won.[67] This mirrored the once vibrant Tasman labour movement, whose dreams of Australasian fraternalism began in the 1880s and ended with New Zealand's 'Great Strike' of 1913. Likewise, while politically organized women remained committed to internationalism, they appeared 'resigned to national vistas' in the Antipodes.[68]

Australasia's afterlives

Yet, if Australasia had fallen from favour among ex-suffragists, the idea still held currency for metropolitan observers of the colonies' experiments in democracy. The seasoned antipodean activists who joined the suffrage diaspora often worked together to 'teach feminists in the Imperial "heartland"'.[69] As one of the few antipodean women to attend the 1893 Chicago World's Columbian Exposition, Catherine Spence tasked herself to speak not only for South Australia, 'but [all of] Australasia, including New Zealand'.[70] A decade later, in 1902, Vida Goldstein represented Australia and New Zealand at the International Woman Suffrage Conference in Washington DC. Her offer to repeat the arrangement in 1904 by organizing a joint delegation to the International Woman Suffrage Alliance's (IWSA) inauguration in Berlin was ignored, foreclosing future Australasian collaboration. The decision left New Zealand women, who for reasons of distance and disorganization lacked a national political association from which to organize internationally, outside of the Alliance until 1926.[71] Australia's presence at the IWSA's biennial meetings failed to assuage the 'unspeakable disappointment' its leadership expressed at the New Zealanders' absence. After all, as the Alliance's president Carrie Chapman Catt complained, what use was an organization pledged to secure 'the enfranchisement of the women of all nations, and to unite the friends of women suffrage throughout the world' if those few who enjoyed the vote would not attend?[72]

New Zealand feminists' decision to avoid Alliance meetings rather than endure representation by an Australian proxy was not the only sign that women had begun to insist on national distinctions. Long before the iconic expatriate newspaper *British-Australasian* (1884–1924) was renamed the *British Australian and New Zealander*, semantically cleaving London's '"Australasian" community', the political tracts ex-suffragists wrote for international audiences in the 1900s considered the former colonies in isolation.[73] Such texts, which elided the southern circulations on which their success rested, offered blueprints for the national suffrage histories written in the twentieth century.[74] In particular, New Zealanders eager to leave a mark on the world felt their achievements had been usurped by their larger neighbour. World's WCTU president Anna Adams Gordon was not alone in confusing Australia and New Zealand, so when she asked Kate Sheppard to lead the World's franchise department in 1906, the American was surprised by the vehemence of her refusal. 'It was a slip of my pen or in my dictation to ask you if there were not some one in <u>Australia</u> who could be your assistant ... I meant New Zealand and it was a stupid blunder for me to make.'[75] Sheppard's ire mirrored that of William Pember Reeves, the colony's agent-general in London, who pointedly eschewed 'that sprawling and unscientific word "Australasia"' when titling his germinal *State Experiments in Australia and New Zealand* (1902). 'Our colony,' he bristled, 'is in no sense an offshoot or outlying province of Australia.'[76] Seven years later, the contrast between Meeson's resplendent banner and its neighbour, a 'plain, red banneret, inscribed in minute letters, "N.Z."', prompted the novelist Edith Searle Grossman to admit that 'my national vanity was not flattered'.[77] Alert to such sensitivities, the International Council of Women's (ICW) Scottish secretary Maria Ogilvie Gordon wrote apologetically to Sheppard when discussing the National Council of Women of New Zealand's dissolution: 'I hope you will not think it very impertinent of me if I, un-officially, ask you whether it might be possible for New Zealand to join the Australasian combination of Councils for the purpose of having one representative at the I.C.W.?'[78] There is no record of Sheppard's reply, but as in

1904, there was little appetite for the idea. Instead, in rejecting the proposal New Zealand women remained absent from the ICW's gatherings until the dormant National Council of Women relaunched in 1918.[79]

Even as colonial demarcations calcified into national distinctions, Australian and New Zealand women collaborated in the British campaign, fashioning a democratic alliance that preceded the Anzac legend. Forged, among other places, in Meeson's Chelsea studio, Goldstein and Anna Stout's friendship formed the axis for the Australian and New Zealand Women Voters' Committee in 1911. The lobby was, as Clare Wright states, a manifestation of 'Australasian kinship', albeit one whose mutability reveals as much about antipodean identities as its existence.[80] The Committee flourished where earlier attempts to fabricate Australasian coalitions failed because imperial ties bound the Dominions in ways that the fledging circuits of international feminism could not match. For Stout, Goldstein and the almost 200 others who joined them, marching behind Meeson's banner was not a sunny display of solidarity with women 'from all corners of the earth', but an assertion of their status as 'the real foundations of Empire'.[81] For this reason they waved 'red, white, and blue streamers ... being the only women who are entitled to wear the "Empire" colors as a right, and not as a privilege'.[82] Established to fix 'a feminist eye' on that year's Imperial Conference, the Committee preoccupied itself with a uniform nationality bill, which would see all British women lose their citizenship upon marriage to foreigners and the loss of members' voting rights in Britain.[83] Nevertheless, the Committee's focus soon superseded the interests of disenfranchised Australasian women. In 1914, it merged with the fledgling British Dominions Woman Suffrage Union, beginning its reinvention as an 'Empire franchise movement'.[84] The transformation concluded with another rebranding, as the British Commonwealth League, in 1925. The organization's remit extended to securing 'equality of liberties, status, and opportunities between men and women' across the empire focusing, paternalistically, on 'women of the less forward races'.[85] Whatever its merits, the expanded League curtailed the moment of Australasian kinship that had invigorated Goldstein and Stout. In its place stood an Anglo-Australian alliance. Despite its stated commitment to racial and regional equality, the League privileged the voices of white British and Australian women, who used it to shape an agenda for women across the empire for two generations.[86]

Conclusion

Dora Meeson entered the Australasian suffrage world as a young Christchurch artist before withdrawing into her work, only throwing herself 'heart and soul into the suffrage movement' after her West London studio was mistaken for a Women's Freedom League venue in 1906. Whether addressing suffrage meetings or, through the Artists' Suffrage League, crafting the iconography of the Edwardian campaign, Meeson drew on a gamut of Australasian experiences.[87] An apprenticeship in the Canterbury suffrage movement meant exposure to British and American suffrage literature, ideas and campaign methods drawn from across the seven colonies, as well as the thrilling sensation that her youthful activism was being transmitted across the Tasman and around the world. Traces of this hybridity, which pepper Meeson's autobiographical writing and laid at the heart of the political movements she joined, have been obscured by her banner's installation at the heart of Australia's democracy. The honour of official recognition, ironically, is one she would have craved, though surely for one of the British impressionist paintings that were more representative of her oeuvre.[88]

The dissipation of Meeson's plural identity, wavering between Britain, Victoria, New Zealand and the Commonwealth she would not visit until 1913, coincided with the diminution of the Australasian suffrage world. As a homesick student in Victorian London, Meeson longed for New Zealand. When she resumed her training in Melbourne, she feared her classmates thought her 'an English girl' who felt herself 'superior to colonial students'. After a decade in Britain, Meeson began to embrace Australia, a transformation accelerated by the exigencies of artistic survival. Sporadic visits to Melbourne – during which Meeson noted 'we were no longer reckoned Australians by the customs authorities – you ceased to be one after five years' absence' – were intended to court the Dominion's 'picture-loving public'. Like those who would historicize her career, Meeson found in Australia a receptive audience and institutions eager to bolster her and Coates's reputation. Neither was assured for an expatriate painter dedicated to Victorian styles in interwar Britain.[89] The pair's wartime experiences intensified their desire to shape the story of the Commonwealth. In 1915, Coates enlisted in the Royal Army Medical Corps. Unable to serve his country of birth, Coates saw an opportunity to make amends in the Australian National War Records Office's 1918 request that he become an official war artist. Yet, the War Office denied his request for a transfer to the Australian Imperial Force. The pair's anguish at the decision striates Meeson's biography of her husband. Stung by the refusal, Coates pursued Australian War Museum Committee commissions after his discharge. The most famous of these, *General William Bridges and His Staff Watching the Manoeuvres of the 1st Australian Division in the Desert in Egypt, March 1915* (1922–6), is credited with Meeson, who worked as a 'ghost' on her debilitated husband's canvasses: sketching compositions, retouching backgrounds and adding fine details.[90]

Yet, if absence and injustice – alongside the pursuit of lucrative commissions – strengthened the pair's identification with Australia, it seldom felt like home. In 1921, Coates refused to make a visit to Melbourne permanent by declining the directorship of his alma mater, the National Gallery School. As Meeson recalled, after half a lifetime in Europe he found himself 'out of sympathy with [Australian] standards' and, in any case, he 'could never be happy so far away from the world's greatest works of art'.[91] If George was an ambivalent Australian, when Dora visited in 1934, there appeared to be little doubt about her allegiances. Alongside her growing presence in public and private collections, she had long served as the London president of the ANZAC Fellowship of Women, a patriotic association which, belying its title, hosted so few New Zealanders that their mere presence was remarked upon.[92] Interviewed by the *West Australian*, Meeson was still fashioning her identity. Overlooking her distant Canterbury adolescence, Meeson insisted that although she had spent 'so many years in the old world, I still love Australia as the land of my birth'. The Australasian moment had passed. Still, Meeson was far from the unambiguously national figure she became when her banner arrived in Canberra fifty-four years later. When pressed for her impressions of the continent she was soon to leave for the final time, Meeson's thoughts drifted: 'The more I come to this part of the world, the more I am struck with its un-Englishness ... I have not become accustomed to the strong light – it is very unlike England.'[93]

Notes

1   Lisa Tickner, *The Spectacle of Women: Imagery of the Suffrage Campaign, 1907–14* (Chicago: The University of Chicago Press, 1988), 122–31.

2   National Archives of Australia, Canberra (hereafter NAA), A363, 1987/2824, Dale Spender to Gillian Bonham, 30 June 1987; Bonham to Edith Hall, 8 July 1987; Bonham to Helen L'Orange, 7 November 1988; NAA, A463, 1987/3770, Janet Ramsay to Ms McIlraith, 1 February 1988; Clare Wright, *You Daughters of Freedom: The Australians who won the vote and inspired the world* (Melbourne: Text Publishing, 2018), 468–9.

3   For an exception to this, led by groups like Women Against Racism, who opposed the NWCC's participation in the celebration of the bicentenary of colonization, see Wright, *You Daughters*, 469–72. On the new nationalism, feminist efforts to upset the overwhelmingly masculine canon of Australian nation-building, and the uses of history in late-twentieth-century Australia, see Ann Curthoys, 'We've just started making national histories and you want us to stop already?', in *After the Imperial Turn: Thinking with and Through the Nation*, ed. Antoinette Burton (Durham, NC: Duke University Press, 2003), 79–81; Kate Laing, 'Reconceiving the nation', in *How Gender can Transform the Social Sciences: Innovation and Impact*, ed. Marian Sawer, Fiona Jenkins and Karen Downing (Basingstoke: Palgrave Pivot, 2020), 78; Mark McKenna, 'The history anxiety', in *The Cambridge History of Australia, Volume 2: The Commonwealth of Australia*, ed. Alison Bashford and Stuart Macintyre (Melbourne: Cambridge University Press, 2013), 571–6.

4   *Commonwealth Franchise Act 1902* (Cth), s. 4; see NAA, A463, 1988/3222/1, Trish Mercer to Kay Daniels, 17 January 1990; Eileen Duhs to Kaye Dal Bon, 1 May 1990; NAA, A463, 1988/3222/2, Carmela Mollica, 'The conservation treatment of the womens [*sic*] suffragette banner', c. June 1990; Justine van Mourik, Director Art Collection & Exhibitions, Department of Parliamentary Services to James Keating, 14 January 2020.

5   Meeson Coates was not oblivious to the Victorian campaign. In 1908, for example, she sent a parcel of Artists' Suffrage League postcards to Vida Goldstein, but the exchange appears to have been a discrete one. State Library of New South Wales, Sydney (hereafter SLNSW), M2309/4, Vida Goldstein 1908 diary, 19 October 1908.

6   Sharon Crozier-De Rosa and Vera Mackie, *Remembering Women's Activism* (New York: Routledge, 2019), 19–22, 44–5; Alison Bartlett and Margaret Henderson, 'Working with feminist things: The *wunderkammer* as feminist methodology', in *Things that Liberate: An Australian Feminist Wunderkammer*, ed. Alison Bartlett and Margaret Henderson (Newcastle upon Tyne: Cambridge Scholars Publishing, 2013), 1–13. On the sartorial differences between New Zealand and British suffragists, see Harriette Richards, 'Fashioning protest: Suffrage as dressed performance in New Zealand and the United Kingdom', *About Performance* 16 (2018): 27–43.

7   This fascination, most recently on display in the National Gallery of Victoria's 2020 exhibition of suffragette ephemera, is not limited to Australia. June Purvis has noted British historians' preference for the spectacle of militancy above peaceful activism,

while Te Papa Tongarewa's 2016 acquisition of expatriate suffragette Frances Parker's Women's Social and Political Union (WSPU) hunger-strike medal typifies a similar impulse in New Zealand. 'Krystyna Campbell-Petty AM and family suffrage research collection', *National Gallery of Victoria*, https://www.ngv.vic.gov.au/exhibition/womens-suffrage-research-collection/, accessed 22 December 2020; Purvis, 'Gendering the historiography of the suffragette movement in Edwardian Britain: some reflections', *Women's History Review* 22:4 (2013): 577; 'Rare suffragette medal goes on display at Te Papa', *Museum of New Zealand Te Papa Tongarewa*, https://tepapa.govt.nz/about/press-and-media/press-releases/2016-news-and-media-releases/rare-suffragette-medal-goes-on, accessed 13 February 2020.

8   Frank Bongiorno, 'Trust the women', *Labour History* 65 (1993), 208–11; Audrey Oldfield, *Woman Suffrage in Australia: A Gift or a Struggle?* (Melbourne: Cambridge University Press, 1992); Myra Scott, *How Australia Led the Way: Dora Meeson Coates and British Suffrage* (2003; North Melbourne: Australian Scholarly Publishing, 2018); '$1 Coin to commemorate the centenary of women's suffrage', Royal Australian Mint, https://www.ramint.gov.au/publications/1-coin-commemorate-centenary-womens-suffrage, accessed 6 September 2021.

9   Sharon Crozier-De Rosa, 'Narratives of democracy, the emotions of politics and memories of militant suffragism: Britain, Ireland, the USA and Australia', in *The British Women's Suffrage Campaign: National and International Perspectives*, ed. June Hannam and June Purvis (London: Routledge, 2021), 187.

10   Wright, *You Daughters*, 473.

11   The biographical details in this paragraph are from Dora Meeson Coates, *George Coates: His Art and His Life* (London: J. M. Dent and Sons Ltd, 1937); Myra Scott, 'The art of George James Coates, 1869–1930 and Dora Meeson Coates, 1869–1955, Volume I' (MFA thesis, University of Melbourne, 1992).

12   At least 30,000 women signed thirteen suffrage petitions in 1893. Of these, only the largest roll has survived. *The Women's Suffrage Petition, Te Petihana Whakamana Pōti Wahine, 1893* (Wellington: Archives New Zealand, Te Rua Mahara o Te Kāwanatanga, National Library of New Zealand, Te Puna Mātauranga o Aotearoa, and Bridget Williams Books, 2017); 'Women's Suffrage Petition 1893 – sheet no. 3', *NZHistory*, https://nzhistory.govt.nz/files/documents/suffrage-pdfs/003.pdf, accessed 24 May 2022.

13   Kate R. Robertson, *Identity, Community and Australian Artists, 1890–1914: Paris, London and Further Afield* (London: Bloomsbury Visual Arts, 2019), 53–74; Angela Woollacott, *To Try Her Fortune in London: Australian Women, Colonialism, and Modernity* (Oxford: Oxford University Press, 2001), 1–9; *Women's Franchise*, 17 September 1908, 127.

14   Rex Butler and A. D. S. Donaldson, 'Cities within cities: Australian and New Zealand art in the 20th century', *Journal of Art Historiography* 4 (2011): 1–2. On the practice of claiming Australasian figures for a particular national canon, see Helen Bones and Karen Fox, 'Re-membering Tasman lives', *New Zealand Journal of History* 56:1 (2022): 67–93.

15   Meeson Coates, *George Coates*, 61–2; Ken Hall, Felicity Milburn, Nathan Pohio, Lara Strongman and Pete Vangioni, 'The world tossed continuously in a riot of colour, form, sound', *Bulletin of the Christchurch Art Gallery* 192 (2018): 8–10; Frances Hodgkins to Rachel Hodgkins, 27 June and 23 October 1902, in *Letters of Frances Hodgkins*, ed. Linda Gill (Auckland: Auckland University Press, 1993), 129–30, 140–2; *The Times*, 14 June 1902, 9.

16 *Dunstan Times*, 9 April 1901, 3. See also *Evening Star*, 27 November 1902, 7; *Auckland Star*, 20 August 1907, 2; *Otago Daily Times*, 1 July 1910, 3.

17 Donald Denoon, 'Re-membering Australasia: A repressed memory', *Australian Historical Studies* 34:122 (2003): 290; Bones and Fox, 'Re-membering Tasman lives'; Marilyn Lake, 'Nationalist historiography, feminist scholarship, and the promise and problems of new transnational histories: The Australian case', *Journal of Women's History* 19:1 (2007): 183–4; Grace Millar, 'Women's lives, feminism and the *New Zealand Journal of History*', *New Zealand Journal of History* 52:2 (2018): 139–40.

18 Judith Collard, 'Blighted camellias: Si(gh)ting women in New Zealand art', *Women's Studies Journal* 10:1 (1994): 104–6; *White Camellias: A Century of Women's Artmaking in Canterbury* (Christchurch: Robert McDougall Gallery, 1993), 39. Despite extensive criticism, the nationalist orthodoxies of the mid-century cast a long shadow in New Zealand. See, e.g., Helen Bones, *The Expatriate Myth: New Zealand Writers and the Colonial World* (Dunedin: Otago University Press, 2018); Brigid Magner, 'A glassy sort of rainbow', *Sydney Review of Books*, https://sydneyreviewofbooks.com/essay/magner-glassy-sort-of-rainbow/, accessed 13 May 2021; Katie Pickles, 'Transnational history and cultural cringe: Some issues for consideration in New Zealand, Australia and Canada', *History Compass* 9:9 (2011): 657–73.

19 *Star*, 19 September 1895, 2; *Lyttelton Times*, 19 September 1895, 4; *Press*, 19 September 1895, 4; 23 September 1895, 4.

20 See, e.g., Robertson, *Identity, Community and Australian Artists*; Scott, *How Australia Led the Way*; Catherine Speck, *Painting Ghosts: Australian Women Artists in Wartime* (Melbourne: Craftsman House, 2004); Wright, *You Daughters*.

21 Greg Dening, 'Empowering imaginations', *Contemporary Pacific* 9:2 (1997): 423.

22 Bones, *The Expatriate Myth*, 72. See Felicity Barnes, *New Zealand's London: A Colony and its Metropolis* (Auckland: Auckland University Press, 2012); Kate Darian-Smith, Patricia Grimshaw and Stuart Macintyre, eds, *Britishness Abroad: Transnational Movements and Imperial Cultures* (Melbourne: Melbourne University Publishing, 2007); Meg Tasker, 'William Pember Reeves, writing the fortunate isles', *Journal of the Association for the Study of Australian Literature* 13:3 (2013): 1–3; Woollacott, *To Try Her Fortune*, 139–80.

23 James Belich, *Paradise Reforged: A History of the New Zealanders from the 1880s to the Year 2000* (Auckland: Allen Lane, 2001), 51.

24 Rollo Arnold, 'The Australasian peoples and their world, 1888–1915', in *Tasman Relations: New Zealand and Australia, 1788–1988*, ed. Keith Sinclair (Auckland: Auckland University Press, 1987), 53–62.

25 Rebecca Mead, *How the Vote was Won: Woman Suffrage in the Western United States 1868–1914* (New York: New York University Press, 2004), 13–14; Patricia Grimshaw, 'Settler anxieties, indigenous peoples, and women's suffrage in the colonies of Australia, New Zealand, and Hawai'i, 1888 to 1902', *Pacific Historical Review* 69:4 (2000): 553–72. Overseas observers of the settlers' 'social experiments' shared this progressive vision of a white Australasia. See especially Marilyn Lake, *Progressive New World: How Settler Colonialism and Transpacific Exchange Shaped American Reform* (Cambridge, MA: Harvard University Press, 2019).

26 Denoon, 'Re-membering Australasia', 290; J. O. C. Phillips, 'Musings in Maoriland – or was there a *Bulletin* school in New Zealand?' *Historical Studies* 20:81 (1983): 51. On the Tasman world, see especially Philippa Mein-Smith, Peter Hempenstall and Shaun Goldfinch, with Stuart McMillan and Rosemary Baird, *Remaking the Tasman World* (Christchurch: Canterbury University Press, 2008).

27 Donald Denoon and Philippa Mein-Smith, with Marivic Wyndham, *A History of Australia, New Zealand and the Pacific* (Oxford: Blackwell, 2000), 1. See, e.g., Arnold, 'The Australasian peoples', 53–62; Rollo Arnold, 'Some Australasian aspects of New Zealand life, 1890–1913', *New Zealand Journal of History* 4:1 (1970): 54–76.

28 In 2019, for example, Alison Bashford argued that 'for historians taught and researching from an Australian base ... the nation no longer holds any historiographical monopoly'. Bashford, 'On nations and states: a reflection on "Thinking the Empire Whole"', *History Australia* 16:4 (2019): 638–9; James Keating, 'Piecing together suffrage internationalism: Place, space, and connected histories of Australasian women's activism', *History Compass* 16:8 (2018): 1–15.

29 SLNSW, MLMSS186/13/535–41, Mary Lee to Lady Mary Windeyer, 23 September 1892.

30 *Daily Telegraph*, 28 November 1893, 5; *Womanhood Suffrage League of New South Wales Annual Report and Balance Sheet for Year Ending June 1st, 1894* (Sydney: Jas. A. Ross Printer, 1894), 5.

31 Catherine Helen Spence to Scott, 20 September 1902, in Susan Margarey, with Barbara Wall, Mary Lyons and Maryan Beams, eds, *Ever Yours, C.H. Spence: Catherine Helen Spence's An Autobiography (1825–1910), Diary (1894), and Some Correspondence (1894–1910)* (Adelaide: Wakefield Press, 2005), 351. See, e.g., *Daily Telegraph*, 11 June 1896, 3; *Freeman's Journal*, 12 March 1898, 12; SLNSW, MAV-FM4-9555, 'Notice of womanhood suffrage public meeting, Protestant Hall, Monday, 4th June, 1900'; *Womanhood Suffrage League of New South Wales, Tenth Annual Report and Balance Sheet for the Year ending June 1st, 1901* (Sydney: S. D. Townsend & Co. Printers, 1901), 5, 21.

32 Nicholas Aroney, *The Constitution of a Federal Commonwealth: The Making and Meaning of the Australian Constitution* (Cambridge: Cambridge University Press, 2009), 158–64; *The Woman's Christian Temperance Union of Australasia, Minutes & Proceedings of First Intercolonial Woman's Christian Temperance Union Convention* (Melbourne: J. J. Howard, 1891), 3.

33 *Union Signal*, 30 July 1891, 10.

34 Two delegates to the Melbourne convention – Caroline Fulton and Mary Kirkland – persuaded their West Taieri branch to affiliate with the Australasian union before the New Zealand executive intervened. *Prohibitionist*, 29 August 1891, 3; *New Zealand Herald*, 25 March 1892, 6; Hocken Collections, Dunedin, ARC-0379, AG613/021, Catherine Henrietta Elliot Fulton diary 1891, 28 April–25 June.

35 SLNSW, MLMSS3641, Sydney WCTU Minute Book 1882–92, 1 February 1888; *Evening News*, 1 May 1894, 2; Alexander Turnbull Library (hereafter ATL), Wellington, 79-057-08/03, Auckland WCTU Minute Book 1889–98, 21 August 1889, 8 March 1893, 28 May 1894, 28 October 1896; 79-057-08/04, Auckland WCTU Minute Book 1898–1902, 12 October 1898, 15 March 1899 and 12 February 1902.

36 ATL, 79-057/08/03, Auckland WCTU Minute Book 1889–98, 13 April 1893; *Eighth Annual Report of the Adelaide Woman's Christian Temperance Union* (Adelaide: G. Hassell & Son, 1894), 1; *Worker*, 5 October 1895, 3; *Brisbane Courier*, 25 September 1896, 2; *Telegraph* [QLD], 18 May 1931, 9.

37 See, e.g., State Library of South Australia, Adelaide (hereafter SLSA), SRG186/748, Annie Schnackenberg to Elizabeth Webb Nicholls, 6 March 1897; SRG186/768, Mary Lodge to Nicholls, 25 April 1898; *Woman's Christian Temperance Union of Australasia, Minutes of the Fourth Triennial Convention* (Adelaide: Hussey & Gillingham, 1900), 11,

61; *Australasian Woman's Christian Temperance Union, Minutes of the 5th Triennial Convention* (Melbourne: Green & Fargher, 1903), 9, 11, 17, 23–5.

38 *WCTU of Australasia, Minutes of First Intercolonial Convention*, 3; SLSA, SRG186/748, Jessie Rooke to Nicholls, 7 March 1899; University of Melbourne Archives, Melbourne (hereafter UMA), 101/85, Box 15/241/1, Sara Nolan and Alice Masterman to Nicholls, 14 September 1899. For examples of intercolonial rivalry, see James Keating, *Distant Sisters: Australasian Women and the International Struggle for the Vote, 1880–1914* (Manchester: Manchester University Press, 2020), 49, 133, 147.

39 ATL, 79-057/08/03, Auckland WCTU Minute Book 1889–98, 19 August 1891. See, e.g., *Australasian WCTU Minutes of the Fourth Triennial Convention*, 30.

40 Canterbury Museum, Christchurch (hereafter CM), ARC176.53/55, Wallace to Sheppard, 18 August 1891; ARC176.53/228, M. E. Kirk to Sheppard, 18 January 1894; *Australasian Woman's Christian Temperance Union Minutes of the Second Triennial Convention* (Sydney: n.p., 1894), 16, 73.

41 *Woman's Christian Temperance Union of South Australia, Minutes of Eleventh Annual Convention*, (Adelaide: A. & E. Lewis, 1899), 10.

42 *Mercury*, 18 April 1894, 3.

43 UMA, 101/85, Box 77/231/2, Nicholls to the Australasian WCTU, 24 August 1896; *Brisbane Courier*, 27 April 1897, 6.

44 CM, ARC176.53/269, Nicholls to Sheppard, 30 April 1895.

45 UMA, 101/85, Box 77/231/2, Nicholls to the Australasian WCTU, 24 August 1896; CM, ARC176.53/310, Mary Ann Müller to Sheppard, 18 August 1898.

46 Dora B. Montefiore, *From a Victorian to a Modern* (London: E. Archer, 1927), 5, 31–3.

47 SLNSW, MLMSS38/33/1, Womanhood Suffrage League of New South Wales Minute Book, 1891–96, 222, 238, 356; *Womanhood Suffrage League of New South Wales Annual Report and Balance Sheet, for the Year Ending June 1st, 1896* (Sydney: Christian World Printing House, 1896), 4–5.

48 ATL, MS-Papers-1784-202/30, Scott to Hall, 6 January 1894.

49 Judith Devaliant, *Kate Sheppard: A Biography* (Auckland: Penguin Books, 1992), 21; Ian Tyrrell, *Woman's World/Woman's Empire: The Woman's Christian Temperance Union in International Perspective, 1880–1930* (Chapel Hill: The University of North Carolina Press, 1991), 224. See *Sixteen Reasons for Supporting Woman's Suffrage* (Christchurch: Smith, Anthony, Sellars & Co., 1891); *Is it Right?* (Christchurch: Smith, Anthony, Sellars & Co., 1892).

50 CM, ARC176.53/55, Catherine Wallace to Sheppard, 18 August 1891; C. P. Wallace, *Manual of the Franchise Department* (Melbourne: Dunn & Wilkinson, 1891); *Prohibitionist*, 27 February 1892, 3.

51 Ryan Cordell, 'Reprinting, circulation and the network author in antebellum newspapers', *American Literary History* 27:3 (2015): 423–9.

52 CM, ARC176.53/70, John Vale to Sheppard, 27 October 1891; CM, ARC176.53/74, 'The Editor, W.S.J.' to Sheppard, 9 March 1892; *Prohibitionist*, 7 November 1891, 3; 12 November 1892, 3; 6 May 1893, 3; *Sixteen Reasons for Supporting Woman's Suffrage* (Adelaide: Holden & Strutton, 1892); Joyce R. Henderson, *The Strength of White Ribbon: A Year-by-Year Record of the Centennial History of the Woman's Christian Temperance Union of Western Australia* (Perth: The Union, 1992), 4.

53 On these titles' history and the conditions that allowed for their efflorescence in an Australasian market, see Keating, *Distant Sisters*, 133–69.

54 *Woman's Voice*, 18 May 1895, 239; 27 July 1895, 299–300; *Australian Woman's Sphere*, May 1901, 69.

55 ATL, MS-Copy-Micro-0694-58/36, Sheppard to Hall, 20 April 1892.

56 Figures from *Dawn*, 1892–1903.

57 *Woman's Voice*, 23 March 1895, 199; *Daybreak*, 1 June 1895, 5–6; 13 July 1895, 1; 20 July 1895, 3; 24 August 1895, 7.

58 *Women's Christian Temperance Union of New South Wales Annual Report of the Fourteenth Convention* (Bathurst: National Advocate, 1896), 54.

59 Figures calculated from the monthly 'subscriptions received' column in *Australian Woman's Sphere* between September 1901 and September 1902; *Dawn*, 1888–1905; and Olive Lawson, ed., *The First Voice of Australian Feminism: Excerpts from Louisa Lawson's The Dawn 1888–1895* (Sydney: Simon & Schuster, 1990), 17–20.

60 Rollo Arnold, *New Zealand's Burning: The Settlers' World in the Mid 1880s* (Wellington: Victoria University Press, 1994), 220–34; Henry Mayer, *The Press in Australia* (Melbourne: Lansdowne, 1964), 12–13. For a more comprehensive content analysis of these titles, see Keating, *Distant Sisters*, 152–5.

61 See, e.g., *Australian Woman's Sphere*, 10 December 1902, 238–9; *Dawn*, 1 June 1897, 10; *Daybreak*, 27 July 1895, 1–2; *Our Federation*, December 1902, 7; *White Ribbon*, 1 January 1903, 1–3.

62 Helen Bones, 'Arthur H. Adams and Australasian narratives of the colonial world', in *Archiving Settler Colonialism: Culture, Space and Race*, ed. Yu-Ting Huang and Rebecca Weaver-Hightower (Abingdon: Routledge, 2019), 41.

63 Carolyn Holbrook, 'Federation and Australian nationalism: Early commemoration of the Commonwealth', *Australian Journal of Politics and History* 66:4 (2020): 560–77.

64 Helen Irving, 'A gendered constitution? Women, federation and heads of power', in *A Woman's Constitution: Gender & History in the Australian Commonwealth*, ed. Helen Irving (Sydney: Hale & Iremonger, 1996), 106.

65 As late as 1948 the visiting Scottish suffragette Helen Archdale would decry the 'stress laid on … narrow … state matters' by Australian feminists. SLNSW, MLMSS/9091/2/2, CY4624, Archdale, 'An interfering female', typescript, c. May 1948. See also Alan Atkinson, 'Federation, democracy and the struggle against a single Australia', *Australian Historical Studies* 44:2 (2013): 262–79; Sharon Crozier-De Rosa, *Shame and the Anti-Feminist Backlash: Britain, Ireland and Australia, 1890–1920* (New York: Routledge, 2018), 95–107; Carolyn Holbrook, '"What sort of nation?": A cultural history of Australians and their federation', *History Compass* 15:11 (2017): 1–10; James Keating, '"An utter absence of national feeling": Australian women and the international suffrage movement, 1900–14', *Australian Historical Studies* 47:3 (2016): 462–81.

66 *Australian Woman's Christian Temperance Union, Minutes of the 13th Triennial Convention* (Brisbane: R. G. Gillies, 1927), 11, 35–6.

67 Erik Olssen, Clyde Griffen and Frank Jones argue that the rapid success which greeted those who strove to make New Zealand more egalitarian than Britain created 'an increasingly self-satisfied society'. Likewise, Clare Wright contends that Australians were 'pleased to the point of self-righteousness' with their 'unique "experiment" in political equality'. By the interwar years, when both countries had shed their world-leading status, feminists would reckon bitterly with what they saw as their forebears' complacency. Olssen et al., *An Accidental Utopia? Social Mobility and the Foundations of an Egalitarian Society, 1880–1940* (Dunedin: Otago University Press, 2011), 188; Wright, '"A splendid object lesson": A transnational perspective on the birth of the Australian nation', *Journal of Women's History* 26:4 (2014): 14; Keating, *Distant Sisters*, 203–4.

68 Melanie Nolan, 'Personalizing class conflict across the Tasman: the New Zealand Great Strike and trans-Tasman biography', *Journal of New Zealand Studies* 18 (2014): 130. It was at this moment that the term 'Australasia' disappeared from maps, replaced by 'Australia and New Zealand'. Philippa Mein Smith, 'Mapping Australasia', *History Compass* 7:4 (2009): 15–20.

69 June Hannam, 'International dimensions of women's suffrage: "At the crossroads of several interlocking identities"', *Women's History Review* 13:3–4 (2005): 554.

70 *Daily Telegraph*, 26 December 1893, 6. Two weeks later, she lectured on Australia and New Zealand at Brown University. *South Australian Register*, 3 January 1984, 6.

71 *Report, First International Woman Suffrage Conference* (New York: International Woman Suffrage Headquarters, 1902); SLNSW, MLMSS 38/41/401–7, Vida Goldstein, 'Report of the Australian sub-committee of the International Woman Suffrage Committee', 10 February 1904.

72 CM, ARC176.53/376, Carrie Chapman Catt to Sheppard, 14 August 1908; *Report, Second and Third Conferences of the International Womanhood Suffrage Alliance* (Copenhagen: Bianco Luno, 1906), 116. See, e.g., ATL, MS-Papers-1376-01, Catt to Sheppard, 24 February 1908, 2, and 4 February 1909; *Press*, 15 November 1913, 6.

73 Simon Sleight, 'Reading the *British Australasian* community in London, 1884–1924', in *Australians in Britain: The Twentieth-Century Experience*, ed. Carl Bridge, Robert Crawford and David Dunstan (Melbourne: Monash University ePress, 2009), paragraph 27.

74 K. Sheppard, *Woman Suffrage in New Zealand* (London: International Woman Suffrage Alliance, 1907); Vida Goldstein, *Woman Suffrage in Australia* (London: International Woman Suffrage Alliance, 1908); Anna Stout, *Woman Suffrage in New Zealand* (London: The Woman's Press, 1911); Nellie Martel, *The Women's Vote in Australia* (London: Woman's Press, 1913). The idea of Australasia as a coherent entity lasted longer in Europe, perhaps because suffragists were less attuned to the distinctions between the former colonies than their British counterparts. See, e.g., Pierre Leroy-Beaulieu, 'L'Australie et la Nouvelle-Zélande: Les expériences sociales – le féminisme', *Revue de Deux Mondes* 136:3 (1896): 626–61; *La Femme et Le Féminisme: Collection de Livres, Périodiques etc. sur la Condition Sociale de la Femme et le Mouvement Féministe*, ed. C. V. Gerritsen and Aletta H. Jacobs (Paris: V. Giard & E. Brière, 1900), 233–4; Gino Rava, *Il Suffragio Femminile in Australasia* (Intra: Tipografia Interese, 1912).

75 CM, ARC176.53/365, Anna A. Gordon to Sheppard, 21 August 1906. Emphasis in original. See also ATL, MS-Papers-1376-01, Catt to Sheppard, 2 February 1909.

76 William Pember Reeves, *State Experiments in Australia and New Zealand*, 2 vols (London: George Allen & Unwin, 1902); W. P. Reeves, 'Attitude of New Zealand', *Empire Review* 1:1 (1901): 111.

77 *Lyttelton Times*, 8 August 1908, 13.

78 CM, ARC176.53/368, Maria Ogilvie Gordon to Sheppard, 23 June 1908.

79 Roberta Nicholls, *The Women's Parliament: The National Council of the Women of New Zealand 1896–1920* (Wellington: Victoria University Press, 1996), 75–113.

80 Scott, *How Australia Led the Way*, 48; Monica Webb, 'A colonial for the cause: Lady Stout (1858–1931), suffrage and New Zealand and an exemplar to the Empire, 1909–1914', in Hannam and Purvis, eds, *The British Women's Suffrage Campaign*, 165–8; Wright, *You Daughters*, 408.

81 *Jus Suffragi*, 15 November 1911, 25–6; *Memento of Women's Coronation Procession to Demand Votes for Women, Saturday June 17, 1911, Order of March and Descriptive*

Programme (London: Woman's Press, 1911); SLNSW, M2309/5, Vida Goldstein album of letters, autographs, and photographs, 'final Albert Hall meeting' speech notes, 1911.

82 *Daily Telegraph*, 29 July 1911, 19.

83 *Woman's Leader and the Common Cause*, 18 May 1911, 105; Harriet Mercer, 'Citizens of empire and nation: Australian women's quest for independent nationality rights 1910s–1930s', *History Australia* 13:2 (2016): 215–17.

84 Woollacott, *To Try Her Fortune*, 116–20; *Woman Voter*, 29 April 1913, 3–4.

85 *Jus Suffragi*, March 1925, 86; Imaobong D. Umoren, *Race Women Internationalists: Activist-Intellectuals and Global Freedom Struggles* (Oakland: University of California Press, 2018), 29–30.

86 Whereas the leadership and composition of the British Dominions Woman Suffrage Union had been shared fairly evenly among its members, by 1929 the British Commonwealth League had thirteen affiliate societies from Australia, twelve from Britain, two from New Zealand, and one each from its remaining members. Sumita Mukherjee, *Indian Suffragettes: Female Identities and Transnational Networks* (Oxford: Oxford University Press, 2018), 104–12; Woollacott, *To Try Her Fortune*, 129; *British Dominions Woman Suffrage Union Report of the Second (Biennial) Conference, London, 1916* (London: G. J. Parris, 1916), 5–10; *British Dominions Women Citizens' Union Report of Work 1917–1918 and of the Third (Biennial) Conference, London, 1918* (Manchester: Percy Brothers, 1918), 10–15.

87 Meeson Coates, *George Coates*, 38–40; Tickner, *The Spectacle of Women*, 16–20; Wright, *You Daughters*, 214–16, 452.

88 Scott, 'Dora Meeson Coates, Vol. I', 62–78; Catherine Speck, 'Women artists and the representation of the First World War', *Journal of Australian Studies* 23:60 (1999): 33.

89 Work like Meeson's remained popular on the Australian market, which largely eschewed modernism, well into the 1930s. John F. Williams, *The Quarantined Culture: Australian Reactions to Modernism 1913–1939* (Cambridge: Cambridge University Press, 1995), 1–14; Meeson Coates, *George Coates*, 9, 61–9, 77–8, 132, 138–41, 148, 191. See, e.g., *Catalogue of Paintings by George Coates and Dora Meeson (Mrs Coates), at the Athenaeum Art Gallery, Collins Street, July 7th to July 19th, 1913* (Prahran: Fraser & Morphet, 1913); *Exhibition of Oil Paintings, Water Colours and Etchings by Dora Meeson, Held at the Fine Art Society's Gallery, 100 Exhibition St., Melbourne, 16th July to 28th July, 1934* (Melbourne: Fine Art Society, 1934).

90 Margaret Hutchison, *Painting War: A History of Australia's First World War Art Scheme* (Melbourne: Cambridge University Press, 2019), 65, 131, 163–7; Meeson Coates, *George Coates*, 1, 86, 118, 173, 187–8; Speck, *Painting Ghosts*, 72–6.

91 Meeson Coates, *George Coates*, 148.

92 SLNSW, MLMSS2109/2/4, Dora Meeson Coates to Mary Booth, 11 May 1932; Meeson Coates, *George Coates*, 169.

93 *West Australian*, 26 September 1934, 4.

7

Circulations of Belonging: Chinese British Subjects in Australasia, 1880–1920

Kate Bagnall

Chinese missionary Timothy Fay LOIE (雷惠和, 1869–c.1940s) was naturalized in New Zealand in May 1906. Earlier that year, his wife WONG Sing Quan (1886–c.1970s) had given birth to their first child, David (雷福榮, 1906–43), at Greymouth, where they lived on the west coast of the South Island. The Rev. Alexander Don first applied for naturalization on T. F. Loie's behalf in 1902, but in the intervening period Loie had travelled to Canton, where he studied at the American Presbyterian College and met and married Wong Sing Quan in 1904, before they returned to resume his missionary work. Loie's 1902 memorial for naturalization noted that he had resided in New Zealand for five years, but his residence in Australasia stretched back to the late 1880s and would stretch forward for another two decades. Over this time, he moved between Victoria, the Northern Territory of South Australia, Victoria, New Zealand, Guangdong, New Zealand and Victoria, before returning finally to live in Hong Kong in 1924. Loie arrived in the colonies as a subject of the Qing Empire but acquired local British subjecthood for himself and his wife through his 1906 naturalization; their New Zealand-born children were British subjects by birth (see Figure 7.1).

T. F. Loie was one of the final handful of Chinese men to be naturalized in colonial Australasia. One by one, as colonies and then as new nations, Australia and New Zealand stopped naturalizing Chinese residents, a right that was not to be restored again until the 1950s. In this chapter, I consider the connected histories of nationality, naturalization and Chinese restriction, following the movement of Chinese British subjects, both naturalized and natural-born, around the Australasian colonies and back to China. Naturalization was used across the British Empire to encourage settlement of non-British migrants in the settler colonies, but, increasingly, Chinese migrants and their locally born children faced legislative and administrative impediments to their settlement in the colonies and abrogation of their rights as British subjects, despite their legal nationality. In considering nationality and naturalization alongside Chinese restriction, I contribute to the growing body of scholarship that considers how race, ethnicity and gender intersect in histories of citizenship in Australia and New Zealand.[1] As much of this work demonstrates, investigating the experiences of people who were not white men provides an opportunity to examine the limits of belonging that British subjecthood offered to colonial subjects.

Figure 7.1 'Mr T.F. Loie and Family', *c*. 1911, New Zealand Chinese Mission, 88/7/12. Image courtesy of the Presbyterian Research Centre Archives, Presbyterian Church of Aotearoa New Zealand.

This chapter focuses on questions of mobility and residence of Chinese British subjects through the example of Timothy Fay Loie, Wong Sing Quan and their New Zealand-born children. Mobility and residency rights are not the only lens through which to examine the rights of Chinese British subjects in the colonies (the franchise and social welfare are two others, for example), but they are perhaps the most significant in the late colonial and early post-Federation period under consideration, when ideas of 'White Australia' and 'White New Zealand' solidified and were enshrined in law. As Tony Ballantyne has noted, 'Mobility was racialized in stark ways: white settlers – who typically remained mobile – were engines of progress, while non-whites, but specifically Chinese, imperilled colonial development.'[2] Following the Loie family's movements, we see the different ways that Chinese people became British subjects, the different types of British subjecthood they held, and how their rights as British subjects were not equal, neither among themselves nor in comparison to white British subjects.

Timothy Fay Loie arrived in Australasia as part of the generation of Cantonese Chinese migrants who came after the initial gold-rush migrations from the 1850s to the 1870s. Chinese men arriving in the 1880s and beyond may have worked in mining, but more likely they worked as market gardeners, agricultural labourers, grocers, hawkers, cabinetmakers or laundrymen, while the small but growing number of women who arrived in the colonies largely migrated as wives, daughters and servants of merchant, storekeeping and missionary families. These migrants joined fluid Chinese communities that had, at their core, men and women who were settled in the colonies, often in cities or rural towns, and often with established families, property and businesses – what Keir Reeves has described as the 'antipodean epicentre' of Chinese immigration.[3] The period when T. F. Loie and his family lived in Australasia, from the 1880s to the 1920s, was also one of community building for Chinese in the colonies, even as the overall population figures fell (see Table 7.1).[4] The size and patterns of these Chinese communities varied, across the different colonies and across time, with each one shaped by their own particular economic, social, political and legal histories. What they had in common was that, despite these differences, colonial governments gradually came together – some enthusiastically, some more reluctantly – to exclude and restrict the rights of Chinese from the 1880s onwards.[5] The presence of Cantonese migrants and their descendants, and the connections they created across the Australasian colonies as mobile individuals and through business and family ties, prompted the circulation of racialized ideas of colonial and national belonging that conflicted with legal definitions of British subjecthood.

Following the paper trail left by the movements of the Loie family, this chapter focuses on New Zealand and Victoria, in comparison to two other Tasman colonies, New South Wales and Tasmania, as well as the Commonwealth of Australia. The legal and administrative histories of nationality, naturalization and Chinese restriction are complex and I hope that focusing on these particular jurisdictions allows for a close and considered reading of legislation alongside official archives of immigration and citizenship. Much scholarship on the history of migration and citizenship takes a national focus, yet such a focus, from either side of the Tasman, overlooks the connections that bound the colonies of Australasia together – from being part of the same imperial system of law, to the continual movement of people back and forth

Table 7.1 Chinese population of the Tasman colonies, 1881–1921

	1881	1891	1901	1911	1921
New South Wales	10 205	13 157	10 222	8 226	7 282
Male	10 141	13 048	10 063	7 942	6 903
Female	64	109	159	284	379
Victoria	11 959	8 489	6 347	4 707	3 162
Male	11 795	8 355	6 236	4 491	2 918
Female	164	134	111	216	244
Tasmania	844	939	506	427	262
Male	842	931	482	400	247
Female	2	8	24	27	15
New Zealand	5 004	4 444	2 857	2 630	3 110
Male	4 995	4 426	2 825	2 542	2 905
Female	9	18	32	88	205

Note: The figures for New South Wales, Victoria and Tasmania do not include numbers of 'half-caste Chinese', which were enumerated separately.

Source: *Official Year Book of the Commonwealth of Australia, No. 18, 1925*, Commonwealth Bureau of Census and Statistics, Melbourne, 1925, 952–3, 955; James Ng, *Windows on a Chinese Past: Volume 1*, Otago Heritage Books, Dunedin, 1993, 209–10.

across the Tasman – as well as the ways that colonial borders, not just later national ones, could impede the movements of mobile subjects within Australasia itself. As the colonies asserted greater control over their borders, it became clear that these were permeable for white British subjects, and often for white 'aliens', yet they were increasingly solid for those who were Chinese or otherwise classified as 'coloured'.

Nationality in Britain, Australasia and China

Until 1949, a person living in Australia or New Zealand was legally classified as either a 'British subject' or an 'alien' (that is, a 'non-British subject' or a 'foreigner'). It was only in the second half of the twentieth century that the *legal* concept of 'New Zealand citizen' or 'Australian citizen' formally came into being, although the terms were used in a cultural sense well before then. The categories of 'British subject' and 'alien' were seemingly binary concepts – a simple either/or – but in reality the categories were much more complex, and malleable, in terms of the citizenship rights they bestowed or denied, based on how and where British subjecthood was acquired and factors such as gender, race and original nationality. British subjecthood could be acquired by birth and acquired or lost through naturalization (voluntary or involuntary).

Birth within the dominions of the British Crown was the most common way to become a British subject, following a principle called *jus soli* (literally 'law of the soil', or birthright citizenship). In the period under discussion, therefore, anyone born within the British Empire was a British subject,[6] regardless of race or parentage, so Chinese born in British territories such as Hong Kong, the Straits Settlements and the Australasian colonies were British subjects under British law. This included the children of T. F. Loie and Wong Sing Quan. Their first baby was a son, David Fook Wing Loie, born in 1906 at Greymouth, who was followed by two daughters: Dora, born 1908, and Hannah, born 1909, also at Greymouth.[7] With their birth in a British colony, the three Loie children acquired British subject status, regardless of the fact that their parents were 'aliens'.

Natural-born British subjects retained their British subject status wherever they travelled within the empire and, strictly, it could not be taken from them, although it could be removed through naturalization by a foreign power. Naturalization – the other means of acquiring British subjecthood – was said to bestow upon a naturalized subject the same rights and privileges as a natural-born British subject, yet British subjecthood acquired through naturalization did not necessarily 'stick' to mobile subjects as they moved around the empire and around the world. Under imperial law (that is, legislation passed by the British Parliament), an alien naturalized in Britain carried their British subject status with them wherever they went, but colonial naturalization only conferred the right of naturalization within the particular colony.[8] This territorial limit meant that a Chinese subject naturalized in Victoria would be regarded as a British subject while in Victoria, but as Chinese when in Britain or another British colony; outside the British Empire they would, however, be regarded as a British subject, except in their own country of birth.

T. F. Loie and Wong Sing Quan were born in Guangdong province, China, in 1869 and 1886, as subjects of the Qing Empire. Chinese nationality had long been based on the principle of *jus sanguinis* (血統主義 *xuetong zhuyi* 'blood lineage') – that is, citizenship by descent – but it was not enshrined in law until the introduction of the Chinese Nationality Law 1909.[9] Writing in 1910, Tsai Chutang noted:

> The law is based on the principle of parentage pure and simple. A child takes the nationality of the father; but should this not be clearly determined, it follows that of the mother. It is only when the nationality of both parents is unascertainable that the principle of place of birth is resorted to.[10]

The law also declared that all Qing subjects who had become naturalized elsewhere 'without permission from the Chinese authorities' would be deemed to be Chinese still 'regardless of circumstances'.[11] After the Qing Empire fell, the Republican government introduced a new nationality law that was, in essence, the same as the earlier Qing law. From the Chinese perspective, therefore, in both the late Qing and early Republican period, Chinese nationality was seen as inalienable, not able to be given or taken away through naturalization by a foreign state; it was also inherited by the children of Chinese nationals abroad regardless of the citizenship law of their country of birth. Historian Shao Dan has noted, citing a Chinese legal scholar writing in 1909, that 'most nationality laws were established in order to include people who wanted to be naturalized, while the Chinese law was established to prevent people from denouncing their Chinese nationality'.[12]

For mobile subjects such as T. F. Loie, Wong Sing Quan and family, the differing principles and legal frameworks of nationality in China, the Australasian colonies and the British Empire more broadly meant that their legal status changed as they moved, creating contradictions and complications. From the British perspective, T. F. Loie and Wong Sing Quan both acquired local British nationality on his naturalization in 1906 but this nationality was only secure while they were in New Zealand; their children, however, were British subjects by birth wherever they went (*jus soli*). From the Chinese perspective, T. F. Loie and Wong Sing Quan remained Chinese nationals regardless of their local naturalization in New Zealand, while their children acquired Chinese nationality from their parents (*jus sanguinis*). Further complicating matters was the fact that in Australasia, legal status and racial identity were often conflated, with Chinese continuing to be viewed as 'aliens' despite their legal status as British subjects.[13] One small example of this was how, in New Zealand, the term 'race alien' was used in official statistics to describe people of non-Māori, non-European descent, including Chinese but also Indians, who were, of course, British subjects by birth.[14]

Until the introduction of the Aliens Act 1844 (UK), naturalization of foreigners in Britain and across the empire was accomplished by individual Acts of Parliament. New Zealand, which was established as a Crown Colony separate from New South Wales in 1841, passed twenty such Acts between 1844 and 1866, when the Aliens Act 1866 (NZ) was introduced. The imperial Aliens Act 1844 (UK) introduced a more straightforward, administrative form of naturalization, and this model was followed in corresponding colonial laws: in New South Wales in 1847, Tasmania in 1861, Victoria in 1863 and New Zealand in 1866. An amendment to the British Act in 1847 had clarified that the 1844 Act would not apply to the colonies – naturalization in the United Kingdom conferred British subjecthood throughout the empire (imperial naturalization), but naturalization in a colony only conferred British subjecthood in that colony (local naturalization). It was not until the early 1920s that naturalization in Australia (1920) and New Zealand (1923) conveyed imperial naturalization, following the introduction of a common code of British nationality across the empire through the British Nationality and Status of Aliens Act 1914 (UK).

At first the colonial laws closely mirrored the imperial law, but over time they were amended and localized to suit Australasian conditions as the colonies and then dominions grew increasingly independent from Britain. Colonial New Zealand enacted Aliens Acts in 1866 and 1880, and Aliens Act Amendment Acts in 1882 and 1892, which related to the naturalization of children and the fees payable for naturalization; under the 1882 and 1892 Acts, the fee was first reduced and then abolished for all applicants other than Chinese. As a dominion, New Zealand consolidated its earlier colonial Acts as the Aliens Act 1908 (NZ); then enacted two Acts relating to the revocation of naturalization in 1917 and 1920; and introduced the British Nationality and Status of Aliens (in New Zealand) Act 1923 (NZ). The 1923 Act made no prohibition on the basis of race and removed the separate fee structure for Chinese, although this was largely a moot point after 1908.

Across the Tasman, nationality and naturalization became functions of the Commonwealth of Australia after Federation in 1901. One new federal law, the Naturalization Act 1903 (Cth), which came into force from 1904, replaced the six separate colonial laws. It recognized the British subject status of those who had earlier taken naturalization in any of the six Australian colonies (which included naturalized Chinese), but prohibited the naturalization of 'aboriginal natives of Asia' and other non-white people.[15] It also limited the territorial effect of Australian naturalization. The race restriction was removed with the introduction of the Nationality Act 1920 (Cth); however, it remained Australian government policy not to naturalize Chinese until the mid-1950s.

Chinese British subjects in Australasia

By the 1880s, a significant proportion of the Chinese population in the Australasian colonies were natural-born and naturalized British subjects, made up of those born locally, those born in other British territories such as Hong Kong and the Straits Settlements, and those who had been naturalized.[16] Estimating their actual numbers is difficult due to the changing definitions of 'Chinese' used in colonial population statistics – sometimes it meant 'birthplace' (i.e. China) and sometimes it meant 'race' – but the 1911 Australian census enumerated the number of British subjects among the 'non-European races' in the country (see Table 7.2). Of the total population of 25,772 people of Chinese 'race' (including mixed-race Chinese) in Australia, 8,196 (32 per cent) were British subjects. Of these Chinese British subjects, 4,816 (18.7 per cent of total Chinese population) were British subjects by birthplace, 70 (0.3 per cent) by parentage and 3,310 (12.8 per cent) by naturalization. Of those who were naturalized, 3,261 were male and only 49 were female; however, the gender distribution was much more even among those who were British by birthplace (male = 2,679; female = 2,137). The majority (92 per cent) of those who were British by birthplace were born in Australasia (n = 4,452), with the rest being born in Hong Kong (n = 320), the Straits Settlements (n = 35), England (n - 5), and one each in British India, Ceylon, Papua and British Polynesia.[17]

If there were more than 3,000 naturalized Chinese living in Australia in 1911 – which would have included naturalized men, their wives and minor children – how many Chinese men had been naturalized over all? Historian Paul Jones's collated Australian figures for Chinese naturalized in the mainland colonies and Tasmania to 1904 come to a total of 4,885: Victoria, 2,969; New South Wales, 908; Tasmania, 592; South Australia, 284; Queensland, 110; and Western Australia, 22.[18] My own research puts the figure of Chinese naturalized in New Zealand at around 500 successful applications up to 1907.[19] James Ng has estimated that around 8,000 Chinese individuals came to New Zealand between 1871 and the turn of the twentieth century, and if this is correct, then we can estimate that around 6 per cent of Chinese arriving in colonial New Zealand became naturalized.[20] Their motivations for naturalization varied, but they largely related to the disadvantages aliens faced under the law as well as certain legal, social and political advantages for Chinese who were naturalized British subjects.

There was no automatic right of naturalization for any alien in the colonies, Chinese or otherwise – as s2 of the Aliens Act 1880 (NZ) stated: 'When any alien friend now residing in or who shall hereafter reside in New Zealand desires to be naturalized, the Governor may, if he think fit, grant to him letters of naturalization.'[21] It was well within the law then for naturalization to be delayed or denied to an individual or group, even

Table 7.2 Chinese British subjects in Australia, 1911

		British subject by			Total Chinese British subjects	Total Chinese
		Birthplace	Parentage	Naturalization		
Male Chinese	Australia	2 679	67	3 261	6 007	23 374
	NSW	914	21	1 041	1 976	8 500
	Victoria	678	28	913	1 619	4 956
	Tasmania	84	1	116	201	450
Female Chinese	Australia	2 137	3	49	2 189	2 398
	NSW	772	1	14	787	855
	Victoria	586	1	12	599	645
	Tasmania	72	–	6	78	79
Total Chinese	Australia	4 816	70	3 310	8 196	25 772
Male 'full Chinese'	Australia	1 168	65	3 259	4 492	21 856
	NSW	354	21	1 040	1 415	7 939
	Victoria	213	28	913	1 154	4491
	Tasmania	34	1	116	151	400
Female 'full Chinese'	Australia	643	3	49	695	897
	NSW	203	1	14	218	284
	Victoria	159	1	12	172	216
	Tasmania	20	–	6	26	27
Total 'full Chinese'	Australia	1 811	68	3 308	5 187	22 753
Male 'half-caste Chinese'	Australia	1 511	2	2	1 515	1 518
	NSW	560	–	1	561	561
	Victoria	465	–	–	465	465
	Tasmania	50	–	–	50	50
Female 'half-caste Chinese'	Australia	1 494	–	–	1 494	1 501
	NSW	569	–	–	569	571
	Victoria	427	–	–	427	429
	Tasmania	52	–	–	52	52
Total 'half-caste Chinese'	Australia	3 005	2	2	3 009	3 019

Source: *Census of the Commonwealth of Australia, 1911, Part VII: Non-European Races.*

if naturalization was possible by law. The administrative steps necessary for naturalization were outlined in legislation and these were broadly the same across the colonies. Legislation further outlined how records of naturalization were to be kept, in New Zealand by the Colonial Secretary, in Victoria by the Chief Secretary, and in Tasmania and New South Wales by the Supreme Court. We can follow the administrative steps outlined in law through T. F. Loie's naturalization under the Aliens Act 1880 (NZ), a process that took place between February and May 1906.

The 'alien friend' was required to present to the Governor a signed memorial that stated: his name, age, birthplace, residence, occupation and length of residence in the colony; his desire to settle in the colony; and a request that letters of naturalization be granted. The memorial was to be verified by a statutory declaration from the memorialist and accompanied by a statement by a magistrate or justice of the peace that the memorialist was known to them and was to the best of their knowledge a 'person of good repute'. Loie completed his memorial on an official printed form in October 1902, making his declaration before E. H. Carew, Stipendiary Magistrate and Justice of the Peace, at Dunedin. Carew also completed the 'certificate as to character' section of the form, and this was accompanied in Loie's application by a separate 'certificate of character' in the form of a letter from Alexander Don.

Don sent Loie's application to the Colonial Secretary in Wellington in November 1902, but due to a delay by the Colonial Secretary's Office and then Loie's departure from New Zealand to study in Canton, the application lay dormant until revived by a letter from Don in February 1906. At that point, Under-Secretary of the Colonial-Secretary's Office Hugh Pollen asked if the local Stipendiary Magistrate at Greymouth, where Loie was then living, could recommend naturalization papers be issued to Loie. W. G. K. Kenrick, SM, did so and Loie's naturalization application was then approved.

Under the Aliens Act 1880 (NZ), if the Governor agreed to grant naturalization, the memorialist had to swear an oath of allegiance and pay any required fee before the Letters of Naturalization would be issued. Loie swore his oath of allegiance before James Ring, Justice of the Peace, at Greymouth on 12 May 1906, and he paid the £1 fee in the form of 20 one-shilling stamps that were affixed to the back of his memorial. Loie's Letters of Naturalization were then prepared and signed on 20 May 1906, and sent to him via Alexander Don. A duplicate copy was 'enrolled' for safe custody in the Colonial Secretary's Office on 23 May 1906. The final step of the process was gazettal – that is, publication of a notice in the government gazette – which took place on 13 September 1906.

T. F. Loie's application for naturalization made no mention of his wife, but according to s14 of the Aliens Act 1880 (NZ), Wong Sing Quan was also 'deemed and taken to be herself naturalized, and have all the rights and privileges of a natural-born subject' through his naturalization. In this regard colonial law reflected the British Naturalization Act 1844 (UK), which provided that a foreign woman acquired British subject status through her marriage to a British subject. There was no legal provision for Wong Sing Quan to retain an independent nationality from her husband, and to my knowledge no foreign-born Chinese woman was naturalized in her own right in Australia or New Zealand in the period under discussion.

Chinese restriction and British subjecthood

Historian Rieko Karatani has argued that the British Acts of 1847 and 1870 'not only confirmed the validity of local naturalization, but they also ended up encouraging colonial governments to strengthen colonial immigration policies of their own', having provided them with 'the power to determine who, among the holders of British subjecthood, were entitled to receive citizenship rights and obligations within their territories'.[22] It was the Chinese – the largest non-white immigrant population in colonial Australasia – who primarily encountered the exclusionary powers of colonial immigration and naturalization law and policy. Together the colonies debated Chinese immigration at Colonial Conventions held in 1881 and 1887, and consequently they decided to implement (more or less) uniform measures to discourage Chinese migrants from settling, even as they criticized them for their sojourning practices; the treatment and rights of Chinese British subjects in the colonies featured in these discussions.[23] Led by New South Wales, the Tasman colonies enacted laws that placed restrictions on Chinese mobility across colonial borders, (re)introducing poll taxes and tonnage restrictions designed to limit the numbers of Chinese entering each colony. Chinese restriction laws were passed in New South Wales, Victoria and New Zealand in 1881 and tightened again in 1888; Tasmania did not introduce its Chinese Immigration Act until 1887.

The New Zealand Chinese Immigrants Act 1881 (NZ) applied to all Chinese regardless of nationality or place of birth. It introduced a poll tax of £10 and a limit of one Chinese passenger to every 10 tons of tonnage, but enabled Chinese residing in New Zealand to apply for a certificate that exempted them from paying the poll tax. Seven years later, the Chinese Immigrants Act Amendment Act 1888 raised the tonnage restriction to one Chinese passenger to every 100 tons and introduced exemptions for Chinese naturalized in New Zealand. Later, the Chinese Immigrants Act Amendment Act 1896 (NZ) raised the poll tax to £100 (the average annual male wage in New Zealand in 1896 was £84) and increased the tonnage restriction to 200 tons.[24] Alongside the immigration restriction Acts, New Zealand discouraged the settlement of Chinese through the cost of naturalization. The original Aliens Act 1866 (NZ) had stipulated an application fee of £1, which was reduced to 2 shillings and sixpence under the Aliens Act Amendment Act 1882 (NZ) and then abolished under the Aliens Act Amendment Act 1892 (NZ) – except for Chinese, for whom it was retained throughout.

T. F. Loie had first arrived in Australasia, in Victoria, in around 1887, a time when under the Chinese Act 1881 (Vic) a £10 poll tax was payable by Chinese to enter the colony. He converted to Christianity in Victoria and by mid-1889 was on his way to Port Darwin in the Northern Territory as a Chinese missionary with the Wesleyan Church. In 1888, South Australia (which administered the Northern Territory) had introduced its first legislation limiting Chinese migration to the Territory, the Chinese Immigration Restriction Act 1888 (SA), with entry by permit and according to tonnage restrictions. When Loie returned to Victoria seven years later, a new Act was in force, the Chinese Act 1890 (Vic), which allowed for special exemptions by proclamation – 'Timothy Loie Fay, of Port Darwin, Chinese Missionary' was granted such an exemption in September 1896, allowing him to land without penalty.[25] After less than a year working for the Salvation Army in Melbourne, Loie was invited by Alexander Don to take up a position with the Presbyterian Church of Otago and Southland, and so he left Victoria for New Zealand.

Loie arrived at Bluff on the SS *Talune* from Melbourne via Hobart in late August 1897. The Chinese Immigrants Act Amendment Act 1896 (NZ) had raised the poll tax to £100 and the tonnage restriction from 100 to 200 tons, but Loie was permitted to land under guarantee from the master of the SS *Talune*, who would be liable for the payment of the £100 poll tax unless permission was received from the Colonial Secretary to remit the amount due. Alexander Don requested remission of the poll tax on Loie's behalf, as he was entering New Zealand to assist Don in his missionary work, and permission was duly granted by the Governor. Loie worked with Don for the Presbyterian Church's Chinese Mission for the next five years, before leaving New Zealand for China in early 1903 to undertake studies at the American Presbyterian College in Canton. When he returned to New Zealand in November 1904, Loie was accompanied by his wife, Wong Sing Quan, who was also granted an exemption from the poll tax.[26]

While T. F. Loie's employment as a missionary smoothed his passage across colonial borders even before he was naturalized, Chinese immigration restriction laws enacted across Australasia from the 1880s onwards included various exemptions for Chinese British subjects, or for those who had been naturalized in the colony in question. These exemptions were introduced to protect the rights of natural-born and naturalized Chinese British subjects, who should have enjoyed the same rights and privileges as other subjects of the Queen. In Victoria, the Chinese Act 1881 (Vic) exempted all British subjects, while the later Chinese Immigration Restriction Act 1888 (Vic) and Chinese Act 1890 (Vic) exempted Chinese who had been naturalized in Victoria. In New Zealand, the Chinese Immigrants Act 1881 (NZ) made no exemptions for British subjects but, in the Chinese Immigrants Act Amendment Act 1888 (NZ) and the Immigration Restriction Act 1908 (NZ), the definition of 'Chinese' (to whom the Act applied) excluded Chinese naturalized in New Zealand. The New South Wales Chinese Restriction and Regulation Act 1888 was the most particular in its exemptions, separately exempting Chinese who could produce evidence of being a British subject by birth, and those who could prove they were a '*bonâ fide* holder' of a certificate of naturalization in New South Wales. Specific exemptions for Chinese British subjects were no longer included after new systems of immigration control were introduced through the Australian Immigration Restriction Act 1901 (Cth) and the New Zealand Immigration Restriction Amendment Act 1920 (NZ).

Comparatively small numbers of Chinese had applied for naturalization in the Australasian colonies until the introduction of the 1880s Chinese immigration laws. Chinese in the colonies had come to know and understand the workings of colonial law and were strategic in the ways they interacted with it, identifying and making use of legal and administrative loopholes.[27] Consequently, applications for naturalization grew dramatically after the introduction of the 1881 anti-Chinese Acts in New South Wales and Victoria. In Victoria, for example, from 1871 to 1881 (inclusive), only 91 Chinese took out letters of naturalization, but after the Chinese Act 1881 came into force, the yearly numbers grew and grew: 317 in 1882, 593 in 1883, 601 in 1884 and

1,178 in 1885. The Victorian Government then decided to issue no more letters of naturalization to Chinese 'unless a sufficient reason was assigned', with the result that 173 Chinese were naturalized in 1886, 16 in 1887 and none thereafter.[28] New South Wales went one step further, prohibiting naturalization of Chinese through its Chinese Restriction and Regulation Act 1888 (NSW), but the island colonies of Tasmania and New Zealand continued to naturalize Chinese settlers into the early years of the twentieth century.[29]

While T. F. Loie was granted naturalization in 1906, his first application for naturalization had been submitted in late 1902, five years after he went to Otago to work with Alexander Don. Don regularly interceded on behalf of Chinese in New Zealand in their dealings with the government and, in November 1902, he wrote to the Colonial Secretary requesting that Loie be granted naturalization, 'even though you have a rule not to issue Naturalization Papers to Chinese who have been less than 15 years resident in the Colony'.[30] Don acknowledged the wisdom of this practice, 'owing to the traffic in such Papers', but argued that Loie should be an exception because of his role with the Presbyterian Church. Loie's reasons for seeking naturalization were, according to Don, because he intended on marrying a New Zealand-born 'Eurasian' woman and wished 'to become by law what his intended wife is by birth, a British subject',[31] and because it would help him to assist other Chinese in their dealings with banks and 'the Customs'. With no response, Don wrote again in January 1903, noting some urgency in the request as Loie was preparing to leave New Zealand to study in Canton for eighteen months; he wrote again in May and June 1903, but by this time, Loie had left for China.[32]

Don's letters highlight a critical point in the history of Chinese naturalization in colonial Australasia – that even when by law there was no impediment to the naturalization of a Chinese settler (providing they met the qualifications and paid the required fee), in practice naturalization of Chinese was subject to the vagaries of colonial politics. As historian Nigel Murphy has detailed, after Liberal Richard Seddon became premier of New Zealand in 1893, 'the political climate immediately became much more conducive to anti-Chinese legislation', with a series of anti-Chinese bills proposed over 1894, 1895 and 1896.[33] In 1896 and again in 1897, Seddon introduced bills into Parliament that would have ended Chinese naturalization; the first of these, the Asiatic Restriction Act 1896 (NZ), was passed through Parliament but denied Royal Assent.[34] The largest number of Chinese naturalizations per year had been granted in 1894 (with 96 Chinese naturalized that year), but the annual number fell to zero in 1897 and remained under five per year until 1904 as administrative decisions were made that reflected the hardening political attitudes towards the Chinese.[35] T. F. Loie's initial application for naturalization had been delayed during that time.

The aim in prohibiting Chinese naturalization in New Zealand was primarily related to concerns about a traffic in naturalization papers, which could enable Chinese migrants to evade the poll tax by entering on papers that were not their own. There is some limited evidence of this occurring in New Zealand, as it did in Victoria and New South Wales,[36] but the cessation of Chinese naturalization in New Zealand seems to have been primarily pre-emptive. In 1908, when the New Zealand government consolidated existing immigration legislation under the Immigration Restriction Act

1908, it also decided to end the naturalization of Chinese; this was done through a decision of Cabinet on 4 February 1908. Only five Chinese were naturalized between then and 1952: Dong Chang Wai and Dong Ching, who had already been naturalized in British Columbia, Canada, in 1910; and the 'exceptional' cases of Frank Kow Kee in 1920, Kathleen Pih in 1928 and Anthony Joe in 1947.[37] In Australia, Chinese naturalization ended with the introduction of the Naturalization Act 1903 (Cth), which prohibited the naturalization of 'aboriginal natives of Asia' and other non-European races.

The Loie family left New Zealand for Melbourne in 1912, where T. F. Loie had accepted a position with the Wesleyan Church. Their entry into Australia was on a twelve-month exemption under the Immigration Restriction Act 1901–1910, granted by the Australian Minister for External Affairs. Without this exemption, they would not have been able to enter and reside in Australia. The exemption was organized by the Church, who negotiated further exemptions over the following years. When the first renewal took place in 1913, the Secretary of the Department of External Affairs, Atlee Hunt, commented that it 'must not be regarded as implying any promise of a permanent exemption', but the exemption was extended without issue every year, and in 1920 permission was also given for Wong Sing Quan's mother, Wong Wai Shong, to come to Australia on exemption.[38]

After eleven years in Australia, however, and with the children growing up and a period of furlough in Hong Kong planned, in late 1923 the Loie family sought security of their future residence. According to historian James Ng, Loie wished to return to New Zealand after the Hong Kong furlough, but the Dunedin Chinese Mission Church had insufficient funds to employ him and Alexander Don could or would not help.[39] In Australia, Rev. Alexander McCallum, President General of the Methodist Church of Australasia, wrote to the Minister for Home Affairs asking whether T. F. Loie's New Zealand Letters of Naturalization could be recognized in Australia and, as the Loie children were British subjects born in New Zealand, whether 'any rights exist for them in the way of claiming their place within the Commonwealth'.

The answer was no, of course, and being Chinese the Loie family were not eligible to be naturalized again in Australia under the Naturalization Act 1903 (Cth), despite their lengthy residence in Victoria. The request did, however, find a sympathetic ear in A. R. Peters, Secretary of the Department of Home Affairs, who advocated to the minister that the family was 'deserving of special consideration' for permanent residence, on the basis of T. F. Loie's long-standing church work and David Loie's 'rather brilliant scholastic career' in Melbourne. Peters was able to negotiate two concessions for the family – that they could be granted an exemption for three years (instead of twelve months) and that each family member could be granted their own exemption certificate, rather than one tied to T. F. Loie's employment by the Church. Writing from Hong Kong in July 1924, where he had found secure employment, David Loie stated that if they 'could get freedom of movement in Australia, we would willingly return, but if we go to Melbourne and there is nothing to look forward to ... then it would not be worth [it]'.[40] They stayed in Hong Kong.

In New Zealand and Australia in the early decades of the twentieth century, Chinese British subjects born and naturalized in Australasia used their legal nationality to negotiate their way through the opaque legal and bureaucratic systems that challenged their rights of mobility and residence based on their race. The Loie family made the decision to remain in Hong Kong, but other individuals and families in Australasia continued to push against the restrictions they faced.[41] In 1919, a landmark case in the New Zealand Supreme Court, *Joe Lum v. Attorney General*, concluded that 'local-born Chinese New Zealanders had the same rights as any other natural New Zealander, unless those rights were taken away by statute'.[42] Naturalized Chinese were exempted from the provisions of the Immigration Restriction Act 1908 (NZ), but the Act had said nothing about Chinese who were natural-born British subjects. In *Joe Lum v. Attorney General,* the Supreme Court concluded that New Zealand-born children could not be counted as Chinese within the meaning of the Act. Despite such legal and administrative victories, Chinese British subjects, both naturalized and natural-born, continued to be confronted by the necessity of applying for re-entry certificates and exemptions under New Zealand and Australian immigration legislation when they moved across national borders.

Conclusion

In 1909, in response to a question about the new Qing nationality law, Chinese Consul-General in New Zealand, Hwang Yung-liang (黃榮良) stated:

> Why Chinese wish to become British subjects passed my understanding . . . I cannot for the life of me see where they are to benefit by becoming British subjects while they are held in contempt by the people who grant them the privilege. I see no objection whatever to their becoming naturalised British subjects providing they are placed on an equality with other British subjects. Otherwise the arrangement is one-sided.[43]

What, indeed, did being 'British' mean to Chinese British subjects in Australasia? In the colonies, in the new nations of New Zealand and Australia, and across the British Empire, there was no single law that defined the results of British subjecthood. The rights of British subjects varied greatly, and the practical effects of British subjecthood were contingent on place of birth, place of domicile, means and place of acquisition, gender and race. The Loie family exemplifies these complexities. After they moved to Melbourne in 1912, T. F. Loie and Wong Sing Quan legally returned to being Chinese subjects – no longer subjects of the Qing Empire but citizens of the new Chinese Republic – while David, Dora and Hannah Loie remained British subjects. This remained the case after the family took up residence in Hong Kong from the mid-1920s. In Hong Kong, David Loie established a career as a chemist in the civil service where his British nationality and Australasian background were known and acknowledged.[44]

As John Chesterman and Brian Galligan have demonstrated in their work on the citizenship of Aboriginal Australians, being a British subject did not guarantee citizenship rights.[45] A range of laws in each jurisdiction set out the rights of subjects and, more commonly, the disabilities of aliens. Some of this legislation focused specifically on nationality, naturalization and aliens, but most concerned other parts of everyday life – travel, immigration, residence, employment, social welfare, property rights and so on. As we have seen in the story of the Loie family, it was in the interpretation and application of these laws, and in the policies and administrative decisions of ministers and bureaucrats, that the rights of Chinese British subjects were tested and clarified. Like many other Cantonese settlers, the lives of the Loie family were shaped by the racialized policing of borders and, ultimately, by hardening ideas about who 'belonged' in the young nations of Australia and New Zealand.

The value of British subjecthood for Chinese in Australasia was precarious, as they continued to be regarded as 'foreigners' and treated as 'aliens' despite their legal status, and as they faced race-based discrimination under anti-Chinese laws. Yet the legal nationality of naturalized and natural-born Chinese British subjects in Australasia allowed them certain rights of residence and mobility, as well as other rights unavailable to alien Chinese, and it provided both a legal and moral foundation for their participation in civil and political society. Significantly, British subjecthood provided Chinese with a weapon to fight against – or at the very least, to negotiate their way around – the racially discriminatory laws and policies that were so central to the governance of New Zealand and Australia over the late nineteenth and early twentieth centuries.

Notes

1   See, e.g., Helen Irving, *Citizenship, Alienage, and the Modern Constitutional State: A Gendered History* (Cambridge: Cambridge University Press, 2016); Margaret Allen, '"I am a British Subject": Indians in Australia Claiming Their Rights, 1880–1940', *History Australia* 15:3 (2018): 499–518; Harriet Mercer, 'Gender and the Myth of a White New Zealand, 1866–1928', *New Zealand Journal of History* 52:2 (2018): 23–41; Peter Prince, 'The "Chinese" Always Belonged', *History Australia* 15:3 (2018): 475–98; Rachel Bright, 'Migration, Naturalisation, and the "British" World, c.1900–1920', *History of Global Arms Transfer* 10 (2020): 27–44; Emma Bellino, 'Married Women's Nationality and the White Australia Policy, 1920–1948', *Law & History* 7:1 (2020): 166–92.

2   Tony Ballantyne, 'Mobility, Empire, Colonisation', *History Australia* 11:2 (2014): 36.

3   Keir Reeves, 'Tracking the Dragon Down Under: Chinese Cultural Connections in Gold Rush Australia and Aotearoa, New Zealand', *Graduate Journal of Asia-Pacific Studies* 3:1 (2006): 53.

4   On the creation of the Chinese community in Australia, see Mei-fen Kuo, *Making Chinese Australia: Urban Elites, Newspapers and the Formation of Chinese-Australian Identity, 1892–1912* (Clayton, Vic: Monash University Publishing, 2013).

5   The 1880s were not the first time that restrictions on Chinese in Australasia were introduced, of course. Victoria and New South Wales implemented a range of anti-Chinese measures in the late 1850s and early 1860s, most notably restrictions on Chinese immigration through the form of poll taxes and tonnage limits. By the 1870s, however, these anti-Chinese immigration laws had been repealed, and there were no limits on Chinese immigration again (other than in Queensland) until 1881.

6   Exceptions were children born to foreigners during a hostile occupation and the children of foreign ambassadors. Alexander Cockburn, *Nationality; or, The Law Relating to Subjects and Aliens Considered with a View to Further Legislation* (London: William Ridgway, 1869), 7–12.

7   Birth registrations for David Fook Wing Loie (1906/7762), Dora Loie (1908/24552) and Hannah Loie (1909/13681), Births, Deaths and Marriages, New Zealand Department of Internal Affairs.

8   Aliens Act 1847 (UK) and Naturalization Act 1870 (UK).

9   Shao Dan, 'Chinese by Definition: Nationality Law, Jus Sanguinis, and State Succession, 1909–1980', *Twentieth-Century China* 35:1 (2009): 5.

10 Tsai Chutang, 'The Chinese Nationality Law, 1909', *American Journal of International Law* 4:2 (April 1910): 407.

11 Tsai, 'The Chinese Nationality Law', 408.

12 Meng Sen, 'Lun zhong-wai guojifa xingzhi zhi butong (On the differences between Chinese and foreign nationality laws)', *Waijiao bao (Journal of Diplomacy)* 250 (10 August 1909), cited in Shao Dan, 'Chinese by Definition', 11.

13 See Peter Prince, 'Aliens in their Own Land: "Alien" and the Rule of Law in Colonial and Post-Federation Australia' (PhD thesis, Australian National University, 2015), in particular ch. 2, 'Chinese Australians: "The Stranger Within your Gates"'.

14 See, e.g., *New Zealand Official Year-Book* from 1898 to 1930, Statistics New Zealand, https://www.stats.govt.nz/indicators-and-snapshots/digitised-collections/yearbook-collection-18932012/.

15 On the Naturalization Act 1903, see Kartia Snoek, 'Empire, Race, Naturalisation: The *Naturalisation Act 1903* (Cth)', *Melbourne Historical Journal* 40:1 (2012) 103–27.

16 Peter Prince has argued that official Census records substantially underestimated the number of Chinese in Australia who were British subjects. See Peter Prince, 'The "Chinese" Always Belonged', 480–5.

17 Census of the Commonwealth of Australia, 1911, Part VII: Non-European Races.

18 Appendix II: Naturalisation Statistics, Table A, in Paul Jones, 'Alien Acts: The White Australia Policy, 1901–1939' (PhD thesis, University of Melbourne, 1998), n.p. For an analysis of the accuracy of Jones's figure for Queensland, see Kevin Wong Hoy, 'Becoming British Subjects 1879–1903: Chinese in North Queensland' (MA thesis, La Trobe University, 2006), 87–92.

19 Analysis of Colonial Secretary's Office / Department of Internal Affairs records of naturalization held in ACGO 8333 [IA1] and ACGO 8377 [IA53].

20 James Ng, 'The Sojourner Experience: The Cantonese Goldseekers in New Zealand, 1865–1901', in *Unfolding History, Evolving Identity: The Chinese in New Zealand*, ed. Manying Ip (Auckland: Auckland University Press, 2003), 8.

21 Aliens Act 1880 (NZ).

22 Rieko Karatani, *Defining British Citizenship: Empire, Commonwealth and Modern Britain* (London: Routledge, 2014), 56–7.

23 Charles A. Price, *The Great White Walls are Built: Restrictive Immigration to North America and Australasia* (Canberra: ANU Press, 1974), 190–8.

24 *New Zealand Official Year-Book 1897*, https://www3.stats.govt.nz/New_Zealand_Official_Yearbooks/1897/NZOYB_1897.html.

25 'Chinese Act 1890 Exemption', *Victoria Government Gazette*, no. 94, 11 September 1896, 3818.

26 'Rev. A Don on the Japanese', *Oamaru Mail*, 26 September 1904, 1, https://paperspast.natlib.govt.nz/newspapers/OAM19040926.2.8; Passenger list for the *Waikare*, arrived Wellington, 2 November 1904, 'New Zealand, Archives New Zealand, Passenger Lists,

1839–1973', *FamilySearch*, https://familysearch.org/ark:/61903/1:1:QJDJ-SR18. My thanks to Helen Wong for her assistance in locating this record.

27 See, e.g., Mark Finnane, '"Habeas Corpus Mongols": Chinese Litigants and the Politics of Immigration in 1888', *Australian Historical Studies* 45:2 (2014): 165–83; Kate Bagnall, '*Potter v. Minahan*: Chinese Australians, the Law and Belonging in White Australia', *History Australia* 15:3 (2018): 458–74.

28 *Victorian Year-Book, 1889–90*, vol. 1, Government Printer, Melbourne, 1891, 131–2.

29 For a discussion of this across the Australian colonies, see Price, *The Great White Walls are Built*, 198.

30 Archives NZ (Wellington): ACGO, Series 8333, Box 866, Item 23, Record 1902/4037 [R24920487].

31 Although not named in Don's letter, the woman in question was Mary Ah Hee, daughter of Yue Ah Hee and Mary Ferguson, born in Otago in 1879. According to James Ng, Don was keen on a match between Loie and Mary Ah Hee, who had gone to China with her mother and siblings in 1890. James Ng, *Windows on a Chinese Past*, vol. 3, 378 n. 32(b); Yue Henry Jackson, 'My Reminiscences, 1890–1917', Micro MSS 112, Alexander Turnbull Library, National Library of New Zealand; Birth registration for Mary Ann Eliza Ah Hee, New Zealand Births, Deaths & Marriages, 1879/10039.

32 Archives NZ (Wellington): ACGO, Series 8333, Box 866, Item 23, Record 1902/4037 [R24920487].

33 Nigel Murphy, *Guide to the Laws and Policies Relating to the Chinese in New Zealand, 1871–1997* (Wellington, NZ: New Zealand Chinese Association, 2008), 33–4.

34 Asiatic Restriction (No. 2) Bill 1896 (NZ), s16; Alien Immigration Restriction Bill 1897 (NZ), s19; Asiatic Restriction Act 1896 (60 Vic n 64) (NZ), s18.

35 For naturalization figures by year, see *New Zealand Official Year-Book*, 1893 to 1908. See Archives NZ (Wellington): ACGO, Series 8333, Box 701, Item 36, Record 1896/1922 [R24817459]; and Archives NZ (Wellington): ACGO, Series 8333, Box 995, Item 1, Record 1906/2506 [R24776159].

36 Such a traffic was known to have existed since the 1880s and it continued on into the twentieth century. See, e.g., 'Chinese Immigration', *The Age*, 3 April 1909, 4, http://nla.gov.au/nla.news-article196123226.

37 Archives NZ (Wellington): ACGO, Series 8333, Box 1517, Item 20/4/369 [R24213749]; Archives NZ (Wellington): ACGO, Series 8376, Box 14, Item 26 [R20964595].

38 National Archives of Australia (NAA): A1, 1924/24996.

39 James Ng, *Windows on a Chinese Past*, vol. 2, 340.

40 NAA: A1, 1924/24996.

41 See, e.g., Kate Bagnall, 'Anglo-Chinese and the Politics of Overseas Travel from New South Wales, 1898 to 1925', in *Chinese Australians: Politics, Engagement and Resistance*, ed. Sophie Couchman and Kate Bagnall (Leiden: Brill, 2015).

42 Murphy, 'Joe Lum v. Attorney General', 59.

43 'Chinamen Abroad', *Southland Times*, 8 April 1909, https://paperspast.natlib.govt.nz/newspapers/ST19090408.2.43.

44 See, e.g., '地下英雄的一羣', 工商晚報 *Kung Sheung Evening News*, 17 April 1947, 4. See also Mary Catherine Cheng and Patrick Chiu, 'An Interview of Mr. Mervyn David Loie, a former Chief Pharmacist at the Department of Medical and Health Services, Hong Kong', *Hong Kong Pharmaceutical Journal* 22:2 (2015): 59–61.

45 John Chesterman and Brian Galligan, *Citizens without Rights: Aborigines and Australian Citizenship* (Cambridge: Cambridge University Press, 1997). See particularly the section 'Empty Subjecthood', 79–83.

Part Three

Environmental Transformations

8

We Keep Down Our Remorse: Anthony Trollope and the Emotional Politics of Australasian Agriculture

Grace Moore

Anthony Trollope's domestic novels are notable for the great compassion shown by their narrators and, to a degree, he brings a similar empathy to the environmental aspects of his writing. Trollope understood that the use of Britain's dominions as gigantic farms to produce agricultural commodities that would circulate through the empire came at a great ecological cost. He also understood better than many the difficulties associated with transposing European farming practices to the arid and unpredictable Australian climate. In mapping the progress of settler pastoralists in Australia, Trollope charted a sequence of transformations of the landscape. Sometimes he did so with great pride, obviously impressed with the rapidity of change and 'improvement', while at others he seemed quite distraught. His empathy for farmers, settlers and some forms of wildlife did not, however, always extend to Australia's Indigenous peoples. In this chapter I shall examine the intersection of Trollope's writing about farming, land clearance and his discussions of race during his Australasian travels, paying particular attention to his time in Australia. Further, I shall argue that he returned repeatedly to this intersection in the years that followed his first trip by revisiting his two Australian novels and reconsidering the conspicuous absence of race, and empathy, from both works.

The historian Patrick Wolfe has drawn attention to the entanglement of agriculture, settler nationalism and 'elimination', and his reminder that 'invasion is a structure not an event' is key to understanding the contradictions and inconsistencies of Trollope's Australasian writing.[1] As Regenia Gagnier has noted, drawing on the work of Raymond Williams, 'Trollope's popularity among colonial readers, like Dickens before him, has a great deal to do with the way he narrativizes and makes visible structures of feeling which cloud and complicate the pursuit of material and social gain.'[2] Gagnier continues to argue, following Lydia Wevers, that 'Trollope's circulation in Australasia had everything to do with the appropriation of land'.[3] She points to the immense popularity of the novel *Orley Farm* (1861–2) in Australia and New Zealand as evidence of a settler society looking for self-validation through its reading practices, reading of characters whose lives, successes and material comforts they aspired to emulate. While I concur with Gagnier's position in relation to Trollope's domestic novels and their colonial popularity, I contend that those 'structures of feeling' become obscured and perhaps even break down in both Trollope's Australasian travelogue and fiction. The emotions that circulate freely both within and in response to those novels that evoked nostalgia in colonial settler readers are blurred in the travel writing because they are too closely tied to the feelings surrounding the structure of invasion and settlement. What ensued was writing that sometimes staged its author's conflicting emotions at some of the more confronting and unpalatable aspects of Australian colonial life, but which also revealed repressed guilt and anxiety.

Trollope twice travelled to Australia in the 1870s. He took one long trip with his wife, Rose, in 1871–2, to visit their younger son Frederic. Fred owned a sheep station, Mortray, in New South Wales, which his father had purchased for him, and then regularly subsidized. This visit, involving an eighteen-month absence from England, was largely funded by a payment of £1,250 from his publishers Chapman & Hall, who commissioned a travelogue from the author. Based on a sequence of articles Trollope wrote for the *Daily Telegraph*, *Australia and New Zealand* appeared in 1873 and was largely unrevised. That Trollope did not edit his writing extensively goes some way to account for its inconsistencies.

Trollope was, by this point in his career, a well-known travel writer, but what makes *Australia and New Zealand* stand apart from his other writings in this genre is that he also viewed the work as a guide for potential migrants. Somewhere between 80 and 100 works about Australia were published between 1840 and 1873, many of which were guides for would-be emigrants. The poet and critic Richard Hengist Horne, in an extended review of *Australia and New Zealand*, commented on the ephemerality of these handbooks, asserting that Trollope's more substantial volumes would have a significantly longer afterlife.[4] As Horne expressed it, 'the volumes of Mr. Anthony Trollope, now under examination ... are the best that have appeared on these, the most extensive and important of the British Colonies'.[5] Horne's plaudits aside, *Australia and New Zealand* received mixed reviews in England. *The British Quarterly Review* commented on the 'tact and open-mindedness' with which Trollope represented Australian settler society.[6] *The Spectator*, however, was rather less kind, remarking: 'It is not possible to read ten pages of this book without feeling what a weariness it must have been to Mr. Trollope to write it'.[7] Australian reviewers were more hostile still. The work's publication was greatly anticipated by the Australian public, and parts of it were published in many local newspapers, where they were met by great outrage from those who had previously greeted Trollope's antipodean excursion with excitement.[8] Many objected to Trollope's criticism of 'blowing', or boasting, and a large number took issue with his prediction that Australia would become independent of the Crown.

Like Trollope's other travelogues, *Australia and New Zealand* mapped a large number of environmental changes, including the impact of imported farm animals upon native flora and fauna in both countries. While industrialism was gradually pushing labourers from the land in England, the colonies seemed to offer opportunities aplenty for those with farming interests, like young Fred Trollope. Himself the son of a bankrupt farmer, Anthony Trollope knew better than many that working the land was a risk-prone venture, and it is a concern he discussed in a number of his novels. Fred, who was not academically inclined, was allowed by his parents to travel to Australia when he was 18, with the condition that he would return to England at the age of 21, to discuss his future intentions. He returned to England in 1868 and emigrated permanently the following year, purchasing the sheep station with his father's assistance, and committing wholesale to colonial life.

Fred Trollope's farm was on Wiradjuri land near Grenfell, 400 kilometres west of Sydney. Grenfell had been a gold-rush town in the 1860s, but by the time of his father's visit, agriculture had become the dominant industry, through both wheat-growing and sheep-farming. 'Mortray' – which Fred owned outright – would have been on cleared land. Trollope tells readers that his son's paddock was 'partially cleared of timber', which suggests that Fred had been extending his grazing land.[9] Fred's presence in Australia was the impetus for his father's trip, as Trollope wrote in his autobiography:

> I went to Australia chiefly in order that I might see my son among his sheep. I did see him among his sheep, and remained with him for four or five very happy weeks. He was not making money, nor has he made money since. I grieve to say that several thousands of pounds which I had squeezed out of the pockets of perhaps too liberal publishers have been lost on the venture. But I rejoice to say that this has been in no way due to any fault of his. I never knew a man work with more persistent honesty at his trade than he has done.[10]

Writing to a friend during his stay, Trollope emphasized how hard his son was working, and expressed real admiration for his efforts: 'Fred, my son here, is always on horseback and seems to me to have more troubles on his back than any human being I ever came across.'[11] Later, when the station failed, Trollope was eager to make it known that it was not for lack of hard work on Fred's part. He was sympathetic to the trials of the farmer, and understood that determination alone was not enough in a hostile, drought-ridden climate.

As might be expected from the father of a small-scale farmer, at many points in *Australia and New Zealand* Trollope takes the time to offer advice to prospective migrants with an interest in agriculture. He shows himself to be particularly sympathetic towards the free-selector, while expressing disdain for the 'pastoral autocrats with acres by the hundreds of thousands'.[12] Seeking to alert the would-be agriculturalist to some of the challenges associated with bush life, Trollope warns the aspiring migrant:

> [H]e must not expect that he will find ploughed fields. He will find forest land, covered more or less thickly with timber, – what all the world in Australia knows as bush, – and it will be his first work to clear that portion of his holding from which he intends to get his first crop.[13]

The idea of 'first work' makes the removal of trees sound all too easy, but as many accounts of the period reveal, it was hard labour. The Australian novelist Louisa Atkinson encapsulates the tribulations in her novel of 1872, *Tressa's Resolve*, when her omniscient narrator declares '[t]o clear even one acre would be the work of Herculean toil'.[14] While Atkinson is highlighting the physical effort involved in preparing the land for a European style of agriculture, the discourse surrounding land clearance that she deployed frequently masked settler efforts to clear people, as well as trees, from the same space. Although Atkinson was more expansive in her journalism about the devastating effects of clearance on *all* of the forest's inhabitants, Trollope seems to have been hesitant to engage with the term's full implications. However, some of the questions with which he approached settler society point to a sense of discomfort with the disparate emotions swirling around the structures of invasion.

Early in the travelogue, when writing of his time in Queensland, Trollope noted the animosity between settler farmers and Indigenous Australians, characterizing the two groups as 'enemies'.[15] Rejecting the notion of *terra nullius* outright, the novelist asked a question that would have been unthinkable for many of his countrymen:

> [H]ad the first English settlers any right to take the country from the black men who were its owners, and have the progressing colonists who still go westward and northward in search of fresh lands the right to drive the black men back, seeing as he does that they cannot live together. If they have no such right, – that is, if they be morally wrong to do it, – then has the whole colonizing system of Great Britain been wrong, not only in Australia, but in every portion of the globe. And had Britain abstained from colonizing under the conviction of conscientious scruples, would it have been better for the human race?[16]

These rhetorical questions would have seemed radical to many of Trollope's Victorian readers, but his answers fall short. Instead of interrogating the concerns he has raised, he falls back on justifications for Britain's occupation of Australia, which are dependent on the idea of Indigenous Australians as lacking in vigour. In a passage delineating resistance and 'battles', Trollope draws the incongruous conclusion: 'It is their fate to be abolished; and they are already vanishing.' Yet he continues, 'Nothing short of abstaining from encroaching upon their lands, – abstaining that is from taking possession of Australia could be of any service to them.'[17] The passage continues in a defensive tone, acknowledging the British invasion, yet contradictorily remarking: 'Of the Australian black man we may certainly say that he has to go.'[18] In a study of what he terms the 'proleptic elegy', Patrick Brantlinger explains the phenomenon of anticipating the demise of an entire race, noting: 'Savagery ... was frequently treated as self-extinguishing. The fantasy of auto-genocide or racial suicide is an extreme version of blaming the victim, which throughout the last three centuries has helped to rationalize or occlude the genocidal aspects of European conquest and colonization.'[19] Wolfe has identified the complexity of settler emotions surrounding this issue, observing:

> [T]he erasure of indigeneity conflicts with the assertion of settler nationalism. On the one hand, settler society required the practical elimination of the natives in order to establish itself on their territory. On the symbolic level, however, settler society subsequently sought to recuperate indigeneity in order to express its difference – and accordingly, its independence – from the mother country.[20]

Although Trollope cannot fully articulate this murderous paradox, Wolfe's incisive summary offers a partial explanation for the novelist's vacillating position on both race and the settler community's sense of entitlement to the land. At the same time, it sheds light on the novelist's frequent displacement of racial concerns onto discussions of trees.

Trollope's consideration of deforestation in *Australia and New Zealand* emphasizes the idea of trees as obstacles to the modernization that settlers have brought to the land, just as he saw Indigenous Australians as an awkward presence to be removed. The widespread felling of trees exacerbated the climate's aridity, and today it is accepted that the destruction of native vegetation since European settlement is responsible for rising temperatures and an increased number of bushfires across the country. The settler community, for the most part, was not aware of the damage it was inflicting, although there were prominent exceptions, including the botanists Ferdinand von Mueller – who warned of the need for 'judicious restraint of consumption' of forest resources – and William Woolls.[21] The farming community regarded themselves as tamers of an unruly landscape, bringing order by clearing misshapen trees and scrubland in favour of neat green fields and sheep. Trollope declared of Australia, 'she is a grazing country', and in the process seemed to align himself with pastoralists, who equated cleared land with prosperity.[22] He was, though, not entirely at ease with the process, as emerges in both the travelogue and some of his later writing.

As I have discussed elsewhere, Trollope displayed considerable discomfort in relation to the non-human victims of the relentless tree-felling.[23] While his knowledge of Australian fauna was somewhat spotty – rather perplexingly, he remarked that 'Australia is altogether deficient in sensational wild beasts' – his travel writing captured its endangerment at the hands of European settlers.[24] While known for his love of hunting, which he pursued keenly during his time down under, Trollope approached most Australian wildlife with a traveller's curiosity.[25] He also revealed deeper insights into some of the effects that settler society was having on precarious ecological and anthropological balances in the Antipodes when he wrote of native animals. Commenting on the kangaroo, Trollope observed:

> They are still very numerous in many parts of the country. I have come upon herds, in which hundreds have been congregated together; – but they are more frequently met by threes and fours. In some districts they are increasing in number, because there are no longer black men to eat them.[26]

Earlier, Trollope had written of the possum, noting that it was one of the few native animals to thrive, because it was no longer being eaten. In neither instance does he explain that the Indigenous consumers of these native animals were themselves critically endangered, as agriculturalists laid claim to the land and drove them from it.[27] While he expresses admiration for those animals able to adapt, Trollope turns discourses of acclimatization and survival of the fittest against Indigenous Australians, asserting that they are 'dying out', 'ineradicably savage' or that the arrival of settlers 'has had no tendency to civilise'.[28] In drawing once more on 'doomed race' ideology, he becomes complicit with the push to drive wildlife and people from the land in the name of modernization.

In a section entitled 'Aboriginals', Trollope compares the taking of an Indigenous life to the killing of a tiger or a snake. This comparison originates from a discussion with a man, whom the author identifies as a Member of Parliament and magistrate, who is responding to a question from Trollope about what he would do 'if stress of circumstances compelled me to shoot a black man in the bush'.[29] As Trollope reports it, his respondent suggests that spearing cattle would constitute grounds for murdering a man and concealing his death: 'He cannot be found, and he is never missed. The distant squatter, whom he attacks or whose beast he kills, knows that he must be red-handed himself, or that the black man will go unpunished.'[30] Several chapters later, Trollope adopts a similar tone when discussing another indigenous pilferer of livestock, the dingo:

> The dingo or wild dog is the squatter's direct enemy. He comes down by night from holes in the hills or out of dense scrubs, and destroys the lambs and drives the sheep. The squatter attempts to rid himself of the dingo by poison, and consequently strychnine is as common in a squatter's house as castor oil in a nursery.[31]

The passage continues with a detailed commentary on various techniques for poisoning dingoes.[32] Given the parallels that Trollope makes throughout the travelogue between Indigenous peoples and native animals, it is not too much of a stretch to draw a comparison between the extermination of dingoes as 'pests' and attempts to eradicate Indigenous peoples through the poisoning of food. Lyndall Ryan has written of instances in which settlers deliberately contaminated flour with arsenic, while Marjorie Barnard has drawn an explicit parallel between dingoes and Indigenous victims of settler poisonings.[33] As Ryan has shown, poisoning was a type of settler massacre, and perpetrators were often shielded from the consequences of their actions.[34] Trollope himself seems to conflate people and wildlife when he writes of non-native animals 'thrusting out the aboriginal creatures of the country', a phrase which might just as easily be applied to the actions of settler farmers.[35]

While travelling through Australia, Trollope was prone to take his cues on racial matters from whoever was hosting that particular leg of his visit.[36] These influences, along with the inherent contradictions of the colonial venture, go some way to account for the travelogue's vacillation between great compassion and the deepest contempt. As scholars including James Buzard and Deborah Denenholz Morse have registered, Trollope's racial politics were often unpleasant.[37] Works like *The West Indies and the Spanish Main* (1859) reveal him to be capable of the type of execrable racism that characterizes the writing of many eminent Victorian writers. Trollope falls back on the palatably romanticized notion of the natural attrition of both 'savagery' and 'wilderness' when faced with the vigour of settler society. Importantly, his pronouncements on settler–Indigenous relations in *Australia and New Zealand* were often sublimated into discussions of the natural world – a somewhat paradoxical way of thinking, given the settler community's determination to sever the connection between the land and its long-term inhabitants. In spite of his best efforts, Trollope frequently interwove issues of race, land ownership and anticipated extinction. Furthermore, while Trollope had, in previous travelogues, dispatched matters of race very swiftly, the Australian trip stuck with him. Part of that stickiness, to adopt Sara Ahmed's usage, is of course connected to the fact that his son had committed to life in the Antipodes.[38] However, Trollope also returned to the issue because Fred was, as a sheep farmer, directly implicated in the system which viewed both trees and human lives as inconveniences to be done away with.[39]

In *Australia and New Zealand*, Trollope writes of land being cleared through ringbarking, describing the process, and noting some of the itinerant characters who wandered from farm to farm killing trees so that land could be cleared for livestock. In his discussion of native fauna, he notes of the possum that 'the hollow, half dead, crumbling gum trees are full of him', casually referencing the carnage inflicted on the landscape to remove canopy for grazing.[40] Several chapters later, he returns to the issue, describing a number of road-making projects (according to his figures, more than 604 miles of road had been completed, with another 1,255 'in various states of incompletion'). As he concludes his thoughts about the roads, he continues to think about clearances and their impact upon the forests that remain:

> This travelling through the endless forest of gum-trees is very peculiar, and at first attractive. After a while it becomes monotonous in the extreme. There is a great absence of animal life. One may go all day through a pastoral country without seeing a sheep or a kangaroo. Now and again one hears the melancholy note of the magpie, or the unmelodious but cheerful gobble of the laughing jackass, and sometimes the scream of a cockatoo; but even birds are not common.[41]

This scene continues, with Trollope reflecting on his occasional meetings with swagmen and squatters. Strikingly absent from this account are Indigenous Australians, and there is an uncanny quality to this empty forest, which is soon to be no more. As Jean-François Vernay and Nathaniel O'Reilly have noted, the Australian landscape can seem most unnerving when it is represented as empty. This discomforting quality, they argue, stems from the knowledge – repressed by settler society – that the land is far from vacant. The cries of native animals and birds take on eerie characteristics, often evoking disproportionate expressions of fear, stemming from latent anxieties relating to people who might emerge from the bush. Trollope's assertions of emptiness and melancholy borrow from this settler aesthetic, while also perhaps anticipating a deeper and more lasting silence in the name of progress.[42]

Indigenous peoples are also conspicuously missing from Trollope's two Australian novels, *Harry Heathcote of Gangoil* (serialized in *The Graphic* and brutally parodied by *Melbourne Punch* in 1873 as 'Harry Hartshorn of Tinfoil, by Anthony Dollup') and his work of 1879, *John Caldigate*.[43] *Harry Heathcote* was a very personal piece of writing for Trollope, who made his affective relationship to the novella very clear when he wrote to his friend Mary Holmes, 'Harry Heathcote is my boy Frederic, or very much the same.'[44] The work is a novel of settler anxiety, in which fear of fire takes centre stage. It also, however, picks up the issue of clearance from the travelogue and revisits the scene of the ringbarked forest:

> Gangoil was surrounded by forest ... through which no path could be made without an axe, but of which the greater portions were open, without any under-wood ... which after rain would be luxuriant, but in hot weather would be scorched

down to the ground ... Immediately round the house ... about one hundred acres had been cleared ... with a few trees left here and there for ornament or shade. Further afield ... the trees had been destroyed, the run of the sap having been stopped by "ringing" the bark; but they still stood like troops of skeletons, and would stand, very ugly to look at, till they fell ... by reason of their own rottenness. There was a man always at work about the place – Boscobel he was called – whose sole business was to destroy the timber after this fashion, so that the air might get through to the grasses, and that the soil might be relieved from the burden of nurturing the forest trees.[45]

As Brett J. Stubbs has noted, ringbarking was topical in New South Wales in the 1870s, which goes some way to explain Trollope's engagement with the issue.[46] Ferdinand von Mueller referred to the practice in 1871 as the 'reckless ringing of trees', notable for its 'improvidence'.[47] While Trollope would have been sympathetic to the needs of farmers, his disdain for ringing is likely to have stemmed from the fact that it tended to be undertaken by large-scale pastoralists, rather than smallholders. Trollope had moved between a number of extremely large sheep stations on his arrival in Queensland, describing them as 'hardly typical bush residences'. These farms of two hundred thousand sheep were, for Trollope, a clear contrast to his son's smallholding of ten thousand sheep on 27,000 acres, which represented life 'in the rough' compared to the affluence of the pastoralists.[48] This comparison might explain his ambivalent attitude to ringing in *Harry Heathcote*.

The farm at Gangoil is situated within an almost impenetrable wilderness, and we can see that the clearance process is ongoing. Boscobel, the employee behind the clearances, turns out to be an appalling scoundrel, and so it is significant that Trollope chooses to make him responsible for ringbarking, rather than the hero Harry, who is distanced from it. There is something accusatory about the way in which the trees loom, 'like troops of skeletons', and their corpses stand as reminders of the deadness that settler culture was bringing to the land, in human and non-human terms. The ecocritic Barbara Holloway has gone so far as to read the trees as the 'undead', bringing together ideas of connectedness across Country to consider how deadness, or what Deborah Bird Rose has termed 'violent unmaking', extends across species and unbalances ecosystems.[49] Writing of 'funereal pines' in an 1879 cantata by Henry Kendall, she asserts that '[d]ying trees open the circumstances for recognising violence against Aboriginal peoples as well as the forest', noting that the forest of which Kendall had written had ceased to exist.[50] Holloway's reading might just as easily encompass the cleared stumps of Gangoil, and their haunting, accusatory presence in the landscape.

Susan K. Martin neatly encapsulates settler society's ambivalence towards trees, which to this day stand as markers of its impact on the land:

In Australian fiction and poetry throughout the nineteenth century, there is ambivalence around the practices of land clearing generally. Ringbarking, which was both visually evident and symbolically significant, was a locus of this ambiguity. At the centre of this ambivalence was the relationship between improvement and destruction that ringbarking represented. The alignment of forest clearing or destruction with progress, civilization of the continent, and notions of suitable labour, meant that ringbarking as part of land clearing was frequently identified as act and signifier of proper and positive behaviour, and identified with settler virtue. However, at the same time it produced a vision of destruction and loss which was lasting and difficult to ignore.[51]

The ringbarked forest is an embodiment of the structures of feeling that I argued, at the beginning of this chapter, Trollope was eliding or repressing. While there are no actual Indigenous characters in *Harry Heathcote*, the skeleton-like trees stand as markers of their absence, and point to Trollope's unresolved emotions with regard to clearance. Furthermore, there are parallels between the violent and systematic destruction of the native trees – as settlers made their way further and further across Australia – and the driving of the traditional custodians from the land. As Wolfe reminds us, 'The reproach of nomadism renders the native removable. Moreover, if the natives are not already nomadic, then the reproach can be turned into a self-fulfilling prophecy through the burning of corn or the uprooting of fruit trees.'[52] For Trollope, the feelings of guilt and anxiety which had attached themselves to Australian agriculturalism were to recur in 1875, when he returned to New South Wales to help Fred sell his farm (which was dispensed with at an enormous loss).[53] Once more, the novelist attempted to reconcile the bloodshed underlying the settler agricultural venture in his own mind, but once again he experienced difficulty in arriving at a consistent position.

As part of his second journey, Trollope wrote twenty letters, which were published in the *Liverpool Mercury* and syndicated to at least eleven other newspapers from 3 July to 13 November 1875. He wrote to the London publisher Nicholas Trübner, who negotiated their sale, 'I shall endeavour to deal chiefly with the social condition of the people among whom I found myself', although in many ways these short missives seemed to be a riposte to the critics of *Australia and New Zealand*.[54] Trollope used the letters to open up concerns from the travelogue once more, including the 'manners and mode' of the people he encountered.[55] The first Australian letters engage overtly with Trollope's critics; as he comments of his return to the state of Victoria, 'on reaching the colony again, I found myself to be regarded as rather a bad man, in having come a second time among people whom I had so grossly maligned'.[56] However, the focus shifts from his sense of being wronged, and he begins to immerse himself in his fascination with colonial wealth and productivity once more.

On one level, it is surprising that Trollope revisits the entanglement of race and agriculture when writing about his second visit. Reviewers of *Australia and New Zealand* had almost nothing to say about his representations of the traditional custodians of the land, meaning that there was no obvious external impetus for his return to the issue. Jill Felicity Durey has argued that Trollope's critics were silenced by the 'forthrightness' of his views on race. As she puts it in an article which offers an overly positive perspective on the novelist's racial politics, 'Evidently, Trollope's outspokenness on the iniquitous way in which Aboriginal peoples were treated shocked his contemporaries into silence, for no critic at that time seemed to respond to his views on the subject.'[57] Richard Hengist Horne was one of the few critics to engage with the matter, and he wrote in a tone of careless entitlement that there was 'no other occupant but the aboriginal lord of these mighty deserts, whose claims have been disposed of in the usual way', neatly evading the genocide behind the 'disposal' of Indigenous claims.[58] The *British Quarterly Review* was more direct, noting that 'his entire reference to the treatment of aboriginal races in colonies is slightly contemptuous, hard, and pagan – à la Carlyle'.[59] Trollope, however, could not leave the issue alone, and it clearly troubled him. The letters from his later visit reveal that he continued to struggle with colonial ideology and that while he sought to redress some of his earlier pronouncements, his thoughts on the interconnection of race and environment remained muddled.

The succinctness of the letter format gave Trollope less room for contradiction and counterargument than the travelogue.[60] Returning to his interest in pastoralism, he is much more explicit about the human cost of land clearance, although he draws again on the language of anticipated extinction. While he expresses regret through phrases like 'it is terrible to think of this extermination', he also presents the expansionism as 'absolutely necessary for carrying on God's purposes with the earth'.[61] In a chilling passage – which is a part of a broader musing on the merits of making colonial inroads into Papua New Guinea – Trollope remarks of Australia:

> Thousands live where only tens lived before … The earth which bore nothing is made subject to the plough. Flocks and herds are multiplied, and the seas are covered with ships. The poor wretch who has perished was an abject, idle, useless creature, hideous to our eyes, a cannibal perhaps, low in intellect, and incapable of being taught. Where the wretch was, a dozen men and women, beautiful to look at, are bringing up their children in the fear of the Lord. With this, perhaps slightly exaggerated, estimate of our glories, we keep down our remorse, and the world is peopled.[62]

The letter continues in the same vein, making arguments for an English duty to colonize and civilize the world, and asserting that, painful though the mission was, it would have been so much the worse for native peoples had other European powers taken up the task. In this respect, Trollope's position corresponds to that identified by Wolfe in his remarks on the settler equation of utility with progress. As Wolfe has observed, 'The ideological justification for the dispossession of Aborigines was that "we" could use the land better than they could, not that we had been on the land primordially and were merely returning home.'[63] Despite Trollope's insistence that 'we keep down our remorse', the novelist is not quite able to do so and concedes: '[Y]et we have to acknowledge to ourselves that in occupying these lands we commit a terrible injustice.'[64] This observation connects back to his questions at the beginning of *Australia and New Zealand* about the justification of settlement, and highlights a continuing tension between Trollope's conscience and settler ideology.

In her compelling discussion of the representation of euthanasia in Trollope's 1880 work *The Fixed Period,* Helen Lucy Blythe has argued that Trollope returned to the issue of race (here in relation to his assertions about Māori extinction) because it 'troubled' him.[65] Blythe reads *The Fixed Period* as a reworking of Trollope's earlier, unpublished work, *The New Zealander* (1856, but published posthumously). According to Blythe, by 1880 'Trollope had begun interrogating his own narrative voice and the imperial ideology it supported.'[66] I concur with Blythe's reading, and argue that the troubled feelings she identifies originated earlier, during Trollope's first voyage to Australia. To a degree, they are played out in the travelogue's pages through the narrative's conflicting and contradictory remarks about race. However, this visit was unlike any of Trollope's travels elsewhere, in that he had invested heavily in the land and the idea of settlement, both financially and emotionally. In the West Indies and other places he had visited, he could position himself as a spectator, but in Australia he was thoroughly implicated in the destructive expansionism of colonial settler culture, and he was too self-aware to be able to put the matter neatly to one side.

Australia and New Zealand was much more commercially successful than Trollope had anticipated. He had seen the work as just another migrants' guide with a short shelf life, yet its opinions circulated widely through both hemispheres, and would-be emigrants were being guided by Trollope's opinions and ideas. He wrote in his autobiography with some astonishment: 'Feeling that these volumes on Australia were dull and long, I was surprised to find that they had an extensive sale.'[67] He continued to note that the first expensive run of 2,000 copies sold out quickly, and remarked that the subsequent cheaper edition in parts had a 'considerable circulation'. His views were thus available to influence colonists, and he had to take some degree of responsibility for his pronouncements on race as they circulated more widely than he had anticipated.

Trollope was responding to a wider climate of discussions surrounding what Seeley was to term 'Greater Britain'. But he was not able to 'keep down' his own remorse in the way that his letter suggested might be possible. He may have tried to do so, by effacing Indigenous peoples from his Australian novels, but they remain visible through their absence. In his travel writing, the remorse bubbles to the surface even as he tries to repress it. Phrases like 'The land becomes ours with its fatness – and the people disappear' sound trite and hollow to the modern reader, and it is clear that Trollope is trying too hard to efface the raw memories of what has happened.[68] Absences, awkward silences, along with the sublimation of racial matters into musings on acclimatization and deforestation, leave the reader with many loose threads. What we are left with when surveying Trollope's Australian writing is a half-articulated regret that sits awkwardly alongside attempts to justify the colonial venture. His Australian writing is at odds with the emotional frankness of his domestic fiction, revealing instead the circulation of a remorse that Trollope could not repress, as structures of feeling and structures of colonization continued to conflict with one another.

Notes

1   Patrick Wolfe, 'Settler Colonialism and the Elimination of the Native', *Journal of Genocide Research* 8:4 (2006): 388.

2   Regenia Gagnier, *Literatures of Liberalization: Global Circulation and the Long Nineteenth Century* (Chamonix: Palgrave Macmillan, 2018), 96.

3   Gagnier, *Literatures of Liberalization*, 97. See also Lydia Wevers, *Reading on the Farm: Victorian Fiction and the Colonial World* (Wellington: Victoria University Press, 2010).

4	Richard Hengist Horne, 'Australia and New Zealand', *The Contemporary Review* 22 (October 1873): 699–730. Horne had himself spent an extended period in Australia, travelling there during the gold rush and not returning to England until 1869.

5	Horne, 'Australia and New Zealand', 705.

6	'Australia and New Zealand, by Anthony Trollope', *British Quarterly Review* 114 (April 1873): 529.

7	'Mr. Trollope's Australasia', *The Spectator*, 10 May 1873, 607.

8	The Sydney edition of the satirical journal *Punch* had published an effusive doggerel welcome to Trollope in October 1871, which characterizes the anticipation surrounding the visit with lines like, 'You'll find our climate hot; but then you'll find / Its warmth about our welcome, for that matter' (*Sydney Punch*, 7 October 1871, 3. With thanks to Sarah Comyn). For an extensive account of Australian reactions to the travelogue, see Nigel Starck, *The First Celebrity: Anthony Trollope's Australasian Odyssey* (Bath: Lansdown Media, 2014).

9	Anthony Trollope, *Australia and New Zealand*, 2 vols (1873; London: The Trollope Society, 2002), 1:300. Fred purchased Mortray as a going concern. The station is mentioned as early as 1851 in a newspaper advertisement for a missing horse (see 'Stolen or Strayed', *The Bathurst Free Press*, 8 February 1851, 8). The adjacent property, Pinnacle Run (which was eventually amalgamated with Mortray in 1877) was established in 1839, so it is likely that Mortray originated at around the same time. I am very grateful to Andrew Sergeant of the National Library of Australia for his generous assistance in tracing Mortray's history.

10	Anthony Trollope, *An Autobiography* (London: Folio Society, 1999), 317.

11	Anthony Trollope, *The Letters of Anthony Trollope, Volume Two, 1871–1882*, ed. N. John Hall (Palo Alto: Stanford University Press, 1983), 659.

12	Trollope, *Australia and New Zealand*, 2:142.

13	Ibid., 2:145.

14	Louisa Atkinson, *Tressa's Resolve* (1872; Canberra: Mulini Press, 2004), 47.

15	Trollope, *Australia and New Zealand*, 1:74.

16	Ibid.

17	Ibid., 1:75.

18	Ibid., 1:76.

19	Patrick Brantlinger, *Dark Vanishings: Discourses on the Extinction of Primitive Races, 1800–1930*. (Ithaca: Cornell University Press, 2003), 2.

20	Wolfe, 'Settler Colonialism and the Elimination of the Native', 389.

21	Ferdinand von Mueller, 'Forest Culture in its Relation to Industrial Pursuits: A Lecture', June 1871, 1, https://www.biodiversitylibrary.org/item/57978-ge/1/mode/1up. Von Mueller was very clear that Australian native forests required a different system of administration to those in Europe, and went so far as to suggest the need to plant more forests (7).

22	Trollope, *Australia and New Zealand*, 1:58.

23	For a discussion of Trollope and the non-human world, see Grace Moore, 'So Wild and Beautiful a World Around Him: Trollope and Antipodean Ecology', in *The Routledge Research Companion to Anthony Trollope*, ed. Deborah Denenholz Morse, Margaret Markwick and Mark W. Turner (London: Routledge, 2017).

24	Trollope, *Australia and New Zealand*, 1:187.

25	Exceptions here are his account of dingo-hunting, and his fascination with Australian kangaroo hunts in a section on Australian sports in volume two of the travelogue. For an account of Trollope's antipodean hunting activities, see Ken Gelder and Rachael

Weaver, *The Colonial Kangaroo Hunt* (Melbourne: Melbourne University Press, 2020), 67–8.

26 Trollope, *Australia and New Zealand*, 1:183.

27 For an extended discussion of Trollope's views on native animals, see Grace Moore, 'Beasts, Birds, Fishes and Reptiles: Anthony Trollope and the Australian Acclimatization Debate', in *Animals in Victorian Literature and Culture: Contexts for Criticism*, ed. Laurence W. Mazzeno and Ronald D. Morrison (London: Palgrave Macmillan, 2017), 65–82.

28 Trollope, *Australia and New Zealand*, 1:67.

29 Ibid., 1:73.

30 Ibid., 1:74.

31 Ibid., 1:188.

32 Ibid.

33 Lyndall Ryan, 'Settler Massacres on the Australian Colonial Frontier, 1836–1851', in *Theatres of Violence: Massacre, Mass Killing and Atrocity throughout History*, ed. Philip G. Dwyer and Lyndall Ryan (New York: Berghan Books, 2012), 103; Barnard is quoted in Jane Lydon and Lyndall Ryan, eds, *Remembering the Myall Creek Massacre* (Sydney: New South Books, 2018), 114.

34 Ryan, 'Settler Massacres', 103–4.

35 Trollope, *Australia and New Zealand*, 1:190.

36 Ge Tang has carefully charted how Trollope's opinions, particularly on matters of race, were swayed according to the views of his hosts, in the process accounting for the labile tone of *Australia and New Zealand*. See Ge Tang, *Travel, Emotions, and Race in Anthony Trollope's Travelogues and Fiction* (PhD thesis in progress, University of Melbourne, projected completion 2023). I have benefited from discussions of many aspects of Trollope's racial politics with Ge Tang.

37 See James Buzard, 'Portable Boundaries: Trollope, Race and Travel', *Nineteenth-Century Contexts* 32:1 (March 2010): 5–18; Buzard, 'Trollope and Travel', in *The Cambridge Companion to Anthony Trollope*, ed. Carolyn Dever and Lisa Niles (Cambridge: Cambridge University Press, 2010), 168–80; and Deborah Denenholz Morse, *Reforming Trollope: Race, Gender and Englishness in the Novels of Anthony Trollope* (Farnham: Ashgate, 2013).

38 Sara Ahmed, *The Cultural Politics of Emotion* (Edinburgh: Edinburgh University Press, 2004), particularly 89–94.

39 As Jane Lydon points out, 'In the minds of the squatters, the debate on Aboriginal rights was closely associated with the issues of land tenure and control.' Jane Lydon, '"no moral doubt . . .": Aboriginal Evidence and the Kangaroo Creek Poisoning, 1847–1849', *Aboriginal History* 20 (1996): 152.

40 Trollope, *Australia and New Zealand*, 1:187.

41 Ibid., 1:259.

42 Nathanael O'Reilly and Jean-François Vernay, 'Terror Australis Incognita?: An Introduction to Fear in Australian Literature and Film', *Antipodes* 23:1 (June 2009): 5–9. Vernay and O'Reilly cite Marcus Clarke's 'Australian Scenery' (1867) as a convincing example of the compounding of settler desolation and guilt (7).

43 Anthony Trollope, *Harry Heathcote of Gangoil: A Tale of Australian Bush Life* (London: Folio Society, 1998) and *John Caldigate* (London: Folio Society, 1995). Simon Grennan's 2015 graphic novel takes issue with this absence, inserting a subplot revolving around a Wiradjuri couple, while highlighting Caldigate's exploitation of

Australian natural resources to fund his English country estate; Greenan, *Dispossession: A Novel of Few Words* (London: Penguin Books, 2015).

44 Trollope, *Letters, Volume Two*, 693.

45 Trollope, *Harry Heathcote of Gangoil*, 6.

46 See Stubbs, 'Land Improvement or Institutionalised Destruction? The Ringbarking Controversy 1879–1884, and the Emergence of a Conservation Ethic in New South Wales', *Environment and History* 4:2 (June 1998): 145–65.

47 von Mueller, 'Forest Culture in its Relation to Industrial Pursuits: A Lecture', 9.

48 Trollope, *Australia and New Zealand*, 1:298.

49 Holloway notes that while 'tree removal was unregulated before the 1870s ... by 1884 the NSW government alone approved ring-barking of two and a half million hectares of trees, and then ... a further three million hectares by 1888' (199). See Barbara Holloway, 'Conversing with the Undead in Australian Woodlands', *Land Dialogues: Interdisciplinary Research in Dialogue with Land* 10 (2016): 196–210; and Deborah Bird Rose, *Wild Dog Dreaming: Love and Extinction* (Charlottesville: University of Virginia Press, 2011), 97.

50 Holloway, 'Conversing with the Undead in Australian Woodlands', 201.

51 Susan K. Martin, '"Tragic Ring-Barked Forests" and the "Wicked Wood": Haunting Environmental Anxiety in Late Nineteenth-Century Australian Literature', in *Victorian Environmental Nightmares*, ed. Laurence W. Mazzeno and Ronald D. Morrison (London: Palgrave Macmillan, 2019), 128.

52 Wolfe, 'Settler Colonialism and the Elimination of the Native', 396.

53 Fred subsequently worked for the New South Wales Lands Department, at first as an inspector of colonial purchases, ensuring that small farmers had satisfied the obligations associated with their land grant. For a discussion of Fred's later career, see Starck, *The First Celebrity*, 120–3. Trollope wrote in a letter to his older son Harry that Fred's foray into farming had cost him more than £4,600 (*Letters, Volume Two*, 679).

54 Trollope, *Letters, Volume Two*, 656.

55 Anthony Trollope, *The Tireless Traveler: Twenty Letters to the Liverpool Mercury* (1875; Berkeley: University of California Press, 1978), 98.

56 Ibid., 89.

57 Jill Felicity Durey, 'Modern Issues: Anthony Trollope and Australia', *Antipodes* 21:2 (December 2007): 174.

58 Horne, 'Australia and New Zealand', 707.

59 'Australia and New Zealand', *British Quarterly Review*, 529. The *BQR* is equally critical of Trollope's defence of Queensland planters, who depended on slave labour from the Pacific Islands.

60 It is understandable that, in a work as long as *Australia and New Zealand*, readers will identify inconsistencies and contradictions.

61 Trollope, *The Tireless Traveler*, 124–5.

62 Ibid., 125.

63 Wolfe, 'Settler Colonialism and the Elimination of the Native', 389.

64 Trollope, *The Tireless Traveler*, 124.

65 Helen Lucy Blythe, *The Victorian Colonial Romance with the Antipodes* (New York: Palgrave Macmillan, 2014), 161.

66 Blythe, *The Victorian Colonial Romance with the Antipodes*, 163.

67 Trollope, *An Autobiography*, 312.

68 Trollope, *The Tireless Traveler*, 124.

9

Brooch Clams and Blind Lobsters: HMS
Challenger in the Australasian Pacific, 1874–5

Gillen D'Arcy Wood

The past, wrote L. P. Hartley, is a foreign country.[1] For the global environment, the past is more like a foreign planet. This is increasingly evident in the world's oceans, which have absorbed the overwhelming majority of extra carbon emissions since industrialization. The current 'velocity' of climate change, the rate at which isotherms shift across space, is up to seven times higher on the ocean than on land.[2]

Marine life is mortally sensitive to these temperature changes. Global ocean biodiversity, prior to industrialization, had been stable for millions of years, with species distributions settled since well before the Pleistocene. Current global warming, however, threatens 'catastrophic phase shifts' in marine communities worldwide.[3] With the increasing tropicalization of temperate zones in the south-west Pacific, for example, species with narrow thermal tolerance for propagation will be forced to migrate, or be driven to extinction. A few accidental winners, like jellyfish, will thrive and accelerate homogenization of the seas. Less well appreciated is warming's scrambling effect on ocean currents. In the Australasian Pacific, weakening currents, strengthening currents and currents changing or extending their course are refashioning marine habitats, rendering them increasingly inhospitable to long-term tenants and friendly to current-driven invaders.[4]

Deep-sea mining likewise threatens marine ecosystems in the Pacific. The fantasy of ocean-floor industrialization dates back to the Victorian age – in the words of Captain Nemo: 'I'm telling you that reserves of zinc, iron, and silver exist at the bottom of the sea, and their exploitation would be eminently practicable.'[5] A century and a half later, with terrestrial reserves of industrial minerals – iron, copper, nickel, zinc and precious metals – in steep decline, serious attention has turned to the ocean floor as a new frontier for ore extraction. Dozens of exploratory licences have been issued this century for vast swathes of the south-west Pacific – a familiar neocolonial land grab, except in the deep sea.[6]

This essay revisits Victorian fascination with the undersea frontier embodied in the Challenger Expedition, 1872–6, the first global survey of ocean temperatures, depths and marine life. HMS *Challenger*, a naval vessel repurposed for oceanographic research, was the first to systematically inventory the biota of Pacific waters. With its cutting-edge systems of trawls, dredges and surveying equipment, it likewise debuted the technologies whose extractivist design leads directly to the deteriorated state of Australasian waters today: a marine environment in crisis from carbon warming, while facing the compound existential threat of industrial-scale mining.

Tracing the route of HMS *Challenger* produces an unfamiliar, biocentric map of the Australasian Pacific, an eco-historical alternative to those conventionally drawn according to the bilateral or multilateral relations between colonial dominions and later nation states. Nor did *Challenger*'s voyage adhere to well-worn maritime trade routes between and among the imperial core and its peripheries. By contrast, with its slow, meandering tour of the south-west Pacific, between ports large and small, across unfrequented seas, *Challenger* brought different coordinates for and biophysical dimensions of Australasia fleetingly into focus with its fifty volumes of published data, if only for an elite, late Victorian audience of Royal Society fellows and Admiralty bureaucrats. In our own period of rapid oceanic change, however, the *Challenger* data mass has newfound importance. It offers a vital pre-industrial baseline against which to measure the rampant bio-colonization of marine Australasia in the century and a half since *Challenger* sailed.

In the spirit of a biocentric environmental humanities – which foregrounds non-human actors in narratives of the Anthropocene – I will focus here on two creatures closely identified with the *Challenger* marine record. The celebrated *Trigonia* shell and the deep-sea lobster *Polycheles* – emblematic 'living fossils' of the Australasian Pacific – served as talking points for Victorian scientists in the epoch-defining debate over Darwinian natural selection. Today, both *Trigonia* and *Polycheles* are under threat from industrial pollution of the Pacific, thereby graduating to our own epochal discourse of Anthropocenic maritime decline. As the stories of the clam and lobster will show, the histories of colonial violence and climate change in the Pacific are intimately tied, as are the decline trajectories of land and sea in the Australasian Anthropocene.

The brooch clam . . .

In April 1827, the French exploring vessel *La Coquille* (The Shell), renamed *L'Astrolabe*, made heavy weather of her passage from the Bay of Islands in New Zealand east to Tongatapu. Armed with the charts of Cook and d'Entrecasteaux, the French commander Dumont d'Urville risked the patchwork of harbour reefs to anchor at Nuku-alofa. But the *Astrolabe* was quickly stranded. On the third day, with the ship's masts tilting towards horizontal, d'Urville passed the word for an orderly abandonment. This included nailing up the ship's weapons in the hold, to prevent his men seeking new employment as armed militia for rival Tongan chiefs, who observed the impending French disaster from their canoes alongside.[7]

The ship's company rushed to the boats, with no room permitted for possessions. This order extended to the ship's naturalists, Jean Quoy and Paul Gaimard, who had a year's worth of meticulously ordered specimen jars crammed in their cabin. After a quick conferral, the two agreed to comply with d'Urville's order, with a single exception. Secreted in his pocket, Jean Quoy brought with him a jar containing a thick-shelled clam swimming in alcohol. The shell bore distinctive ornamentation: pearly and iridescent, with curved ridge-lines diverging from a central rib, and an impressive hinge. This mollusc, called *Trigonia*, was the expedition's great scientific prize, destined for the desk of Jean-Baptiste Lamarck at the *Muséum d'histoire naturelle* in Paris. As the ship christened 'The Shell' faced submersion, her Trigonian namesake, lifted from the depths of the Tasman Sea and now floating in spirits, entered nineteenth-century scientific lore as a 'living fossil' of the Antipodes, a contested, protean symbol of the history of life.

More than a quarter-century had passed since Lamarck declared an end to shell collecting as 'a vain object of amusement'. Fossilized molluscs uncovered at sites from the suburbs of Paris to the Alps had disclosed a deep-time Earth history marked by successive inundations of the continents and the abrupt overturn of fauna. Lamarck, however, like the majority of his contemporaries, resisted the idea of catastrophic extinction events. To effectively defend against the extinction paradigm, Lamarck impressed how 'very essential' it was 'to seek out and identify living analogues to the great number of fossilized shells' now unearthed.[8] The *Trigonia* shell was among the most cosmopolitan and diverse of these in European strata, abundant throughout the Mesozoic, but with no apparent descendants beyond the abrupt end-Cretaceous event. To find a living *Trigonia* clam would sink extinction, with its uncomfortable religious and political overtones, and affirm Lamarck's 'transformist' view of the infinite adaptability of species in response to environmental stress.

Three short years after Lamarck's 1799 essay, in which he had first classified the *Trigonia*, a young naturalist named François Péron, travelling with the Baudin expedition to Australia, discovered a separated *Trigonia*-like shell on a beach at Bruny Island in south-east Tasmania. Back on board, he presented his discovery to his senior colleague, René Maugé, who was confined to his cot with dysentery. At the sight of the living *Trigonia* shell, even one half of it, the dying man burst into tears.[9] Lamarck, unsurprisingly, rushed into print to announce the existence of *Trigonia margaritacea*, which he named for its pearly lustre. 'Among the numerous conquests naturalists are making, on a daily basis, among the productions of nature,' he wrote in the museum journal, 'none is more interesting than one we held out so little hope for.'[10]

With proof that the *Trigonia*, having disappeared from northern oceans some 65 million years ago, was alive and well in the south-west Pacific, it remained only to find a complete, healthy specimen. Enter Quoy and Gaimard who, in late 1826, trawled Bass Strait and Westernport Bay across 'un vaste espace' in search of the fabled mollusc, without success. Just when hope seemed lost, on a calm night off Cape Dromedary along the New South Wales coast, the net pulled a fresh trove of clams onto the *Astrolabe*'s deck. Barely distinguishable among the heap was a single living *Trigonia*, with its distinctive iridescent purple shade on the interior of the shell.[11] This famous survivor of the Cretaceous extinction, and near-shipwreck in Tongatapu, duly arrived in Paris in early 1829.

The scallop-shelled *Trigonia* occupied the next generation of European naturalists, divided over the post-Lamarckian transformist paradigm of evolution. Louis Agassiz opened his 1840 monograph on fossil molluscs with an essay devoted to 'les trigonies'. Contra Lamarck, Agassiz interpreted the discovery of the living fossil in the Tasman Sea as proof of catastrophic overturn in biological history, not the continuity of species.

Because no *Trigonia* shell had yet been identified from the Tertiary period – *between* the late Cretaceous and the modern *Trigonia magaritacea* – it was not possible in 1840, Agassiz argued, 'to uphold the principle of the filiation of species of the same type across different geological epochs'. For Agassiz, who published his catastrophist theory of Ice Ages that same seminal year, the patchiness of the fossil record represented not gaps in modern knowledge but rather 'shocking interruptions' in the history of life itself, by which different regimes of plants and animals successively inhabited the Earth. The modern *Trigonia* clam marked an instance of a species's 'surprising return' after prior extinction.[12]

Inevitably, at least in the terms of the scientific grand narrative I am rehearsing here, Tertiary *Trigonia* deposits were soon found to fill the embarrassing gap, once again along the bridgewaters of the Pacific and Southern Oceans, in a beachside cliff face at Torquay in Victoria. Probably because the first official custodian of these new *Trigonia*, Frederick McCoy of the University of Melbourne, was a fierce opponent of the just-released *Origin of Species*, the new *Trigonia* discovery went unpublished. The Torquay fossil did, however, appear in a display case at the 1861 Melbourne Exhibition, and from there travelled to the London Exhibition of 1862, where it came to the notice of a progressive geologist named H. M. Jenkins, who duly publicized the Miocene *Trigonia subundulata* as fresh evidence of Darwin's theory of 'descent with modification'. Jenkins concludes his brief 1865 essay with reflections, common at the time, on the apparent asynchrony of northern and southern zoology – how the Jurassic period in Europe lived on in the marsupials and mussels of Australasia.[13] And with that, the *Trigonia*'s public career, as a 'living fossil', fetish object, and scientific debate point, came to an abrupt close.

A decade after the *Trigonia*'s exhibition in London, in April 1874, the pioneering ocean research vessel HMS *Challenger* sailed into view along the coast of New South Wales. *Challenger* had arrived late on the scene of southern Trigonian discoveries, claimed by the French of an earlier generation, but not too late to escape a form of ritual, crazed homage to the iconic clam. While at anchor in Sydney Harbour, the *Challenger* expended every spare moment, and precious steam power, in wholly unscientific dredging for *Trigonia* shells.[14] Everyone on board, not just the scientists, averred a sudden interest in the tedious work of dredging because, in colonial New South Wales, the ancient *Trigonia* occupied a fresh niche as a fashion accessory. The women of Sydney wore their pink shells as earrings inlaid with gold, or as 'brooch clams'. Word was there was money to be made in these pretty shells (as there is still today).

Molluscs, it was evident to the *Challenger* scientists, functioned as keystone species of the east Australian seaboard. While in Sydney, naturalist Henry Moseley made the pilgrimage to Browera Creek, a cornucopia of marine life where the Hawkesbury River meets the waters of the Pacific Ocean. Along the banks of the Browera, Moseley came across evidence of the long symbiotic history between Australians, molluscs and their shells:

> beyond the extreme beauty of its wild and rocky scenery, the Browera Creek has yet another interest; it was in old times the haunt of numerous aborigines, who lived on its banks in order to eat the oysters, mussels, and the fish. On every point

or projection ... is to be seen a vast kitchen midden or shell mound. So numerous are these heaps of refuse, and so extensive, that it has been a regular trade, at which White men have worked all their lives, to turn over the heaps and sift out the undecomposed shells, for making lime by burning them ... There is now not a single Black on the creek. Many of the mounds are very ancient, and it must have taken a very long time for such heaps to accumulate.[15]

For the source of these very large middens, Moseley cast his gaze upward to the sandstone 'shelters and low-roofed caves along the creek banks. It was in these caves or "gunyas", that the blacks used to camp, and in front of all of them, a mass of shells slopes down towards the creek.'[16] On the walls of the caves, Moseley observed ancient hand paintings, alongside more recent images of what appeared to be white man invaders in hats.

Moseley had journeyed to Browera Creek to study the unique freshwater and marine ecology – to 'sit on a gum tree and fish for sharks', as he put it. But he is more affected instead by the creek as a scene of violent displacement. He reflects with surprising candour on the abandoned shell middens as an index of the human costs of white colonialism, then nearly a century old:

> Delightful though it was at Sydney to make so many friends amongst one's countrymen, after so long a voyage from home, and to enjoy their far-famed hospitality, one could not, as a naturalist, help feeling a lurking regret that matters were not still in the same condition as in the days of Captain Cook, and the colonists replaced by the race which they have ousted and destroyed, a race far more interesting and original from an anthropological point of view.[17]

The official *Challenger* narrative excerpts Moseley's account of his visit to Browera Creek in full, with the conspicuous exception of this spasm of anti-colonial regret with which he concludes. Australia, the *Challenger* text implies, is *terra nullius* – a biotic wonderland uncomplicated by people or history. Australian molluscs, ancient and modern, are the empire's by right.

Thirty miles out of Port Jackson in June 1874, the *Challenger*, laden with profitable *Trigonia* souvenirs, met with a great boundary current, channelling volumes of tropical water southward. The entire south-western Pacific, *Challenger* ultimately determined, is characterized by this 'striking extension southward of [warm ocean] temperature'.[18] The East Australian Current (EAC) – an alternative, oceanic definition of an Australasian border – snakes all the way from Sandy Island off Queensland along the New South Wales coast, then splits in two – one branch tailing eastward to New Zealand, the other bringing residual warmth to Bass Strait north of Tasmania. The water temperature, which had been 62 degrees (°F) in the harbour, rose to above 70 in the heart of the current. When, after a 30-mile traversal, the sea surface temperature abruptly dropped, so the drag of the current vanished with it.[19] The high temperature readings of the EAC directly affected the relative wealth of the *Challenger*'s haul with the tow net and dredge. Offshore warm waters from the north, Moseley and his fellow naturalists guessed, were nutrient poor, depressing the volume and diversity of marine life, in contrast to the cooler, less turbid Harbour waters, with their molluscs in dizzying abundance.

Today, the EAC, first systematically described by the *Challenger*, is a poster child for climate change impacts on ocean circulation, and a threat to marine ecosystems along the Australian seaboard. The EAC, 'an intense, narrow, poleward boundary current', is at least 20 per cent more powerful than a half-century ago.[20] It now extends its reach southward 350 kilometres beyond its historical limit at the north-east tip of Tasmania, along the entire east coast, even bathing the south coast with warm water drawn from the faraway tropics. With the southward extension of the East Australian Current, the map of Anthropocene Australasia is expanding.

This enhanced EAC belongs to a larger oceanographic phase shift, the so-called 'spin-up' of the South Pacific gyre, which affects thermohaline circulation across the entire hemisphere.[21] With a more powerful EAC, sea levels have risen along the south-east Australian coast, and the western Tasman Sea has become a climate change 'hotspot'.[22] Waters along the Tasmanian east coast are heating *four times* faster than the global average – the hottest of hotspots in the southern hemisphere. Seasonal extreme events, so-called marine heatwaves, pose a threat to entire undersea communities. Westerly winds keep the EAC well offshore along the New South Wales and Victorian coasts, to some extent preserving coastal marine life from the current's heat and invasive biota. But the east coast of Tasmania lies in the direct path of a steroidal EAC.

In the 1980s, increasing ocean temperatures began to lay waste to the keystone kelp forests of the south-west Tasman Sea. At Bruny Island, where François Péron collected the first living *Trigonia* shell, the kelp forest is now 98 per cent vanished. This has precipitated 'vast changes' to the marine ecosystem of the Tasmanian east coast.[23] Approximately 370 different algae and 150 invertebrate species have disappeared along with the keystone seaweed, as well as three dozen native fish species.

Into this vacuum created by the kelp crisis, an invader from the north has seized the opportunity for territorial expansion. Migrating south at the rate of 160 kilometres a decade, the *Centrostephanus rodgersii*, a rapacious sea urchin with the 'ability to catastrophically overgraze seaweed beds' has transformed the ancient kelp-rich coastal reefs of the north and central Tasmanian coasts into 'barrens', an unrecognizable ecosystem characterized by impoverished reefs, invasive tropical species and drastically lowered diversity.[24] Incipient colonies of the destructive northern sea urchin have now been spotted off Tasmania's south coast. The immediate biological future of this once biodiverse region is, in a sense, utterly predictable. Faced with the twin threats of warming and new biotic aggressors, and with no attainable land mass to the south, the native inshore marine communities of the south-west Tasman Sea face mass extinction.

This includes a multitude of mollusc species. South-east Australia boasts one of the richest mollusc populations in the world, the *Trigonia* and others having radiated outward from tropical seas over tens of millions of years.[25] Geographical isolation since the final break up of Pangaea, and the creation of the polar oceans, mean that 95 per cent of Australian mollusc species are endemic. But in just fifty years, warm currents have returned to the temperate mollusc habitats of the Tasman Sea, threatening mass mortality. Warmer water depletes oxygen and raises mollusc metabolic rates to mortal levels, inhibiting growth and narrowing the window for successful propagation. More dangerous still is the increasing acidity of the ocean water, which reduces the availability of carbonate minerals for shell formation.

The death blow, conceivably, will be the demise of the caretaker kelp forests. A recent study has shown that nearshore kelp stands provide a daytime refuge from acidic waters, and potential deliverance for shell-building invertebrates in acidifying oceans.[26] Beyond this, however, today's high sea temperatures are really just the beginning. A further 3 degrees (°C) of warming is predicted by 2070, which will push almost all native marine fauna well outside their climate envelope.[27] And with coastal reef systems stripped of kelp, the indigenous marine taxa, mussels included, will have nowhere to hide.

Australian settler colonialism was approaching its first centenary when naturalist Henry Moseley reflected on the displacement of Indigenous peoples from the rich marine environs of Browera Creek. Evidence of the once thriving human community, and their place in the local ecosystem, lay in the great piles of shells at the mouth of now empty caves in the cliffside banks. Fast forward a further century and a half, and not only has the terrestrial south-east coast of Australia undergone massive, highly visible anthropogenic change – deforestation and biotic invasion most conspicuously – but the offshore habitat for endemic mussels, and thousands of other marine species, has witnessed a 'catastrophic phase shift' triggered by the decimation of its foundational kelp forests.

The close relation here between climate and colonialism – and between colonialist violence on land and sea – is worth dwelling on. Notwithstanding Moseley's regrets regarding the dispossession of native lands at Browera Creek, his vessel, HMS *Challenger*, had recently been a direct agent of just such acts of violent dispossession. In August 1868, during her career as a naval patrol ship based at the Australian station, *Challenger* was sent to the Fijian islands to 'shell villages' for the purpose of 'punishing the hostile tribes' implicated in the death of a missionary: 'it is supposed that several of the natives were killed,' reported the *Nautical Magazine* in the operation's aftermath. *Challenger* marines then raided and burnt a second village whose inhabitants had refused to vacate territory in favour of a settler. According to a report in the *Sydney Morning Herald*, the gun battle resulted in the death of an unspecified number of Fijians, in addition to a village's destruction.[28] *Challenger*'s forgotten participation in the history of colonial violence in the Pacific spotlights a more-than-symbolic connection between the extractivist work of the vessel's trawl net scouring the ocean depths and the employment of its guns and men in clearing Pacific territories of its Indigenous peoples.

As these threads of the *Challenger* story suggest, a continuum exists in the Australasian Anthropocene between terrestrial and marine realms, where impacts, albeit less visible to us, are mirrored physically. The bio-depleted ecological 'barrens' of the modern, intensively developed Australian coast mirror the undersea barrens habitat now established along its shores, from New South Wales to Tasmania. Thinking through this abbreviated historical narrative of *Trigonia* shells and rapacious sea urchins, we arrive at a view of European colonialism and anthropogenic climate change as not simply historical links in a chain, or figurations of each other, but materially belonging to a shared continuum of catastrophic environmental change. Invasion, displacement, extinction and bio-homogenization are characteristic of both the colonization of Australasia and the more recent impacts of climate change in its regional waters. Colonialism – via genocide, deforestation and bio-clearance of its domains – established a template for its own global products, which include climate change.

As for the charismatic mollusc, the *Trigonia*, which was for the Victorians proof of Darwinian continuity in the history of life (not to mention a fashionable accessory in the Australian colony), the modern variants of that attractive shell now re-emerge as figures of loss, extinction and the Anthropocene. In unnaturally heated waters off Tasmania, the once-celebrated 'living fossil' *Trigonia* is quietly disappearing from view, to be interred like its forebears in the vast midden heap of extirpated life, terrestrial and marine – a once and future fossil in the inglorious landfill of the Sixth Extinction.

The blind lobster . . .

Challenger's deadly 1868 raids were sufficiently fresh in Fijian memory that, on the ship's return in late July 1874, many fled the coast in fear of renewed violence. They 'mistook' the marine research vessel for a weaponized agent of colonial rule. The research legacy of *Challenger*'s 1874–5 tour of the Australasian Pacific is likewise double-sided. Navigating the archipelagos of south-west islands – from Tonga to Fiji, Vanuatu, Cape York and Papua New Guinea, and afterwards French Polynesia – the *Challenger* recovered a hitherto unknown marine life of stunning abundance.[29] But the same nets, trawling the ocean floor 2–3 miles down in the blue deep, also generated first evidence of the Pacific Ocean floor's great mineral wealth.

In the early twenty-first century, these twin natural endowments of the Australasian Pacific – its rich biodiversity and mineral reserves – are now staked against each other in an all-too-familiar tale of neocolonial resource exploitation. From the north coast of Papua New Guinea to the Cook Islands, multinational mining companies have acquired rights to thousands of square miles of seabed. Billions of dollars' worth of industrial metals – iron ore, copper, nickel and zinc – as well as rare and precious metals essential to high-tech and 'green' industries – sit ripe for the taking.[30]

Multinational companies have long histories in land-based resource extraction in the Pacific Islands (phosphate mining in Nauru is a devastating example). Now, with terrestrial mining reserves increasingly depleted, the deep sea represents an alluring new resource frontier. Needless to say, industrialization of the Pacific Ocean floor will devastate marine ecosystems on which Indigenous islanders depend. As we saw in the example of the *Trigonia* shell, the swift, easy pivot from terrestrial to marine exploitation exemplifies the tight analogies between land and sea in the history of Australasian colonialism past and present. Similarly, too, the current resource battle between Pacific Islander communities, with their conservationist allies, and multinationals committed to mining the south-west Pacific floor has direct connections to the 1870s *Challenger* expedition.

At two dredging stations in the harbour at Tongatapu in July 1874, the *Challenger*'s nets raised up more than 120 distinct marine species – including dozens unknown to science. Among them were original feather stars, sea urchins, molluscs, stingrays, a snake eel, colourful fusilier fish, porcelain crabs and an octopus. Subsequently, during a more-than-two-week cruise among the Fijian islands, *Challenger* naturalists identified more than 350 species of corals, crustaceans and reef-dwelling creatures, over a third new to science.

Most notably, the tour of the south-west Pacific produced a 'living fossil' from the abyssal ocean plains – the multi-clawed crustacean *Polycheles*, or blind lobster. Examples of the Mesozoic ancestor to the lobster *Polycheles* – called *Eryonidae* – had been found preserved in limestone deposits in England and Bavaria. A single living relative, fished off Sicily in the early 1860s and dubbed *Polycheles helleri*, was not widely publicized. In half-mile deep waters off the Kermadec Islands north of New Zealand, the *Challenger* trawl disgorged *Polycheles helleri*, with its signature eye orbits shrivelled to nothing. Then at Fiji, three more new species of blind lobster emerged, before *Polycheles helleri* reappeared in the Bismarck Sea north of Papua New Guinea, this time at more than a mile's depth. In addition to the charismatic red crustacean, the Bismarck Sea stations yielded an astounding cornucopia of heretofore unknown marine life: 115 distinct species of corals, invertebrates and fish, including many dozen starfish, shrimp, sea snails, flounder, goosefish and deep-sea ridgeheads. But the blind lobster *Polycheles*, now established as resident across the entire Australasian Pacific, was the most startling find of all – clear evidence of thriving marine biodiversity at depth.

One hundred and fifty years after the *Challenger*'s spectacular research cruise, the biodiverse waters of the Bismarck Sea north of Papua New Guinea are at high risk for destruction, courtesy of the first deep-sea mining licences awarded in the Australasian Pacific. In the 1970s, during research missions that marked the centenary of the *Challenger*, hydrothermal vents were discovered along volcanic arcs at multiple locations in the Pacific deep sea. The finding revolutionized modern marine biology – the vents 'support vast communities of organisms' – while also bringing the ocean floor to the attention of the mining industry and venture capital.[31]

Hydrothermal vents send plumes of superheated water from beneath the ocean floor. As the plume cools, dissolved metals in the water column bind into sulphide particles and sink to the bottom, eventually forming tall, chimney-shaped structures replete with copper, zinc, gold and silver, all at higher concentrations than terrestrial deposits.[32] These so-called massive sulphides also contain elements vital to ubiquitous products of the emerging global high-tech economy, such as smartphones, LEDs and batteries for electric vehicles. In 2011, the Papua New Guinea government licensed a Canada-based conglomerate named Nautilus Minerals, which already enjoyed prospecting rights across the south-west Pacific, to begin mining in the Bismarck Sea.

Extracting massive sulphides from the deep-sea floor involves deployment of giant, remotely operated machines to drill, suck and pump the ore deposits to an accompanying surface vessel. Natural sedimentation rates of the ocean floor are estimated at a few millimeters per 1,000 years.[33] A sulphide mining operation in the Bismarck Sea would displace more than a million tons of that sediment *per year*, creating heated, particle-dense plumes destructive of all marine life in the vicinity, including blind lobsters. Recovery time frames for mined seabed habitats are estimated in decades at best, while directly impacted sites may never meaningfully recover. Because global demand for minerals will not likely abate, the fortuitous bankruptcy of Nautilus Minerals in 2019, without having drilled a single day, might prove to be only a temporary reprieve for marine life in the Bismarck Sea, and the local communities dependent on it.

Alarmed by the catastrophic prospect of deep-sea mining, a research expedition sponsored by the French government and the University of Papua New Guinea visited the proposed drilling sites in August to October 2010 to promote recognition of the Bismarck and adjacent Solomon Seas as 'epicenter(s) of global marine diversity and a priority region for conservation'.[34] The mission's prize exhibit was a collection of blind lobsters. It identified no fewer than eight species of the famed Polychelidae – first recovered in Pacific waters by HMS *Challenger* in February 1875 – as directly threatened by the Nautilus mine. For the marine biologists on the mission, the vulnerability of these 'emblematic components of deepwater soft bottom habitats' argued for a renewed 'sense of urgency to the exploration of a unique, barely explored region up for destructive exploitation'.[35]

In a charged historical irony, this 'wild west' mining venture in the Australasian Pacific owes its original geological prospect directly to HMS *Challenger*. On their Southern Ocean approach to south-east Australia in March 1874, the *Challenger* net, trawling the seabed at a depth of 3 miles, gathered a quantity of so-called manganese nodules – mineral-rich rocks ranging in size from a marble to a potato and larger. Sliced open, the nodules revealed an astonishing visual record of marine deep time. The interior, often formed about a fossilized shark's tooth or bone fragment, contained shards of whalebone and ancient shells set in concentric circles of volcanic glass shading from light in the centre to dark at the rim.

At multiple deep-sea stations across the Pacific, *Challenger* recorded manganese nodules 'in extraordinary abundance. Over a peck of heavy, very compact oval nodules was obtained from 2750 fathoms of the 11th September [1874] . . . On the 16th September, from 2350 fathoms, the trawl brought up more than half a ton of manganese nodules which filled two small casks.'[36] In the deep ocean between Japan and the Hawai'ian islands, the *Challenger*'s haul of manganese nodules increased in frequency and size, culminating in a bumper crop in the waters of French Polynesia. Here the Penrhyn Basin – an area of 750,000 square kilometres spanning from the Cook Islands to Tahiti and north – contains manganese nodule deposits with the highest known concentrations of iron and valuable cobalt. Penrhyn Basin, accordingly, is the focus of multiple exploratory mining licences issued by the International Seabed Authority (ISA), the UN agency charged with management of the ocean floor outside national waters.[37]

These deep-sea mineral deposits, so richly available on the Pacific Ocean floor, are eons in the making, and require a stable aquatic environment to form. Dissolved metals in sea water precipitate over time around a bone, tooth or shell at the stately rate of 10 millimetres per million years. Inevitably, the industrial harvesting of manganese nodules would involve the irreversible loss of this one-time natural endowment, along with devastation of all marine biota dependent on them. The *Challenger* nodules were routinely covered in polyps and algae – even adhered to by sea squirts and worms. Likewise for greater vertebrate marine life, a 2006 study determined the manganese nodule ecosystem a unique habitat for seabed megafauna.

As with mining of hydrothermal vents, the harvesting of manganese nodules in industrial quantities requires the deployment of massive dredging equipment on the seafloor, designed to operate 24 hours a day for years on end. This churning up of millions of tons of soft sediment will not only destroy the seabed habitat itself but, through the release of sedimentary plumes into the surrounding water column – compounded by extreme light and noise pollution in the silent deeps – will decimate marine communities across the Australasian Pacific.[38] In 2016, a research team revisiting the site of an experimental manganese nodule mine from the late 1980s found a wasted seafloor devoid of marine life.[39] Like a horror image of the unique lobsters whose habitats they will destroy, these latter-day dredges of the sea floor – giant, mechanical, blind – will both fulfil the techno-extractivist logic of the *Challenger* colonial research mission, while annihilating vivid exempla of the marine record that was *Challenger's* great legacy to science.

With its sesquicentenary approaching, how should the *Challenger* mission be assessed? Inevitably, the popular science media will promote the long-rehearsed heroic narrative that casts the Challenger Expedition as a trailblazer of modern marine biology and oceanography. The fifty volumes of *Challenger* data, now digitized, speak to this achievement, as well as the self-conscious Victorian monumentality of its form and objectives. If anything is lacking from this stock narrative, it is a household name. For every layperson who has heard the *Challenger* story, a thousand know Darwin and the *Beagle*. *Challenger's* formalist 'big data' approach to marine science, at the expense of any larger, organizing speculation, explains this muted popular appeal, while also placing the burden on historians to fashion the larger world narratives its fifty volumes effectively smother.

The *Challenger's* vast empirical returns undid some fanciful strains of Victorian theory, notably of a barren deep sea, and of the southern hemisphere as living sanctuary of ancient forms of life. But while it exploded multiple myths nurtured by the Royal Society, *Challenger's* massive data trove opened new mythic trajectories for maritime colonialism and capitalization of the world's oceans. The expedition established baselines for marine chemistry and temperatures, while also operating at the vanguard of industrial economies already in the business of acidifying seas and destabilizing climate. It advanced knowledge, but also destructive, Nemo-like fantasies of the Australasian Pacific – as an inexhaustible fishery and mineral lode just now coming within reach of neocolonial extractive technologies. In that sense, *Challenger* offers a tricky double legacy. Its fifty volumes represent both foundational texts of modern marine science, without which the ocean conservation movement could not exist, and a mining prospectus for Nautilus Minerals Inc.

Notes

1   L. P. Hartley, *The Go-Between* (London: Hamish Hamilton, 1953), 9.
2   Malin Pinksy et al., 'Marine Taxa Track Local Climate Velocities', *Science* 341: 6151 (2013): 1240.
3   Craig R. Johnson et al., 'Climate change cascades: Shifts in oceanography, species' ranges and subtidal marine community dynamics in eastern Tasmania', *Journal of Experimental Marine Biology and Ecology* 400:1 (2011): 17–32.

4　Laura J. Wilson et al., 'Climate-Driven Changes to Ocean Circulation and their Inferred Impacts on Marine Dispersal Patterns', *Global Ecology and Biogeography* 25:8 (2016): 923–39.

5　Jules Verne, *Vingt milles lieue sous les mers* (Paris: J. Hetzel, 1871), 84.

6　L. M. Wedding et al., 'Managing mining of the deep seabed', *Science* 349:6244 (2015): 144.

7　Jules-Sébastien-César Dumont d'Urville, *Voyage de la corvette l'Astrolabe . . . pendant les années 1826, 1827, 1828, 1829*, 5 vols (Paris: J. Tatsu, 1830–4), 4:10–52.

8　Jean-Baptiste Lamarck, 'Prodrome d'une Nouvelle Classification des Coquilles', *Mémoires de la Societé Histoire Naturelle de Paris* 1 (1799): 63.

9　François Péron, *Voyage de découvertes aux terres Australes . . . pendant les années 1800, 1801, 1802, 1803 et 1804* (Paris: De L'Imprimerie Impériale, 1807), 1:240.

10　Jean Baptiste Lamarck, 'Sur une Nouvelle Espèce de Trigonie . . .', *Annales du Muséum d'histoire naturelle* 4 (1804): 551.

11　D'Urville, *Voyage de la corvette l'Astrolabe*, 3:475.

12　Louis Agassiz, *Etudes Critiques sur les Mollusques Fossiles* (1840, New York: Arno Press, 1980), 3.

13　H. M. Jenkins, 'On the Occurrence of a Tertiary Species of Trigonia in Australia', *Quarterly Journal of Science* 2 (1865): 362–4.

14　H. N. Moseley, *Notes by a Naturalist: An Account of Observations Made during the Voyage of HMS Challenger Round the World in the Years 1872–1876* (London: John Murray, 1892), 239.

15　Moseley, *Notes by a Naturalist*, 236.

16　Ibid., 237.

17　Ibid., 239.

18　Alexander Buchan, 'Report on Oceanic Circulation', in *Report on the Scientific Results of the Voyage of H.M.S. Challenger during the years 1872–76: A Summary of the Scientific Results, Second Part* [Appendix] (London: Sir C. Wyville Thomson and John Murray, 1895), 15.

19　C. Wyville Thomson and John Murray, eds, *Report on the Scientific Results of the Voyage of HMS Challenger during the years 1873–6*, 2 vols (London: Longmans & Co, 1885), 1:464.

20　K. R. Ridgway and J. R. Dunn, 'Observational Evidence for a Southern Hemisphere Oceanic Supergyre', *Geophysical Research Letters* 34:13 (2007): L13612 [p. 4].

21　D. Roemmich et al., 'Decadal Spinup of the South Pacific Subtropical Gyre', *Journal of Physical Oceanography* 37:2 (2007): 162.

22　E. C. J. Oliver et al., 'Projected Tasman Sea Extremes in Sea Surface Temperature through the Twenty-First Century', *Journal of Climate* 27:5 (2014): 1980.

23　S. D. Ling, 'Range expansion of a habitat-modifying species leads to loss of taxonomic diversity: a new and impoverished reef state', *Oecologia* 156:4 (2008): 891.

24　S. D. Ling, 'Climate-Driven Range Extension of a Sea Urchin: Inferring Future Trends by Analysis of Recent Population Dynamics', *Global Change Biology* 15:3 (2009): 720.

25　J. Alistair Crame, 'Evolution of Taxonomic Diversity Gradients in the Marine Realm: Evidence from the Composition of Recent Bivalve Faunas', *Paleobiology* 26:2 (2000): 188–214.

26　M. Wahl et al., 'Macroalgae May Mitigate Ocean Acidification Effects on Mussel Calcification by Increasing pH and its Fluctuations', *Limnology and Oceanography* 63:1 (2018): 3–21.

27 Tan Kar Soon and Juaiping Zheng, 'Climate Change and Bivalve Mass Mortality in Temperate Regions' in *Reviews of Environmental Contamination and Toxicology. Volume 251*, ed. P. de Voogt (Cham: Springer, 2019), 112.

28 'Visit of H.M.S. Challenger to Fiji', *Sydney Morning Herald*, 9 September 1868.

29 Thomson and Murray, *Report on the Scientific Results of the Voyage of HMS Challenger*, 1:474–541, 696–800.

30 Wedding et al., 'Managing mining of the deep seabed', 144–5.

31 Kathryn A. Miller et al., 'An Overview of Seabed Mining Including the Current State of Development, Environmental Impacts, and Knowledge Gaps', *Frontiers in Marine Science* 4 (2018): 3.

32 *World Ocean Review 3: Marine Resources, Opportunities and Risks* (Hamburg, 2014), 82–93.

33 Miller et al., 'An Overview of Seabed Mining', 9, 15.

34 Bella S. Galil, 'On a collection of Polychelidae from Papua New Guinea (Crustacea, Decapoda, Polychelida)', *Zoosystema* 35:4 (2013): 496.

35 Galil, 'On a collection of Polychelidae from Papua New Guinea', 495.

36 Thomson and Murray, *Report on the Scientific Results of the Voyage of HMS Challenger*, 1:774–5.

37 *World Ocean Review 3: Marine Resources, Opportunities and Risks*, 66–73.

38 Miller et al., 'An Overview of Seabed Mining', 15.

39 Ann Vanreusel et al., 'Threatened by mining, polymetallic nodules are required to preserve abyssal epifauna', *Scientific Reports* 6:1 (2016).

10

Gorse is People

Thomas McLean

In his 2008 essay, 'The Unlikely Redemption of Gorse', Chris Orsman suggests that kōwhai, a native tree, and gorse, 'this hardy colonial', might together become Aotearoa New Zealand's national flowers.[1] Orsman's suggestion might seem facetious: while both gorse and kōwhai produce attractive yellow flowers, and both can be found across New Zealand, the similarities end there. Kōwhai are popular natives whose distinctive bell-shaped flowers are a favourite of gardeners and artists. They provide an important food source for indigenous birds, and Māori have traditionally valued their medicinal properties. Today, new citizens often receive a young kōwhai as a sign of welcome. Gorse, by contrast, is considered one of New Zealand's worst introduced pests, a shrub covered in inch-long thorns with pods that explode in summer heat, hurling seeds five metres from the parent plant. Once established, gorse is almost impossible to remove: its seeds can lie dormant in the earth for thirty years, and it is often the first and least welcome plant to reappear after fire.

Yet there is some value in Orsman's suggestion. If New Zealand's gardeners continue to dread gorse, its farmers once welcomed it, and its artists and writers have celebrated gorse's scent and colour for more than a century. Katherine Mansfield, in her early poem 'Vignette – Through the Autumn Afternoon', describes a desire to escape 'out of the city streets and on to the gorse golden hills', from where the whole city and harbour seem to resemble 'golden beckoning flowers'.[2] Many New Zealanders have followed Mansfield in seeing gorse as a memorable and perhaps even essential element of the New Zealand landscape. More recently, artists and writers, including Orsman, have called attention to gorse's capacity to aid the growth of native plants.

Orsman's essay is a recent addition to a little-known and even less studied vein of British and New Zealand literature. In the nineteenth century, references to the thorny evergreen shrub known as whin, furze or gorse proliferated in British and Irish literature, much as the plant was proliferating in distant corners of the British Empire. Gorse is common in Britain, where it was long burned in fires and used as a farmland hedge and shelter. Imported to Australasia to serve as a natural border, gorse spread rapidly into hills and cleared fields, transforming landscapes across New Zealand, Tasmania and southern Australia. It remains a visual marker of settler culture in both countries, thus representing one of colonization's more unruly circulations.

Gorse has also left its mark on New Zealand's literature and art. If, in the nineteenth century, gorse was a literary symbol of settler ascendancy, its appearance in twentieth-century New Zealand culture more often intimated youth, wild possibilities and a nostalgia for such ideas. More recently, as gorse's attributes have been better understood, and as Pākehā (New Zealanders of European descent) have recognized the impact of introduced species on native flora and fauna, gorse has taken on a more ambivalent presence.

This essay considers the history of gorse in the literary and visual imaginations of Britain and New Zealand, examining its changing representation over the past two hundred years. While most literary scholars will immediately think of the Egdon Heath landscape in Thomas Hardy's 1878 novel *The Return of the Native*, gorse (often under its more popular Victorian name, furze) finds its way into a wide variety of works and landscapes. More importantly, its meanings go far beyond the desolate landscapes of Hardy's imagination. My argument traces gorse's arrival from the old world to the new, mapping its unanticipated, rapid spread across the New Zealand landscape, and its transformation from a useful boundary-marker to overgrown invader. In the final section, I turn to Dan Davin's collection *The Gorse Blooms Pale*, Janet Frame's short story 'Gorse is not People' and a body of works by the sculptor Peter Nicholls. If Davin and Frame find an untamed, Romantic wildness in the spiky shrub, Nicholls suggests a different way forward, informed by New Zealand's complex history and new insights on gorse's environmental possibilities.

*   *   *

The genus Ulex encompasses about twenty species of thorny evergreen shrubs. Its most familiar species, *Ulex europaeus*, is known by three different names which, according to the *Oxford English Dictionary*, appeared over some seven centuries: gorse (c.725), furze (c.888) and whin (c.1400). Gorse's long blooming season inspired an aphorism first recorded in Middle English:

> Whanne bloweþ þe brom
> þanne wogeþ þe grom
> whanne bloweþ þe furs
> þanne wogeþ wurs

which might be translated as 'When flowers the broom / then woos the groom / when flowers the furze / then woos he worse' (broom is a European shrub sometimes confused with gorse; it has similar yellow flowers but no thorns). Variants popular since the nineteenth century include 'When the furze is in bloom, my love's in tune', and 'When the gorse is out of bloom, kissing's out of fashion'.[3] All of these expressions suggest that the yellow flowers of gorse (and broom) are, like love, almost always observable. The medieval aphorism probably reflects the long flowering periods of both shrubs, along with the fact that several varieties of gorse bloom at different times in Britain. But the expression has taken on a new meaning in New Zealand, where *Ulex europaeus* often blooms twice per year.

There seems to have been some confusion as to whether gorse, furze and whin named separate shrubs. In Shakespeare's *The Tempest* (1623), Ariel describes to Prospero the fate of Caliban, Trinculo and Stephano:

so I charmed their ears
That calf-like they my lowing followed, through
Toothed briars, sharp furzes, pricking gorse and thorns,
Which entered their frail shins.[4]

By the eighteenth century, there was clearer consensus, especially after Carl Linnaeus, who visited England in 1736, identified the thorny shrub as a single species. Which name to use remained unclear. All three appear in Samuel Johnson's *Dictionary* (1755) as defining the same shrub: furze comes first alphabetically and receives the lengthiest definition and the most examples. For the adjective 'furzy', Johnson quotes from John Gay's 'Rural Sports', which calls attention to the dangers faced by hounds who pursue their prey into gorse-covered hovels: 'Wide through the furzy field their rout they take, / Their bleeding bosoms force the thorny brake'.[5]

The thorny shrub appears occasionally in British Romantic literature. Robert Burns anticipates its later presence in Victorian Gothic texts when he describes Tam o' Shanter approaching Kirk Alloway: 'And thro' the whins, and by the cairn, / Whare hunters fand the murder'd bairn'.[6] Wordsworth notes the 'hanging islands of resplendent furze' in 'It was an April Morning', while in 'The Idiot Boy', the searchers can find 'neither Johnny nor his horse' while out on his midnight ride 'Among the fern or in the gorse'.[7] In the opening description from 'The Ruined Cottage', the narrator registers 'the tedious noise' in summer 'Of seeds of bursting gorse that crackled round'.[8] It appears most memorably in Samuel Taylor Coleridge's conversation poem, 'Fears in Solitude', which opens with a description of heathy hills, covered in part 'with the never-bloomless furze'. In the poem's final passage, its scent brings the narrator back to the present moment: 'But now the gentle dew-fall sends abroad / The fruit-like perfume of the golden furze'.[9]

Gorse assumes an even greater presence in the Victorian era. Under its various names, but most often as furze, it appears in Victorian literature as a symbol of uncultivated, hardscrabble life. Its most memorable appearances call attention to the shrub's thorniness; indeed, it seems a favourite of Gothic texts. In Emily Brontë's *Wuthering Heights* (1847), Catherine warns Isabella that Heathcliff is 'an arid wilderness of furze and whinstone'.[10] Catherine is really only lightly revising the housekeeper Nelly's earlier description of Heathcliff as 'Rough as a saw-edge, and hard as whinstone!'[11] In Christina Rossetti's 'Goblin Market' (1862), Lizzie hurries from her encounter with the Goblin men:

In a smart, ache, tingle,
Lizzie went her way;
Knew not was it night or day;
Sprang up the bank, tore thro' the furze,
Threaded copse and dingle,
And heard her penny jingle
Bouncing in her purse, –

Lizzie's mission to save her sister Laura becomes a little more heroic (and painful) via the furze, which also adds a double meaning to 'tore': Lizzy rends both the shrub and herself. It also chimes nicely with the story's other gold, the one bouncing in her purse.[12] At century's end, in Bram Stoker's *Dracula* (1897), a newspaper reports that 'another child, missed last night, was only discovered late in the morning under a furze bush' in Hampstead Heath. Nature seems to provide a foreboding contrast and cover for the unnatural 'tiny wound' that appears on the young victim's throat.[13]

Surely the British writer most associated with furze was Thomas Hardy. There are passing references to furze in a number of Hardy's novels and stories, though its most notable appearance – in Hardy and in British Victorian literature – occurs in *The Return of the Native* (1878). In one of the most famous openings in Victorian literature, Hardy describes the gloomy landscape of Egdon Heath – a 'heathy, furzy, briary wilderness' – as hilltop fires light up the Fifth of November night sky.[14] The boys and men carry furze branches, cut and collected for the fire, 'upon the shoulder by means of a long stake sharpened at each end for impaling them easily – two in front and two behind'.[15] In Hardy's description, the carriers are transformed into a moving furze forest: 'Every individual was so involved in furze by his method of carrying the faggots that he appeared like a bush on legs till he had thrown them down.'[16] Hardy is clearly aware of the labour of such work; he describes the furze-cutter Humphrey as 'a somewhat solemn young fellow' who 'carried the hook and leather gloves of a furze-cutter, his legs, by reason of that occupation, being sheathed in bulging leggings as stiff as the Philistine's [i.e. Goliath's] greaves of brass'.[17] Later, when the protagonist Clym Yeobright becomes a furze-cutter, he borrows from Humphrey 'leggings, gloves, a whetstone, and a hook', working 'from four o'clock in the morning'.[18] It is Clym's utter exhaustion after furze-cutting that precipitates his mother's death and much of the ensuing tragedy.

While Hardy's evocation of the land is often celebrated for its literary pyrotechnics, his presentation of Wessex (or Dorset) heathlands is misleading. His narrator describes a landscape where 'everything around and underneath had been from prehistoric times as unaltered as the stars overhead'.[19] While such a setting provides a powerful objective correlative for the trapped, fated lives of Hardy's protagonists, it does little justice to natural reality. In fact, a heathland is a delicate ecosystem that depends on a high degree of human involvement. As John MacNeill Miller has recently shown, Charles Darwin had written on the fragility of British heathlands in *The Origin of Species* (1859), some two decades before Hardy's novel. Examining the Surrey heathlands, Darwin realized that the landscape depended on the presence of cattle to browse tree seedlings so that they never grow high enough to shade (and therefore kill) the heath around them. 'Darwin,' writes Miller, 'leaves unsaid what contemporary readers could easily infer: cattle are human introductions to such landscapes, so these apparently timeless heaths owe their continued existence to agricultural and pastoral practices.'[20]

Hardy's dark vision of Egdon Heath also depends on his denial of some of the sensory impressions of gorse. His narrator is keen to call attention to touch as well as sound: he tells us that women's 'skirts were scratched noisily by the furze'.[21] But the colour and smell of gorse are hardly noted. Only once are we told that Clym's preferred flowers were 'the purple bells and yellow furze'.[22] In the same passage, we learn that Clym was 'permeated' with the 'odours' of the heath, but those odours are never fully described.

This might seem pedantic, save for the fact that many of Hardy's contemporaries were celebrating just those aspects of gorse in their writings. In R. D. Blackmore's *Lorna Doone* (1869), a book that Hardy had read with pleasure in 1875, Lorna exults in her return to Exmoor, telling her soon-to-be in-laws, 'the scent of the gorse on the moors drove me wild'.[23] In his poem 'Gorse', Irish poet William Allingham revels in how the plant 'Harbours the wren, the furzeling, and the coney'.[24] In Alfred Tennyson's *In Memoriam* (1850), the narrator notes the 'Calm and deep peace on this high wold, / And on these dews that drench the furze, / And all the silvery gossamers / That twinkle into green and gold'.[25] John Everett Millais reimagined Tennyson's lines in his painting *Dew-Drenched Furze* (1889–90), and the eagle-eyed viewer will spot a pheasant finding refuge under the thorny branches. 'I sit like a miser,' writes Katherine Tynan in her poem 'Gorse', where the flower's smell and golden colour become symbols of a natural wealth: 'Miles on miles of the golden cups and the nutty wine'.[26]

There is a whole subset of literary works that focus on one gorse-related anecdote: Linnaeus's supposed encounter with gorse in Britain. *The Cornhill Magazine* in March 1894 puts it thus: 'When "the great and good Linnaeus" first saw gorse in blossom on Wimbledon Common, he fell on his knees, says the veracious legend, and thanked God audibly then and there for having created so glorious and unique a combination of colour and perfume'.[27] While it is true that gorse does not grow in colder climates like Scandinavia, and it would have thus been a sight of interest to the eighteenth-century visitor, the anecdote is almost certainly spurious.[28] But this did not stop Allingham from mentioning it in 'Gorse', or Oscar Wilde from recounting the story in *De Profundis*,[29] or Elizabeth Barrett Browning from celebrating the episode in 'Lessons from the Gorse':

> Mountain gorses, since Linnæus
> Knelt beside you on the sod,
> For your beauty thanking God, –
> For your teaching, ye should see us
> Bowing in prostration new!
> Whence arisen, – if one or two
> Drops be on our cheeks – O world, they are not tears but dew.[30]

The anecdote of Linnaeus reappears in religious magazines and books for young people throughout the nineteenth century, and this serves as a reminder of gorse's presence and associations with the literature of childhood. Several earlier mentioned works, like *Lorna Doone* and 'Goblin Market', were popular among young readers. In many Victorian versions of the story of the Three Little Pigs, the unfortunate second pig's house is made not from just any sticks, but a 'bundle of furze'.[31] In the opening story of Rudyard Kipling's collection *Stalky & Co.*, titled 'In Ambush', the narrator begins by announcing: 'In summer all right-minded boys built huts in the furze-hill behind the College – little lairs whittled out of the heart of the prickly bushes'.[32] The story centres on the schoolboys' loss of one furze hut and discovery of a new one. And in A. A. Milne's *Winnie-the-Pooh*, Pooh climbs a tree for honey, only to fall into a gorse-bush. Later, in a possible nod to Kipling's young imperialists in the making, Pooh, Owl and Piglet discuss the difference between an ambush and a gorse-bush:

'An Ambush,' said Owl, 'is a sort of Surprise.'
'So is a gorse-bush sometimes,' said Pooh.[33]

*　*　*

Empire has spread gorse around the globe, and it has been considered an environmental pest in Chile, the United States and Tasmania. But its impact and expansion in New Zealand is particularly striking. In 1949, Andrew Hill Clark noted that a 'shrewd prophet could have predicted in the mid-nineteenth century' the spread of gorse across cleared farmland.[34] Charles Darwin came close. In apparently the earliest reference to gorse in New Zealand, Darwin, visiting New Zealand aboard the *Beagle* in 1835, noted seeing 'gorse for fences' at the Waimate mission station in the Bay of Islands.[35] While he did not predict gorse's spread, he understood the dangerous potential of imported flora and fauna and was distressed to see several unwelcome plants. His journal entry for 24 December notes:

> In many places I noticed several sorts of weeds, which, like the rats, I was forced to own as countrymen. A leek has overrun whole districts, and will prove very troublesome, but it was imported as a favour by a French vessel. The common dock is also widely disseminated, and will, I fear, for ever remain a proof of the rascality of an Englishman, who sold the seeds for those of the tobacco plant.[36]

Soon there was legislative support for the spread of gorse. According to Michael Bagge, 'a Government regulation introduced in the early 1850s required that Crown land leased to smallholders should be fenced using either gorse or hawthorn'.[37] As Bagge notes, while various 1860s ordinances regulated the growth of gorse within towns, farmers were still encouraged to grow the shrub as a fence and windbreak, and contemporary colonial newspapers regularly advertised the sale of gorse plants and seeds.

By the time of Anthony Trollope's visit to Australasia, its presence was alarming. Describing Christchurch in 1872, Trollope writes:

> In regard to the hedges it may be well to remark that the gorse ... has taken so kindly to its new home that it bids fair to become a monstrous pest. It spreads itself wide over the land and lanes, and unless periodically clipped claims the soil as its own. But each periodical clipping, with rural labour at 6s. a day, is a serious addition to the expense of farming.[38]

This impending botanical disaster did not stop New Zealand writers from celebrating the gorse. In his 1884 'Lecture on Acclimatisation', W. T. L. Travers claims with pride: 'Our hedges of hawthorne, sweetbriar, holly, and gorse, or whin, are almost unexampled in luxuriance and rapidity of growth.'[39] In an 1884 poem, 'The Canterbury Pilgrims', the appropriately named Thomas Bracken – most famous today for composing the national anthem 'God Defend New Zealand' – celebrates the settlers who transformed the South Island landscape in just 'three half-score years':

Behold their work! Revere their names!
Green pictures set in golden frames,
Around the City of the Stream,
Fulfil the Pilgrim's brightest dream;
With them a fairer England grew
'Neath speckless skies of sunny blue.[40]

Bracken was surely aware of the extraordinary change required to create 'a fairer England', and especially in the Canterbury region. As scholars have recently noted, the island landscape had been 'ecologically transformed': before introducing sheep and cattle, British colonists had to

> fell and fire forests, clear shrub lands, drain wetlands, periodically burn tracts of tussock to encourage growth of palatable and nutritious new shoots, cultivate flat to rolling ground in preparation for sown pasture, and broadcast seeds of pasture plants on steeper and higher land.[41]

Only then could the 'golden frames' of Bracken's poem – the gorse hedges enclosing livestock – make their appearance.

Despite the relentless efforts required for such a transformation, the spread of gorse and other introduced species remained, for some observers, a sign of settler strength and native weakness. As W. T. L. Travers wrote to Joseph Hooker, 'the young native vegetation appears to shrink from competition with these more vigorous intruders'.[42] Similar imagery appears in John Liddell Kelly's 1901 sonnet, 'In Maui's Island', which fits Patrick Brantlinger's model of proleptic elegy.[43] Kelly's narrator leaves the wintry cold of the South Island for warmer, 'exotic' landscapes in the north:

From Southern glooms, that chilled my blood erewhile,
    I seek the milder Northern clime's caresses –
    The longer day, the warmer sun that blesses,
In the true Maoriland, old Maui's isle.
Steep hills, deep vales, extend here, mile on mile,
    Streams twinkle sweet in ferny, far recesses,
    Where sombre bush, like Maori maiden's tresses,
Hangs shimmering, glossy, in the Sun-God's smile.

If Kelly's octave reads like a proto-tiki lounge manifesto, the sestet employs more troubling imagery, as the expanding gorse becomes nature's sign of settler dominance:

And yet I note, with lurking discontent,
    The dark bush dwindles, golden gorse spreads free;
So is the vigour of the Maori spent,
    So thrives the fair-haired race from sea to sea.
May conquering and conquered blood be blent,
    And breed new beauty and virility.

Even the back-and-forth rhyme scheme links the spread of gorse and the 'fair-haired race' with 'virility', while the narrator's 'discontent' and the native peoples' exhausted vigour leads only to compromise ('blood be blent').

Nevertheless, some feathered natives were finding ways to make gorse work to their advantage, undermining the seeming logic of settler conquest. In a paper presented to the Wellington Philosophical Society on 17 October 1888, Edward N. Liffiton lamented the failure of introduced pheasants to thrive in the Whanganui district. He identified the culprits as weka, native flightless birds that were no longer hunted by dogs belonging to now-dispersed Māori communities. Finding a comfortable new hiding place in the ever-expanding gorse, weka were stealing pheasant eggs. Liffiton writes: 'The Acclimatization Society for years spent a considerable sum in buying wekas' heads, and thousands were paid for each year, but no perceptible decrease has been noticed, and at last the society have discontinued the practice.'[44]

*   *   *

This recognition of the troublesome nature of gorse in the New Zealand landscape would make its way into the nation's art and literature. Ironically, a shrub that was intended to create borders and limits was instead out of control, reshaping the land and reclaiming its Gothic imagery, creating the 'the gorse golden hills' of Mansfield's early poem. The most famous reference to gorse in New Zealand literature is surely in the title of Dan Davin's 1947 collection, *The Gorse Blooms Pale*. Employing a variety of protagonists, Davin's short stories chart his own autobiography: from Southland childhood to university study, first in New Zealand and then at Oxford, and then military service. While several of Davin's stories make passing references to gorse, particularly the stories of youth, its key appearance is in the poem that opens the collection:

> God blazed in every gorsebush
> When I was a child.
> Forbidden fruits were orchards,
> And flowers grew wild.
>
> God is a shadow now.
> The gorse blooms pale.
> Branches in the orchard bow
> With fruits grown stale.[45]

While Davin's modernist stories are deservedly celebrated for capturing the life of southern Irish Catholic Pākehā, his introductory verse harkens back to the childish pleasures of gorse in Kipling and Milne, and perhaps to the evangelical tone of the Linnaeus anecdote. His contribution is to look past the beauty and see instead the eventual rot. There is a long literary history, from Horace to A. E. Housman, of using flowers as a trope for the passage from promising youth to jaded adulthood. Davin may be the first to use gorse for such purposes. The wild/child rhyme links youth with freedom, while the beauty of wildflowers is silenced by the funereal thumping of three strong stresses in 'The gorse blooms pale'.

Janet Frame, remembering her time at the Sunnyside Mental Hospital near Christchurch, wrote:

> My only writing was in letters to my sister and parents and brother, and these were always censored, and sometimes not mailed: I remember one instance of a letter . . . where I was actually quoting from Virginia Woolf, in describing the gorse as having a 'peanut-buttery smell'. This description was questioned by the doctor who read the letters, and judged to be an example of my 'schizophrenia'.[46]

Frame was perhaps remembering Virginia Woolf's essay 'A Sketch of the Past', which includes a description of the Cornish landscape: 'Little paths led up to the hill, between heather and ling; and our knees were pricked by the gorse – the blazing yellow gorse with its sweet nutty smell.'[47]

Frame wrote 'Gorse is not People' in 1954, offering it to Charles Brasch for *Landfall*, New Zealand's leading literary journal. Brasch had published other works by Frame, but he declined 'Gorse is not People', thinking the story too painful, and it was only published posthumously in 2008. It tells of Naida, an orphan and small person who, since the age of 10, has resided in a mental hospital. The story takes place on her twenty-first birthday, and she expects to be released from the hospital on this day. Driving into town with the nurse for a celebratory birthday lunch and a meeting with a board of doctors, Naida notices the gorse flowers on the hills, with their 'heavy drunken perfume':

> 'What is it?' Naida asked.
> 'Gorse. The farmers' curse.'
> 'Is it always there, yellow like that?'
> 'As far as I know. It has no definite season – no birthday, so to speak.'
> Naida was delighted. 'No birthday,' she repeated, fingering the brooch on her breast. 'It's out in the paddocks there without a birthday.'[48]

For the nurse, gorse is an unwanted pest ('the farmer's curse'), but for Naida, it provides a model for hope, living beyond the rules of society.

Naida and her nurse wander through the town, watching puppets in a department store window as they seem to build a brick structure, only to have the performance start again from scratch. 'It doesn't build,' says Naida. The interview does not go well, and the story ends with Naida back at the hospital, and there to stay:

> In the ward office, the nurse handed to the sister the paper that the three men had signed. The wording on the paper began, 'Registered under the Mental Defectives Act, 1928. This is to certify that Naida Wilma Tait, aged twenty-one . . .'

And so on. The same thing, over and over; brick puppetry; and gorse is not people.

Frame's story owes a debt to Davin, both in the aural echo of its title and in its borrowing of gorse as a symbol of wild, unfulfilled promise. Narrated in a tone that suggests both children's literature and a sermon ('Do you remember your twenty-first birthday? . . . I would like to tell you about Naida's twenty-first birthday'), the story moves inexorably towards a heart-breaking ending. Naida, like a citizen of Winesburg, Otago, will be trapped in the mental hospital for the rest of her life. The closing, elliptical sentence suggests that, while in the natural world, the prickly beauty of gorse thrives, our civilized world has no room for people who are different from the norm, in appearance or in outlook.

*   *   *

The appearance of gorse as a metaphor for the human condition in these works by Davin and Frame, rather than its more narrow use as a symbol of settler culture, suggests the normalization of gorse in New Zealand literature. Like the jacaranda in Australia and South Africa, it was no longer an import; it was a part of the landscape. Only in the late twentieth century would a new thinking about gorse gradually appear. Chris Orsman has described this cognitive shift, as New Zealanders began to understand what Charles Darwin had noted about the Surrey heathlands 150 years earlier:

> By the [19]90s there was evidence of a change in thinking, not perhaps a quantum change, but gorse, once cursed and maligned, was rehabilitated. The spraying and hacking tailed off. The new emphasis – on gorse as a nursery plant of young native flora – was built on facts that had been long known: that it is an excellent soil former, stabilising wind and moisture and temperature at ground level. That its extensive root system tunnels into the ground, breaking it up and piping in nitrogen. That large amounts of litter (humus) further this process, and the denseness of the stands of gorse inhibit erosion and litter wash, so that a moist microclimate is maintained below.[49]

The most visible evidence of this shift is to be found at the Hinewai Reserve on Banks Peninsula, just above Akaroa, which has grown from 109 hectares in 1987 to 1250 hectares today. According to its website, the reserve uses 'a management strategy of minimal interference' in order to 'foster the natural regeneration of native vegetation and wildlife . . . exotic gorse is a hated weed of pastoral farming but is tolerated on Hinewai because it serves as a highly effective temporary nurse canopy for native regeneration'.[50] As Hugh Wilson, botanist and manager of Hinewai, puts it, gorse might be seen 'not as a friend, but as an ally'.[51]

Chris Orsman captures this ambivalent reclamation in his 1994 poem, 'Ornamental Gorse'. The narrator describes gorse as 'yellowing our quaint history / of occupation and reprise'. Gorse is lovable only 'from a distance', where its curves and colour among the hills seem to offer 'a topiary under heavens / cropped by the south wind'. In the closing lines, gorse becomes a religious martyr, 'burnt' and 'hacked' for our sins, as well as a national symbol: the narrator offers us 'this crown of thorns' as New Zealand's 'reluctant emblem'.[52]

One artist whose work, like Orsman's poem, contends with the complexities of gorse, is the late sculptor Peter Nicholls (1936–2021).[53] For Nicholls, the question of environmental responsibility was personal: a maternal ancestor, the missionary and botanist Richard Taylor (1805–73), had spread the Christian gospel among the people of the North Island's Whanganui region, while also scattering European seedlings throughout the land. Many of Nicholls's key works from the 1990s take their inspiration from this ambivalent legacy. *Whanganui* (1990), today in the Sarjeant Art Gallery, is one of several Nicholls sculptures that snake along the ground, tracing the movement of the Whanganui River where Taylor lived and worked in the 1840s. Nicholls created *Whanganui* out of a mixture of woods from native trees (totara, rimu) as well as from those introduced by his ancestor (willow, poplar), and he embedded various objects in the work – an adze head, a compass, a cross – that call to mind both the Māori and Pākehā settlers who left their mark on the river.

Nicholls expanded this meditation on the meeting of Indigenous and settler in *Synthesis*, a later series of small sculptures constructed from two kinds of wood, swamp kauri and gorse. Kauri forests once blanketed the North Island. After decades of logging, however, only a few protected forests survive. Swamp kauri dates from prehistoric time; buried in North Island peat for hundreds or thousands of years, it is now excavated and used for high end furniture or art. By combining these two woods – a quintessential ancient and indigenous timber, and a quintessential invader – Nicholls nods towards Aotearoa New Zealand's troubled immigrant history: the British and other European settlers who rapidly and violently displaced long-established Māori communities, just as the upstart gorse has displaced kauri.

But Nicholls was aware of the shift in thinking about gorse, and he picks up on its paradoxical qualities. Gorse's role as an aid to native regrowth is nicely represented in his heart-like sculpture *Sustain* (2010), where the rough lines of the withered gorse branch form the aorta to the smooth, marbled sheen of the kauri heart. The materials have a sensual beauty in their variety, and there is surely the suggestion of sexuality in the work. But this seems far from the colonial fantasy of John Liddell Kelly's sonnet. The connection between the kauri and gorse is not natural: it has been forced, and the evidence of that brutality is the charcoal burn Nicholls leaves at the point of union. If the charcoal specifically brings to mind the vast indigenous forests burned by Europeans to clear space for new settlements, it more generally suggests the violence of encounter. Two elements, naturally disparate, are sutured together to make something new.

In a related work, *Dream* (2010), a triangular piece of polished kauri balances precariously upon a three-pronged gorse branch. Viewed from one direction, *Dream* brings to mind a boat grounded on a shore. Viewed from another, it suggests a bird on a branch, about to take flight. Both representations are fitting. One conjures the long boats that carried Māori to Aotearoa 900 years ago, and the sailing vessels that carried Europeans to New Zealand 500 years later. The other suggests the rich antipodean bird life that developed over millennia, as well as more recent arrivals brought over by nineteenth-century Britons nostalgic for the sounds of home. A seemingly simple work, *Dream* evinces motifs of nation, migration and ecology. If its central conceit sounds naive, even utopian . . . well, the sculpture *is* titled *Dream*.

* * *

Gorse has a long presence in British and New Zealand art and literature. Not simply the farmer's curse, or a grim feature of the Wessex heathlands, its representation encompasses a wide and varied range. In New Zealand, its image has shifted, from being a marker of settler presence or even dominance, to a symbol of unruly nature and, more recently, to a sign of reconciliation. It seems likely that more artists and writers will follow Orsman and Nicholls in seeing gorse in a new light. If their vision is hopeful, it is also surprisingly pragmatic. Gorse is as likely to disappear from New Zealand as Pākehā are likely to all return to their ancestral homes. In this sense, Janet Frame's narrator had it wrong: Gorse is People.

Notes

1   Chris Orsman, 'The Unlikely Redemption of Gorse', *New Zealand Geographic* 94 (November–December 2008), https://www.nzgeo.com/stories/chris-orsman-the-unlikely-redemption-ofgorse/.
2   Katherine Mansfield, 'Vignette – Through the Autumn Afternoon', in *Poems of Katherine Mansfield*, ed. Vincent O'Sullivan (Auckland: Oxford University Press, 1988), 2–3.
3   Jennifer Speake, ed., *The Oxford Dictionary of Proverbs* (Oxford: Oxford University Press, 2015), 123, 136–7.
4   William Shakespeare, *The Tempest*, ed. David Lindley (Cambridge: Cambridge University Press, 2002), 4.178–81.
5   Samuel Johnson, 'Furze' and 'Furzy', *A Dictionary of the English Language*, 2 vols (London: J. and P. Knapton et al., 1755).
6   Robert Burns, 'Tam o' Shanter: A Tale', in *Burns: Poems*, ed. William Beattie and Henry W. Meikle (London: Penguin Books, 1977), 153–60.
7   William Wordsworth, 'It was an April Morning' and 'The Idiot Boy', in *The poetical works of William Wordsworth*, ed. E de. Selincourt (Oxford: Clarendon Press, 1940–9), 112, 74.
8   William Wordsworth, 'The Ruined Cottage', in *Wordsworth and Coleridge: Lyrical Ballads & Other Poems*, ed. Martin Scofield (Ware: Wordsworth Editions, 2003), 95.
9   Samuel Taylor Coleridge, 'Fears in Solitude', in *The Complete Poems*, ed. William Keach (London: Penguin Books, 1997), 239–44.
10 Emily Brontë, *Wuthering Heights*, ed. Pauline Nestor (London: Penguin Books, 2003), 102.
11 Brontë, *Wuthering Heights*, 35. 'Whinstone' is occasionally used to refer to whin, but in these cases it clearly refers to the Yorkshire basaltic rock.
12 Christina Rossetti, 'Goblin Market', *Goblin Market and Other Poems* (London: Macmillan and Co., 1862). Earlier, Laura had assured the goblins, 'all my gold is on the furze' (7). Three times in the poem, Rossetti rhymes furze and purse (7, 18, 24).
13 Bram Stoker, *Dracula*, ed. Maurice Hindle (New York: Penguin Books, 1993), 230.
14 Thomas Hardy, *The Return of the Native*, ed. Tony Slade (London: Penguin Books, 1999), 11.
15 Hardy, *The Return of the Native*, 18–19.
16 Ibid., 19.
17 Ibid., 24.
18 Ibid., 246.
19 Ibid., 12.
20 John MacNeill Miller, 'Mischaracterizing the Environment: Hardy, Darwin, and the Art of Ecological Storytelling', *Texas Studies in Literature and Language* 62:2 (2020): 163.

21 Hardy, *The Return of the Native*, 38. See also 53.

22 Ibid., 173.

23 R. D. Blackmore, *Lorna Doone: A Romance of Exmoor*, 3 vols. (London: Sampson Low, Son & Marston, 1869), 3:308.

24 William Allingham, 'Gorse', in *Flower Pieces and Other Poems* (London: Reeves and Turner, 1888) 14; furzeling is another name for the English warbler.

25 Alfred Lord Tennyson, *In Memoriam*, ed. Erik Gray (London: Norton, 2004), 13, stanza xi.

26 Katherine Tynan, 'Gorse', in *Irish Poems* (London: Sidgwick & Jackson, 1914), 106–7.

27 'Defence not Defiance', *The Cornhill Magazine* 22:129 (March 1894), 286.

28 C. Pierpoint Johnson, *The Useful Plants of Great Britain: A Treatise* (London: William Kent & Co., 1862), 68.

29 Oscar Wilde, *The Annotated Prison Writings of Oscar Wilde*, ed. Nicholas Frankel (Cambridge, MA: Harvard University Press, 2018), 285.

30 Elizabeth Barrett Browning, 'Lessons from the Gorse', in *Poems*, 3 vols (London: Chapman & Hall, 1862), 3. 134–5.

31 James O. Halliwell, ed., *The Nursery Rhymes of England, Collected Chiefly from Oral Tradition*, 5th edition (1842, London: John Russell Smith, 1853), 37; Mrs. Valentine, ed., *Nursery Rhymes, Tales and Jingles. The Camden Edition* (London: Frederick Warne & Co., n.d.), 459.

32 Rudyard Kipling, *Stalky & Co.* (London: Macmillan & Co., 1952), 1.

33 A. A. Milne, *Winnie-the-Pooh* (1926; London: Methuen & Co., 1965), 116.

34 Andrew Hill Clark, *The Invasion of New Zealand by People, Plants and Animals* (New Brunswick: Rutgers University Press, 1949), 376.

35 Charles Darwin, *Journal of Researches into the Natural History and Geology of the Countries Visited During the Voyage of H.M.S. "Beagle" Round the World* (London: Ward, Lock and Co., 1890), 309.

36 Darwin, *Journal*, 311.

37 Michael Bagge, 'Valuable Ally or Invading Army? The Ambivalence of Gorse in New Zealand, 1835–1900', *Environment and Nature in New Zealand* 9:1 (February 2014): 135, http://environmentalhistory-au-nz.org/wp-content/uploads/2014/03/ENNZ_2014_February.pdf. See also Joan Druett, *Exotic Intruders: The Introduction of Plants and Animals into New Zealand* (Auckland: Heinemann, 1983), 63.

38 Anthony Trollope, *Australia and New Zealand*, 2 vols (London: The Trollope Society, 2002), 2:379.

39 W. T. L. Travers, 'Lecture on Acclimatisation', *New Zealand Country Journal* 8:5 (1884): 500.

40 Thomas Bracken, *Lays of the Land of the Maori and Moa* (London: Sampson Low, Marston, Searle, & Rivington, 1884), 118.

41 Peter Holland, Paul Star and Vaughan Wood, 'Pioneer Grassland Farming: Pragmatism, Innovation and Experimentation', in *Seeds of Empire: The Environmental Transformation of New Zealand*, ed. Tom Brooking and Eric Pawson (London: I.B. Tauris, 2011), 51.

42 J. D. Hooker, 'Note on the Replacement of Species in the Colonies and Elsewhere', *The Natural History Review* 13 (January 1864): 124. See also Tom Brooking and Eric Pawson, 'The Contours of Transformation', in *Seeds of Empire*, ed. Brooking and Pawson, 32.

43 John Liddell Kelly, 'In Maui's Island', *New Zealand Illustrated Magazine*, 1 September 1901, 908. See also Patrick Brantlinger, *Dark Vanishings: Discourse on the Extinction of Primitive Races, 1800–1930* (Ithaca: Cornell University Press, 2003) 3–4.

44 Edward N. Liffiton, 'Notes on the Decrease of Pheasants on the West Coast of the North Island', *Transactions and Proceedings of the Royal Society of New Zealand* 21 (1888): 226.

45 Dan Davin, *The Gorse Blooms Pale* (London: Nicholson & Watson, 1947), vi.

46 Janet Frame, *An Angel at My Table: The Complete Autobiography* (Berkeley: Counterpoint, 2017), 285.

47 Virginia Woolf, 'A Sketch of the Past', in *Moments of Being: Autobiographical Writings*, ed. Jeanne Schulkind (London: Pimlico, 2002), 138.

48 Janet Frame, 'Gorse is not People', *The New Yorker*, 25 August 2008, https://www.newyorker.com/magazine/2008/09/01/gorse-is-not-people

49 Orsman, 'The Unlikely Redemption of Gorse'.

50 Hinewai Reserve, 'Goals', https://www.hinewai.org.nz/about/

51 Interview with the author, 9 April 2021.

52 Chris Orsman, *Ornamental Gorse* (Wellington: Victoria University Press, 1994), 49.

53 This section incorporates passages from Thomas McLean, 'Remembering Peter Nicholls', *Los Angeles Review of Books*, 3 July 2021, https://lareviewofbooks.org/article/remembering-peter-nicholls/.

Part Four

Texts in Motion

11

Antipodean Perspectives: The Politics and Economics of Being Topsy-Turvy

Sarah Comyn

Responding to the London *Spectator*'s indulgence of 'hypercritical remarks' regarding the colony of Victoria's adoption of the term 'Parliament', the Melbourne newspaper, the *Age*, described in 1858 a series of social, political and economic developments in the colony, jesting at the *Spectator*'s audacity in providing advice to 'presuming colonials':[1]

> We Antipodals, Anthropophagi, whom you suppose to be walking topsy-turvy, wearing our heads between our shoulders, are taking the wind out of your heavy sails ... Confidentially, we begin to look down on you in a patronising sort of way, now that every man of us has his vote and can look for his rights as well as his nugget – now that we have got the ballet-box, and aspire to mount the dromedary by way of 'high-horse'! Of course you will stare, and perhaps grunt and grumble at the airs of this preposterous child, taking his parent under his wing![2]

In this satirical rebuke, the *Age* uses the metaphor of antipodean inversion – both through its references to 'walking topsy-turvy' and to the 'preposterous child' colony outgrowing and overshadowing its parent – to respond to the *Spectator*'s (and through it, the British metropole's) claims of political and economic superiority. Adopting what Bernard Smith calls the 'antipodean point of view' and Paul Giles terms the 'antipodean imagination', the *Age* highlights the recent economic and political achievements in the colony (the gold rush, responsible government and male suffrage) and reverses the presumed economic, political and social relations of power between metropole and colony. This brief passage from the *Age* demonstrates, moreover, the political and satirical efficacy of the Antipodes-as-metaphor and is suggestive of the categories of antipodean inversion that will form the focus of this chapter.

Identifying a series of antipodal tropes and figures, this chapter will explore how nineteenth-century newspapers in the colonies of Australia and New Zealand mobilized and adapted this metaphor of antipodean reversal and its accompanying mode of 'topsy-turvyness' to both celebrate and critique the Australasian colonies, induce and address intercolonial rivalry, and shape Australasian political and economic debates. Examining the use of antipodal relations, journeys and figures – such as the parent–child relationship of metropole–colony, the return journey and Macaulay's 'New Zealander' – in newspaper depictions of settler life, this chapter will demonstrate the ways settler colonists were processing transportation, emigration and invasion, while attempting to forge new identities by reclaiming the myth of antipodality.

Envisaged in European mythology as a place of embodied opposites where people walk upside down, their feet face the opposite directions, or the inhabitants are characterized by their backwardness or belatedness, the belief in the Antipodes was intertwined with the search for *Terra Australis*, the great southern continent that was necessary to 'balance the weight of the land in the northern hemisphere'.[3] While occupying a 'symbolic space' defined by its 'otherness' in the geographic imagination of early geographers and explorers, by the eighteenth century the Antipodes 'comes to designate an area in Oceania' and by the nineteenth century was frequently associated with Australia and New Zealand.[4] In deploying this antipodean association with satirical and critical intent, nineteenth-century Australasian newspapers frequently rely on *Terra Australis*'s relational connotations of balance and its counterweight – imbalance or topsy-turvyness – to examine the antipodean relations between metropole and colony. As Smith has noted, 'the antipodes are not a place, but a relationship ... a spatial and cultural relationship between north and south'.[5] Drawing on this relational quality of the antipodes, Giles argues that a 'heightened version of comparative consciousness' defines the 'antipodean imagination' where the 'phenomenological selfhood of any given culture is refracted through alternative perspectives'.[6] This relational quality of the antipodean imagination is crucial to this chapter's analysis of the constant renegotiation not only of metropolitan power but intercolonial distinctiveness and rivalry in the Australasian colonies through the adaptations of the Antipodes' metaphor of inversion.

A highly malleable and mobile metaphor, the Antipodes, like the concept of Australasia is 'ambiguous, fluid and arbitrary'.[7] It is this very fluidity and arbitrariness that makes it such a popular trope and mode of critique for nineteenth-century newspapers and the perfect site for investigating the evolution of the hybrid settler-colonial identities in Australasia. Used both as a knowing wink at the mocking depictions of colonial belatedness and backwardness, *and also* as the subversion of this very stereotype, the Antipodes depicted in nineteenth-century Australasian newspapers provides an example of what John Eperjesi refers to as a 'territorializing or articulatory practice'. The Antipodes of Australasian newspapers is representative, this chapter argues, of the 'discursive battles' that surround the 'spatializing keywords' dominating an 'imperialist imaginary' in Australasia.[8] A 'Eurocentric phenomenon', to be 'an Antipodean in Australia' is, as Ian McLean reminds us, 'to be out of place in one's place' – to be a European in Australia – and this attachment to metropolitan sensibilities and identities is critical to understanding the hybridity of antipodean sympathies and characteristics in the nineteenth century.[9] Deryck M. Schreuder and Stuart Ward have demonstrated, for instance, how 'Australian migrants were both colonists and citizens at one and the same moment ... remain[ing] attached to their British imperial beginnings', such that the 'Australian sense of nationality was a hybrid ideology, one that drew both from a tenacious race identity of Britishness, together with an increasingly assertive sense of material self-interest, and an environmental sense of place'.[10] Building on Schreuder and Ward's argument, this chapter includes New

Zealand in its analysis of the antipodean-tinted sense of place. While part of the Antipodes agglomerated, the Australian and New Zealand colonies nonetheless applied the antipodean imagination in ways that emphasized their distinctive political, economic and environmental histories.

The Antipodes as political and economic critique

Recognized as a powerful metaphor of critique, accusations of antipodean thinking and behaviour were frequently levelled against the political establishments of the various colonies. The critical evaluations of the political economy of the Australasian colonies demonstrate, moreover, how adaptable the antipodean critique could be across period and geography. As early as 1826, the New South Wales newspaper, the *Monitor*, criticized the taxation policies of New South Wales and Van Diemen's Land for not providing enough protection to local industries:

> When will ye open your eyes to the gloomy obtrusive fact and every-day-matter of experience, that the fountains of industry … should never be taxed? but if meddled with at all be encouraged by bounties? Because we live at the Antipodes, is the *horn-book* of political economy to be only read? Is Adam Smith to be read like the [H]ebrew tongue, *backwards*, and his principles to be considered topsy-turvy?[11]

By 1856, a letter to the editor of the *Hobart Courier* was using the same trope of antipodean inversion, but this time to deplore the protectionist economic policies operating in Tasmania claiming that 'the antipodes of geographical position – the world turned upside down – are politically maintained'.[12] While in the colony of Victoria, the *Geelong Advertiser* featured this short poem in response to the news of an increase in 'public' land prices in 1840:

IMPROMPTU
ON HEARING OF THE UPSET PRICE OF LAND BEING RAISED.

At the Antipodes, they say
The world is topsy-turvy turned,
Their north is south, their night is day,
Their summer chill, their winter burned.

All their affairs are upside down;
Their Governor, no one can doubt,
Must have his conscience outside in,
The settlers' pockets inside out.[13]

Seemingly arbitrary, the very malleability of the antipodean metaphor of backwardness and the world-turned-upside-down heightened its appeal as satirical shorthand for the

Australian colonies' status as the negative inversion of the metropole in geography, politics, economics and culture.

The Antipodes' signature mode of the topsy-turvy could signal anything from ineptitude to corruption (whether moral, economic and/or political) to injustice. Systems of colonial justice, for example, were frequently indicted by the press for their antipodean applications. In 1829 the *Australian* reprinted a lengthy article from Britain's *New Monthly Magazine* that declared: 'Botany Bay is quite as much at the Antipodes of British Justice, as New Zealand is of Britain itself.' Acknowledging that not all of the article's views 'coincide[d]' with those of the newspaper, the *Australian* nonetheless justified the reprint 'in order to shew our readers here the sort of privilege which freedom of discussion is allowed in England in contrast to Botany Bay'.[14]

Propelled by the achievement of responsible government in Victoria, an 1856 letter to the editor of the *Age* in contrast displays no qualms or uneasiness about expressing their opinion freely, thereby revealing the evolution in colonial free speech as well as an assertiveness in the public critique of antipodean forms of justice and governance:

> Have you any doubt whatever that you are at the antipodes? Go to certain courts. It may indeed happen that there you are convinced that you have indeed arrived at the antipodes of justice; at the antipodes of morals; at the antipodes of decorum; at the antipodes of gentlemanly conduct.[15]

Through these critiques, systems of colonial justice, politics and economics become the characteristic sign of the Antipodes as the metropole's negative inverse, but they could also be deployed as a symbol of intercolonial difference and rivalry. 'A Misfit' (see Figure 11.1), an illustration from *Melbourne Punch* in 1861, portrays the antipodean inversion of political economy immortalized as protection, but instead of representing an antipodean collective, the colony of Victoria is singled out as the antipodean misfit.

Dressed in old-fashioned, masculine and funereal black clothes, Miss Victoria forms the negative to the other Australian colonies here basking in the light offered by a future of free trade. Instead of looking towards the future as her sister colonies do, Miss Victoria appears to be shielding herself from this vision and looking to the past. Portraying a mode of topsy-turvy embodiment, Miss Victoria is positioned awkwardly, as if she may lose her footing at any moment in true antipodean fashion. The inscription reads: 'Miss Victoria prudently (?) arrays herself in the left-off wearing apparel of her papa. While her less cautious sisters remain exposed to the dangers of plenty.'[16] The question mark in parenthesis that follows the word 'prudently' registers, as Shu-Chuan Yan argues, *Melbourne Punch*'s 'doubt[s] about Victoria's unwillingness to participate in free trade with the mother country' and the newspaper's ongoing 'adherence to imperial economic policy'.[17] *Melbourne Punch* therefore uses the political and economic implications of being antipodal and topsy-turvy to heighten intercolonial competition and thereby censure the Victorian government's approach to trade.

The antipodean metaphor could also be mobilized against neighbouring colonies as a means of emphasizing positive colonial attributes. In a scathing critique launched against the 'relics of the old regime' in New South Wales – the 'deposed autocracy of the vegetative era' – the *Melbourne Leader* celebrates the electoral reform achieved in the

A   M I S F I T.

MISS VICTORIA PRUDENTLY (?) ARRAYS HERSELF IN THE LEFT-OFF WEARING APPAREL OF HER PAPA, WHILE HER LESS CAUTIOUS SISTERS REMAIN EXPOSED TO THE DANGERS OF PLENTY.

Figure 11.1 'A Misfit', *Melbourne Punch*, Thursday 29 August 1861, 5.

colony of Victoria that distinguishes it from those 'more backward populations' in its neighbouring colonies. The article's severest contempt is levelled at the politician and pastoralist Matthew Henry Marsh who, having previously served on the New South Wales legislative council, was then a representative for Salisbury in the House of Commons. Attacking Marsh for his pastoralist sympathies and his representation of Victorian legislators as 'in every way antipodal and topsy-turvy', the *Melbourne Leader* satirizes Marsh for 'his long-cherished horror of the ballot and our other popular encroachments on halcyon antiquity'. The *Melbourne Leader*'s celebration of Victoria's 'hideous example of disobedience to the previously passive husbandmen and townspeople of New South Wales' both advocates for antipodean opposition and works to differentiate Victoria from its neighbours. In doing so, the *Melbourne Leader* also campaigns for further political and economic reform in the antipodean colonies. Playing on the intercolonial competitiveness in politics and economics, Victoria declares that it has 'rattled [its ballot box] long enough for empty praise, and we must try in future to rattle it for substantial benefit'.[18] There is a political assertiveness here of a *positive* antipodean position that demonstrates how the Antipodes could surpass expectations and how the attribute of topsy-turvyness, especially in political matters, could be seen as progressive rather than regressive.

A letter to the editor of the *South Australian Register* in 1858 (the same year as the *Melbourne Leader*'s critique appeared) echoes this sense of political achievement and entitlement. Titled 'Ultra Reform' the letter states: 'We are considered geographically to be at the antipodes of Britain; but we are antipodal in many other ways besides the geosense.' After listing the numerous environmental factors that distinguish Australia from Britain, the letter argues that 'the colonists' 'resolved' to take their 'example from Dame Nature' and therefore

> rescind many of those antiquated laws to which they had been accustomed to yield a willing obedience, and inaugurated a new code, embodying political and social rights to such a degree as was only imagined by the wildest dreamer in the old country, and which has caused us to be looked upon with envious eyes by thousands in the old world.

This celebration of settler-colonial achievements in South Australia has the same feeling of triumphant spirit that animated the *Age* article (again from 1858) that this chapter began with, and emphasizes the sense that the colonial independence achieved through responsible government in the 1850s could reverse the power relations between metropole and colony. The colonies could, in fact, display their antipodal nature as a badge of honour, occupying a 'van of progress in reform' that leaves 'older nations in the rear'.[19]

As these examples also suggest, this reversal of power relations was frequently imagined as the fledgling colony outsoaring its parent. A common trope, Simon Sleight has argued that 'once established, the trope of Australia as a youth poised perpetually on the threshold of adulthood, would prove difficult to transcend'.[20] This trope of youthful exuberance did, however, have an antipodal energy of subversion that allowed newspapers to imagine these young colonies as outgrowing expectations and outwitting their parents' attachment to tradition. The most famous portrayal of this trope is possibly John Leech's 1850 'Lord John Taking Measure of the Colonies' (see Figure 11.2). A metropolitan perspective of the colonies, the illustration is a response, as Richard Scully notes, to the 'Australian Colonies Government Act (1850), which enabled the separation of the Port Phillip District from New South Wales as the colony of Victoria'.[21] Towering over the other colonies (characterized by Leech's racialized depictions), Australia's portrayal as what Scully describes as a 'gangly youth' that

LORD JOHN TAKING THE MEASURE OF THE COLONIES.

Figure 11.2 John Leech, 'Lord John Taking Measure of the Colonies', *Punch*, 1850.

captured both the 'extraordinarily youthful' population demographic and Victoria's age as a colony, is nonetheless also suggestive of the potential this youthful colony has to overpower their parent and thereby disrupt the traditional power relations between metropole and colony. In contrast to Australia's appreciative smirk at its growth spurt, New Zealand (pictured in the right-hand corner) appears to still be coming to terms with his image. Grimacing, New Zealand appears to be struggling against his ill-fitting jacket, a reference perhaps to the colonies struggles for democratic reform prior to the New Zealand Constitution Act of 1852.

An 1868 satire in *Melbourne Punch* imagines a female counterpart to Leech's stripling with 'Miss Australia' writing to 'Mrs. Britannia'. While describing herself as a 'big girl for my age', Miss Australia is eager to disabuse her 'Dear Mother' of the 'fibs about your daughter at the far off antipodes' even while admitting: 'My trees bark every year, but my native dogs never do anything of the kind.' Playing with the metaphor of the body politic she confesses that although she is 'too fond of a [political] crisis' she must assert that 'for all this my *constitution* is all right'.[22] This youthfulness could signal ignorance and naivety, especially political and economic naivety, but it could also be seen as a sign of future possibility.

A 'hypothetical space', the Antipodes (with *Terra Australis*) has a long tradition, Alfred Hiatt argues, of being viewed both as promising 'colonial expansion' and 'correction'. It is at once 'a learned invention and incitement to exploration, a goad and reproach to vanity and ambition'. The Antipodes could be seen 'as retreat or recess', a 'check on ambition or power' generative of the process of self-reflection.[23] The Antipodes could therefore present a site of potential social and moral renewal. A courtship and emigration poem from as early as 1824 in New South Wales, for example, points to the convict shame that distinguishes the colony from the metropole, contrasting the light of freedom shining in Britain with the 'sombre wing' of slavery associated with transportation. But it also foresees a future bright where

> The Sons of Australasia's Clime
> Shall soon redeem their Country's shame;
> No more the penal 'Land of Crime,'
> But Nurse of Science, Truth, and Fame![24]

Reclaiming the shame of transportation, the poem envisions the Australian colonies as a place of rejuvenation and enlightenment. The 'comparative consciousness' that the Antipodes inspires is on full display in the *Argus* adaptation of an E. L. Blanchard poem performed and made famous by Henry Russell, 'There's Room Enough For All'. Inserting the two italicized lines at the end of the poem, the *Argus* designates Australia as the place that has 'room enough for all' in contrast to the 'typhus-tainted alleys' of home:

> In this fair region, far away,
> Will labour find employment;
> A fair day's work, a fair day's pay,
> And toil will earn enjoyment.
> . . .
> *From rags and crime, Australia's clime*
> *Will free the pauper's thrall:*
> Take fortune's tide – the world is wide –
> Has room enough for all.[25]

The *Argus* featured a postscript to the poem declaring that during a performance of this song in England, Henry Russell claimed he 'never saw yet a lovelier spot then the rich savannahs and fertile plains of New South Wales' and that he hoped 'the present emigration movement throughout Great Britain will be means of removing many from the scenes of toil and want at home, to one of comparative independence at the antipodes'.[26]

An emigration poem, 'At the Antipodes', attributed to Matthias Barr and reprinted in at least seven Australian newspapers in the 1860s, builds on this theme of antipodean prosperity in contrast with a starving and suffering England:

> 'TWAS care and want in England,
> My own dear wife;
> Our means were scant in England,

My own dear wife:
But here around us everywhere
Enough we have, wife, and to spare;
Ah, Kate! We bade adieu to care
The day we left old England.[27]

These poems mobilize antipodean opposition and contrast to reshape the metropolitan concepts and colonial shame attached to emigration and transportation. In doing so they imagine the Antipodes as a place of endless space and opportunity that completely elides the existence of Indigenous Australians and suggests instead *terra nullius*. Rather than a topsy-turvy land where the Anthropophagi roam, the Antipodes is reshaped as a blank canvas for future projects. As Justin Clemens and Thomas Ford have argued, rather than a 'conservative doctrine', *terra nullius* was 'put in service of liberalising projects of colonial development that progressively displaced present conditions with those of a perfect state to come', where the 'arbitrary actions of government were restrained by the fundamental liberties of its citizens'. The 'future-oriented progressiveness' Clemens and Ford associate with *terra nullius* is equally applicable to the discursive battles over the definition of antipodality in nineteenth-century Australian newspapers.[28] Instead of denoting a place of moral, social, political and economic topsy-turvyness, the widespread use of the trope of antipodean inversion in these newspapers began to portray the Antipodes as a place of rejuvenation where the young settler colonies could assert their own political identity that nonetheless always evoked their British metropolitan relations.

Great Britain in the Antipodes

Unlike the Australian colonies, where antipodean contrasts were regularly embraced and adapted and the commitment to *terra nullius* became sacrosanct, New Zealand was frequently described as the 'Britain of the Southern Hemisphere'. Referring to the 'New Zealands' as 'the two or three most noble islands in the entire Southern Hemisphere', an article reprinted in the *New Zealander* in 1866 argues, for example, that New Zealand represents 'geographically the future Great Britain of the South'. Though the colonies of Britain are numerous, 'none', the article continues, 'are possessed of such vital interest as New Zealand' where the 'temperate climate' has blessed the colony with 'fertile soil, and great mineral wealth' so that it 'must assume in the imaginations of intending emigrants all the charms of a new paradise'. Described as the 'young bantling Britain of the Antipodes', it is not surprising, then, that there are fewer instances of colonial New Zealand newspapers deploying the antipodean metaphor of inversion.[29] There are, however, some examples of the newspapers using antipodean negatives to critique religion, politics and even cemeteries in a similar way to that of their Australian counterparts. An 1880 poem called 'Topsy-Turvy' published in the *Evening Star*, for instance, uses the familiar tropes of opposites and backwardness to describe the separation of lovers across the hemispheres. Writing from a northern perspective and direction, the poem has the speaker contemplating his 'somebody' in 'Dunedin, Otago, New Zealand':

The fancy quite pleased me when lonely
    To think – though we severed had been –
Our feet were together, with only
    Rotundity rolling between.

That if some new Isambard Brunel
    Could pierce through a world rather wide
I had only to drop through the tunnel
    And stand upside-down by her side.

The darkness opposed to the whiteness,
    Here autumn – there spring in its bloom
On her earth all sunshine and brightness,
    On mine all the dullness and gloom.

But tho' the world's hard as we've found it
    And don't do at all as it's bid;
A woman can always come round it,
    And that's what my somebody did.

No longer we know different weather,
    No more oppose morning and night;
In England we share them together,
    And serve the Antipodes right.[30]

Despite these instances of antipodean satire, more frequently than not the Antipodes was used in a denotative rather than a connotative sense by colonial New Zealand newspapers. With the New Zealand colonies seen as a replica of Britain in the south, the Antipodes-as-metaphor lost some of its satirical resonance and inversive potential for their newspapers.

Antipodal tropes were used, however, to mark settler-colonial resentment towards missionaries, the colonial and imperial officials and metropolitan humanitarian policies during and following the 'New Zealand Wars'. As James Belich argues, a key 'feature in the British interpretation' of the 'fall of Kororareka' in 1845, for example, was to 'attribute the defeat to the exceptional incompetence or treachery of the leading figures in it'. One widely held belief was that the 'soldiers and sailors . . . had somehow been betrayed by the local missionaries'.[31] In assessing the response to the 'shock of defeat' by the British and the settler colonists, Belich concludes that the 'New Zealand scapegoat hunt was unusual both in degree if not kind': 'Of the thirteen Imperial and colonial officers who held independent commands of any importance during the Wars, not one escaped severe criticism.'[32] In carrying out this critique, colonial New Zealand newspapers could deploy the antipodean accusation with damning effect.

A reimagining of *A Christmas Carol* (1843) published as a short series by the *Nelson Examiner and New Zealand Chronicle* in 1845 uses an antipodean approach to explore these themes of colonial betrayal. Set in 1870, 'A Christmas Carol in New Zealand' opens with England as a place, not of Macaulay's ruins (which will be explored in more detail below), but of stagnation where 'her statesmen acknowledged that, without any decay being perceptible in her commerce or her retrogression in her institutions, she had reached the zenith of her power, and would advance no more'. In contrast to this moral and economic stagnation, 'a spirit of advancement' was 'becoming manifest' in the colonies, 'the effect of which would cause them to dispute the seat of civilization and power with the countries of the northern world'. This backdrop of antipodal inversions being laid, the story follows 'C–D–, a civilian having been appointed to the government of New Zealand', who having almost arrived at New Zealand is suddenly arrested by the Phantom – 'the spirit to whom the watch of this land is entrusted' – who transports him to a hall of sculptures where he encounters sculptures of such 'eminent characters' as Captain Cook, Jules Dumont d'Urville and Captain Hobson. At each sculpture of the European figures deemed pivotal in the history of the colony, C–D– and the Phantom assess their impact with Arthur Wakefield described, for example, as inducing immediately a sense of the 'character of him whose name was the brightest and whose memory the most beloved'.[33]

When the pair approach the statue of Governor Robert FitzRoy, however, the shame and sense of betrayal associated with FitzRoy's defeats in the 1840s results in the second visitation, with the Phantom declaring: 'I will not by description or relation create in your mind any impression favourable or otherwise to the memory of this man, but I will introduce you to the events characteristic of his time and illustrative of his policy, the results of which you are already acquainted with'. The second transportation sees the pair in London attending a meeting of the 'Aborigines Paternal Sympathetic Association'. Launching a scathing critique of the Aborigines' Protection Society, the story satirizes the members of the society and those attending the meeting as having but 'one object before them – a desire to be accredited for morality, disinterestedness, and philanthropy'.[34] Persuaded of the ill effects of this metropolitan interference, the third transportation takes the pair to the Legislative Assembly in Auckland 'with the recent annihilation of the Bay of Islands settlements fresh before them'. Here C–D– witnesses the debate between FitzRoy and the other members about how best to manage the increasing conflict between the settlers and Māori, and the passing, presumably, of the 1844 Debenture Act, which is described in the story as evidence of FitzRoy's 'incapacity' and as a 'measure of arrogance, suggested in difficulty and completed in precipitance'. In these debates, local opinions and advice are ignored, and settler-colonial interests are constantly deferred through obfuscation by FitzRoy. The council chamber is lambasted for 'being the showroom of predetermined decisions and preconcerted majorities'.[35] With its future-tense setting, 'A Christmas Tale in New Zealand' allows the settler colonists to process their current defeats and sense of metropolitan duplicity in the managing of their affairs. Travelling forward to travel backwards in order to reassess the political present, this adaptation of *A Christmas Carol* uses antipodal inversions both of time and place to imagine a future New Zealand where '[a]ll was animated; and the manifestations of activity bore witness to the thriftiness of those who had made New Zealand their home'.[36]

With the continuation of the wars, however, this future-oriented reconciliation between the politics of the colony and metropole becomes less imaginable and settler resentment frequently becomes dogma. A sardonic catechism called 'The Philo-Maori Creed', published in the *Southern Cross* and reprinted in the *Hawke's Bay Weekly Times*, featured seven principles, including that '[t]he natives can do no wrong', that the Treaty of Waitangi is only binding for the government, that 'all confiscated lands taken during the war ... shall be restored immediately to the wronged and much-injured natives', and concluding:

> Human nature amongst the New Zealanders has assumed an entirely different degree of development known in the world before: consequently all the experience of ancient and modern sages, both sacred and profane, must be set at naught, and, living as they do at the antipodes, all previous histories and rules must necessarily be reversed.[37]

Through the recital of this mantra, settler-colonial feelings of resentment are nurtured by an understanding of the Antipodes as embodying treachery and betrayal. Although not bearing the same connotative weight in New Zealand as it did in the Australian colonies, the subversive and inversive potential of the Antipodes-as-metaphor could still be used by colonial newspapers to signal their contempt for imperial and colonial governance.

Macaulay's New Zealander as Australasian political archetype

Distinctive in their use of the Antipodes as a metaphor of contrasts and critique, the Australian and New Zealand colonies nonetheless share an approach in their adaptation of that most antipodal figure of future-history: Macaulay's New Zealander.[38] Drawing on the popular trope of tourists visiting imperial ruins, Thomas Babington Macaulay imagines a day when 'some traveller from New Zealand shall, in the midst of a vast solitude, take his stand on a broken arch of London Bridge to sketch the ruins of St. Paul's'.[39] In the colonial Australasian newspapers Macaulay's New Zealander becomes a means of registering cultural cringe and satirizing colonial politicians when they show any signs of self-aggrandizement or when they travel to the metropole as colonial representatives. Demonstrating its imperial sympathies, for example, *Sydney Punch* published a full-page illustration of W. H. Cooper as 'Macaulay's New Zealander Anticipated' after Cooper had 'denounced the British Empire' during his election bid for the Parramatta borough in New South Wales. 'Every school-boy knows the story of Macaulay's New Zealander,' writes *Sydney Punch*, 'but what nobody knew till the other day was that the famous illustrator of departed glories was destined to be, not a New Zealander at all, but a New South Welshman.' Relishing Cooper's failed election attempt, *Sydney Punch* concludes by asking, given this failure, if 'the British Empire [is] any nearer irremediable ruin than before, or reprieved from instant dusty death – at any rate, for the present?'.[40]

Emblematic of colonial presumption, Macaulay's New Zealander was frequently used to signal doubt about colonial politicians' visits, returns and relocations to the metropole. Both the *New Zealand Herald* and Adelaide's *Evening Journal* used Macaulay's New Zealander in 1879 to poke fun at the former premier of New Zealand, Julius Vogel, who was then residing in London as the agent-general for the colony.

Deriding Vogel's proposal to have Britain provide security for all colonial loans, the *New Zealand Herald* mused that it is this very proposal that will bring about the prophecy of the Empire's ruin:

> One cannot help but cast his mind forward when such mighty projects are made to loom before him. One can behold Macaulay's New Zealander sitting on the ruins of London Bridge, and being hardly able to fulfil his duty of sketching the ruins of St Paul's for the tears evoked by the consciousness that England has perished by the lavishness with which she has nourished her dependencies.[41]

Upon hearing the news that Vogel now intended to stand for the Falmouth constituency, the *Evening Journal* featured a ditty titled, 'The "New Zealander" Has Arrived At Last', which predicted the coming of Vogel as the coming of imperial dissolution:

> The great modern Babylon fairly may fear
> That the hour of her downfall is now drawing near,
>   And St. Paul's from its dome to its crypt well may tremble;
> For if only the Jingoes of Falmouth agree,
> Then Macaulay's New Zealander London will see
>   In St. Stephen's when Parliament next shall Assemble.[42]

Vogel's metropolitan political career is, therefore, mocked by both Australian and New Zealand newspapers for the colonial transgression of self-aggrandizement.

Melbourne Punch used a similar satirical tactic in a lengthy feature parodying the visit of the Victorian and New South Wales premiers, George Turner and George Reid, to London for the 1897 Colonial Conference during Queen Victoria's Diamond Jubilee. Titled 'The Career of Colonial Premiers on the Imperial Wallaby in England. Or, the Reign of the Two Georges', this feature mock-history lampoons the overconfident sense of colonial achievement that attached itself to the event, imagining again in antipodal fashion the future light in which this event would be read through Macaulay's artist:

> When Macaulay's New Zealander goes home from the Bridge and writes the history of the present century, the Maori Historian will not fail to note that two great events occurred in the ends of the century. In 1815 the ever-memorable and glorious Battle of Waterloo was fought and won. In 1897 the AUSTRALIAN PREMIERS VISITED ENGLAND. How they came, what they saw and whom they conquered will be truthfully, if feebly, recorded in these pages.[43]

In its transformation of Macaulay's New Zealander into an historian and its jesting comparison of the colonial visit with the Battle of Waterloo, *Melbourne Punch* undermines the assumed precociousness of the colonial politician and minimizes the scale of their political reach and authority. Humorous and dismissive, the antipodal adaptation of Macaulay's New Zealander subverts any attempts of colonial grandstanding in the imperial sphere.

This shared appreciation by Australia and New Zealand of the antipodean nature of Macaulay's New Zealander is captured in a poem by J. Brunton Stephens that frames this artist-historian as an Australasian figure. Fittingly published in the Melbourne newspaper, the *Australasian*, Stephens's poem positions Macaulay's New Zealander as the speaker of the poem desperate to no longer be an idle observer and chronicler but to share his knowledge of the past and future:

> Here three-and-thirty years* I've stood estranged,
> A dream of ruin all around me stretching;
> And centuries shall see me yet unchanged,
> Ever in act to sketch, but nothing sketching;
> Mutely immutable, constrain'dly still,
> With nought to stand against, except my will.

Although standing in London 'immovable and dumb', the poem's 'New Zealander' hears 'inklings' of the scientific, economic, political and industrial discoveries and advancements. He hints that he

> Could tell how empire shall have changed its place
> But must not 'blow,' although an Australasian
> Could tell you which shall be the ruling race,
> But may not shock the orthodox Caucasian,
> Nor dare your curiosity assuage,
> Lest I should make half-castes become the rage; – [44]

Simultaneously challenging and fulfilling Anthony Trollope's accusations of an Australasian penchant for bragging or 'blowing' in Australia and New Zealand, Stephens embraces the self-aggrandizement through an antipodean inversion of the imperial centre. Described in the poem as a 'literary popinjay', Stephens's New Zealander is nonetheless also an intercolonial and international figure: a nineteenth-century Australasian in the heart of the metropole. Macaulay's New Zealander, therefore, embodies the antipodal negotiation of settler-colonial identity that is always relational to the British metropole, even when imagining the relocation of the imperial centre to the Antipodes.

Stephens's antipodal reversal of empire nonetheless leaves the question of white supremacy in this new imperial imaginary ambiguous. The New Zealander of Stephens's poem and its antipodal conversions therefore emphasize the fears and anxieties of Australasian settler colonists as they negotiate their imperial relationships. Fears of colonial ignorance and anonymity, imperial indifference, miscegenation, and racial and social degeneration. These anxieties are, however, always implicit in the antipodean jest through its evocation of a cultural, political or economic opposite: from the Australian projection of a continent with 'room enough for all' that erases Indigenous presence entirely, to the 'Philo-Maori' creed that registers shame at military defeats and a deep fear of the loss of racial supremacy while couched in the superior tone of mockery.

The ability to emphasize contrasts and reversals between colony and metropole is what makes the Antipodes-as-metaphor, and antipodal figures like Macaulay's New Zealander or the usurping colonial child, such an appealing satirical tool for settler-colonial newspapers. It is also what makes it such an adaptable mechanism for exploring the changing dynamics between and within the Australasian colonies and the British Empire in the nineteenth century. By mobilizing the metaphor of inversion as both positive and negative reflections of Britain, the newspapers mediate the discursive battles of what it means to be the Antipodes of Britain, and equally what it means to be Australasian.

While always associative by their very nature, antipodean tropes could also be useful in developing a hybrid political identity for settler colonies ready (sometimes presumptively so) to assert themselves on the imperial stage. While some newspapers, like the Melbourne and Sydney *Punch*, had imperial sympathies, many of the examples explored in this chapter demonstrate the anti-establishment potential of antipodal thinking, whether the establishment in question was colonial or metropolitan. The antipodean metaphor could be used to ridicule presuming colonial politicians as well as arrogant metropolitan officials, but it could also be used to process the shame associated with transportation, the need to emigrate or military defeat. Its malleability is exactly what made it such a useful means of mediating the equally pliable settler-colonial Australasian identity within the ever-shifting imperial imaginary of the British Empire.

Notes

1   *Age*, Tuesday 16 March 1858, 5, http://nla.gov.au/nla.news-article154855450; *Age*, Tuesday 15 June 1858, 5, http://nla.gov.au/nla.news-article154856424.
2   *Age*, Tuesday 15 June 1858, 5.
3   Alfred Hiatt, *Terra Incognita: Mapping the Antipodes Before 1600* (Chicago: The University of Chicago Press, 2008), 19. See also Paul Arthur, 'Antipodean Myths Transformed: The Evolution of Australian Identity', *History Compass* 5:6 (2007): 1862–78; Matthew Boyd Goldie, *The Idea of the Antipodes: Place, People and Voices* (London: Routledge, 2010); Avan Judd Stallard, *Antipodes: In Search of the Southern Continent* (Melbourne: Monash University Publishing, 2016).
4   Arthur, 'Antipodean Myths Transformed', 1863; Goldie, *The Idea of the Antipodes*, 165.
5   Bernard Smith, *Modernism's History: A Study in Twentieth-Century Art and Ideas* (Sydney: UNSW Press, 1998), 7.
6   Paul Giles, *Antipodean America: Australasia and the Australasia and the Constitution of U.S. Literature* (New York: Oxford University Press, 2014), 24, 41. For a longer discussion of the 'comparative consciousness' at operation in nineteenth-century Australian newspapers and how they both use and collapse the myth of the Antipodes, see Sarah Comyn, 'Southern Doubles: Antipodean Life as a Comparative Exercise', in *Worlding the South: Nineteenth-Century Literary Culture and the Southern Settler Colonies*, ed. Sarah Comyn and Porscha Fermanis (Manchester: Manchester University Press, 2021).
7   Phillipa Mein Smith, 'Mapping Australasia', *History Compass* 7:4 (2009): 1099.

8   John Eperjesi, *The Imperialist Imaginary: Visions of Asia and the Pacific in American Culture* (Hanover, NH: Dartmouth College Press, 2004), 90, 5.

9   Giles, *Antipodean America*, 24; and Ian McLean, *White Aborigines: Identity Politics in Australian Art* (Cambridge: Cambridge University Press, 1998), 94.

10   Deryck M. Schreuder and Stuart Ward, *Australia's Empire* (Oxford: Oxford University Press, 2008), 9–10.

11   *Monitor*, Friday 24 November 1826, 4, http://nla.gov.au/nla.news-article31758006.

12   'Topsy Turvy', *Hobart Courier*, Saturday 24 January 1857, 2, http://nla.gov.au/nla.news-article2457584.

13   'Impromptu', *Geelong Advertiser*, Saturday 21 November 1840, 2, http://nla.gov.au/nla.news-article92675360.

14   'Cabinet Portraits', *Australian*, Friday 20 November 1829, 2, http://nla.gov.au/nla.news-article36865606.

15   W. Schultz, 'The Administration of the Law', *Age*, Wednesday 5 November 1856, 4, http://nla.gov.au/nla.news-article154869158.

16   'A Misfit', *Melbourne Punch*, Thursday 29 August 1861, 5, http://nla.gov.au/nla.news-article174526779.

17   Shu-Chuan Yan, '"Kangaroo Politics, Kangaroo Ideas, and Kangaroo Society": The Early Years of Melbourne Punch in Colonial Australia', *Victorian Periodicals Review* 52:1 (Spring 2019): 95.

18   'Reform!', *Age*, Friday 27 August 1858, 6, http://nla.gov.au/nla.news-article154874055. The *Age* indicates that the article is a reprint from the *Melbourne Leader*.

19   G. L. C. 'Ultra Reform', *South Australian Register*, Tuesday 20 July 1858, 3, http://nla.gov.au/nla.news-article49779172.

20   Simon Sleight, 'Wavering between Virtue and Vice: Constructions of Youth in Australian Cartoons of the Late-Victorian Era' in *Drawing the Line: Using Cartoons as Historical Evidence*, ed. Richard Scully and Marian Quartly (Clayton: Monash University ePress, 2009), 05.13.

21   Richard Scully, 'Britain in the *Melbourne Punch*', *Visual Culture in Britain* 20:2 (2019): 158.

22   'Miss Australia to Miss Britannia', *Melbourne Punch*, Thursday 23 April 1868, 1, http://nla.gov.au/nla.news-article174537257.

23   Alfred Hiatt, '*Terra Australis* and the Idea of the Antipodes', in *European Perceptions of Terra Australis*, ed. Alfred Hiatt et al. (London: Routledge, 2011), 15, 18.

24   'To Miss ******: On Her Arrival in New South Wales', *Sydney Gazette and New South Wales Advertiser*, Thursday 29 April 1824, 3, http://nla.gov.au/nla.news-article2182850.

25   'There's Room Enough For All', *Argus*, Monday 23 July 1849, 4, http://nla.gov.au/nla.news-article4773685. The italicized lines (my emphasis) replace these lines from the original poem: 'Oh! Fellow men, remember then, / Whatever chance befall'.

26   'There's Room Enough For All', *Argus*, Monday 23 July 1849, 4.

27   'At the Antipodes', *Sydney Morning Herald*, Tuesday 15 June 1869, 4, http://nla.gov.au/nla.news-page1461957. Reprinted in numerous papers in 1869, including the *Kiama Independent and Shoalhave Advertiser*, *Evening Journal*, and *The Manaro Mercury, and Cooma and Bombala Advertiser*, the poem was republished again in a number of newspapers in 1871 as 'The Husband's Reply'. See, for example, the illustrated version in *Australian Town and Country Journal*, Saturday 9 September 1871, 21, http://nla.gov.au/nla.news-article70468965.

28   Thomas H. Ford and Justin Clemens, 'Barron Field's *Terra Nullius* Operation', *Australian Humanities Review* 65 (2019): 16.

29 'England and its Antipodes', *New Zealander*, 25 April 1866, 3, https://paperspast.natlib. govt.nz/newspapers/NZ18660425.2.18.

30 'Topsy Turvy', *Evening Star*, 12 February 1880, 2, https://paperspast.natlib.govt.nz/ newspapers/ESD18800212.2.13.7.

31 James Belich, *New Zealand Wars and the Victorian Interpretation of Racial Conflict* (1986; Auckland: Auckland University Press, 2015), 39.

32 Belich, *New Zealand Wars*, 314.

33 Flit, 'A New Zealand Christmas Carol', *Nelson Examiner and New Zealand Chronicle*, 28 June 1845, 68, https://paperspast.natlib.govt.nz/newspapers/NENZC18450628.2.12.

34 Flit, 'A New Zealand Christmas Carol', *Nelson Examiner and New Zealand Chronicle*, 5 July 1845, 71–72, https://paperspast.natlib.govt.nz/newspapers/NENZC18450705.2.12.

35 Flit, 'A New Zealand Christmas Carol', *Nelson Examiner and New Zealand Chronicle*, 12 July 1845, 75–6, https://paperspast.natlib.govt.nz/newspapers/NENZC18450712.2.11.

36 Ibid., 76.

37 'The Philo-Maori Creed', *Hawke's Bay Weekly Times*, 21 December 1868, 105, https://paperspast.natlib.govt.nz/newspapers/HBWT18681221.2.5.

38 For an examination of the popularity of this theme and view of history, see Kelly J. Mays, 'Looking Backward, Looking Forward: The Victorians in the Rearview Mirror of Future History', *Victorian Studies* 53:3 (2011): 445–56.

39 Thomas Babington Macaulay, review of Leopold von Ranke's *The Ecclesiastical and Political History of the Popes During the Sixteenth and Seventeenth Centuries* [*Die römische Papste*], trans. S. Austin (London, 1840); *Edinburgh Review* 72 (October 1840): 227–58. For a study of the history of 'Macaulay's New Zealander' and other popular tourists of London in ruins, see David Skilton, 'Contemplating the Ruins of London: Macaulay's New Zealander and Others', *Literary London: Interdisciplinary Studies in the Representation of London* 2:1 (2004): n.p., http://www.literarylondon. org/london-journal/march2004/skilton.html#2; and 'Tourists at the Ruins of London: The Metropolis and the Struggle for Empire', *Cercles* 17 (2007). 93–119; John Strachan, ed., *Parodies of the Romantic Age* (London: Pickering & Chatto, 1999), II, 199–200.

40 'Macaulay's New Zealander Anticipated' and 'Occasional Notes', *Sydney Punch*, Saturday 3 November 1877, 1, 4, http://nla.gov.au/nla.news-article253642369.

41 *New Zealand Herald*, 24 May 1879, 4, https://paperspast.natlib.govt.nz/newspapers/ NZH18790524.2.1.

42 'The "New Zealander" Has Arrived At Last', *Evening Journal*, Saturday 15 November 1879, 2, http://nla.gov.au/nla.news-article197732711.

43 'The Career of Colonial Premiers on the Imperial Wallaby in England. Or, the Reign of the Two Georges', *Melbourne Punch*, Tuesday 27 July 1897, 3, https://trove.nla.gov.au/ newspaper/article/174626712.

44 'Macaulay's New Zealander', *Australasian*, Saturday 25 October 1873, 7, http://nla.gov. au/nla.news-article137583213.

12

Pedestrian Touring, Racial Violence and Bad Feeling in Trans-Tasman Settler Fiction

Porscha Fermanis

Midway through Thorpe [Frances Ellen] Talbot's novel *Philiberta, An Australian Story* (1882), Harper Parkinsson, colonial entrepreneur and founder of the theatrical newspaper 'The Novel Notion', writes to beg money of Madge Fitzroy, one of Melbourne's leading burlesque and pantomime actresses. Modelled on Estella in Charles Dickens's *Great Expectations* (1860), Madge is a cold-hearted and vestigial version of the sentimental heroine, a disingenuous actress whose studied theatricality is offset by the emotional superfluity of Parkinsson's parasitical dandy:

> I am reluctantly forced to appeal to you as my only friend in this heartless hemisphere. Unless you immediately forward me £5 … I shall have to sleep on Collins Street's hard pavement, or on the Yarra's green banks (perhaps in the Yarra's green waters … ?), or on the Queen's wharf, or in the Peripatetic Philosopher's favourite gas-pipe, this night. Forgive my incoherency, dear one of my heart – I am mad with humiliation and despair.[1]

In a strategic reversal of Harold Skimpole's cruel eviction of Jo the crossing sweeper in *Bleak House* (1853), Parkinsson's potential destitution raises the unwelcome spectre of white pauperism in the settler-colonial context, artfully referencing Marcus Clarke's weekly column for the *Australasian* newspaper, 'The Peripatetic Philosopher', the observations of a 'shoeless vagabond' inhabiting the second gas-pipe on Cole's Wharf.[2] Itself heavily influenced by Dickens's urban ethnography, Clarke's column reclaims the downward social mobility of the vagrant by deliberately focusing on the shallow and ephemeral content of passing interest, adopting a mask of unfeeling indifference that ironically exposes the Skimpole-like callousness of Melbourne's sensation-loving appetite crowds and penny publics.[3]

Mobilizing the Philosopher's flâneurial spirit of social critique and invoking two of Dickens's least compassionate characters, *Philiberta*'s exchange of false sentiment in the epicentre of the 'heartless hemisphere' brings to the surface the racialized biopolitics of feeling on which both humanitarian sentiment and Dickensian pathos rest. Far from being merely a standard trope of sentimental fiction, Parkinsson's phrase 'heartless hemisphere' originally circulated in evangelical humanitarian critiques of moral conduct in the southern colonies, where advocacy for the 'heart-rending' suffering of Indigenous peoples was often met with resistance from settler political elites.[4] On the one hand, Madge's gradual transformation from Dickensian villain into philanthropic Victorian heroine redirects *Philiberta*'s moral discourse away from Indigenous suffering and towards white pauperism, thereby consolidating the racial exclusions inherent to Dickens's rejection of 'telescopic philanthropy' in *Bleak House*. On the other hand, the novel deflates settler origin myths of humanitarian benevolence by depicting examples of extreme violence towards Indigenous peoples, as well as identifying repeated failures in the 'affect-saturated' institutions of family and home that supposedly animate white settler states.[5]

Using *Philiberta*'s invocation of heartlessness as its primary reference point, this chapter examines how false, deceptive, cruel, violent and otherwise negative feelings circulate between Australia and New Zealand in nineteenth-century settler fiction. It focuses on a small cluster of peripatetic narratives of trans-Tasman touring or crossing in order to demonstrate the importance of regional affiliations in constructing (and deconstructing) sentimentalized forms of white nationalism, addressing three interrelated issues: first, the performative nature of settler identity and the ways in which affective attachment is used to cultivate an ontological priority to Indigenous land; second, the use of affective registers to 'manage' Indigenous peoples and to demarcate convicts and other politically precarious subjects from 'compassionate' white settler populations; and third, the ways in which the racial logic of settler violence reflects distinctively regional problems of vagrancy, carcerality and exploitative indentured labour practices across Australasia and the wider South Pacific.[6]

Treating the geopolitical landscape of pre-Federation Australasia as simultaneously 'territorial and emotional', the chapter argues for the close connection between affective states, racial ontologies and the rise of settler nationalism. However, it also seeks to recover the neglected role of Australasia as a scalar category that both supplements and revises the movement towards continental nationhood. In foregrounding a regional rather than a national spatial imaginary, trans-Tasman novels provide a basis for re-evaluating foundational national stories and retrospective constructions of colonial nationalism while simultaneously participating in the ongoing production of racial geographies. The fragile yet lingering presence of Australasia as a constructed white space suggests that we must understand the genealogy of settler nationalism as subject to complex, hybrid and shifting scales of emotional identification across intra-, inter-, and transcolonial spaces.[7]

Performing nation: mobility, Melbourne and melodrama

Described by the *Newcastle Morning Herald* as a 'truly Australasian story', Talbot's picaresque novel, documenting its wandering heroine's travels 'vagabondizing' 'up the bush' in New Zealand and 'on the wallaby track' in Australia, points to a history of settler touring, travelling, wandering and working across Australia and New Zealand, often by foot. *Philiberta*'s depiction of 1860s trans-Tasman gold-rush travel begins and ends in the colony of Victoria, but much of it is set in Dunedin, Canterbury and Southland on the South Island of New Zealand, problematizing its self-characterization as an 'Australian story' and reflecting Talbot's own bifurcated identity between a protean childhood in Victoria and an adult residence in Dunedin.[8]

As James Belich has pointed out in his advocacy of the 'Tasman world' as a conceptual frame, 'the Tasman sea was more bridge than barrier' in the mid- to late nineteenth century with pre-Federation colonists seeing themselves as 'shifting and wandering within a single system' or 'linked constellation'.[9] Passenger shipping routes from Sydney and Hobart to Auckland were established in the 1840s, and from 1875 transport and communication links between Melbourne and the South Island of New Zealand were consolidated by the Union Steam Ship Company. By 1883, the Melbourne *Argus* noted that the 'commercial interests of [the lower] South Island are closely allied to Victoria'.[10] Colonial governors across Australasia were, however, quick to notice the relationship between unregulated trans-Tasman movement, 'the nomadic sociality of the diggings' and the 'capitalist excesses' of large cities like Melbourne, using vagrancy laws as tools to prevent crime, drunkenness and prostitution, and to preserve class hierarchies and settled family life following gold-rush population booms.[11]

Urban 'almost from its inception', Parkinsson's letter to Madge invokes Melbourne's capitalist pretensions to wealth, modernity and sophistication, as well as its self-representation as a cosmopolitan 'world' city, the 'London' of the southern hemisphere.[12] While early-nineteenth-century British maps show Port Jackson (or Sydney) as the mother colony of the Pacific region, by the 1860s the gold rush had transformed Melbourne into an intellectual and cultural centre.[13] Talbot's treatment of Melbourne as a place of accelerated modernity and pandemic theatricality most likely drew its inspiration from the city's theatrical culture, visual extravagance and famous night-time spectacles. However, it also recalls Dickens's own interest in stage design and the moral potential of the melodrama. For Parkinsson and Madge, the colonial world is a stage and, as in Dickens's novels, those who view the world as *theatrum mundi* are contrasted in *Philiberta* with those who possess deeper and right-directed feelings.[14]

The restless performativity of settler identity is an explicitly gendered trope in the novel, with theatrical touring linked to an identitarian crisis of belonging that undercuts the domestic fetishism of the white bourgeois home and eventually results in Philiberta becoming 'unsexed': 'What a very vagabond I feel!' said Philiberta ... 'Unsexed, too: trying to live the life of a man while there is all too much of the woman in me.'[15] Anne McClintock has noted the extent to which both vagrancy and 'sumptuary panic' came to 'overdetermine' anxieties about changing identities and 'commutable or absent selves' in the settler colonies.[16] These anxieties were, as Leigh Boucher has argued, partly driven by gendered ideals surrounding personal autonomy in colonial settings.[17] Despite the regular occurrence of cross-dressing in melodramas and pantomimes on the nineteenth-century stage, anti-theatrical tracts worried about the denaturalizing threat that theatrical exhibitionism posed to ideals of domesticity, sincerity and femininity, linking the theatre to prostitution and sexual availability.[18]

Yet while *Philiberta* emphasizes the 'ontological instability of play-acting' and works to show how colonial identities are performatively shaped and contested, it also intimates the ways in which the theatre – and the novel – could strive to produce more communal and long-lasting sentiments. As Anita Callaway has noted, a key feature of the burlesque version of the pantomime of which Madge is Melbourne's undisputed queen was the so-called 'transformation' scene or, more accurately, 'a technically sophisticated sequence of unfolding scenes' that used allegorical dioramas, panoramas or transparencies to represent the 'seemingly inevitable progression' from a 'prosaic colonial present' to a glorious white Australian future.[19]

The racialization of these allegorical scenes was overt, either representing Aboriginal peoples ethnographically as primitive spectacle or encoding the settler 'right to land' through landscape spectacle with its visual depictions of pastoral fantasy.[20] Along with other forms of middlebrow culture, colonial melodramas and their stage-sets appealed to an emergent sense of Australian nationalism and the teleological presumptions of a white settler future, replacing deadly frontier warfare with mythic substitutes and symbolic resolutions. As such, they tended to downplay Australia's carceral past by depicting 'virtuous convicts' and 'amiable bushrangers' as well as representing Australia as a 'nascent neo-classical civilisation'.[21]

Bain Attwood has noted the extent to which the white settlement of Australia has always been rhetorical and performative, seeking to consolidate consensus-driven 'stories of rightful possession' in ways that secured a new 'point of origin' for the nascent nation. If settlers attempted to discredit autochthonous ways of preserving knowledge, relegating the embodied memory systems of Indigenous peoples to the non-archival and the anachronistic, their own performances deployed ritualized and reiterative practices.[22] In evading the differences between myth and material reality, colonial melodramas increasingly sought to use the staged or performed nation as a way of eliding the archival nation, whose material records, however incomplete, contained evidence of mass murder, indentured labour, crime and carcerality – evidence that continued to circulate across Australasia in the storeyed and sometimes shadowy layers of oral memory, serialized fiction and other forms of local print culture.[23]

Archival nation: frontier violence, convictism and collective feeling

Despite being Australian-born, Philiberta has little emotional attachment to the colony of Victoria, describing her feelings of patriotism as 'vague' rather than 'definite'. This failure of affective attachment is attributed to the violent events of her childhood, which cyclically prevent her from establishing those white 'alchemies of indigeneity' through which novels of settlement tend to legitimize land claims and dispossession.[24] The novel's opening depiction of the 'roaring destruction' of a drought and bush fire in Merlyn Creek, Victoria, quickly gives way to the death of Philiberta's mother and the loss of her first abortive home. Later adopted by the Scottish station owner John Campbell, Philiberta internalizes various settler subjectivities in the process of adolescence, modelling herself first on a fanatical missionary preacher and then a scientific 'hybrid evolutionist', before taking up her place as landowner at Morven station near Emu Creek (originally Burnagulla and home to the Djargurd Wurrung people).[25]

Philiberta's discursive shift from the paternalistic language of Christian universalism to evolutionary discourses reflects the hardening of biological race theory in the 1860s, when a racialized scientific orthodoxy increasingly questioned the humanity of Aboriginal peoples. Indeed, Philiberta's second home is destroyed by an apocalyptic sequence of events set in process by the deliberate mass poisoning of the Aboriginal tribe who live near Morven station, resulting in a reprisal party of fifty Aboriginal men attacking Morven and causing Campbell and his wife to commit suicide, as well as initiating 'a conflagration that devastated all the country for miles'.[26] The novel's mass killing is a fictional rendering of the 'Murdering Gully' (Puuroyup) massacre that occurred in October 1839 near Camperdown, Victoria, when thirty-five men, women and children of the Tarnbeere Gundidj tribe were shot dead by Frederick Taylor and station hands from Glenormiston station in retaliation for killing sheep. The massacre effectively destroyed the tribe and did not result in any reprisals.[27]

As Marilyn Lake has pointed out, the Australian colonial frontier was a place where white men could do as they liked and where male citizenship involved both an unspoken 'right' and a 'preparedness to kill', resulting in hundreds of frontier massacres of Aboriginal peoples over the first 140 years of the settler occupation of Australia. Paradoxically, the frontier, a place 'on the borders', became increasingly emblematic of Australian national experience, with settler print culture representing pioneering settlers as suffering victims rather than as perpetrators of violence.[28] Notwithstanding the convictions of settler perpetrators following the Myall Creek Massacre of 1838, images of frontier conflict – with the Aboriginal foe depicted as 'primitive' and 'savage' and settlers as 'genteel' and 'vulnerable' – were reproduced repeatedly in nineteenth-century print culture.[29] These sentimentalized images of European vulnerability were, as Rachel Standfield has argued, ultimately productive of more rather than less violence, with settlers responding with disproportionate aggression to subjugate 'dangerous' Indigenous peoples.[30]

The intimacy of the frontier violence in *Philiberta*, with the Aboriginal victims well known to their murderers, points to the quotidian, everyday nature of colonial violence, and the rapid escalation of small acts of theft to mass murder.[31] While the 'swollen black distorted bodies' of the murdered Aboriginal victims, lying 'in all possible attitudes begotten of pain and death' in a 'grotesque tableaux', are mentioned in passing as a 'horrible sight', the crime of concealing the poison in consumables is attributed to the depraved and covert acts of ex-convict station hands. The novel thereby frames 'frontier atrocity as a convict' rather than a settler crime, detaching complicity in Indigenous murder and dispossession from both state-sanctioned government forces and the honest, compassionate, middle-class settler.[32]

The heartlessness of the convict figure is a common theme in Australian settler fiction. However, the idea of the convict as the original 'source of colonial sin and contagion' has a special resonance in trans-Tasman novels, where the convict taint is imported to free New Zealand from penal Australia, both by first-generation escaped convicts and their mobile second-generation offspring. While the New Zealand settlements saw convictism as an opportunity to separate themselves from the Australian colonies and to characterize themselves as the most 'English' of the southern settler colonies, the convict figure repeatedly resurfaces across antipodean print culture, problematizing the geographic juxtaposition of free and carceral spaces, and providing 'a disruptive counterpart to the supposed triumphal progression of Anglo-Saxon culture and blood'.[33]

In W. M. Southan's *The Two Lawyers*, published in Dunedin in 1881 but set between Timaru, Melbourne and Hobart, John Hobart, the 'degenerate' son of a 'lifer' and 'a true specimen of what his father was', is represented as 'congenitally' unable to 'belong to the national household [or] family'.[34] Setting up contrastive pairings between Timaru and Melbourne/Van Diemen's Land, the novel's plot hinges on the conscious dissimulation that characterizes the homosocial friendship between the honest Frank Perryman and the deceptive bigamist Hobart.[35] It is Hobart's lack of ability to feel the quotidian bonds of civic manhood, domesticity and friendship – his monstrous dandified antipathy – that places him outside the bounds of the socially and civically constituted colonial subject. The intergenerational taint of convict blood, represented as an atavistic heredity ('blood will tell'), means that Hobart must be returned to and contained within Van Diemen's Land, leaving both Melbourne and Timaru free from the threat of the convict class.[36]

Hobart's heartlessness is suggestive of the 'epistemological function' of the emotions in defining the differences between the human and the non-human, the determined and the free, and the citizen and the subject in settler fiction.[37] In *Philiberta* the convict figure and threat is largely contained within Australia, but the novel's 'heartless' acts follow a similarly regional logic, contrasting an 'old' degenerate and heartless Australia with a 'young' morally healthy New Zealand, albeit one that is increasingly impacted by the oceanic interconnection of labour regimes and commodity markets across the South Pacific. Talbot's depiction of the massacre of a hundred Chinese passengers on a ship called the *Star* bound for Hong Kong, as well as Philiberta's inadvertent part in a blackbirding scheme involving Indian indentured labourers intended for the Colonial Sugar Refining Company in Fiji, integrates these spaces into the novel's cartographic imaginary of a 'heartless hemisphere', reflecting Fiji's status as the 'cultural terminus' of the white Pacific.[38]

The novel's racialization of mobility is evident in Philiberta's early friendships with Chinese traders in Victoria, who are largely excluded from white European communities. Later the threat of Chinese immigration, and its 'transactional' quality, becomes more pronounced. As Tony Ballantyne has pointed out, from 1865 onwards anxieties about mobility in New Zealand centred on groups of Cantonese miners in Otago. As large numbers of immigrants came into New Zealand from Guangdong via Canton and Hong Kong, arguments in favour of tighter border controls were debated in the New Zealand Parliament, with a particular source of anxiety resting on the perceived lack of Chinese commitment to permanent settlement and the fact that the bodies or bones of their dead were returned to China – the very custom that causes the sailors (on the ship on which Philiberta travels) to mutiny and massacre Chinese passengers, who carry with them 'their dead for burial in their native land'.[39]

Philiberta's self-suppression of both the blackbirding scheme and the massacre on the *Star* is suggestive of the novel's tendency to raise European atrocities and then to repress or withhold their details, allowing violent acts to re-emerge in uncanny forms. This tendency is particularly evident in Philiberta's interactions with Indigenous peoples. While ill on the road during a provincial theatrical tour to small digging townships in Victoria, Philiberta is tenderly nursed back to health by a compassionate but 'ignoble' Aboriginal woman Queen Mary, 'a scraggy old lubra of most repulsive appearance', herself on a 'pedestrian tour' of various pubs surrounding the townships.[40] Part of the emerging discourse of the 'Aboriginal vagrant', Queen Mary's state of undress, destitution and drunkenness suggests that she is one of the dispossessed Indigenous 'underclass' living on the margins of colonial cities and towns following the explosive demographic transformations produced by the Victorian gold rush.[41]

An 'Aboriginal mother' in a novel lacking in functioning mother figures, Queen Mary mistakes Philiberta first for a 'piccaninny' and then for a boy – the emaciated Philiberta is now, quite literally, the white waif of Dickensian fiction – nursing her back to health in a reversal of the paternalistic discourses of white philanthropy and protectionism. When Philiberta refuses to give her rum in return because it is 'a type of poison', Queen Mary asks for actual poison, performing a mock death scene falling 'lengthwise on the ground, writhing, struggling, kicking; giving altogether a fine dramatic representation of the agonies of death by poison'.[42]

Queen Mary's belated re-enactment of the agonies of the mass-poisoning scene at Morven station is suggestive both of the performativity of violence and of its traumatic and uncanny temporalities, in which lingering manifestations of dead or disappeared Indigenous peoples return in anachronistic ways to haunt the white settler state. Yet if Indigenous 'ghosts' are part of a larger narrative that Simone Bignall calls 'the negative aboriginal state', Philiberta's repressed memory of violence is not so much a sign of settler guilt as the natural consequence of a settler-colonial logic that extends to all settler–Indigenous and, via corrupting exposure to European violence, to Indigenous–Indigenous relations: 'Strick-a-neene, ar-sa-nikee kill um dingo dead? Whitefellow, blackfellow dead?'[43] Hauntingly elongated by Queen Mary's pidgin English, a marker of colonial assimilation and linguistic genocide, the exchange of sentiment between Philiberta and Queen Mary is always subject to the limits imposed by the settler-colonial state, with poison acting as the uncanny sign of colonial exchange relations.

Touring nation: New Zealand, gender reversal and 'homecoming'

Thanks to Queen Mary, Philiberta survives her illness. Yet two fires, the death of her birth mother, the mass murder of over a dozen Aborigines, the suicide of her adoptive parents and the total destruction of her second home occur rapidly in the first half a dozen chapters of the novel, establishing the colony of Victoria as a place of racial violence and climatic disaster. As Bernard Smith has noted, the image of Australia as a country that 'taxed human endurance to the limit' developed and spread during the second half of the nineteenth century. Anxieties about the hostility of the environment, the aridity of the country's inland areas, and its susceptibility to flood, fire and drought are reproduced in numerous climatic disaster narratives in Australian settler fiction.[44]

The South Island of New Zealand, by contrast, is represented as relatively free of environmental catastrophe and racial tensions, with the Otago and Canterbury settlements depicted as orderly Wakefieldian towns based on systems of hired labour and racial assimilation. In E. Simeon Elwell's *The Boy Colonists; or Eight Years of Colonial Life in Otago, New Zealand* (1878), Otago is completely free of racial violence, whereas shearers' tales from the 'other side' detail escalating levels and scales of violence in frontier Australia, from the casual shooting of Aboriginals, to 'fearful and ghastly' massacres, to 'hideous and dismal' reprisals and counter-reprisals.[45] The commodity most emblematic of the growth and wealth of the Australasian colonies thus enables the circulation of tales of violence via mobile shearers and moveable goods 'in which the memories of places have been left encrypted', exposing feelings of horror and disgust at the heart of the global commodity market.[46]

Sickened by shepherd life in Australia and the 'terrible' and 'indiscriminate slaughter' of Aboriginal peoples, Clifford, the shearer in *The Boy Colonists*, leaves for New Zealand, where the 'great war' on the North Island is represented as an organized equitable campaign unrelated to the punitive killings that characterize Australian settler violence. Angela Woollacott has demonstrated the extent to which military volunteerism contributed to violence against Indigenous peoples in the settler colonies, arguing that military forces installed cultures of heroic masculinity that escalated frontier killings. Here, however, the war is said to reduce frontier violence by preventing the 'great cruelties [that] would have been practised' by the settlers, 'cruelties such as the soldiers would not have been permitted to indulge in'.[47]

In *Philiberta*, too, there is a marked contrast between depictions of Victoria and Otago. Unlike the densely populated, hyper-urban Melbourne with its cold-hearted theatrical upstarts, the self-consciously genteel Dunedin is a 'fair white city' of 'slender graceful spires'. Philiberta's first friend is Emma Retlaw, 'a woman of intense feeling and boundless sympathy', as well as a freethinker opposed to religious orthodoxy, whose sincerity opposes the valorization of surfaces that characterizes the theatrical milieu in Melbourne. Retlaw's freethinking colleagues belittle the 'galloping rhymes' of Philiberta's favourite poet, the colonial balladeer Adam Lindsay Gordon, as maudlin 'poetry of a purely emotional type', arguing in favour of Wordsworthian 'depth, reflection, and philosophy in verse'. Despite her critique of Wordsworth's 'dreariness', Philiberta's eventual rejection of the distinctively Australian idioms of Gordon's verse suggests that the narrative shift from Victoria to Otago is one from unfeeling transactionalism to emotional depth, and from frontier violence to Wakefieldian order.[48]

Philiberta's second visit to the South Island, a theatrical tour during which she passes as a male violinist, similarly reflects the slow time of Wordsworthian attachment and reflection. Christchurch in the Canterbury region is described as a 'garden city'; and the landscape she encounters while travelling by foot in the Naseby and Maniototo districts is an 'orderly', 'homely' and 'domestic' settler terrain known as 'Thompson's Farm-yard'. A notorious racial theorist, whose 'Barata' theory argued that Māori were descendants of an archaic 'Negroid' race of India, John Turnbull Thompson was Government Surveyor in Otago from the 1850s to the 1870s. His place names replaced Māori names with those of farm animals in his local Northumbrian dialect (Kyeburn, Sowburn, Swineburn, Hogburn etc.).[49]

The strong regional identities in settler New Zealand – with the South Island representing a 'new Scotland' and the North Island a 'new England' – reproduced and internalized some of Britain's own archipelagic and provincial affiliations, albeit in a geographically inverted form.[50] Far more than the North Island, the green and enclosed South Island was an ideal foil for the hyper-modern Melbourne and the colony of Victoria more generally. While depictions of the South Island as a domesticated 'farm for England' and an idyllic, pre-industrialized 'Little England' in the South Seas became something of a cliché in emigration literature, they were premised on the actual and discursive erasure of Māori and therefore performed 'important ideological work', inscribing settler values onto the local environment, evacuating colonial landscapes of prior Indigenous cultures and eliding uncomfortable questions about the cross-cultural violence that effected Indigenous removal.[51]

Some reviewers dismissed this section of the novel as a 'tedious' 'itinerary of New Zealand', but Philiberta's pedestrian tour of the South Island enables a utopian mapping of settler terrain cleared of any Māori presence, celebrating a place where 'you have nothing to fear from treacherous blacks'.[52] In Australia, on the other hand, the Indigenous presence and 'threat' persists, even if in *Philiberta* that threat is increasingly redirected inwards towards 'white society's "darker self"'.[53] Philiberta's third and final attempt at 'homing' after her prolonged theatrical tour in New Zealand is to work in disguise for her former lover Edward Paget at his station Yoanderruk outside of Melbourne. Yoanderruk has an impressive homestead but it is yet another broken settler home in which the domestic ideal is a thin veneer covering the alcoholism that turns Paget's wife into a 'devilish' caricature of her sentimentalized suffering self.[54]

The gothic tropes of this part of the novel invited comparisons in reviews with Charlotte Brontë's *Jane Eyre* (1847). However, *Philiberta*'s deflation of the white bourgeois home also anticipates the 'New Woman' fiction of Olive Schreiner and others, as Philiberta, disguised as Phil Tempest, takes on the most hyper-masculine of roles in nascent Australian national culture, the stockman or bushman, later a key symbol of Australian nationalism.[55] By co-opting a masculine construction that defines itself against the feminine principle, Phil's paid work as a cross-dressing man undermines the value of the sentimental domestic ideal, already undercut in the novel by Philiberta's vocation as an actress and by Paget's wife, who in crippling her own son is incapable of nurturing motherhood in the way intended by the fetishization of middle-class domesticity.[56]

The destabilizing, queer potential of Philiberta's cross-dressing becomes even more apparent when her loss of femininity renders her unrecognizable to her former lover, thus deflating the sentimental power of the 'recognition' scene that motored the melodramatic fictions and theatricals of the period. Overhearing Paget's unrequited declaration of love to Madge, by now transformed into a more acceptable version of Victorian womanhood through her philanthropic endeavours, Philiberta is displaced from her third broken home and takes off on her final pedestrian tour into the Victorian desert, where, this time, no compassionate Aboriginal mother appears to guide or nurse her: 'And below, a ragged, travel-stained, dead woman – at rest, at rest.'[57]

Deconstructing nation: genres, canons and foundation myths

For a colonial reading public saturated in the ritualized death scenes of Victorian melodrama, Philiberta's suicide in the Australian interior was almost inexplicable.

Despite praise for its local colouring and the realism of its 'every-day records of Australian travel', various reviews in the colonial press described the novel as 'glaringly improbable' and 'disappointing', and declared its 'tragic termination' 'needless and absurd'. A female reader writing from Geelong on 11 July 1882 noted in a letter to the Melbourne *Leader* that she was not prepared for Philiberta's 'unhappy fate' or for the 'unnatural termination' of the novel, complaining: 'I cannot perceive any truth or moral in the tale.' Feeling cheated by the novel's denial of either a romantic reconciliation or a morally transformative 'good death', readerly consensus is that the cursory nature of Philiberta's death did not allow the expected tears to flow and failed to reproduce the immersive experience of Dickensian affect.[58]

The novel certainly fails to conform either to the allegorical transformation scene of the melodrama or to the new national fictions that were emerging in Australia in the 1880s. While Philiberta is initially established as one of those independent-minded, Australian-born girls representing the spirit of the future nation, the novel seriously questions the kind of idealized femininity and heteronormative domesticity on which both Australian girlhood novels and masculine nationalist fantasies so often rest.[59] If Philiberta's final pedestrian tour could be said to look forward to the mythologizing trope of the 'heroic failure' and 'death in the interior' that came to ground white Australia's necronationalism in the land, there is nonetheless no functioning nuclear family in the novel, just as there is no successful romantic relationship that can provide the basis for permanent settlement, patriarchal lineage and affective nationality.[60] With little sense of emotional or spiritual belonging, and frequent failures to invest in home, the novel seems to 'write unsettlement'.[61]

Jason Rudy's insight about how '*reproducing Britain* [in the colonies] meant *reproducing sentiment*' takes on new significance here, where the reproduction of sentiment involves the mobilization of negative affect associated with Dickens's villains and where the novel substantially revises the cultural expectations associated with both the colonial and metropolitan melodrama.[62] The performance of nationhood is, of course, always a reiterative and citational practice, involving the machinery of allusion and intertextuality. In this case, however, Dickensian allusion is not deployed 'in deliberate anticipation' of 'a felt national tradition' or in consolidation of the territorial identity of the nation, but rather to showcase settler anxieties about precarity, impermanence and the impossibility of collective feeling, as well as to invoke emotional affiliations that are both smaller and greater than continental nationhood.[63]

What then are we to make of the broken settler and Indigenous homes in *Philiberta*? And what do novels like *Philiberta* reveal about 'the cartographic imaginary of that time before nation'? In some ways, *Philiberta* and other trans-Tasman novels work to replace metropolitan touchstones of 'home' and 'abroad' and 'old world' and 'new world' with more local and regional ones, shifting dominant perspectives away from metropolitan centres.[64] By projecting such radically different affective geographies of (and within) Australia and New Zealand, the novels seem, on the one hand, to anticipate the eroticized cultural differences that nation states cultivate. On the other hand, such novels place a regional relationship at the centre of their vision, involving a geographic repositioning of the affective bonds that mark out the relationship between old worlds and new. London increasingly becomes the periphery rather than the affective or imagined centre of Australasian colonial plots, a place where minor characters such as Madge depart but where the central resolution of the novel cannot take place.[65]

By the 1890s, Thorpe Talbot had herself been co-opted into a national proto-canon of 'distinctively Australian literature', which included, according to the *Daily Northern Argus*, 'Marcus Clark, Mrs. Campbell Praed, Helen Mathers, Mr. B. L. Fargeon, Mr. Fergus Hulme, Rolf Boldrewood, Thorpe Talbot, and a long procession of lesser worthies' that will produce 'a record of national genius' and 'intellectual achievement worthy of our Anglo-Saxon descent'.[66] A decade later, this white genealogical settler canon – closely linked to globe-spanning 'Greater Britain' discourses about white supremacy and racial destiny – would be whittled down to remove Fargeon, Talbot, Praed and Mathers, reflecting both the self-consciously nationalist attitudes that turned their back on Australasian ties following Federation in 1901, and the explicitly masculinist discourses associated with the Sydney *Bulletin* group.[67] As well as being 'racist, anti-Semitic, anti-Imperialist and loudly misogynist', this group promoted a project of cultural separation from New Zealand and the Pacific Islands as much as from Britain, reifying a decidedly isolationist 'island nation' via songs, oral stories and other 'rituals of possession' that ironically involved, as Jonathan Dunk has pointed out, the 'heterologous appropriation of a collection of signifiers of Aboriginality'.[68]

The hardening of colonial demarcations into national distinctions following Australian Federation in the first decade of the twentieth century has had a profound effect on the ways in which we retrospectively understand nineteenth-century settler fiction and its rendering of highly contested colonial spaces, particularly from the 1950s onwards when intellectuals idealized the 1890s as part of a search 'for roots that might sustain a post-war resurgence of Australian literary culture'.[69] While this view of the 1890s has long been critiqued, not least by the transnational turn in Australian Studies, the problem of scale persists in understandings of Australian literary history. If, as Alan Atkinson has suggested, we need to begin 'imagining Australia in parts rather than as a preordained unity', we equally need to see Australia and New Zealand as interconnected parts of what Robert Dixon calls the 'complex scalar mosaic of the pre-Federation era'.[70] As Donald Denoon has put it, Australasia, 'dismembered' at the time of Australian Federation, needs to be 're-membered' in accounts of colonial identity and canon formation.[71]

Thinking about novels like *Philiberta* as 'Australasian' rather than 'Australian' means that we can read settler fiction with an alertness towards the contemporary fluidity of sociopolitical space as well as the actual mobility of people and characters within that space. In returning the past to its own present, it is particularly important to understand representations of settler violence towards Indigenous and non-European peoples within a local and regional rather than just a national or proto-national scalar framework. Amanda Nettelbeck and Robert Foster have argued that both violence and the remembrance of violence against Aboriginal peoples should be examined on a regional scale, 'providing opportunities for altering or reshaping narratives of foundation that are more generic or resilient on the national scale'. As they point out, the 'great Australian silence' on the significance of Aboriginal peoples and their history in the story of European settlement was 'never . . . total at the regional' or local level.[72]

It is precisely this opportunity for re-evaluating foundational stories that so-called minor novels like *Philiberta* and other trans-Tasman novels present. As Gilles Deleuze and Félix Guattari have argued, minor literature is nearly always 'affected by a high coefficient of deterritorialization.'[73] Unlike those settler novels organized spatially and ideologically around the homestead, regional novels of transit or touring tend to be set outside of the privatized domestic spaces of homes and drawing rooms, with their action taking place in and on roads, pubs, goldfields and other public places. And unlike the typical colonial *Bildungsroman* where the rootless protagonist eventually domesticates 'itinerant (false) tendencies' and gains 'a legal or moral right' to Indigenous land, such novels allow for an 'unhomely reversal' of the affective ties of bourgeois domesticity and territorial possession.[74] Whereas in canonical novels of nationalist sentiment the violence of the frontier tends to give way to tales of either pioneer hardship or domestic cohesion, the immediatism of trans-Tasman touring portrays Indigenous erasure as it happens. A renewed focus on pre-Federation narratives – most of them serialized in local print culture – can therefore disrupt retrospective performances of colonial nationalism by emphasizing highly explicit accounts of localized violence towards Indigenous peoples, who themselves experienced sovereign boundaries in ways very different to those enshrined in settler performances of nationhood.[75]

Notes

1   Thorpe [Frances Ellen] Talbot, *Philiberta. A Novel* (Melbourne: E. W. Cole, 1882), 162. For Madge's affinities with Estella, see ibid., 165–6, 179. *Philiberta* was first published serially in the Melbourne *Leader* in 1882 and subsequently in the *Newcastle Morning Herald* in 1895. In serialized form, it was sub-titled 'An Australian Tale' or 'An Australian Story'. See Lawrence Jones, 'The "strangely curious career" of *Philiberta*: A "Lost" New Zealand Novel', *Kotare* 1:1 (1998): 20–4.

2   Marcus Clarke, *The Peripatetic Philosopher* (Melbourne: George Robertson, 1869), 31. On the Dickensian dandy and Skimpole's heartless elegance, see Juliet John, *Dickens's Villains: Melodrama, Character, and Popular Culture* (Oxford: Oxford University Press, 2003), 157–67.

3   David Conley, 'Marcus Clarke: The Romance of Reality', *Australian Studies in Journalism* 9 (2000): 51–74; and Mary L. Shannon, *Dickens, Reynolds, and Mayhew on Wellington Street: The Print Culture of a Victorian Street* (London: Routledge, 2006), 177, 205.

4   *Report of the Parliamentary Select Committee on Aboriginal Tribes (British Settlements)* (London: William Ball, 1837), v–vi, 55. See, e.g., Penelope Edmonds and Anna Johnson, 'Empire, Humanitarianism and Violence in the Colonies', *Journal of Colonialism and Colonial History* 17:1 (2016): https://muse.jhu.edu/article/613279.

5   Talbot, *Philiberta*, 228; Jane Lydon, *Imperial Emotions: The Politics of Empathy Across the British Empire* (Oxford: Oxford University Press, 2020), 100–22; Lauren Berlant, *The Female Complaint: The Unfinished Business of Sentimentality in American Culture* (Durham, NC: Duke University Press, 2008), 12.

6   On affective control, see Ann Laura Stoler, 'Affective States', in *A Companion to the Anthropology of Politics*, ed. David Nugent and Joan Vincent (Oxford: Blackwell Publishers, 2007), 4–20.

7   Naomi Greyser, *On Sympathetic Grounds: Race, Gender, and Affective Geographies in Nineteenth-Century North America* (Oxford: Oxford University Press, 2018), 4, 1.

8   Anon, 'New Tale. Philiberta', *Newcastle Morning Herald and Miners' Advocate*, 28 March 1895, 4; *Philiberta*, 298, 180, 187; Jones, '*Philiberta*', 20–4.

9   James Belich, *Making Peoples: A History of New Zealanders, from Polynesian Settlement to the End of the Nineteenth Century* (London: Penguin Books, 1996), 134, and *Paradise Reforged: A History of the New Zealanders from the 1880s to the Year 2000* (Honolulu: University of Hawai'i Press, 2001), 47–8.

10 Michael Stevens, '"A Defining Characteristic of the Southern People": Southern Māori Mobility and the Tasman World', in *Indigenous Mobilities Across and Beyond the Antipodes*, ed. Rachel Standfield (Canberra: ANU Press, 2018), 95; 'The Vagabond', 'Roundabout New Zealand. The Bluff to Dunedin', *Argus*, 26 May 1883, 13.

11 Philip Steer, 'Greater Britain: Jevons, Trollope, and Settler Colonialism', *Victorian Studies* 58:3 (2016): 447. See, e.g., Catharine Coleborne, 'Law's Mobility: Vagrancy and Imperial Legality in the Trans-Tasman Colonial World, 1860s–1914', in *New Zealand's Empire*, ed. Katie Pickles and Catharine Coleborne (Manchester: Manchester University Press, 2016), 89–101.

12 Anita Callaway, *Visual Ephemera: Theatrical Art in Nineteenth-Century Australia* (Sydney: UNSW Press, 2000), 36. On Melbourne as a world city, see, e.g., Frederick Sinnett, 'The Fiction Fields of Australia', *Journal of Australasia* 1 (1856): 97–105, 199–208; and Francis W. L. Adams, 'Melbourne and her Civilization', in *Australian Essays* (Melbourne: William Inglis & Co., 1886), 1–10.

13 Philippa Mein Smith, 'Mapping Australasia', *History Compass* 7:4 (2009): 1105, 1108. On Dickens and popular middlebrow entertainments in Australia, see Susan K. Martin and Kylie Mirmohamadi, *Colonial Dickens: What Australians Made of the World's Favourite Author* (North Melbourne: Australian Scholarly Publishing, 2012).

14 John, *Dickens's Villains*, 169.

15 Talbot, *Philiberta*, 296.

16 Anne McClintock, *Imperial Leather: Race, Gender and Sexuality in the Colonial Contest* (London: Routledge, 1995), 174, 133.

17 Leigh Boucher, 'Race, Rights and the Re-forming Settler Polity in Mid-nineteenth Century Victoria', *Journal of Australian Colonial History* 15 (2013): 92–3.

18 See, e.g., Jane Woollard, 'The Elasticity of Her Spirits': Actresses and Resilience on the Nineteenth-Century Colonial Stage', *Australian Drama Studies* 70 (2017): 7–34; and Lucy Chesser, 'More Playful Than Anxious: Cross-Dressing, Sex-Impersonation and the Colonial Stage', *Australian Drama Studies* 52 (2008): 148–64.

19 Emily Allen, *Theatre Figures: The Production of the Nineteenth-Century British Novel* (Columbus: Ohio State University Press, 2003), 17; Callaway, *Visual Ephemera*, viii.

20 Patricia Smyth, 'Landscape and Identity in Australian Melodrama', *Journal of Victorian Culture* 21:3 (2016): 363–86.

21 Gabrielle Wolf, 'Innocent Convicts and Respectable Bushrangers: History and the Nation in Melbourne Melodrama, 1890–1914', *Journal of Australian Studies* 28:81 (2004): 73, 75; David Higgins, 'Writing to Colonial Australia: Barron Field and Charles Lamb', *Nineteenth-Century Contexts* 32:3 (2010): 219.

22 Bain Attwood, *Possession: Batman's Treaty and the Matter of History* (Melbourne: Miegunyah Press, 2009), 101; Amanda Nettelbeck and Robert Foster, 'Commemorating Foundation: A Study in Regional Historical Memory', *History Australia* 7:3 (2010): 53.3; Diane Taylor, *The Archive and the Repertoire: Performing Cultural Memory in the Americas* (Durham, NC: Duke University Press, 2003), 3.

23 Ann Laura Stoler, *Along the Archival Grain: Epistemic Anxieties and Colonial Common Sense* (Princeton: Princeton University Press, 2009), 22. On violence in the colonial

short story, see Rachael Weaver, 'Colonial Violence and Forgotten Fiction', *Australian Literary Studies* 24:2 (2009): 33–53.

24 Talbot, *Philiberta*, 110; Audra Simpson, 'From White into Red: Captivity Narratives as Alchemies of Race and Citizenship', *American Quarterly* 60:2 (2008): 251–7.

25 Talbot, *Philiberta*, 5, 6, 21, 23, 27.

26 Ibid., 49.

27 Leaving for India in early 1840, Taylor eventually returned to Australia in 1844, where he was later involved in multiple massacres of the Gunai people in Gippsland. See, e.g., Ian D. Clark, *Scars in the Landscape: A Register of Massacre Sites in Western Victoria 1803–1859* (Acton: Aboriginal Studies Press, 1995), 103–18. See also the University of Newcastle Massacre Map, which suggests that large-scale reprisals by Aboriginal people were rare: https://c21ch.newcastle.edu.au/colonialmassacres/map.php.

28 Marilyn Lake, 'Frontier Feminism and the Marauding White Man', *Journal of Australian Studies* 20:49 (1996): 12–20.

29 Lydon, *Imperial Emotions*, 53.

30 Rachel Standfield, 'Violence and the Intimacy of Imperial Ethnography: The Endeavour in the Pacific', in *Moving Subjects: Mobility, Intimacy and Gender in an Age of Empire*, ed. Antoinette Burton and Tony Ballantyne (Champaign: University of Illinois Press, 2008), 33.

31 See, e.g., Penelope Edmonds and Amanda Nettelbeck, eds, *Intimacies of Violence in the Settler Colony: Economies of Dispossession Around the Pacific Rim* (Basingstoke: Palgrave Macmillan, 2018).

32 *Philiberta*, 38; Jane Lydon, 'Anti-slavery in Australia: Picturing the 1833 Myall Creek Massacre', *History Compass* 15 (2017): 6.

33 Ibid.; Anna Johnson, 'Travelling the Tasman World: Travel Writing and Narratives of Transit', in *New Zealand's Empire*, ed. Pickles and Colebourne, 80.

34 W. M. Southan, *The Two Lawyers* (Dunedin: John Mackay, 1881), 25. Southan was himself a fraudster and failed businessman, who did three years of hard labour.

35 Vanessa Smith, *Intimate Strangers: Friendship, Exchange and Pacific Encounters* (Cambridge: Cambridge University Press, 2010), 111.

36 Ibid., 137; Southan, *Two Lawyers*, 197.

37 Rachel Ablow, 'Introduction: Victorian Emotions', *Victorian Studies* 50:3 (2008): 375.

38 Talbot, *Philiberta*, 128–9, 130; Mein Smith, 'Mapping Australasia', 1108.

39 Tony Ballantyne, 'Mobility, Empire, Colonisation', *History Australia* 11:2 (2014): 34–5; *Philiberta*, 128, 129.

40 Ibid., 247, 185.

41 Amanda Nettelbeck, 'Creating the Aboriginal Vagrant: Protective Governance and Indigenous Mobility in Colonial Australia', *Pacific Historical Review* 87:1 (2018): 92, 93, 80.

42 Talbot, *Philiberta*, 187, 188.

43 Simone Bignall, *Postcolonial Agency: Critique and Constructivism* (Edinburgh: Edinburgh University Press, 2010), 77–91; Talbot, *Philiberta*, 188.

44 Bernard Smith, ed., *Documents on Art and Taste in Australia 1770–1914* (Melbourne: Oxford University Press, 1975), 128.

45 E. Simeon Elwell, *The Boy Colonists; or Eight Years of Colonial Life in Otago, New Zealand* (London: Simpkin, Marshall & Co., 1878), 73.

46 Josephine McDonagh, 'On Settling and Being Unsettled: Legitimacy and Settlement Around 1850', in *Legitimacy and Illegitimacy in Nineteenth-Century Law, Literature and History*, ed. Margot Finn et al. (Basingstoke: Palgrave Macmillan, 2010), 58.

47 Angela Woollacott, *Gender and Empire* (Basingstoke: Palgrave Macmillan, 2006), ch. 3; Elwell, *Boy Colonists*, 74, 97.

48 Talbot, *Philiberta*, 78, 84, 85.

49 Wilbert Wong Wei Wen, 'John Turnbull Thompson and the *Hikayat Abdullah*', *New Zealand Journal of Asian Studies* 17:2 (2015): 110.

50 Joel Barnes, 'The View from the Margins: John Pocock and the Antipodean Origins of Four Nations History': https://fournationshistory.wordpress.com/2015/09/28/the-view-from-the-margins-john-pocock-and-the-antipodean-origins-of-four-nations-history/ (accessed 25 March 2021).

51 Johnson, 'Travelling the Tasman World', 72, 76; Philip Steer, *Settler Colonialism in Victorian Literature: Economics and Political Identity in the Networks of Empire* (Cambridge: Cambridge University Press, 2020), 135.

52 See, e.g., Anon, 'The Ubiquitous English Novel', *South Australian Register*, 20 August 1884, 7; Elwell, *Boy Colonists*, 66.

53 Penny van Toorn, 'The Terrors of *Terra Nullius*: Gothicising and De-Gothicising Aboriginality', *World Literature Written in English* 32:2 (1992): 87.

54 Talbot, *Philiberta*, 302, 323.

55 *South Australian Register*, 20 August 1884, 7; Heather Smyth, 'Mollies Down Under: Cross-Dressing and Australian Masculinity in Peter Carey's *True History of the Kelly Gang*', *Journal of the History of Sexuality* 18:2 (2009): 188, 190. Described as 'an early example of the emancipated woman', Talbot signed two women's suffrage petitions in New Zealand in 1892 and 1893. See Geoff Adams, *Judge Ward* (Dunedin: Geoff Adams, 2011), 12.

56 McClintock, *Imperial Leather*, 160, 162.

57 Talbot, *Philiberta*, 366.

58 *Newcastle Morning Herald*, 28 March 1895, 4; *South Australian Register*, 20 August 1884, 7; Anon, 'English Novels from Four Quarters of the Globe', *Sydney Mail and NSW Advertiser*, 16 August 1884, 305; Emily, 'Philiberta. To the Editor of the Leader', *Leader Supplement*, 22 July 1882, 2; Louisa D. Morris, 'Philiberta. To the Editor of the Leader', *Leader*, 12 August 1882, 25.

59 See, e.g., Mandy Treagus, *Empire Girls: The Colonial Heroine Comes of Age* (North Terrace: University of Adelaide Press, 2014).

60 Mark Byrne, *The Outback Within: Journeys into the Australian Interior* (Newcastle upon Tyne: Cambridge Scholars Publishing, 2016), 18–19.

61 Michael Farrell, *Writing Australian Unsettlement: Modes of Poetic Invention 1796–1945* (Basingstoke: Palgrave Macmillan, 2015).

62 Jason R. Rudy, *Imagined Homelands: British Poetry in the Colonies* (Baltimore: Johns Hopkins University Press, 2017), 65.

63 Robert Dixon, 'Before the Nation: Rolf Boldrewood and the Problem of Scale in National Literatures', *Australian Literary Studies* 30:3 (2015): 7.

64 Ibid., 6; Johnson, 'Travelling the Tasman World', 85.

65 Grace Moore, *Dickens and Empire: Discourses of Class, Race and Colonialism in the Works of Charles Dickens* (Aldershot: Ashgate, 2004), 7.

66 *Daily Northern Argus*, 30 August 1890, 4.

67 Donald Denoon, 'Re-Membering Australasia: A Repressed Memory', *Australian Historical Studies* 34:122 (2003): 299.

68 Ibid., 298; Jonathan Dunk, 'Short Fiction Short Nation: The Ideologies of Australian Realism', *Australian Literary Studies* 33:3 (2018): 6.

69 Martin Lyons, 'Introduction', *A History of the Book in Australia, 1891–1945: A National Culture in a Colonised Market*, ed. Martyn Lyons and John Arnold (St Lucia: University of Queensland Press, 2001), xvi.

70 Alan Atkinson, *The Europeans in Australia: Volume 3 Nation* (Sydney: NewSouth Publishing, 2014), 103; Dixon, 'Before the Nation', 25.

71 Denoon, 'Re-Membering Australasia', 292.

72 Nettelbeck and Foster, 'Commemorating Foundation', 53.2, 53.3.

73 Gilles Deleuze and Félix Guattari, *Kafka: Toward a Minor Literature* (Minneapolis: University of Minnesota Press, 1986), 16–17.

74 Robert P. Marzec, 'Enclosures, Colonization, and the *Robinson Crusoe* Syndrome: A Genealogy of Land in a Global Context', *boundary 2* 29:9 (2002): 132; Lydon, *Imperial Emotions*, 101.

75 Katherine Bode, *Reading by Numbers: Recalibrating the Literary Field* (London: Anthem Press, 2012), 33.

13

When Detection Goes South: Ngaio Marsh's Wartime 'New Zealand' Novels, 1937–45

Antoinette Burton

New Zealand stands like a cranky little coda, at the bottom of the world.
Ngaio Marsh, *New Zealand* (1942)

What happens when English detective fiction goes south? And what does it mean when one of the Golden Age Queens of Crime sends her chief inspector from Britain to New Zealand – that 'cranky little coda, at the bottom of the world' – in three consecutively written novels? We might expect a world turned upside down, and in many ways that is what we find. Roderick Alleyn, a World War I veteran and a detective with a considerable reputation by 1937, when *Vintage Murder* appears in print, is incognito here, in *Colour Scheme* (1943) and *Died in the Wool* (1945). In all three novels he is known only to a few (including local police) even as he is caught up in murder investigations that end up revealing his true identity. Each plot revolves around this masquerade, using Alleyn to caricature both Scotland Yard and New Zealand law enforcement and to explore the colonial relationship between the two forces. While it is true that New Zealand and New Zealanders appear in other Ngaio Marsh novels, this trio is unusual because in each one the entire story takes place there.[1] And because they were published serially and in such a tight time frame, it is tempting to view this simply as her New Zealand period: a mere detour into the south in an otherwise north-facing, metropolitan body of work. One of Marsh's biographers, Joanne Drayton, calls this the 'Death Down Under' chapter in Marsh's life of crime, sandwiched in between her early years as a minor writer in London in the 1920s and her transatlantic fame as a million-reader author in the 1950s.[2] Given the frankly unsatisfying ways that contemporaries and critics then and now have tried to explain Marsh's New Zealandness, viewing these novels as a kind of antipodean aberration in her otherwise anglo-facing corpus seems as good an explanation as any.[3]

What I want to explore here, in the context of 'southern circulations', is the ways that Marsh's novels do not merely get transported to New Zealand but are changed by them – indeed, how they are transformed from detective fiction into spy fiction as they head south. Appreciating that transformation requires that we take seriously the impact and experience of World War II on Marsh and on her expatriate contemporaries as well. As a global conflict, an imperial enterprise and an ongoing experiment in local naval defence, World War II turns detective work into spycraft – backlighting the Anglophilia of the Golden Age of Crime and its colonial connections as well. In this process, indigenous stories go in and out of view while Marsh works through the largely naturalized whiteness of her national-imperial vision. Reading Marsh through the war means reading Alleyn through the lens of spy fiction[4] – both of which mean returning these so-called New Zealand novels *back to* the imperial and proto-decolonizing worlds of the twentieth century in which they were written and read. I want to suggest, too, that doing so requires us to blur the lines between detective fiction and spy novels and to historicize as well as challenge the genre distinction between them.[5] Rather than setting the stage for the age of the full-fledged espionage novel of the Cold War era, wartime detective fiction like Marsh's allows us to see with greater clarity how earlier iterations of the genre, with its defence-of-the-imperial-realm patriotism, its sociological take on Englishness and (by extension) white settlement, and its northern orientation, anticipated the literary terrain of the post-war world. Written about the south and from the south, Marsh's spy novels point northward towards a metropolitan centre under duress, reminding us in turn of how important it is to think of circulation as an effect of historical change as well as an index of it, especially at a time of war 'without and within'.[6]

In *Vintage Murder*, going south is disorienting for DCI Roderick Alleyn: he is like any other tourist encountering New Zealand's beauty and its strangeness for the first time. He talks of falling in love with the landscape, the wine and 'the smell of old New Zealand' – 'a kind of dark wet smell like the native forest'.[7] He is routinely mesmerized by the scenery – the wet moss, the sound of birds – which make him lose his train of thought and forget his expertise and even his identity as a Scotland Yard detective. True to character, Alleyn has an ostensibly witty take on this, labelling his New Zealand adventure 'The Man from the Yard in the Virgin Bush'. It is an early sign of his myopia when it comes to the politics of race, nation, empire and whiteness *in situ*. And unsurprisingly perhaps, it is Māori culture and community that are the recurrent objects of his fascination. That fascination serves in turn as a major plot line for his disorientation: in the course of a backstage murder, a *tiki* is stolen, drawing him into conversation with a local Māori man, Dr Rangi Te Pokiha, and into ruminations about Indigenous cosmologies, the sacred and the forbidden. Alleyn's reflections begin by being cringeworthy and end up enabling outright racist scenes. These include exchanges where the "N-word" is mooted alongside denials that a colour bar exists in New Zealand; a brutal physical attack on the doctor when he is considered, erroneously, as suspect in the murder; and a recurrent theme of what percentage of 'civilized' Māori remains 'savage'.

It is worth noting that Dr Te Pokiha has an Oxford degree and a pronounced if uneasy secular distance from his grandparents' generation and from their reverence for ancestors and ancient local history. This elite/hybrid Māori identity is obviously not lost on Marsh, but it is, by all indications, lost on Alleyn, who thrills to the authentic access he thinks Te Pokiha gives him to Indigenous ways of knowing. Once south, Alleyn outdoes even the locals in this regard: he has been told that the percentage that remains 'savage' in Māori is 10 per cent but he repeats it as 20 per cent when he observes Te Pokiha responding with counterforce as he is assaulted and accused of being implicated in the murder.[8]

Meanwhile, his inability to fathom the workings of the white settler security state – the local constabulary, by any other name – by virtue of his southern turn actively competes with and ultimately subordinates the Māori plot in *Vintage Murder*. Despite the fact that he has come to New Zealand voluntarily, seeking a respite from the rigours of his day job, and wishes his identity to be concealed, he is drawn into the murder investigation because Detective Wade recognizes him from press coverage about an earlier case. This is the first sign among many that even within his peer group – white men and professional detectives to boot – the normally rational and self-possessed Alleyn is not fully in control of himself in New Zealand. He may wish to think of himself as a tourist – the man in the bush – but the local police have him pegged as 'The Handsome Sleuth or the Man who Never Gives Up'.[9] Among them, he is unsure and dithering; it is here we get a sense of Marsh's interest in 'the unease that quivered just below the surface of New Zealander–British relationships'.[10] Alleyn is hobbled by not knowing *pakeha* vocabulary – he cannot work out the New Zealand meaning of 'crook' or the sense of 'dikon' – and by not understanding his place in the settler pecking order. He does not want to come across as superior English but soon realizes he need not worry because from the start he misreads the crime scene as an accident scene, embarrassing himself in front of the indulgent but quietly smirking New Zealand detectives.[11]

To be sure, Alleyn's own authority in the case is not in question. Wade and his mates treat him respectfully, some even admiringly given his Scotland Yard affiliation. They also see him as a naif, instructing him in local ways and in the meaning of their work as well. Wade casts it simply, if pedagogically: '[P]eople spend half their time wondering about each other. That's what sells this detective fiction, I reckon.' Alleyn, for his part, is not about to be completely outdone, let alone undone. Notwithstanding the turbulence of this particular experience of southern circulation, he ends up reconfirmed in his identity as a detective at heart. He writes to Fox that despite arriving incognito, he could not help but get involved (a significant rewriting of the story we have just witnessed, where Wade and Company actually unmask him). Alleyn goes on: 'I confess I am surprised at myself and can only suppose I must *like* teckery – an amazing discovery.' It is quite a cliché, this particular discovery narrative: the inveterate English go native when they travel south but they always return with self-knowledge that shores up their original sense of identity.[12]

In Alleyn's case, that is definitely an English imperial identity, stoked by a white liberal 'appreciation' for the flora and fauna of the southern hemisphere and, of course, for Māori culture and people. Is this a war novel? Not technically, written as it was in 1937. But it sets up Marsh's first true spy novel in important ways. In *Colour Scheme*, published in 1943, Alleyn is again in disguise upon arrival in New Zealand, this time more intentionally and successfully as Septimus Falls, sent by Scotland Yard to keep an eye on enemy activity off the coast of the North Island.[13] Here the Māori plot line is much more prominent, and actually fulfils Toni Morrison's argument about the foundational role of characters of colour in shaping the storyline and creating, here, the real drama around the murder mystery in an Indigenous setting.[14] The story centres around a therapeutic resort run by an expatriate Raj family, Colonel Claire and his wife and children. Their spa turns out, literally and figuratively, to be the centre of major intrigue when a visitor disappears and ends up murdered in the proximity of the hot springs that is the main attraction. The Māori community are the true stewards of the thermal areas and both *pakeha* and the variety of colonial visitors who pass through the resort concede their authority in fanciful, 'orientalist' and racist ways. Indeed, Māori sovereignty and environmental agency are often perceived as one. The earth around the springs trembles and those who approach it 'moved across a skin ... [whose] organism beneath was restless'. Of the hot mud it is said, '[I]t was impossible to escape the notion that Taupotapu had some idiotic purpose of its own.'[15]

The Māori family at the heart of *Colour Scheme* offers a slightly different model minority example than Dr Te Pohika of *Vintage Murder*. The head of this clan, Rua Te Kahu, is a former journalist and MP who is a royalist and loyalist: he arrives at the spa in 'the suit he bought in 1936 to welcome the Duke of Gloucester ... he's a Maori version of the Last of the Barons'. He is uninvolved in the spy drama except insofar as the springs themselves represent Māori cosmological power and thereby serve some explanatory function for how the victim died. In fact, it is implied for much of the narrative that it is the springs themselves which are the murderer, because it is in the springs that the dead body is found. And down to the end of the novel, it is the imagery of pots of boiling mud set alight by indigenous rituals and woven through the local imagination through Māori song about maidens sent to their deaths in boiling mud cauldrons that tethers the danger threatening the spa and all it represents to unseen yet menacing Māori landscapes and cosmologies.

Here the appearance of Māori women is noteworthy, in both the person of the young girl and kitchen servant to the Claires, Haui, and the stately matron and 'princess' of the Te Rawaras, Mrs Te Papa. The former is described as looking 'like a Polynesian goddess who had assumed, on a whim, some barbaric disguise'.[16] Little more than props, they are also indicative of the ornamental function of all the Māori characters in the novel. While they are never direct suspects, they are nonetheless considered presumptively suspicious – curiosities who dot the landscape of the novel and mystery plot at its heart. If Marsh intended these distortions to be a send-up of white liberal New Zealand attitudes, she hardly succeeds, the glossary of 'Maori words used in the text' at the front notwithstanding. The whole narrative enterprise of *Colour Scheme* is saturated by the racism of 'progressive' satire – the kind that reproduces the very stereotypes it is ostensibly aiming to trouble.[17]

As with *Vintage Murder*, the Indigenous characters and plot lines are subordinated to the drama between and among various white people: from the settler inhabitants of New Zealand to the Australian murder victim and suspected fifth columnist Maurice Questing to the bumbling Raj refugees, the Claires. Espionage is the theme from the opening pages. There is a ship off the coast, the *Hippolyte*, which has been sunk, raising alarms about the wider activity of the Germans in the Pacific and the possibility of invasion of New Zealand itself. This is followed, at the start of chapter seven, by the torpedoing of the *Hokianga* which had been on its way to the United States loaded with bullion. While no officials – police or otherwise – are signalling a state of high alert, the denizens of the Claires' spa are abuzz with conviction that there must be a spy among them. Up to midway through the novel, everyone is a suspect: the Claires for hosting a possible transmitting station and even Septimus Falls himself, because of his mysterious air and questionable whereabouts at the time of Questing's disappearance. The most interesting character here is Dikon Bell, a white New Zealander by birth who has lived abroad for years, working for a famous English actor with whom he has travelled to the spa to secure some rest and relaxation for his boss. His return to his native land in the context of war and the prospect of invasion makes him the most baldly nationalist character in the novel, and possibly in all of Marsh's detective fiction.

Dikon takes up a disproportionate amount of space in a cast which has almost twenty characters moving in and out of the storyline. He is notable for his simultaneously fearful and patronizing attitude towards Rua and his clan. He is full of suspicion about Questing and ready to believe that the spa is a nest of spies. He is determined to see the flashes of light along the coast as Morse code and thereby to force security-minded interpretations of what is happening in and around the Claires to the front of discussions. And at the end of the novel, he enlists for New Zealand to fight the good fight for the empire. These outsized performances exhibit a form of expatriate white masculinity newly energized by the spectre not just of war but of the nation's enemies from within. His identification with certain forms of white settler manliness is enhanced by his suspicion of all the other men in the plot (save Rua who does not register as a man to him); by his ongoing display of competition with Septimus Falls over theories about who the spy really is; by his recurrent pathologizing of Māori land and customs; and by his romantic pursuit of the Claires' daughter Barbara, the only eligible white woman on the scene. Though few critics have noted it, preferring to see Ngaio's wartime 'patriotism' especially aimed at Britain, I would go so far as to say that it is Dikon's character who continuously reminds us that this is not a mere detective story but a spy story because of his endless comments to all concerned that New Zealand national security is under threat because of what is happening within (the thermal pools) and beyond (the coastline) waters of the Northland.[18]

In the character of Dikon, then, the war can be seen to have catalysed New Zealand provincialism, often a source of discomfort (or worse) for Marsh, into an unbridled expression of national patriotism, specifically through his preoccupations with espionage.[19] The historical verisimilitude of Dikon's anxieties is worth underscoring here. 'Pacific Coastwatchers' had been in place since the early 1930s, alert to the Japanese takeover of Manchuria and to the challenges to traditional Western imperial hegemony it signalled globally, but especially in antipodal waters. Fears of German activity in the Pacific and Indian Oceans were active from 1938 onwards, generating tensions between Wellington and London over strategies for and costs of protecting the coastlines equally.[20] Threats to the coastline ran the gamut of German raiders and Japanese submarines; the mining of the waters; even 'human torpedos', that is, mini subs or explosive motorboats that might evade the radar. And the blowing-up of ships like the ones in *Colour Guard* was not fiction: German raiders cruised offshore and sank several ships in late 1940, taking prisoners of war and bombarding shore installations with significant impact on the nation's economy as well as on its nerves.

In *Colour Scheme*, which is clearly a spy novel, this posture towards the realities of war manifests itself in interesting ways – namely, via discussions about whether the crisis they are facing – murder in wartime – warrants the work of detection per se. Marsh and her fellow Queens of Crime often indulged in dialogues internal to their narratives where characters opined about the life of detective fiction as a lived, social form.[21] Dikon announces early on in discussions of fifth columnists that he is sceptical of 'detective-fiction' mongers, which suggests that he sees the plot they are involved in as something different. He carries on with this sentiment when one of the spa guests, Dr Ackrington, opines that Questing's disappearance has been staged. Dikon strenuously disagrees, arguing that that is 'the kind of thing they do in thrillers' and it is too neat, it leaves 'no lee-way for jolts'. Ackrington concedes: 'I have no doubt that Webley, in the best tradition of the worst type of fiction, will suspect each of us in turn.'[22]

In *Colour Scheme* (and as we shall see shortly, *Died in the Wool* as well) Marsh toggles uneasily between detection and spycraft, allowing Dikon to be the mouthpiece of a new way of thinking about murder and its detection at a time of national peril and global war. The line between the two genres – between the puzzle plot and the thriller – is an ever-shifting one, dependent on historical contingency and in this case, the storyline itself.[23] For in the end, Questing was not a secret agent. And it is Septimus Falls, revealed as Roderick Alleyn in the last pages of the novel, who tells us so. After running through various theories of the murder, including what he calls 'the Maori element', he discloses that the murderer (Herbert Smith, local roustabout) knew that Questing was colour-blind and took advantage of his not being able to read the warning flags along the edges of the hot springs, which in turn caused him fatally to fall in. The motive was a sacred and valuable Māori adze that Gaunt wanted and Questing had.[24] Still speaking as Septimus Falls, Alleyn says that he remains a devotee of detective fiction, defending it as 'the slow amassment of facts sufficient to justify the arrest of someone who has been more or less suspect from the moment the crime was discovered'.[25] In saying so, he backs off a bit from his earlier observation in the 1940 novel *A Surfeit of Lampreys* that the investigation of homicide was 'a dull enough business' of which detective fiction has made too much.[26] But at the end of *Colour Scheme*, Alleyn also reveals that his public position – that is, what he says in front of the Claires and their guests – is not exactly his professional one. 'I'm afraid we've only caught a sprat,' he tells the local superintendent of police, 'but at least it will show the seriousness of the position.'[27] And he lets us in on a stage secret: that his rather hackneyed 'all possible suspects and motives' show at the Claires' was part of a choreographed performance, done with the help of Colonel Claire, who was in on his disguise and on the intelligence threats that fifth columnists and raider activity really did signify.

Colour Scheme is Alleyn's victory, not Dikon's; the latter is none the wiser. And by 1943, when Scotland Yard goes south in Marsh's novel, the CID (Crime Investigation Department, London) and the CID (Committee on Imperial Defence, Wellington) are practically one in the same. That is to say, keeping up the fiction that what Alleyn is doing at the thermal baths is detective work is part of imperial defence and security. That makes *Colour Scheme* spy fiction masquerading as detective fiction, in theory and practice. And embracing the category of detective fiction, cleaving to that genre itself against lots of evidence to the contrary, becomes part of British patriotic duty in a changing world, as imagined and governed by those in the English professional class (including, here, *pakeha* policemen) who are engaged in the war effort on all fronts, in the Antipodes and beyond. Interestingly, Marsh considered it her best-written novel.[28]

If *Colour Scheme* navigates the transition from pre-war to post-war order by trying to manage genre difference in a bicultural world, *Died in the Wool* emerges in 1945 as fully formed spycraft in defence of the predominantly white nation and the wider British world. And if Marsh's trilogy of New Zealand novels exhibit 'a narrowness of vision ... that she never managed to shake off', it was Māori society that was practically narrowed out of existence by this time. For in contrast to her two previous 'New Zealand' novels, Māori make no appearance in these pages – though this does not prevent a random reference to 'working like a black' from arising unbidden into dialogue.[29] It is the South Island, 1943, and Alleyn arrives at Mount Moon sheep station incognito again. His cover lasts only a dozen or so pages, due in part to the heightened suspicion of locals that any stranger could be a fifth columnist or enemy alien. 'We pictured you in a false beard, dodging around geysers,' Fabian Losse tells him (whereupon the reader cannot suppress the thought that no, that is the plot for *Colour Scheme*: a thought Marsh no doubt relished the possibility of our thinking).[30] Alleyn is open with Fabian but tries to keep his identity shrouded from the larger community of Mount Moon, where the murder of a prominent woman MP over a year before his arrival becomes the centre of his counter-espionage work. Raptures about the beauty of the landscape abound here as they do in *Vintage Murder* and *Colour Scheme* but Alleyn is self-professedly all business, and frankly so. He tells Fabian: 'I think I ought to warn you. I'm a bit of state machinery. Anyone can start me up but only the state can switch me off.'[31] Detection has become impersonal and controlled from afar; it is not too much to say, riffing off that line, that Alleyn has become weaponized in the service of the war effort. The difference between 1943 and 1945 is two years and a new realpolitik about the relationship between detection and spycraft: they are one and the same.[32]

There is a familiar coziness to a drawing room 'suspect line-up' – a coziness for which the Queens of Crime had a celebrated predilection. But Alleyn is not simply a detective now, and as if to prove that he subordinates the quest for Flossie's killer to his furtive investigation of chemical experiments that Fabian and Douglas are involved in, thinking it is linked to plans for violence and sabotage. His instincts are compromised briefly insofar as he imagines Fabian might be the one. As above, it is not being in New Zealand that has him off balance, it is the complexities of the war and the possibility of double identities and double agents that wobbles him. Ultimately, it is Douglas who is revealed to be the closet German; he uses the chemical compounds to blow himself up and tries to take Alleyn with him. In his summary letter to Inspector Fox back in London, Alleyn characterizes the relationship between detective fiction and the spy novel at a time of war: 'My job was to find the agent. As a working proposition I imagined he was also the murderer. If, then, the murderer was the agent, the two likeliest bets were Losse and Grace.'[33] In this particular instance, when English detection went south, it unequivocally became spycraft – or, as it was termed in the parlance of MI6, simply 'spy detection'.[34]

William Tell Gifford has argued that the choice of place is 'swallowed up by war' in both *Colour Scheme* and *Died in the Wool*, but I think this is mistaken.[35] The New Zealand setting matters, especially if we acknowledge that this trio of novels, written 'in a cranky little coda at the bottom of the world', serve as important evidence of how World War II transformed Marsh into a spy writer, at least temporarily. And New

Zealand matters as a place because the security of the Antipodes was the key to Allied military success in a decidedly Australasian theatre of war – reminding us of how global militarism was as consequential in shaping that formation as post-Enlightenment trade, migration or even white settlement itself.[36] Despite Marsh's own tendencies to provincialize the islands, they nonetheless 'press against the ascendancy of an aggregated and naturalized national history' precisely because of how detection becomes catalysed as espionage in a regional and global war where New Zealand played a consequential role – as bellwether, as bulwark, as 'place-holder' for empires past, present and future in the 1940s.[37] Alleyn's southern circulations across these three stories represent his metamorphosis from domestic detective to an instrument of the global imperial security apparatus – a supra-national spymaster as well as a master of disguise by virtue of his class mobility, his manliness and his English credentials. But if we are to truly press against the ascendancy of white nationalism, as above, we must acknowledge that New Zealand's south-ness is not a historical fact but a convenient fiction. At the very least, it is an instituted perspective (whose south? at the bottom of whose world?) that depends very much on who you are and where you are looking from – a perspectival view of Australasia as a whole that is worthy of sustained consideration.[38] Recent work by Frances Steel and colleagues affirms this claim over the long durée, arguing for both New Zealand's archipelagic character and its position 'not as the remotest colony, but in the flux of globalizing traffic and exchange'.[39]

What reading Marsh's 'New Zealand' novels allows us to see with particular vividness is not how southern they are but how careful we need to be when we talk about the locative position of detective fiction as a genre. For when we invoke detective fiction we often mean, without naming, its anglophone iteration – and its Anglocentric, north-facing orientations. Denaturalizing detective fiction by calling out its politics of whiteness and investigating its relationship to histories of colonialism is one way of decolonizing the genre. In so doing, we can better see and appreciate the south as a categorical effect of a specific, if often unspoken, imperial form of detective work, even as we recognize its ongoing rhetorical power. That is to say, even when we acknowledge it as a convenient fiction, we must concede that the south nonetheless does critical ideological and material work. For when Marsh wrote in her short book on New Zealand commissioned during the war, 'in the south island the traveler may feel that he is forever crossing thresholds', she reiterated English colonial Pacific south-ness upon which her identity, reputation and popularity as a writer entirely depended.[40] The South Island she invokes is, of course, also synecdochical: the South Island stands for itself and stands in for New Zealand as a southern outpost, reminding us that instituted perspectives always happen at multiple scales – and allowing us to glimpse a version of Australasia as she saw it.[41]

The structure of *Colour Scheme* and *Died in the Wool* are also very similar, suggesting how quickly this new genre might exhaust itself – how quickly spy fever might turn to spy fiction overkill, even in the oeuvre of a single popular author. Marsh may have held this view as early as 1943. 'Somehow,' says Rua halfway through *Colour Scheme*, 'I have never been able to enjoy spy stories. They always seem to me to be incredible.'[42] Spending the war in New Zealand turned Marsh into a kind of quick-change spy novelist; her isolation due to the war and later to her father's old age kept her away from

London until the early 1950s. So, the war must be reckoned with as a major historical event in her literary life – and her theatrical one as well. For she spent much of this period involved in the New Zealand theatre scene in the context of what one recent study has called 'Bloomsbury South'.[43] Back in Britain, a decade after the war had ended, Graham Greene and his brother Hugh published an anthology called the *Spy's Bedside Book*, which gathers excerpts from authors as diverse as John Buchan to O. Henry that might qualify as spy stories.[44] The Greenes wanted to suggest how broad a spectrum of stories could be encompassed by spy writing, including texts that dated well before World War II. They were also collecting these examples in a decade when the facts of Cold War espionage were as strange as fiction, and when literary figures like Graham Greene himself – and many others – might be taken for spies because of their political affiliations or the company they kept. Even as detective fiction carried on, new forms of surveillance and new-found awareness of Cold War spycraft made spy fiction feel just as relevant, just as familiar. Spy fiction may also have felt just as English, where Englishness (still white, still class-based, still male) conjures a disposition towards the observation of people: intelligence-gathering by any other name.[45]

Neither Marsh nor Christie nor Elizabeth Bowen appear in the Greenes' anthology. And only one of them has ever been considered even remotely linked to actual spy activity.[46] Their absence from the Greenes' consideration undoubtedly has a lot to do with gender; the spy novel from Buchan through to Ian Fleming (and beyond) has mainly been written by men.[47] Perhaps this explains, too, the consensus that one requirement of spy fiction as a genre is 'an attractive male hero who acquires a body of information the significance of which he does not understand, so that he himself is at risk but does not know why he is at risk'. Whereas we might say of detective fiction, as Bruce Mason did of Marsh's work upon her death in 1982, that the real question is 'who is guilty?' – a question that conjures the kind of ethical communitarianism that social scientists have associated with white middle-class respectable women like Marsh and her readers.[48] Marsh thus went against type, if only briefly, in her wartime New Zealand novels. The impact of the war on her may thus be said to be profound, insofar as it not only found her embracing spy fiction but drawing women readers, who typically read crime writing rather than spy novels, into an unfamiliar generic terrain as well.[49] That this new terrain was also New Zealand underscores the entanglement of gender, genre and place in this particular example of 'southern circulations'. It also suggests how the detective novel might be considered a consequential example of the kinds of 'material forms' Tony Ballantyne talks about in his Introduction to this volume.

What does it mean to decolonize Ngaio Marsh's fiction? As a method, decolonization takes many forms. To echo the late, great Tracey Banivanua Mar, it involves showing how the ends of empire 'radiated from the peripheries' in ways that can only be seen from the time and space of the Pacific, and via the work of Australasia in the global south by extension.[50] It also requires taking up larger arguments about the ways that the Queens of the Golden Age of Crime Fiction (Christie, Sayers, Allingham and Marsh) recruited the presumptive whiteness of English colonial society at home and abroad in their mystery plots in highly naturalized ways – and the pass they have been given by critics who routinely sidestep questions of empire in the scholarship on detective fiction. One consequence is the way that 'detective fiction' as a genre category has been effectively equated with Englishness *tout court* in the global marketplace of twentieth-century popular literature, via mass consumption of paperbacks, the TV serials and major motion pictures. There are, of course, French and German and South African and South Asian traditions of detective and spy stories, but these require geographical qualification in ways that the English variant does not. Despite her identity as a New Zealander and of course because of it, Ngaio Marsh's popularity is thus much more than a 'cranky little coda' to the story of The Golden Age of Imperial Crime Writing, as it ought to be called. Like so much relegated to the so-called 'bottom of the world', her fiction is an index of geopolitical forces that cannot be fully appreciated without a set of simultaneously historical, anti-imperial and geographically subversive reading practices of the kind I have tested out here.

Notes

1   Marsh's penultimate novel, *Photo Finish* (1980), also takes place in New Zealand.
2   Joanne Drayton, *Ngaio Marsh: Her Life in Crime* (Auckland: HarperCollins, 2008), 106 ff.
3   For a recent original take on Marsh *in situ*, see Peter Simpson, *Bloomsbury South: The Arts in Christchurch, 1933–1953* (Auckland: Auckland University Press, 2016).
4   Which Robin Winks calls an 'out-rider' to detective fiction in his edited collection, *Detective Fiction: A Collection of Critical Essays* (Woodstock, VT: The Countryman Press, 1988), 251.
5   For extensive reflections on this kind of project, see Laura Mayhall and Elizabeth Prevost, eds, *British Murder Mysteries* (forthcoming), especially Mayhall's '"Indecently Preposterous": The Interwar Press and Golden Age Detective Fiction'.
6   I borrow here from Philip H. J. Davies, *MI6 and the Machinery of Spying* (Abingdon: Frank Cass, 2005), ch. 4.
7   Ngaio Marsh, *Vintage Murder* (1937; New York: Felony and Mayhem Press, 2012), 170. Without irony, William Tell Gifford calls this 'detection of place'. See his 'Sense of Place in Detective Fiction: The Case of Ngaio Marsh's First New Zealand Novel', *Clues: A Journal of Detection* 20:1 (1999): 36.
8   *Vintage Murder*, 263.
9   *Vintage Murder*, 96–7. This is an interesting twist on *Murder Must Advertise* (Dorothy L. Sayers, Harper, 1933).
10 Kathryn Slate McDorman, *Ngaio Marsh* (Boston, MA: Twayne Publishers, 1991), 22. She reads the trilogy I bundle here as part of Marsh's extended series of 'Commonwealth novels' (ch. 3).
11 Marsh found New Zealanders crude and was especially disdainful of their language/ idioms. See Carole Acheson, 'Cultural Ambivalence: Ngaio Marsh's New Zealand Detective Fiction', *Journal of Popular Culture* 19:2 (1985): 162, 173 ('English is such a superb language and they really do bastardize it').
12 Ibid., 95, 165.
13 Though Alleyn's disguises are a kind of folly, Rhodri Jeffreys-Jones reminds us that this stealth approach reflects the aspirations of wartime British intelligence culture, where 'the MI5 man was trained to follow and observe' in contrast to the less subtle practices of surveillance used by, say, the FBI. See his *We Know all About You: The Story of Surveillance in Britain and America* (Oxford: Oxford University Press, 2017), 112.

14 Toni Morrison, *Playing in the Dark: Whiteness and the Literary Imagination* (Cambridge, MA: Harvard University Press, 1992).

15 Ngaio Marsh, *Colour Scheme* (1943; New York Jove Books, 1982), 75–6.

16 Ibid., 13.

17 While generally happy to acknowledge Marsh's ambivalence about white settler New Zealand, her biographers and literary critics are less willing to call out her white liberal racism. Carole Acheson, for example, thinks Marsh 'paints an observant and sympathetic picture' of Māori manners in a tone that is 'light and amusing' in *Colour Scheme* ('Cultural Ambivalence', 169). For an equally appreciative gloss of Marsh's liberal racism toward Maori characters, see Tell, 'Sense of Place', 33, where he, astonishingly, attributes all the racial slurs to the New Zealand detectives and praises Alleyn's 'reverential' attitude towards Dr Te Pokiha (34). McDorman calls Marsh's representations of Māori 'probing but sympathetic portraits' even as she admits Marsh can be said to have 'imput[ed] savagery to them' (25, 29). And Bruce Harding lets Marsh's 1940 claim that in their quest for 'New Zealand at all costs' New Zealand writers 'overloaded their poems and short stories and novels with local color, Maori words and colonial slang' pass unremarked. Yet *Colour Scheme* surely fulfils this remit perfectly. See his '"The Great and True Amphibian": The New Zealand/England Polarity in the Short Fiction of Ngaio Marsh' in *Ngaio Marsh: The Woman and her Work,* ed. B. J. Rahn (Metuchen, NJ: Scarecrow Press, 1995), 220.

18 For a discussion of Marsh's heightened British patriotism during the war, see Margaret Lewis, *Ngaio Marsh: A Life* (Wellington: Bridget Williams Books, 1991), 83.

19 Thanks to Laura Mayhall for helping me to see this point.

20 Beyond the Pacific, the weakest arena of British intelligence heading into the war was the Naval Intelligence Directorate. See Wesley K. Wark, 'British Military and Economic Intelligence: Assessments of Nazi Germany Before the Second World War', in *The Missing Dimension: Government and Intelligence Communities in the Twentieth Century*, ed. Christopher Andrew and David Dilks (London: Macmillan, 1984), 89.

21 There is quite a lot of this kind of talk in Dorothy L. Sayers's *Gaudy Night*, for example (1936; New York: HarperCollins, 2012).

22 *Colour Scheme*, 124, 211.

23 Thanks to Mike Saler for this characterization.

24 I will note that the drama over the adze, and its relationship to sacred Māori traditions, is an important contrapuntal line in the novel, and that one form of postcolonial/anti-imperial reading would be to see it as the *sine qua non* of the plot. I do not disagree with that interpretive thrust but I also do not want to recuperate Maori agency simply as a counter to Marsh's own patronizing and frankly racist attitudes in *Colour Scheme*. In the interpretive frame of detection/spy fiction I am working with here, Māori knowledge (via the adze) may be said to compete with security knowledge (via Morse code/flashing lights). That indigenous knowledge is certainly consequential to the plot, in Toni Morrison's terms. But, structurally and affectively, it is and remains completely *subordinated* to the white masculine truth-telling that Dikon and Alleyn are seen to master. To me this is an equally critical counter-reading that requires us to interrogate Marsh's liberal racist treatment of Māori practices and peoples without granting that her version of them represents anything like admiration, let alone equality, for them. Or that 'admiration' is simply one more effect of her problematic representations of Māori in the novel.

25 Ibid., 266.

26 Quoted in Carole Acheson and Carol Lidgard, *Return to Black Beech: Papers from a Centenary Symposium on Ngaio Marsh* (Christchurch.: Centre for Continuing Education, University of Canterbury, 1996), 79.

27 *Colour Scheme*, 279.

28 Lewis, *Ngaio Marsh*, 87.

29 For the narrowness of vision quote, see Lewis, *Ngaio Marsh*, 75. The complete erasure of Māori in this novel has escaped critics like Carole Acheson, who sees only pride in an expanding 'national culture' (and also completely elides the spy story). See 'Cultural Ambivalence', 172.

30 Ngaio Marsh, *Died in the Wool* (1945; New York: HarperCollins omnibus edition, 2009), 15.

31 Ibid., 26.

32 For reference to this long-standing genre debate, see Winks, *Detective Fiction*, 253.

33 Ibid., 222.

34 Davies, *MI6 and the Machinery of Spying*, 145.

35 Gifford, 'Sense of Place in Detective Fiction', 28.

36 See Philippa Mein Smith, 'Mapping Australasia', *History Compass* 7:4 (2009): 1113.

37 Tony Ballantyne, 'On Space, Place and Mobility in Nineteenth Century New Zealand', *New Zealand Journal of History* 45:1 (2011): 54.

38 As Kristian Jensen, Denmark's finance minister, put it elegantly if pointedly in 2017: 'There are two kinds of European nations . . . there are small nations and there are countries that have not yet realized they are small nations.' Quoted by Elizabeth Buettner, 'How Unique is Britain's Empire Complex', in *Embers of Empire in Brexit Britain*, ed. Stuart Ward and Astrid Rasch (London: Bloomsbury Academic, 2019), 37. See also Tony Ballantyne, 'Mobility, Empire, Colonisation', *History Australia*, 11:2 (2014): 7–37.

39 Frances Steel, ed., *New Zealand and the Sea: Historical Perspectives* (Wellington: Bridget Williams Books, 2018), especially her introductory essay, 17.

40 Ngaio Marsh with R. M. Burden, *New Zealand* (London: William Collins, 1942), 42.

41 I am riffing here on Donald Denoon, 'Re-membering Australasia: A Repressed Memory', *Australian Historical Studies* 34:122 (2003): 293.

42 *Colour Scheme*, 58.

43 See Simpson, *Bloomsbury South*.

44 Graham Greene and Hugh Greene, eds, *The Spy's Bedside Book* (London: Rupert Hart-Davis, 1957).

45 I borrow from Maurice Oldfield, former head of MI6, here: 'Intelligence is about people and the study of people.' Attributed in Richard Deacon, *C: A Biography of Sir Maurice Oldfield, Head of MI6* (London: Futura, 1985).

46 For Agatha Christie's wartime proximity to what was apparently a hotbed of spies in Hampstead, see David Burke, *The Lawn Road Flats: Spies, Writers and Artists* (Woodbridge: Boydell Press, 2014), ch. 6.

47 For a run-down of the long line of men writing about spies before the Cold War, see 'Spy Fiction' in *The Oxford Companion to Crime and Mystery Writing*, ed. Catherine Aird and John M. Reilly (Oxford: Oxford University Press, 1999), 426–8. Theirs is not a list that takes empire into account; such a list would certainly include Conrad's *The Secret Agent* and even, perhaps, Kipling's *Kim*. See Jon Thompson, *Fiction, Crime and Empire: Clues to Modernity and Postmodernism* (Champaign: University of Illinois Press, 1993) especially ch. 4, 'The Heroic Spy Novel: Kim and the Rhetoric of the Great

Game'; and, for *Kim* as spy fiction, Robin Winks, *Modus Operandi: An Excursion in Detective Fiction* (Boston, MA: David R. Godine, 1982), 55.

48 Robin Winks, 'Spy Fiction – Spy Reality: From Conrad to Le Carré', *Soundings: An Interdisciplinary Journal* 76:2–3 (1993): 224; and Bruce Mason, 'In Memoriam: Dame Ngaio Marsh, 1899–1982', *Landfall* 36:2 (1982): 241. See also Carol Gilligan, *In a Different Voice: Psychological Theory and Women's Development* (Cambridge, MA: Harvard University Press, 1982).

49 Aird and Reilly, eds, *Oxford Companion* ('Spy Fiction'), 428. Thanks to Mike Saler for pointing me towards this source and helping me think through the gendered meanings of Marsh's generic turn.

50 Tracey Banivanua Mar, *Decolonization and the Pacific: Indigenous Globalization and the Ends of Empire* (Cambridge: Cambridge University Press, 2016).

Conclusion. Perpetual Flight: Relationships in Space and Time

Tony Ballantyne

This volume has explored changing conceptions of Australasia, competing visions of the region, and the forms of mobility and circulations that gave this spatial imaginary real weight. Drawing upon the work of the art historian Bernard Smith, Peter Beilharz has observed that the Antipodes are a culturally significant formation and that they are best 'understood as a relationship more than a place' and that these forms of interdependence are produced through 'processes of cultural traffic'.[1] That line of argument can work for Australasia as well as the Antipodes. We have seen throughout this volume that Australasia was essentially a relational construction. It was and is, however, a multi-axial one. Through this concept, some have defined southern lands and waters in relation to Asia; it has frequently been used to characterize these places through contrasts to northern lands and peoples, especially Europeans, and in particular Britain and its culture; and, it has been built around visions of the connections and commonalties that link the peoples that inhabit the region, often in terms of a shared colonial inheritance, but also as a result of integrative circuits of mobility.

Smith also suggested that Australian artists were like 'migratory birds', drawing cultural energy from 'perpetual flight', navigating routes between the old world and the new.[2] Although the gravitational pull of Europe in the imaginations of Australians, New Zealanders and Pacific peoples has shifted significantly since Smith made this observation in the 1950s, the metaphor of migratory birds resonates widely. It is an image that has long currency in the New Zealand case, too: the annual global movement of godwits, between Alaska and New Zealand, has become a significant metaphor for the mobility and cultural restlessness of New Zealanders.[3] Given that this volume has signalled the importance of shared agents of environmental change and biological connections, it is worth remembering that the movement of birds has laced New Zealand and Australia together as well: the white-faced heron, common around New Zealand waterways now, is one of the very recent arrivals.[4] Returning to the symbolic realm, it is also important to note that birds are central metaphors in Māori cultural tradition in discussions of movement, music and politics; people and birds are also closely associated in this cultural world, in keeping with deep Pacific traditions.

Smith's vision of 'perpetual flight' also speaks to the unsettled-ness of so-called 'settlers' (and their descendants). Mobility was a defining characteristic of colonists and the working of empires was dependent on movement and circulation, a key argument of this book. But we must not replicate long-standing oppositions between mobile Europeans and Indigenous peoples fixed in time and space: this volume has also repeatedly stressed the importance of Indigenous peoples on the move. We might note, for example, the importance of Poihākena (Port Jackson/Sydney) in the nineteenth-century Māori world, a set of connections that have been emphasized in recent work by Rachel Standfield, Michael Stevens and Rohan Howitt, while some of the resonances of these connections have been explored by Alice Te Punga Somerville.[5] Important relationships to Australia are also fashioned by Pacific peoples from the Realm of New Zealand: the Cook Islands population in Australia grew in the 1980 and 1990s, primarily through migration via New Zealand itself; this pattern has been replicated on a smaller scale for Niue and Tokelau. These are a particular set of linkages within the wider fabric of the manifold connections woven by Pacific people who continue to move, work and build families between the islands of Te Moananui-a-Kiwa, New Zealand and Australia.

These bonds remind us of how mobile people connect societies and how links are fortified by the movement of goods and money, words and ideas, values and aspirations. Poignant scenes of reunion in airports and on docksides in Australia, New Zealand and the Pacific during the COVID-19 pandemic have reminded us of the emotional impact when 'perpetual flight' or even more routine journeys are paused. These images have underscored the affective ties that disregard national borders, but that can be constrained by their continued power to limit mobility. In both the modern world shaped by empire and in our contemporary moment, families and communities are made and remade, often in expansive ways, where affective ties and lines of descent reach out in time and space. These far-reaching webs of connection often elude what Mimi Sheller and John Urry have termed the 'a-mobile' and sedentary vision of dominant approaches in social sciences (and, one could add, the humanities, too).[6]

The histories of some of these types of movement, experiences of mobility, forms of association and affiliation, and ways of thinking could be recovered by new literary and historical work organized around the unit of Australasia, but in my view they are best placed in a variety of ways. The scale and shape of human activity and thought – whether local, regional, national or transnational – should determine the contours of the analytical frames adopted by historians. James Belich, whose early writing reshaped New Zealand's national historiography in profound ways but now largely works on a broader canvas, noted in the second volume of his history of New Zealand, *Paradise Reforged*, that 'national packaging falsifies history. The actual past, especially in culture, is no respecter of national boundaries.'[7] And as some of the essays collected here demonstrate, national boundaries can also propel the exclusion of peoples on the grounds of difference, excising them from imagined national communities and their particular historical vision as well.

In recovering some particular ways of imagining Australasia, this volume has both traced the history of a spatial imaginary that was entangled with imperial aspirations and charted the cultural traffic that produced a particular kind of cartographic consciousness. Inevitability, it is incomplete, but the chapters gathered here provide important vantage points on these histories, recovering a range of voices and offering glimpses of people and ideas in motion. It repeatedly returns to the restlessness of the peoples that made their homes in these southern lands in the shadow of empire, how they made sense of their world, and imagined future possibilities for these southern lands and peoples. While those visions were rarely fully realized, they offer important windows into the aspirations of earlier generations who were convinced that they had both the right and capability to remake the world.

Notes

1   Peter Beilharz, 'Bernard Smith: The quality of marxism', *Thesis Eleven* 114:1 (2013): 94–102; see also Peter Beilharz, *Thinking the Antipodes: Australian Essays* (Clayton: Monash University Publishing, 2015).

2   Beilharz, 'Bernard Smith'.

3   James Belich, *Paradise Reforged: A History of the New Zealanders from the 1880s to the Year 2000* (Auckland: Penguin Press, 2001), 331 3; also see Jon Bywater, 'Interrupting Perpetual Flight: a Local Practice of Locational Identification', *Afterall: A Journal of Art, Context and Enquiry* 13 (2006): 101–6.

4   Michael King, *Being Pakeha: An Encounter with New Zealand and the Maori Renaissance* (Auckland: Hodder & Stoughton, 1985), 51.

5   Rachel Standfield, 'The Parramatta Māori Seminary and the Education of Indigenous Peoples in Early Colonial New South Wales', *History of Education Review* 41:2 (2012): 119–28; Michael Stevens, '"A Defining Characteristic of the Southern People": Southern Māori Mobility and the Tasman World', in *Indigenous Mobilities: Across and Beyond the Antipodes*, ed. Rachel Standfield (Canberra: ANU Press, 2018); Rohan Howitt, 'Māori Workers in Colonial New South Wales, c. 1803–40', *History Workshop Journal* 93 (2022): 1–21; Alice Te Punga Somerville, 'Living on New Zealand Street: Maori Presence in Parramatta', *Ethnohistory* 61:4 (2014): 655–69, Also see Paul Hamer's survey of the long-term development of Māori communities in Australia, *Māori in Australia: Ngā Māori i Te Ao Moemoeā* (Wellington: Te Puni Kokiri, 2007).

6   Mimi Sheller and John Urry, 'The New Mobilities Paradigm', *Environment and Planning A* 38:2 (2006): 207–26, especially 208.

7   Belich, *Paradise Reforged*, 338.

Selected Bibliography

Introduction. Southern Circulations and the Making and Remaking of Australasia *Tony Ballantyne*

Ballantyne, Tony. *Entanglements of Empire: Missionaries, Māori, and the Question of the Body*. Durham, NC: Duke University Press, 2014.

Ballantyne, Tony. 'Mobility, Empire, Colonisation'. *History Australia* 11:2 (2014): 7–37.

Ballantyne, Tony. 'On place, space and mobility in nineteenth-century New Zealand'. *New Zealand Journal of History* 45:1 (2011): 50–70.

Ballantyne, Tony. *Orientalism and Race: Aryanism in the British Empire*. Basingstoke: Palgrave, 2002.

Ballantyne, Tony. *Webs of Empire: Locating New Zealand's Colonial Past*. Wellington: Bridget Williams Books, 2012.

Bayly, C. A. *Imperial Meridian: The British Empire and the World, 1780–1830*. London: Longman, 1989.

Belich, James. *Making peoples: A History of the New Zealanders: From Polynesian Settlement to the End of the Nineteenth Century*. London: Allen Lane, 1996.

de Brosses, Charles. *Histoire des navigations aux terres australes: contenant ce que l'on sait des mœurs & des productions des Contrées découvertes jusqu'à ce jour ; & où il est traité de l'utilité d'y faire de plus amples découvertes, & des moyens d'y former un établissement*. Paris: Durand, 1756.

Clark, Anna, Anne Rees and Alecia Simmonds, eds. *Transnationalism, Nationalism and Australian History*. Singapore: Palgrave Macmillan, 2017.

Comyn, Sarah and Porscha Fermanis, eds. *Worlding the South: Nineteenth-Century Literary Culture and the Southern British Colonies*. Manchester: Manchester University Press, 2020.

Curthoys, Ann, and Marilyn Lake, eds. *Connected Worlds: History in Transnational Perspective*. Canberra: ANU E Press, 2005.

Denoon, Donald. 'The isolation of Australian history: historical reconsiderations'. *Historical Studies* 22:87 (1986): 252–60.

Denoon, Donald. 'Re-Membering Australasia: A repressed memory'. *Australian Historical Studies* 34:122 (2003): 290–304.

Denoon, Donald, and Philippa Mein Smith with Marivic Wyndham. *A History of Australia, New Zealand, and the Pacific*. Oxford: Blackwell, 2000.

Harlow, Vincent T. *The Founding of the Second British Empire, 1763–1793*. 2 vols. London: Longmans, Green & Co, 1952–64.

Mein Smith, Philippa. 'Mapping Australasia'. *History Compass* 7 (2009): 1099–122.

Mein Smith, Philippa, Peter J. Hempenstall and Shaun Goldfinch. *Remaking the Tasman World*. Christchurch: Canterbury University Press, 2008.

Salesa, Damon Ieremia. 'New Zealand's Pacific'. In *The New Oxford History of New Zealand*, ed. Giselle Byrnes, 149–72. Melbourne: Oxford University Press, 2009.

Salesa, Damon Ieremia. '"Travel-happy" Samoa: colonialism, Samoan migration and a "brown Pacific"'. *New Zealand Journal of History* 37:2 (2003): 171–88.

Sinclair, Keith, ed. *Tasman Relations: New Zealand and Australia, 1788–1988*. Auckland: Auckland University Press, 1987.

Standfield, Rachel ed. *Indigenous Mobilities: Across and Beyond the Antipodes*. Canberra: ANU Press, 2018.

Standfield, Rachel. *Race and Identity in the Tasman World, 1769–1840*. London: Pickering & Chatto, 2012.

Steel, Frances, ed. *New Zealand and the Sea: Historical Perspectives*. Wellington: Bridget Williams, 2019.

Steel, Frances. *Oceania under Steam: Sea Transport and the Cultures of Colonialism, c.1870–1914*. Manchester: Manchester University Press, 2011.

1 Framing Australasia: Empire, Colonization and the Cartographic Imagination *Tony Ballantyne*

Armitage, David. *The Ideological Origins of the British Empire*. Cambridge: Cambridge University Press, 2000.

Ballantyne, Tony. 'Empire, Knowledge and Culture: from Proto-Globalization to Modern Globalization'. In *Globalization in World History*, ed. A. G. Hopkins, 115–140. W. W. Norton & Co.: New York, 2002.

Ballantyne, Tony. 'The State, Politics, and Power, 1769–1893'. In *The New Oxford History of New Zealand*, ed. Giselle Byrnes, 99–125. Melbourne: Oxford University Press, 2009.

Bayly, C. A. *The Birth of the Modern World, 1780–1914: Global Connections and Comparisons*. Oxford: Blackwell, 2004.

Burton, Antoinette, and Isabel Hofmeyr, eds. *Ten Books That Shaped the British Empire: Creating an Imperial Commons*. Durham, NC: Duke University Press, 2014.

Callander, John. *Terra Australis Cognita: or, voyages to the Terra Australis, or Southern hemisphere, during the sixteenth, seventeenth, and eighteenth centuries*. Edinburgh: A. Donaldson, 1766–8.

Douglas, Bronwen. '"Terra Australis" to Oceania: Racial Geography in the "Fifth Part of the World"'. *The Journal of Pacific History* 45:2 (2010): 179–210.

d'Urville, Jules-Sébastien-César Dumont. 'Sur les îles du Grand Océan'. *Bulletin de la Société de Géographie* 17 (1832): 1–21.

Eisler, William Lawrence. *The Furthest Shore: Images of Terra Australis from the Middle Ages to Captain Cook*. Cambridge: Cambridge University Press, 1995.

Lake, Marilyn, and Henry Reynolds. *Drawing the Global Colour Line: White Men's Countries and the Question of Racial Equality*. Cambridge: Cambridge University Press, 2008.

Marshall, P. J., and Glyndwr Williams. *The Great Map of Mankind: Perceptions of New Worlds in the Age of Enlightenment*. London: Dent, 1982.

Ryan, Tom. '"Le Président des Terres Australes": Charles de Brosses and the French Enlightenment Beginnings of Oceanic Anthropology'. *Journal of Pacific History* 37:2 (2002): 157–86.

Scott, Anne M., and Alfred Hiatt, Claire McIlroy and Christopher Wortham, eds. *European Perceptions of Terra Australis*. Farnham: Ashgate, 2011.

Tcherkézoff, Serge. 'A Long and Unfortunate Voyage Towards the "Invention" of the Melanesia/Polynesia Distinction 1595–1832'. Translated from French by Isabel Ollivier. *The Journal of Pacific History* 38:2 (2003): 175–96.

2 Circulating Texts on Circulating People: Mobilities, Epistemic Injustice and the Creation of the Imagined Australasian *Rachel Standfield*

Busby, James. *Authentic Information relative to New South Wales, and New Zealand.* London: Joseph Cross, 1832.

Fricker, Miranda. *Epistemic Injustice: Power and the Ethics of Knowing.* Oxford: Oxford University Press, 2007.

Leane, Jeanine. 'Tracking Our Country in Settler Literature'. *JASAL: Journal of the Association for the Study of Australian Literature* 14:3 (2014): 1–17.

Matthew, Patrick. *Emigration fields: North America, the Cape, Australia, and New Zealand, describing these countries, and giving a comparative view of the advantages they present to British settlers.* Edinburgh: Adam and Charles Black, 1839.

Medina, José. 'Epistemic Injustice and Epistemologies of Ignorance'. In *The Routledge Companion to the Philosophy of Race*, ed. Paul C. Taylor, Linda Martin Alcoff and Luvell Anderson, 247–60. New York: Routledge, 2017.

Melville, Henry. *The present state of Australasia: including New South Wales, Western Australia, South Australia, Victoria, and New Zealand: with practical hints on emigration; also, Remarks on prison discipline: with suggestions for obviating the difficulties attending the transportation of convicts; to which are added the land regulations, and description of the aborigines and their habits.* London: G. Willis, 1851.

Piesse, Jude. *British Settler Emigration in Print, 1832–1877.* Oxford: Oxford University Press, 2015.

Rose, Deborah Bird. *Reports from a Wild Country: Ethics for Decolonisation.* Sydney: UNSW Press, 2004.

Shaw, John. *A tramp to the diggings: being notes of a ramble in Australia and New Zealand in 1852.* London: Richard Bentley, 1852.

Standfield, Rachel, ed. *Indigenous Mobilities: Across and Beyond the Antipodes.* Canberra: ANU Press, 2018.

Standfield, Rachel and Michael J. Stevens. 'New Histories But Old Patterns: Kāi Tahu in Australia'. In *Labour Lines and Colonial Power: Indigenous and Pacific Islander Labour Mobility in Australia*, ed. Victoria Stead and Jon Altman, 103–31. Canberra: ANU Press, 2019.

Veracini, Lorenzo. *Settler Colonialism: A Theoretical Overview.* New York: Springer, 2010.

Wagner, Tamara S. 'Introduction: The Nineteenth-Century Pacific Rim: Victorian Transoceanic Studies Beyond the Postcolonial Matrix'. *Victorian Literature and Culture* 43:2 (2015): 223–34.

3 Triangular Formation: Fiji, New Zealand and Australia *Frances Steel*

Fieldhouse, D. K. 'New Zealand, Fiji and the Colonial Office'. *Historical Studies: Australia and New Zealand* 8:30 (1958): 113–30.

Irving, Helen. 'Making the federal Commonwealth, 1890–1901'. In *The Cambridge History of Australia*, ed. Alison Bashford and Stuart Macintyre, 242–66. Melbourne: Cambridge University Press, 2013.

Paisley, Fiona. 'Sexuality, Nationalism, and "Race": Humanitarian Debate about Indian Indenture in Fiji, 1910–18'. *Labour History* 113 (2017): 183–207.

Ross, Angus. *New Zealand Aspirations in the Pacific in the Nineteenth Century.* Oxford: Clarendon Press, 1964.

Steel, Frances. *New Zealand and the Sea: Historical Perspectives.* Wellington: Bridget Williams Books, 2018.

Steel, Frances. *Oceania under Steam: Sea Transport and the Cultures of Colonialism, 1870–1914.* Manchester: Manchester University Press, 2011.

Steel, Frances. 'Re-routing Empire? Steam age circulations and the making of an Anglo Pacific, c.1850–90'. *Australian Historical Studies* 46:3 (2015): 356–73.

Steel, Frances. 'Servant Mobilities between Fiji and New Zealand: The transcolonial politics of domestic work and immigration restriction, c.1870–1910'. *History Australia* 15:3 (2018): 519–39.

Thompson, Roger. *Australian Imperialism in the Pacific: The Expansionist Era, 1820–1920.* Melbourne: Melbourne University Press, 1980.

Veracini, Lorenzo. '"Emphatically not a white man's colony": Settler colonialism and the construction of colonial Fiji'. *Journal of Pacific History* 43:2 (2008): 189–205.

Young, John. *Australia's Pacific Frontier: Economic and Cultural Expansion into the Pacific, 1795–1885.* Melbourne: Cassell, 1967.

4 'A Splendid Thing': Imagining Australasian Federation *Frank Bongiorno*

Broeze, Frank. *Island Nation: A History of Australians and the Sea.* St Leonards: Allen & Unwin, 1998.

Dixon, Robert. '"A Nation for a Continent": Australian Literature and the Cartographic Imaginary of the Federation Era'. *Antipodes* 28:1 (June 2014): 141–54.

Fairburn, Miles. 'New Zealand and Australasian Federation, 1883–1901'. *New Zealand Journal of History* 4:2 (1970): 138–59.

Hirst, John. *The Sentimental Nation: The Making of the Australian Commonwealth.* South Melbourne: Oxford University Press, 2000.

Martin, Ged. *Australia, New Zealand and Federation, 1883–1901.* London: Menzies Centre for Australian Studies, King's College London, 2001.

Mein Smith, Philippa. 'New Zealand Federation Commissioners in Australia: One Past, Two Historiographies'. *Australian Historical Studies* 34:122 (2003): 305–25.

Mein Smith, Philippa, Peter J. Hempenstall and Shaun Goldfinch. *Remaking the Tasman World.* Christchurch: Canterbury University Press, 2008.

Official Record of the Proceedings and Debates of the Australasian Federation Conference, 1890, held in The Parliament House, Melbourne. Melbourne: Robert S. Brain, Government Printer, 1890.

Sinclair, Keith. 'Why New Zealanders are not Australians: New Zealand and the Australian Federal Movement 1881–1901'. In *Tasman Relations: New Zealand and Australia, 1788–1988,* ed. Keith Sinclair, 90–102. Auckland: Auckland University Press, 1988.

Tapp, E. J. 'New Zealand and Australian Federation', *Historical Studies: Australia and New Zealand* 5:19 (1952): 244–57.

Wood, F. L. W. 'Why did New Zealand not join the Australian Commonwealth in 1900–1901?'. *New Zealand Journal of History* 2:2 (1968): 115–29.

5 Cosmopolitan Pacific: Pan-Pacific Internationalisms in the Mid-Twentieth Century *Fiona Paisley and Helen Gardner*

Akami, Tomoko. *Internationalising the Pacific: The United States, Japan and the Institute of Pacific Relations in War and Peace, 1919–45.* London: Routledge, 2002.

Anderson, Warwick, Miranda Johnson and Barbara Brookes, eds. *Pacific Futures Past and Present*. Honolulu: University of Hawai'i Press, 2018.

Armitage, David, and Alison Bashford, eds. *Pacific Histories: Ocean Land People*. Basingstoke: Palgrave Macmillan, 2013.

Banivanua Mar, Tracey. *Decolonisation and the Pacific: Indigenous Globalisation and the Ends of Empire*. Cambridge: Cambridge University Press, 2016.

Bhambra, Gurminder K., and John Narayan, eds. *European Cosmopolitanism: Colonial Histories and Postcolonial Societies*. London: Routledge, 2017.

Carey, Jane, and Francis Steel. 'Introduction on the Critical Importance of Colonial Formations'. *History Australia* 15:3 (2018): 399–412.

Cheah, Pheng, and Bruce Robbins, eds. *Cosmopolitics: Thinking and Feeling Beyond the Nation*. Minneapolis: University of Minnesota Press, 1998.

Choy, Catherine Ceniza, and Judy Tzu-Chun Wu. *Gendering the Trans-Pacific World*. Leiden: Brill, 2020.

Crocombe, Ron. *The Pacific Way: An Emerging Identity*. Suva, Fiji: Lotu Pasifika Productions, 1976,

Denoon, Donald, Philippa Mein-Smith and Marivic Wyndham, eds. *A History of Australia, New Zealand and the Pacific*. Oxford: Blackwell Publishers, 2000.

Gibson, Jason, and Helen Gardner. 'Conversations on the Frontier: Finding the Dialogic in Nineteenth-Century Anthropological Archives'. *History Workshop* 88 (Autumn 2019): 4–65.

Gorman, Daniel. *The Emergence of International Society in the 1920s*. Cambridge: Cambridge University Press, 2012.

Johnson, Miranda. 'The Pacific Way'. In *The Land in our History: Indigeneity, Law, and the Settler State,* ed. Miranda Johnson, 133–60. Oxford: Oxford University Press, 2016.

Keesing, Felix. *The South Seas in the Modern World*. New York: John Day Company, 1946.

Keesing, Marie. 'Cultural Contributions of Pacific Countries'. *Pan-Pacific* (April–June 1939): 10.

Mara, Ratu Sir Kamisese. *The Pacific Way: A Memoir*. Honolulu: University of Hawai'i Press, 1997.

Paisley, Fiona. *Glamour in the Pacific: Cultural Internationalism and Race Politics in the Women's Pan-Pacific*. Honolulu: University of Hawai'i Press, 2009.

6 'We Seem To Shake Hands across the Seas': Dora Meeson Coates and the Lost World of Australasian Suffrage Activism *James Keating*

Bashford, Alison. 'On nations and states: a reflection on "Thinking the Empire Whole"'. *History Australia* 16:4 (2019): 638–41.

Bones, Helen. *The Expatriate Myth: New Zealand Writers and the Colonial World*. Dunedin: Otago University Press, 2018.

Crozier-De Rosa, Sharon. 'Narratives of democracy, the emotions of politics and memories of militant suffragism: Britain, Ireland, the USA and Australia'. In *The British Women's Suffrage Campaign: National and International Perspectives*, ed. June Hannam and June Purvis, 179–98. London: Routledge, 2021.

Crozier-De Rosa, Sharon, and Vera Mackie. *Remembering Women's Activism*. New York: Routledge, 2019.

Curthoys, Ann. 'We've just started making national histories and you want us to stop already?'. In *After the Imperial Turn: Thinking with and Through the Nation*, ed. Antoinette Burton, 70–89. Durham, NC: Duke University Press, 2003.

Keating, James. *Distant Sisters: Australasian Women and the International Struggle for the Vote, 1880–1914*. Manchester: Manchester University Press, 2020.

Keating, James. 'Piecing together suffrage internationalism: Place, space, and connected histories of Australasian women's activism'. *History Compass* 16:8 (2018): 1–15.

Lake, Marilyn. 'Nationalist historiography, feminist scholarship, and the promise and problems of new transnational histories: The Australian case'. *Journal of Women's History* 19:1 (2007): 180–6.

Scott, Myra. *How Australia Led the Way: Dora Meeson Coates and British Suffrage*. 2003; North Melbourne: Australian Scholarly Publishing, 2018.

Woollacott, Angela. *To Try Her Fortune in London: Australian Women, Colonialism, and Modernity*. Oxford: Oxford University Press, 2001.

Wright, Clare. *You Daughters of Freedom: The Australians Who Won the Vote and Inspired the World*. Melbourne: Text Publishing, 2018.

7 Circulations of Belonging: Chinese British Subjects in Australasia, 1880–1920 *Kate Bagnall*

Bagnall, Kate. 'Anglo-Chinese and the Politics of Overseas Travel from New South Wales, 1898 to 1925'. In *Chinese Australians: Politics, Engagement and Resistance*, ed. Sophie Couchman and Kate Bagnall, 203–38. Leiden: Brill, 2015.

Ballantyne, Tony. 'Mobility, Empire, Colonisation'. *History Australia* 11:2 (2014): 7–37.

Bright, Rachel. 'Migration, Naturalisation, and the "British" World, c.1900–1920'. *History of Global Arms Transfer* 10 (2020): 27–44.

Chesterman, John, and Brian Galligan. *Citizens without Rights: Aborigines and Australian Citizenship*. Cambridge: Cambridge University Press, 1997.

Irving, Helen. *Citizenship, Alienage, and the Modern Constitutional State: A Gendered History*. Cambridge: Cambridge University Press, 2016.

Karatani, Rieko. *Defining British Citizenship: Empire, Commonwealth and Modern Britain*. London: Routledge, 2014.

Kuo, Mei-fen. *Making Chinese Australia: Urban Elites, Newspapers and the Formation of Chinese-Australian Identity, 1892–1912*. Clayton, Victoria: Monash University Publishing, 2013.

Mercer, Harriet. 'Gender and the Myth of a White New Zealand, 1866–1928'. *New Zealand Journal of History* 52:2 (2018): 23–41.

Murphy, Nigel. *Guide to the Laws and Policies Relating to the Chinese in New Zealand, 1871–1997*. Wellington: New Zealand Chinese Association, 2008.

Ng, James. *Windows of a Chinese Past*. 4 vols. Dunedin: Otago Heritage Books, 1993.

Prince, Peter. 'The "Chinese" Always Belonged'. *History Australia* 15:3 (2018): 475–98.

Reeves, Keir. 'Tracking the Dragon Down Under: Chinese Cultural Connections in Gold Rush Australia and Aotearoa, New Zealand'. *Graduate Journal of Asia-Pacific Studies* 3:1 (2006): 49–66.

8 We Keep Down Our Remorse: Anthony Trollope and the Emotional Politics of Australasian Agriculture *Grace Moore*

Blythe, Helen Lucy. *The Victorian Colonial Romance with the Antipodes*. New York: Palgrave Macmillan, 2014.

Brantlinger, Patrick. *Dark Vanishings: Discourses on the Extinction of Primitive Races, 1800–1930*. Ithaca: Cornell University Press, 2003.

Gagnier, Regenia. *Literatures of Liberalization: Global Circulation and the Long Nineteenth Century*. Chamonix: Palgrave Macmillan, 2018.

Martin, Susan K. '"Tragic Ring-Barked Forests" and the "Wicked Wood": Haunting Environmental Anxiety in Late Nineteenth-Century Australian Literature'. In *Victorian Environmental Nightmares*, ed. Laurence W. Mazzeno and Ronald D. Morrison', 121–43. London: Palgrave Macmillan, 2019.

Moore, Grace. 'Beasts, Birds, Fishes and Reptiles: Anthony Trollope and the Australian Acclimatization Debate'. In *Animals in Victorian Literature and Culture: Contexts for Criticism*, ed. Laurence W. Mazzeno and Ronald D. Morrison', 65–82. London: Palgrave Macmillan, 2017.

Moore, Grace. 'So Wild and Beautiful a World Around Him: Trollope and Antipodean Ecology'. In *The Routledge Research Companion to Anthony Trollope*, ed. Deborah Denenholz Morse, Margaret Markwick and Mark W. Turner', 399–411. London: Routledge, 2017.

Tang, Ge. *Travel, Emotions, and Race in Anthony Trollope's Travelogues and Fiction*. PhD thesis in progress, University of Melbourne, projected completion 2023.

Trollope, Anthony. *Australia and New Zealand*. 2 vols. 1873; London: The Trollope Society, 2002.

Trollope, Anthony. *Harry Heathcote of Gangoil: A Tale of Australian Bush Life*. London: Folio Society, 1998.

Trollope, Anthony. *John Caldigate*. London: Folio Society, 1995.

Trollope, Anthony. *The Letters of Anthony Trollope, Volume Two, 1871–1882*, ed. N. John Hall. Palo Alto: Stanford University Press, 1983.

Trollope, Anthony. *The Tireless Traveler: Twenty Letters to the Liverpool Mercury*. 1875; Berkeley: University of California Press, 1978.

Wolfe, Patrick. 'Settler Colonialism and the Elimination of the Native'. *Journal of Genocide Research* 8:4 (2006): 387–409.

9 Brooch Clams and Blind Lobsters: HMS *Challenger* in the Australasian Pacific, 1874–5 *Gillen D'Arcy Wood*

Agassiz, Louis. *Études Critiques sur les Mollusques Fossiles*. 1840; New York: Arno Press, 1980.

Dumont d'Urville, Jules-Sébastien-César. *Voyage de la corvette l'Astrolabe . . . pendant les années 1826, 1827, 1828, 1829*. 5 vols. Paris: J. Tatsu, 1830–4.

Lamarck, Jean-Baptiste. 'Prodrome d'une Nouvelle Classification des Coquilles'. *Mémoires de la Societé Histoire Naturelle de Paris* 1 (1799).

Johnson, Craig R., et al. 'Climate change cascades: Shifts in oceanography, species' ranges and subtidal marine community dynamics in eastern Tasmania'. *Journal of Experimental Marine Biology and Ecology* 400:1 (2011): 17–32.

Miller, Kathryn A., et al. 'An Overview of Seabed Mining Including the Current State of Development, Environmental Impacts, and Knowledge Gaps'. *Frontiers in Marine Science* 4 (2018).

Moseley, H. N. *Notes by a Naturalist: An Account of Observations Made during the Voyage of HMS Challenger Round the World in the Years 1872–1876*. London: John Murray, 1892.

Oliver, E. C. J., et al. 'Projected Tasman Sea Extremes in Sea Surface Temperature through the Twenty-First Century'. *Journal of Climate* 27:5 (2014): 1980–8.

Ridgway, K. R., and J. R. Dunn. 'Observational Evidence for a Southern Hemisphere Oceanic Supergyre'. *Geophysical Research Letters* 34:13 (2007): L13612, 1–5.

Soon, Tan Kar, and Juaiping Zheng. 'Climate Change and Bivalve Mass Mortality in Temperate Regions'. In *Reviews of Environmental Contamination and Toxicology. Volume 251*, ed. P. de Voogt, 109–29. Cham: Springer, 2019.

Thomson, C. Wyville, and John Murray, eds. *Report on the Scientific Results of the Voyage of HMS Challenger during the years 1873–6*. 2 vols. London: Longmans & Co, 1885.

Wedding, L. M., et al. 'Managing mining of the deep seabed'. *Science* 349:6244 (2015): 144–5.

Wilson, Laura J., et al. 'Climate-Driven Changes to Ocean Circulation and their Inferred Impacts on Marine Dispersal Patterns'. *Global Ecology and Biogeography* 25:8 (2016): 923–39.

10 Gorse is People *Thomas McLean*

Barrett Browning, Elizabeth. 'Lessons from the Gorse'. In *Poems*. 3 vols. London: Chapman & Hall, 1862.

Brooking, Tom, and Eric Pawson. *Seeds of Empire: The Environmental Transformation of New Zealand*. London: I.B. Tauris, 2011.

Davin, Dan. *The Gorse Blooms Pale*. London: Nicholson & Watson, 1947.

Frame, Janet. 'Gorse is not People'. *The New Yorker*. 25 August 2008. https://www.newyorker.com/magazine/2008/09/01/gorse-is-not-people

Hardy, Thomas. *The Return of the Native*, ed. Tony Slade. London: Penguin Books, 1999.

Kelly, John Liddell. 'In Maui's Island'. *New Zealand Illustrated Magazine*. 1 September 1901, 908.

McLean, Thomas. 'Remembering Peter Nicholls'. *Los Angeles Review of Books*. 3 July 2021. https://lareviewofbooks.org/article/remembering-peter-nicholls/

Miller, John MacNeill. 'Mischaracterizing the Environment: Hardy, Darwin, and the Art of Ecological Storytelling'. *Texas Studies in Literature and Language* 62:2 (2020): 149–77.

Orsman, Chris. *Ornamental Gorse*. Wellington: Victoria University Press, 1994.

Orsman, Chris. 'The Unlikely Redemption of Gorse'. *New Zealand Geographic* 94 (November–December 2008). https://www.nzgeo.com/stories/chris-orsman-the-unlikely-redemption-ofgorse/

Rossetti, Christina. 'Goblin Market'. *Goblin Market and Other Poems*. London: Macmillan and Co., 1862.

11 Antipodean Perspectives: The Politics and Economics of Being Topsy-Turvy *Sarah Comyn*

Age. Tuesday 15 June 1858, 5. http://nla.gov.au/nla.news-article154856424.

Arthur, Paul. 'Antipodean Myths Transformed: The Evolution of Australian Identity'. *History Compass* 5:6 (2007): 1862–78.

Comyn, Sarah. 'Southern Doubles: Antipodean Life as a Comparative Exercise'. In *Worlding the South: Nineteenth-Century Literary Culture and the Southern Settler Colonies*, ed. Sarah Comyn and Porscha Fermanis', 58–77. Manchester: Manchester University Press, 2021.

Flit. 'A New Zealand Christmas Carol'. *Nelson Examiner and New Zealand Chronicle*. 28 June 1845, 68; 5 July 1845, 71–2; 12 July 1845, 75–6.

Giles, Paul. *Antipodean America: Australasia and the Constitution of U.S. Literature*. New York: Oxford University Press, 2014.

Goldie, Matthew Boyd. *The Idea of the Antipodes: Place, People and Voices*. London: Routledge, 2010.

Hiatt, Alfred. *Terra Incognita: Mapping the Antipodes Before 1600*. Chicago: The University of Chicago Press, 2008.

Hiatt, Alfred. 'Terra Australis and the Idea of the Antipodes'. In *European Perceptions of Terra Australis*, ed. Alfred Hiatt et al., 9–44. London: Routledge, 2011.

Macaulay, Thomas Babington. Review of Leopold von Ranke's *The Ecclesiastical and Political History of the Popes During the Sixteenth and Seventeenth Centuries [Die römische Papste]*. Trans. S. Austin. London, 1840. *Edinburgh Review* 72 (October 1840): 227–58.

Schreuder, Deryck M., and Stuart Ward. *Australia's Empire*. Oxford: Oxford University Press, 2008.

Sleight, Simon. 'Wavering between Virtue and Vice: Constructions of Youth in Australian Cartoons of the Late-Victorian Era'. In *Drawing the Line: Using Cartoons as Historical Evidence*, ed. Richard Scully and Marian Quartly, 05.1–05.26. Clayton: Monash University ePress, 2009.

Smith, Bernard. *Modernism's History: A Study in Twentieth-Century Art and Ideas*. Sydney: UNSW Press, 1998.

12 Pedestrian Touring, Racial Violence and Bad Feeling in Trans-Tasman Settler Fiction *Porscha Fermanis*

Berlant, Lauren. *The Female Complaint: The Unfinished Business of Sentimentality in American Culture*. Durham, NC: Duke University Press, 2008.

Callaway, Anita. *Visual Ephemera: Theatrical Art in Nineteenth-Century Australia*. Sydney: UNSW Press, 2000.

Clarke, Marcus. *The Peripatetic Philosopher*. Melbourne: George Robertson, 1869.

Edmonds, Penelope, and Anna Johnson. 'Empire, Humanitarianism and Violence in the Colonies'. *Journal of Colonialism and Colonial History* 17:1 (2016).

Elwell, E. Simeon. *The Boy Colonists; or Eight Years of Colonial Life in Otago, New Zealand*. London: Simpkin, Marshall & Co., 1878.

Greyser, Naomi. *On Sympathetic Grounds: Race, Gender, and Affective Geographies in Nineteenth-Century North America*. Oxford: Oxford University Press, 2018.

Johnson, Anna. 'Travelling the Tasman World: Travel Writing and Narratives of Transit'. In *New Zealand's Empire*, ed. Katie Pickles and Catharine Coleborne, 71–88. Manchester: Manchester University Press, 2016.

Lydon, Jane. *Imperial Emotions: The Politics of Empathy Across the British Empire*. Oxford: Oxford University Press, 2020.

Standfield, Rachel. 'Violence and the Intimacy of Imperial Ethnography: The Endeavour in the Pacific'. In *Moving Subjects: Mobility, Intimacy and Gender in an Age of Empire*, ed. Antoinette Burton and Tony Ballantyne', 31–48. Champaign: University of Illinois Press, 2008.

Stoler, Ann Laura. 'Affective States'. In *A Companion to the Anthropology of Politics*, ed. David Nugent and Joan Vincent, 4–20. Oxford: Blackwell Publishers, 2007.

Stoler, Ann Laura. *Along the Archival Grain: Epistemic Anxieties and Colonial Common Sense*. Princeton: Princeton University Press, 2009.

Talbot, Thorpe [Frances Ellen]. *Philiberta. A Novel*. Melbourne: E. W. Cole, 1882.

Wolf, Gabrielle. 'Innocent Convicts and Respectable Bushrangers: History and the Nation in Melbourne Melodrama, 1890–1914'. *Journal of Australian Studies* 28:81 (2004): 73–81.

13 When Detection Goes South: Ngaio Marsh's Wartime 'New Zealand' Novels, 1937–45 *Antoinette Burton*

Acheson, Carole. 'Cultural Ambivalence: Ngaio Marsh's New Zealand Detective Fiction'. *Journal of Popular Culture* 19:2 (1985): 159–74.
Ballantyne, Tony. 'On Space, Place and Mobility in Nineteenth Century New Zealand'. *New Zealand Journal of History* 45:1 (2011): 50–70.
Banivanua Mar, Tracey. *Decolonization and the Pacific: Indigenous Globalization and the Ends of Empire*. Cambridge: Cambridge University Press, 2016.
Davies, Philip H. J. *MI6 and the Machinery of Spying*. Abingdon: Frank Cass, 2005.
Drayton, Joanne. *Ngaio Marsh: Her Life in Crime*. Auckland: HarperCollins, 2008.
Harding, Bruce. '"The Great and True Amphibian": The New Zealand/England Polarity in the Short Fiction of Ngaio Marsh'. In *Ngaio Marsh: The Woman and her Work,* ed. B. J. Rahn, 57–76. Metuchen, NJ: Scarecrow Press, 1995.
Lewis, Margaret. *Ngaio Marsh: A Life*. Wellington: Bridget Williams Books, 1991.
Marsh, Ngaio. *Colour Scheme*. 1943; New York: Jove Books, 1982.
Marsh, Ngaio. *Died in the Wool*. 1945; New York: HarperCollins omnibus edition, 2009.
Marsh, Ngaio. *Vintage Murder*. 1937; New York: Felony and Mayhem Press, 2012.
Simpson, Peter. *Bloomsbury South: The Arts in Christchurch, 1933–1953*. Auckland: Auckland University Press, 2016.
Winks, Robin. *Detective Fiction: A Collection of Critical Essays*. Woodstock, VT: The Countryman Press, 1988.

Conclusion. Perpetual Flight: Relationships in Space and Time *Tony Ballantyne*

Beilharz, Peter. 'Bernard Smith: The quality of marxism'. *Thesis Eleven* 114:1 (2013): 94–102.
Beilharz, Peter. *Thinking the Antipodes: Australian Essays*. Clayton: Monash University Publishing, 2015.
Belich, James. *Paradise Reforged: A History of the New Zealanders from the 1880s to the Year 2000*. Auckland: Penguin Press, 2001.
Howitt, Rohan. 'Māori Workers in Colonial New South Wales, c. 1803–40'. *History Workshop Journal* 93 (2022): 1–21.
Sheller, Mimi and John Urry. 'The New Mobilities Paradigm'. *Environment and Planning A* 38:2 (2006): 207–26.
Standfield, Rachel. 'The Parramatta Māori Seminary and the Education of Indigenous Peoples in Early Colonial New South Wales'. *History of Education Review* 41:2 (2012): 119–28.
Stevens, Michael J. '"A Defining Characteristic of the Southern People": Southern Māori Mobility and the Tasman World'. In *Indigenous Mobilities: Across and Beyond the Antipodes*, ed. Rachel Standfield, 70–114. Acton, ACT: ANU Press, 2018.
Te Punga Somerville, Alice. 'Living on New Zealand Street: Maori Presence in Parramatta'. *Ethnohistory* 61:4 (2014): 655–69.

Index

9 781350 264168